The Passion of Fāṭima

Critiquing Kitāb Sulaym Ibn Qays

by

Abdullah Al-Rabbat

Kindle Direct Publishing

First Edition, 2021

ISBN: 9798732852769

Published by Kindle Direct Publishing

In memory of Aḥmed Ibn Muḥammad Ibn ʿAmmār al-Shahīd (d. 317/930), the eminent young ḥadīthist who was beheaded afront the Kaʿba by Qarmatian invaders as they pillaged the city of Mecca, hence attaining the honorable rank of martyrdom in shāʾa Allāh.

Transliteration

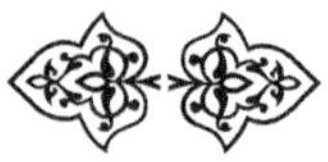

The transliteration system I have utilized in this book is a slightly modified *International Journal of Middle Eastern Studies* (IJMES) system.

When translating Arabic texts, I generally aimed to translate everything into English. However, there were certain terms that I opted to keep untranslated, usually because they are common and well-known Arabic terms that are readily understood and used by English speakers acquainted with discussions on Islamic textual criticism.

I should also note that this book contains several multipage Arabic passages. Since this book is primarily written in English, the multipage Arabic texts are to be read from left to right, as opposed to the standard right-to-left direction of Arabic texts across pages.

CONTENTS

INTRODUCTION

بسم الله الرحمن الرحيم، عونك اللهم.

أقول، وبالله الثقة:

The annals of history are replete with divergent ideas, beliefs, faiths, and values that developed within human societies throughout the passage of time. The factors behind the emergence of such ideas and values within a prospective society are plenty, but perhaps one of the most significant and influential of them all are the stories that are taught and inherited across generations. Such stories and narratives are, in many respects, the foundation(s) for many of our values, sensibilities and collective wisdoms of the past, present and future.

The drastic power and influence of stories over human societies are inescapable; however, the utility and value of such stories and narratives will vary depending on a philosophical quandary: what is the purpose of a story? Some stories, such as those of Aesop's fables, evidently were meant to be vessels of ideas, values and wisdoms that transcended the bounds of historicity. Hence, most readers of the book, upon engaging with its material, would not be led to believe that its dialogues that occur between animals were intended to be descriptive of true historical events. Rather, they clearly are a composition of stories written with metaphorical imagery and prose, and their author(s) was not invested in convincing the reader that his stories bore any semblance of historicity. Stories written in this context are usually judged by their prose, cohesion and efficacy in the delivery of their meanings to their intended audience(s). Other stories, however, are sought to ascertain historical truths pertaining to past events and figures. Such stories may prove to embody various values and wisdoms; however, their intended purpose, first and foremost, is to document and convey historical truths. Hence, they are judged in accordance to a variety of parameters relating to the historicity of their content, accuracy and transmission. In between these two archetypical "storytypes" is a spectrum of narrative and stories that may prioritize one objective at the expense of another.

One of the major divides that continue to unravel in several Muslim societies is the Sunnī-Shīʿite schism, which commenced over 14 centuries ago. Though the differences between the majority of Muslims and their Shīʿite counterparts often are quite intricate, they do, in many instances, come down to diverging stories told in both communities about a shared past. The Shīʿite text being studied in this book, *Kitāb Sulaym Ibn Qays*, is but a microcosm of that reality. While the vast majority of Muslims, the Sunnīs, Ibāḍīs, and several Muʿtazilite and Zaydī strands, generally maintain that the Prophet's ﷺ companions, Abū Bakr and ʿUmar, lived virtuous lives before and after the Prophet's ﷺ death, many Twelver Shīʿites today revile both men as deviant apostates, heretics and/or hypocrites who murdered the Prophet's ﷺ daughter shortly after his death. The origins of this alternate narrative are unclear; however, one of the sources cited most to justify it is no other than *Kitāb Sulaym Ibn Qays al-Hilālī*, which was allegedly compiled by a direct disciple of ʿAlī b. Abī Ṭālib.

Amir-Moezzi accurately summarizes *Kitāb Sulaym Ibn Qays'* contents saying, "In short, the Book of Sulaym is the account of a conspiracy, hatched long before the Prophet's death, and aiming to remove the latter and the closest members of his family, to alter the very nature of his religion in order to take hold of power and wrest Muslims away. The protagonists of this diabolical conspiracy were ʿUmar, Abū Bakr, and Abū ʿUbayda b. al-Jarrāḥ, their accomplice."[1]

The text is filled with grievous, detailed scenes that resemble, in several respects, those of a tragedic theatrical script. As an example, an account in the book describes a purported event when Abū Bakr and ʿUmar's accomplices stormed into ʿAlī and Fāṭima's house, forcing ʿAlī to pledge his allegiance to Abū Bakr. *Kitāb Sulaym's* author said:

> He [ʿUmar] commanded a group of men around him to carry the firewood, so they carried it with him, and they placed it around the house of ʿAlī, Fāṭima and their two sons. ʿUmar then yelled until ʿAlī and Fāṭima were able to hear him, and he said, "O ʿAlī, by Allah, you shall come out of your house and pledge your allegiance to the caliph of the Messenger of Allah ﷺ or I will [otherwise] set your house on fire!"

1 The Silent Quran and the Speaking Quran (p. 22)

> Fāṭima then responded saying, "O ʿUmar, what have you to do with us?!" ʿUmar responded saying, "Open the door, or we shall otherwise burn your house down upon you!"
>
> She told him, "O ʿUmar, do you not fear Allah such that you want to enter my house?!" ʿUmar refused to leave.
>
> ʿUmar then asked for a fire, and he set the door on fire and then he shoved it and entered the house. Fāṭima confronted him and shouted, "O father! O Messenger of Allah!"
>
> "ʿUmar then raised his sword as it was in its sheath, and he beat her with it on her side. She thus screamed, "O father!" "ʿUmar then raised his whip and struck her with it on her arm, to which she called out, "O Messenger of Allah! Evil is what Abū Bakr and ʿUmar have done after you!"[1]

قال سليم: قال سلمان: [...] ثم أمر أناسا حوله أن يحملوا الحطب فحملوا الحطب وحمل معهم عمر، فجعلوه حول منزل علي وفاطمة وابناهما عليهم السلام. ثم نادى عمر حتى أسمع عليا وفاطمة عليهما السلام: والله لتخرجن يا علي ولتبايعن خليفة رسول الله وإلا أضرمت عليك بيتك النار فقالت فاطمة عليها السلام: يا عمر، ما لنا ولك؟ فقال: افتحي الباب وإلا أحرقنا عليكم بيتكم.فقالت: يا عمر، أما تتقي الله تدخل على بيتي؟ فأبى أن ينصرف. ودعا عمر بالنار فأضرمها في الباب ثم دفعه فدخل فاستقبلته فاطمة عليها السلام وصاحت: يا أبتاه! يا رسول الله! فرفع عمر السيف وهو في غمده فوجأ به جنبها فصرخت: يا أبتاه! فرفع السوط فضرب به ذراعها فنادت: يا رسول الله، لبئس ما خلفك أبو بكر وعمر!

Since the book is claimed to have been authored by a disciple of ʿAlī b. Abī Ṭālib, it is not only said to be the oldest extant Shīʿte ḥadīth collection, but it is also incorrectly claimed to be the earliest extant Islamic ḥadīth collection as well. Until recent times, the book was widely unknown to Sunnī scholarship, which is mostly due to the book's secretive transmission within Rāfiḍite circles. For this reason, most early criticism of *Kitāb Sulaym* was posed by Twelver scholarship. The Twelver scholar, al-Mufīd (d. 413), for example, stated that book was unreliable and that its text had undergone corruption and falsification.[2] Al-Mufīd was followed by another fifth-century Twelver critic, Ibn al-Ghaḍāʾirī, who concluded that the book was

1 Kitāb Sulaym Ibn Qays (p. 150)
2 Taṣḥīḥ Iʿtiqādāt al-Imāmiyya by al-Mufīd (p. 149-150)

fabricated without a doubt.[1] Nevertheless, these Twelver authorities' criticisms of *Kitāb Sulaym* are countered by statements from other Twelver authorities, such as the fourth century Muḥammad b. Ibrāhīm al-Nuʿmānī, who said:

> There is no disagreement among all of the Shīʿa who have carried knowledge and transmitted it from the Imāms that *Kitāb Sulaym b. Qays al-Hilālī* is an *aṣl* that is one of the largest among the *uṣūl*, which were transmitted by the carriers of *Ahlulbayt's* ḥadīth, and the oldest [of them]. That is because all of its content is relayed from none other than the Messenger of Allah, the Commander of the Faithful, al-Miqdād, Salmān al-Fārisī, Abū Dharr and their likes from those who witnessed and heard from the Messenger of Allah ﷺ and the Commander of the Faithful. It is among the *uṣūl* that are referenced and relied upon by the Shīʿa.[2]

قال النعماني في «الغيبة»: وليس بين جميع الشيعة ممن حمل العلم ورواه عن الائمة (عليهم السلام) خلاف في أن كتاب سليم بن قيس الهلالي أصل من أكبر كتب الاصول التي رواها أهل العلم من حملة حديث أهل البيت (عليهم السلام) وأقدمها لان جميع ما اشتمل عليه هذاالاصل إنماهوعن رسول الله(صلى الله عليه وآله) وأمير المؤمنين (عليه السلام) والمقداد وسلمان الفارسي وأبي ذر ومن جرى مجراهم ممن شهد رسول الله (صلى الله عليه وآله) وأمير المؤمنين (عليه السلام) وسمع منهما، وهو من الاصول التي ترجع الشيعة إليها ويعول عليها.

The Twelver community today, like the Twelver communities of the fourth and fifth centuries, are not in unison regarding the book's authenticity. Nevertheless, the book of Sulaym is believed to be an authentic text by many contemporary Shīʿite clerics and institutions, and it is hence cited, alongside other texts, to justify the hatred and condemnation of Abū Bakr, ʿUmar and their associates as the murderers of Fāṭima, the Prophet's daughter ﷺ.

This purported first century Shīʿte text does not come from a vacuum: in the second century, there were Rāfiḍite and staunch Shīʿite transmitters who fabricated traditions that vilified certain companions of the Prophet ﷺ who were perceived as enemies of *Ahlulbayt* by the Shīʿa. As an example, Ibn Ḥibbān (d. 354) described the forger, Abū al-Jārūd Ziyād b. al-Mudhir (d. 151), saying:

---

1 Al-Rijāl by Ibn al-Ghaḍāʾirī (p. 63)
2 Al-Ghayba by al-Nuʿmānī (p. 103)

> He was a Rāfiḍīte who used to fabricate reports about the blunders (*mathālib*) of the Prophet's ﷺ companions, and he used to transmit reports in the merits of *Ahlulbait* that are baseless. It is impermissible to transcribe his transmission.[1]

قال ابن حبان: كَانَ رَافِضِيًّا يضع الْحَدِيث فِي مثالب أَصْحَاب النَّبِي صَلَّى اللَّهُ عَلَيْهِ وَسَلَّمَ ويروي عَن فَضَائِل أهل الْبَيْت أَشْيَاء مَاله أصُول لَا تحل كِتَابَة حَدِيثه.

Abū al-Jārūd was condemned by other critics for forgery as well. Ibn ʿAdī (d. 365) described another suspect Shīʿite forger, ʿAbdulGhaffār al-Fuqaymī (d. 202), saying:

> He is suspected [of forgery] whenever he transmits anything pertaining to the merits [of *Ahlulbayt*]. The predecessors used to accuse him of fabricating reports in the merits of *Ahlulbayt* and in the blunders (*mathālib*) of others.[2]

قال ابن عدي: وَهو مُتَّهَمٌ إِذَا رَوَى شَيْئًا مِنَ الْفَضَائِلِ وَكَانَ السَّلَفُ يَتَّهِمُونَهُ بِأَنَّهُ يَضَعُ فِي فَضَائِلِ أَهْلِ الْبَيْتِ وَفِي مَثَالِبِ غَيْرِهِمْ وَلِعَمْرٍو غَيْرَ مَا ذَكَرْتُ مِنَ الْحَدِيثِ.

Abū Saʿīd b. Yūnus described the Rāfiḍite forger, Jaʿfar b. Aḥmed b. ʿAlī b. Bayān, saying:

> He was a lying Rāfiḍite who used to fabricate ḥadīths that disparage the Prophet's ﷺ companions.[3]

قال أبو سعيد ابن يونس: كَانَ رَافِضِيًّا كذابا يضع الحَدِيث فِي سبّ أَصْحَاب رَسُول الله صلى الله عَلَيْهِ وَسلم.

Jaʿfar b. Aḥmed's student, Ibn ʿAdī (d. 365), dedicated an insightful entry for him in *al-Kāmil* where he expounded his forgery and dubious practices in transmission.[4] A plethora of other unreliable Rāfiḍite transmitters were condemned for fabricating traditions in the merits of *Ahlulbayt* and/or the blunders of the *ṣaḥāba.*

This genre of forgery, where traditions were forged for the condemnation and vilification of one's theological opponents, was not exclusive to Rāfiḍite forgers. Some staunch Ḥanafī partisans, as an example,

---

1 Al-Majrūḥīn by Ibn Ḥibbān (1/306)
2 Al-Kāmil fī Ḍuʿafāʾ al-Rijāl (6/253)
3 Al-Ḍuʿafāʾ wa-l-Matrūkūn by Ibn al-Jawzī (1/170)
4 Al-Kāmil fī Ḍuʿafāʾ al-Rijāl (2/400-405)

forged prophetic traditions that condemned one of the chief antagonists of Ḥanafī jurisprudence, Muḥammad b. Idrīs al-Shāfiʿī (d. 204). Ibn Ḥibbān (d. 354) described the transmitter, Ma'mūn b. Aḥmed al-Sulamī, saying:

> He transmitted a ḥadīth from Aḥmed b. ʿAbdillāh, from ʿAbdullāh b. Maʿdān al-Azdī, from Anas that the Prophet ﷺ said, "There shall be in my nation a man by the name of Muḥammad b. Idrīs who shall be more harmful upon my *Umma* than Iblīs (the devil); and there shall be a man in my nation called Abū Haniīfa. He shall be the torchlight of my *Umma*."
>
> [Ibn Ḥibbān said:] Whoever transmits reports like these ones or parts of them should not be listed among the people of knowledge. I merely listed him [in this book] because the beginner students of Khurāsān transcribed his ḥadīths [and] so that his lies in ḥadīth and intentional slander of the people of knowledge are known.[1]

قال ابن حبان: وَرَوَى عَنْ أَحْمَدَ بْنِ عَبْدِ اللَّهِ عَنْ عَبْدِ اللَّهِ بْنِ مَعْدَانَ الأَزْدِيِّ عَنْ أَنَسٍ عَنِ النَّبِيِّ صَلَّى اللَّهُ عَلَيْهِ وَسَلَّمَ قَالَ, "يَكُونُ فِي أُمَّتِي رَجُلٌ يُقَالُ لَهُ مُحَمَّدُ بْنُ إِدْرِيسَ أَضَرُّ عَلَى أُمَّتِي مِنْ إِبْلِيسَ. وَيَكُونُ فِي أُمَّتِي رَجُلٌ يُقَالُ لَهُ أَبُو حَنِيفَةَ هُوَ سِرَاجُ أُمَّتِي."

فَمَنْ حَدَّثَ بِهَذِهِ الأَحَادِيثِ أَوْ بِبَعْضِهَا يَجِبُ أَنْ لَا يُذْكَرَ فِي جُمْلَةِ أَهْلِ الْعِلْمِ وَإِنَّمَا ذَكَرْتُهُ لأَنَّ الأَحْدَاثَ بِخُرَاسَانَ قَدْ كَتَبُوا عَنْهُ لِيُعْرَفَ كَذِبُهُ فِي الْحَدِيثِ وَتَعَمُّدُهُ فِي الإِفْكِ عَلَى أَهْلِ الْعِلْمِ.

Many other "pro-Sunnī" and "anti-Sunnī" traditions that embodied criticisms and condemnations of certain figures or sects were fabricated at various points in history, and a careful study of Ibn al-Jawzī's *al-Mawḍūʿāt* and earlier works of *ʿIlal* that amassed defective traditions will prove to be quite insightful in this regard.

Eventually, a particular genre of ḥadīth literature arose, mostly within Shīʿite circles, which was known as the *mathālib.* This genre of ḥadīth literature mostly revolved around the defects, flaws and blunders of the Prophet's ﷺ companions who were disliked by the Shīʿa, and it mirrored the *faḍā'il* literature, which often revolved around the merits of *Ahlulbayt*, the Prophet's ﷺ companions and others. Evidently, passionate hatred or love of a historical figure is a rather powerful incentive to forge traditions about that individual, and the *faḍā'il* literature was hence recognized as one of the

---

1 Al-Majrūḥīn by Ibn Ḥibbān (3/46)

most compromised genres that were replete with forgeries and exaggerations.

Ibn Ḥajar (d. 852), when commenting on a statement of Aḥmed b. Ḥanbal on three genres of ḥadīth literature that are replete with weak and forged reports, said:

> The *faḍā'il* (merits) should be added to them, for these are the valleys of weak and fabricated ḥadīths, since the dependence in *maghāzī* is on the likes of al-Wāqidī, and in *tafsīr* on the likes of Muqātil and al-Kalbī, and in *malāḥim* on the *Isrā'īliyyāt*. As for the *faḍā'il*, how much the Rāfiḍites had fabricated in the merits of *Ahlulbayt* is innumerable. The ignorant from *Ahlussunna* countered them first with the merits of Muʿāwiya and then the merits of Abū Bakr and ʿUmar, and Allah has sufficed them both and elevated their ranks beyond [needing] such fabrications.[1]

قال ابن حجر: ينبغي أن يُضاف إليها الفضائل، فهذه أودية الأحاديث الضعيفة والموضوعة، إذ كانت العمدة في المغازي على مثل الواقدي، وفي التفسير على مثل مقاتل والكلبي، وفي الملاحم على الإسرائيليات، وأما الفضائل فلا تُحصى كم وضع الرافضة في فضل أهل البيت، وعارضهم جهلة أهل السنة بفضائل معاوية بدأ، وبفضائل الشيخين، وقد أغناهما الله وأعلى مرتبتهما عنها.

In this regard, the eminent ḥadīthist, Abū Yaʿlā al-Khalīlī (d. 446), described the proliferation of forgery in some Shīʿite circles saying:

> The weak transmitters among the people of Kūfa are innumerable. One of the *ḥuffāẓ* said, "I have observed what the people of Kūfa have fabricated in the merits of ʿAlī and his household, and it amounted to more than 300,000 [ḥadīths]."[2]

قال الخليلي في «الإرشاد»: ولأهل الكوفة من الضعفاء ما لا يمكن عدهم. قال بعض الحفاظ: تأملت ما وضعه أهل الكوفة في فضائل علي وأهل بيته فزاد على ثلاثمائة ألف.

The contents of *Kitāb Sulaym* are some of the most extreme and most developed extant manifestations of the *mathālib* literature. In fact, the book's alleged transmitter, Abān b. Abī ʿAyyāsh, is even quoted saying in its forefront:

1 Lisān al-Mīzān by Ibn Ḥajar (1/207)
2 Al-Irshād fī Maʿrifat ʿUlamā' al-Ḥadīth by al-Khalīlī (p. 145)

> My chest tightens as a result of some things in this book, for it embodies the imminent destruction of the *Umma* of Muḥammad head-on from the *Muhājirin*, the *Anṣār*, and the successors (*tābiʿīn*), except you, *Ahlulbayt*, and your Shīʿa.[1]

قال أبان: إنه ليضيق صدري ببعض ما فيه، لأن فيه هلاك أمة محمد صلى الله عليه وآله رأسا من المهاجرين والأنصار والتابعين، غيركم أهل البيت وشيعتكم.

Like any text that is claimed to originate from the first century of Islam, *Kitāb Sulaym Ibn Qays* certainly is worthy of scrutiny before its ascription can be deemed authentic and historical. The book's extreme polemical nature and its embodiment of controversial and contested historical claims should warrant even more scrutiny and caution. Hopefully, the need for such scrutiny should be multifacetedly self-evident: a text that touches on controversial events and particularly vilifies certain historical figures who have been the epicenter of much sectarian strife and discord is a text with much room for error and many incentives for forgery and fabrication. Alas, that alone would not necessarily be sufficient evidence to dismiss the text in its entirety, but it should, at least, warrant careful inspection and study of its origins. Furthermore, the book's transmission and text embody various discrepancies and defects, as shall be expounded in this book, and such observations certainly warrant even more intensified scrutiny of this purported first century text.

In this book, I intend to touch on several topics pertaining to *Kitāb Sulaym Ibn Qays* and related texts: (i) an analysis of its transmission, (ii) an analysis of its contents, (iii) and, ultimately, a dating of the book's authorship. The first two chapters are preliminary studies of the text, and chapter three effectively is the synopsis and materialization of all my notable observations and findings regarding *Kitāb Sulaym Ibn Qays*. After these three chapters is an essay I had written that provides an overview and contextualization of the correct historical narrative surrounding Abū Bakr's inauguration at the *Saqīfa* of Banī Saʿida and its immediate aftermaths.

What differentiates this work from past critiques of *Kitāb Sulaym* is that I have benefired from Sunnī and, to a lesser extent, Zaydī sources alongside Twelver sources when assessing the text, and this will prove to be quite fruitful later in this book. In this regard, many Orientalist and Twelver Shīʿite assessments of the book are limited, as they tended to disregard non-

1 Kitāb Sulaym Ibn Qays (p. 128)

Twelver primary and biographical sources throughout their studies of the text, and that may prove to be the byproduct of inaccurate assumptions about *Kitāb Sulaym* and perhaps Twelver ḥadīth literature as well.

Kitāb Sulaym Ibn Qays is not the only Shīʿite source cited as evidence for Fāṭima's purported murder at the hands of the *ṣaḥāba*, namely Abū Bakr and ʿUmar. Rather, a few other seemingly independent reports are also cited to justify this Rāfiḍite narrative, and I have assessed many of them throughout this book. *Kitāb Sulaym*, however, according to many Shīʿites, is the earliest source to embody this notion. Additionally, it provides the most detailed, gruesome and complete rendition of this narrative, and it effectively can be described as the backbone of Fāṭima's passion in Twelver literature. In fact, the reader may be surprised to learn that an entire high-budget movie is currently being produced by an extremist Twelver institution in the West that utilizes *Kitāb Sulaym Ibn Qays* as some of its main source material, and it is expected to soon be aired in international theaters. Hence, the once obscure *Kitāb Sulaym Ibn Qays* has become more relevant than ever.

Today, the average Twelver layman is often introduced to this narrative being told that key components of it can be substantiated from Sunnī sources, something which I suppose is intended to grant some credibility to this otherwise bizarre Twelver conception of the historical events immediately after the Prophet's ﷺ death. Nonetheless, like any controversial theo-historical matter of much emotional significance, this debate tends to bring out the worst in its interlocutors: dishonesty, logical fallacies, selective readings, desperation and exaggeration etc. It is, in several respects, akin to the behavior described by George Orwell in his essay on nationalism, *Notes on Nationalism*. He said:

> For those who feel deeply about contemporary politics, certain topics have become so infected by considerations of prestige that a genuinely rational approach to them is almost impossible. Out of the hundreds of examples that one might choose, take this question: Which of the three great allies, the U.S.S.R., Britain and the U.S.A., has contributed most to the defeat of Germany? In theory it should be possible to give a reasoned and perhaps even a conclusive answer to this question. In practice, however, the necessary calculations cannot be made, because anyone likely to bother his head about such a question would inevitably see it in terms of competitive prestige. He would therefore *start* by deciding in favour of Russia, Britain or America as the case might be, and only *after*

> this would begin searching for arguments that seemed to support his case. And there are whole strings of kindred questions to which you can only get an honest answer from someone who is indifferent to the whole subject involved, and whose opinion on it is probably worthless in any case.

Not withstanding the irony in how Shīʿite polemicists who claim that key elements of Fāṭima's purported murder could be substantiated from Sunnī sources often concurrently argue that Sunnī sources were part of some massive conspiracy to censor and conceal that very same narrative, Twelver polemicists and apologists regularly approach non-Shīʿite sources with the assumption and presumption that the claims within *Kitāb Sulaym Ibn Qays* and similar sources are true. Their consequent readings and takeaways from Sunnī sources in this regard hence tend to be clouded by their preliminary assumptions about these purported historical events. The careful observer of Twelver appeals to Sunnī and non-Sunnī sources that attempt to substantiate the narrative of *Kitāb Sulaym* is able to witness a string of logical fallacies and spurious appeals, most notably, the Texas sharpshooter fallacy.

The Texas sharpshooter fallacy is a logical fallacy in which the proponent of a conclusion/argument (over)emphasizes similarities between data points while discarding and ignoring pertinent differences between those points, leading to fallacious and inaccurate conclusions and associations. The name of this fallacy derives from the imaginary story of a Texan cowboy with a firearm who arbitrarily discharged his firearm at a barn wall. He then approached the wall and began to draw circles around large clusters of holes on the wall, giving the impression that he was shooting precisely at a designated target at the center of that arbitrarily drawn circle. The reality of the matter, however, is that there was no target on the wall: the circle drawn by the cowboy around certain clusters does not describe any substantive relationship between the arbitrarily selected datapoints. The negative effects of such fallacious reasoning in the assessment of historical sources and claims are twofold: (1) it leads to selection bias and the dismissal of sources that conflict with the presumed historical truth and (2) it leads to the inaccurate interpretation of the selected sources in light of the presumed historical truth.

Hence, we return to the initial point on Sunnī sources being cited by Twelver polemicists to substantiate the narrative of *Kitāb Sulaym Ibn Qays* and related sources: do Sunnī sources provide reasonable basis for this staunch Twelver narrative? The answer to that question can only be "yes" if the questioner conveniently disregards vast swaths of data that conflict with this narrative in Sunnī (and non-Sunnī sources) while also projecting preemptive external conclusions onto the arbitrarily selected (and otherwise neutral) datapoints within Sunnī literature. The unsurprising reality is that a careful reading of Sunnī sources in this regard will not only prove that the Twelver narrative of *Kitāb Sulaym* is unfounded therein, but it will also demonstrate that Sunnī sources embody the antithesis to the narrative and the means to deconstruct and disprove this later Twelver narrative.

My primary intention in this book is to dissect the Twelver Shīʿite text known as *Kitāb Sulaym Ibn Qays*, though I do believe that my analysis' implications transcend the mere authenticity of *Kitāb Sulaym Ibn Qays* in multiple regards. The implications of my findings in this book will hopefully prove to be useful in understanding and decoding the origins of the Twelver Shīʿite narrative surrounding the purported murder of Fāṭima by the Prophet's ﷺ companions.

Prior to my exposition of *Kitāb Sulaym Ibn Qays*, I must make something clear: I have come to terms with the fact that the conclusions and arguments in my book are bound to offend and enrage some zealous Shīʿite proponents of the Shīʿite narrative. The clash of divergent historical narratives is bound to result in inescapable tension, especially when such narratives are rooted in competing religious traditions. Nonetheless, my objective in this work is to illustrate the ahistoricity of a narrative that can be demonstrably shown to rest on quite flimsy grounds. In this respect, my arguments and conclusions surrounding *Kitāb Sulaym Ibn Qays* transcend the narrow scope of Sunnī-Shīʿite polemical discord: they are questions of history that should hopefully appeal to any reasonable inquirer, regardless of his/her faith and background. Though it would be great if we are able to bypass the overbearing and neverending drama associated with contemporary Sunnī-Shīʿite polemical discourse through good faith and emphasis on objectivity, I must disgruntedly admit that such an aspiration seems to me untenable. Alas, my objective in this book of mine never was to please or gain the approval of all its potential readers, as such an endeavor is nothing short of a fool's errand.

CHAPTER 1: TRANSMISSION

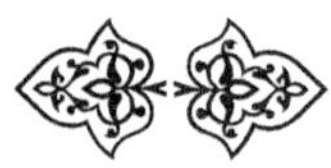

Prior to assessing *Kitāb Sulaym's* contents, it is imperative that its transmission is dissected and examined for a more accurate understanding of its origins, especially considering that the book's isnāds embody serious entanglements and discrepancies.

Various manuscripts for *Kitāb Sulaym* were referenced by Shīʿite figures after the fourth century. However, only 26 manuscripts survive today, and most were copied after the tenth century.[1] This is one of the initial noteworthy observations pertaining to the book's transmission, for the earliest mention of *Kitāb Sulaym* as a book was by the Twelver al-Nuʿmānī (d. ~360) in his book, *Kitāb al-Ghayba.* Therein, he stated that *Kitāb Sulaym* was one of the oldest and largest *uṣūl* referenced by the Shīʿa.[2] Around that time, the fourth century Twelver traditionist, al-Kashshī, referenced the book as well.[3] Another reference to the book appears shortly after that by Ibn al-Nadīm (d. ~380) in his *Fihrist,* where he described the book as the first book to emerge among the Shīʿa.[4] After Ibn al-Nadīm, the Twelver theologian, al-Mufīd (d. 413), mentioned *Kitāb Sulaym* and noted that it was untrusted and that it had undergone corruption and falsification.[5] Later, the fifth century Twelver scholars, al-Ṭūsī (d. 460), Ibn al-Najāshī (d. 450) and Ibn al-Ghaḍā'irī made reference to the book in their prosopographical works, though Ibn al-Ghaḍā'irī concluded that the book was fabricated without a doubt.[6]

Some fragments of *Kitāb Sulaym Ibn Qays* can also be found relayed in the works of al-Ṣaffār (d. 290), al-Kulaynī (d. 329), Ibn Bābawayh Sr. (d. 329), Ibn Bābawayh Jr. (d. 381) and other Shīʿite traditionists via their isnāds to

---

1 Kitāb Sulaym Ibn Qays (p. 92-97)
Al-Majlisī (d. 1111) noted that he came across an "old manuscript of *Kitāb Sulaym Ibn Qays*" that was copied in 609, though it seems that this manuscript has been lost today. See Tanqīḥ al-Maqāl fī ʿIlm al-Rijāl (32/426).

2 Kitāb al-Ghayba by al-Nuʿmānī (p. 103)

3 Rijāl al-Kashshī (p. 82)

4 Al-Fihrist by Ibn al-Nadīm (p. 271)

5 Taṣḥīḥ Iʿtiqādāt al-Imāmiyya by al-Mufīd (p. 149-150)

6 Al-Fihrist by al-Ṭūsī (p. 134-135), Rijāl al-Najāshī (p. 10), al-Rijāl by Ibn al-Ghaḍā'irī (p. 36, 63-64)

Sulaym b. Qays. However, given al-Mufīd's assertion regarding the text's corruption and the ample evidence of falsification occurring within the book (which shall be demonstrated later), the nature of *Kitāb Sulaym* during those respective eras is unclear. It cannot be assumed that past recensions of the book are identical to the extant recension, and it hence cannot be concluded that the likes of al-Ṣaffār (d. 290), who only relayed four brief traditions through Sulaym in *Baṣā'ir al-Darajāt,* necessarily had access to the large book we possess today in its final form.[1] Similarly, the Twelver traditionist, al-Kulaynī (d. 381), relayed only twelve traditions through Sulaym in *al-Kāfī,* two of which do not exist in the extant recension of *Kitāb Sulaym.*[2] Additionally, some of Sulaym's traditions referenced by al-Kulaynī clearly were developed and altered later in history, as can be observed in the extant recension of *Kitāb Sulaym Ibn Qays,* and more will come on that later in this book. In fact, it is possible, if not likely, that the pre-fourth century *Kitāb Sulaym Ibn Qays* was a significantly different text than the extant post-tenth century recensions of the book.

The book's routes of transmission are plagued with numerous entanglements, discrepancies and divergences. To simplify and clarify the transmission of *Kitāb Sulaym,* I constructed an isnād schematic that outlined all the book's isnāds, as seen in Figure 1.1 below.

1 Baṣā'ir al-Darajāt (p. 58, 114, 234, 413-414)

2 See Al-Kāfī by al-Kulaynī (1/25, 1/26, 1/37, 1/112, 1/179-180, 1/339-340, 1/346, 2/231-232, 8/36, 8/182-183). One of the traditions refenced by al-Kulaynī through Sulaym b. Qays is a voluminous tradition that cannot be found in Kitāb Sulaym, and the other tradition is a shorter report. The contemporary editor of Kitāb Sulaym added these two traditions to the appendices of Kitāb Sulaym Ibn Qays. See al-Kāfī of al-Kulaynī (2/187, 2/220) and Kitāb Sulaym Ibn Qays (p. 471-474, 477).

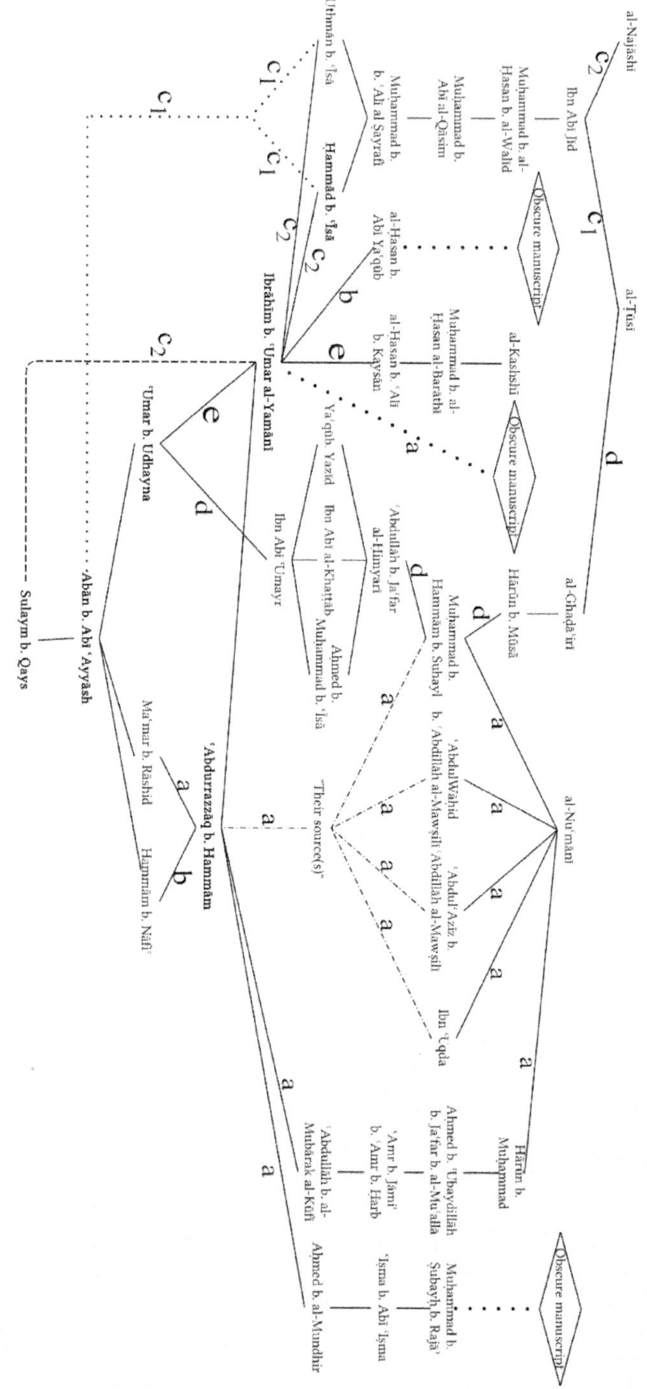

Figure 1.1 A schematic outlining all the different isnāds for *Kitāb Sulaym Ibn Qays*

As observed in figure 1.1, I have divided the book's isnāds into five main routes, A, B, C, D and E. I will provide an exposition of the book's routes and then assess the pivotal transmitters upon its isnāds revolve.

Route A

Route A of *Kitāb* Sulaym cites the prominent Yemenite *muḥaddith*, ʿAbdurrazzāq al-Ṣanʿānī (d. 211), relaying the book from Maʿmar b. Rāshid (d. 154) ⟶ Abān b. Abī ʿAyyāsh (d. 138) ⟶ Sulaym b. Qays.

This route has three main sources: (1) the Twelver, al-Nuʿmānī (d. ~360), who cited two isnāds back to ʿAbdurrazzāq, (2) an obscure manuscript cited by Āghā Bozorg (d. 1389), and (3) an obscure manuscript that commences with Muḥammad b. Ṣubayḥ b. Rajāʾ in its isnād.

Al-Nuʿmānī's Two Isnāds

In *Kitāb al-Ghayba*, al-Nuʿmānī said:

> And from *Kitāb Sulaym b. Qays* is what Aḥmed b. Muḥammad b. Saʿīd b. ʿUqda, Muḥammad b. Ḥammām b. Suhayl, and ʿAbdulʿAzīz and ʿAbdulWāḥid, the sons of ʿAbdullāh b. Yūnus al-Mawṣilī, transmitted from their sources, on the authority of ʿAbdurrazzāq b. Hammām, from Maʿmar b. Rāshid, from Abān b. Abī ʿAyyāsh, from Sulaym b. Qays.[1]

قال النعماني: ومن كتاب سليم بن قيس الهلالي ما رواه أحمد بن محمد بن سعيد ابن عقدة، ومحمد بن همام بن سهيل، و عبدالعزيز وعبدالواحد ابنا عبدالله بن يونس الموصلي، عن رجالهم، عن عبدالرزاق ابن همام، عن معمر بن راشد، عن أبان بن أبي عياش، عن سليم بن قيس.

Al-Nuʿmānī did not list the source(s) in transmission for the four figures he cited in his isnād, and this isnād is hence unreliable. Assuming al-Nuʿmānī was truthful in his citation of his four aforementioned sources, it must be noted that several intermediaries were omitted in this disconnection between them and ʿAbdurrazzāq, which should further compound the weakness of this alleged route. As an example, some Shīʿite

1 Kitāb al-Ghayba by al-Nuʿmānī (p. 74)

sources purport instances were Aḥmed b. Muḥammad b. Saʿīd had three intermediaries between him and ʿAbdurrazzāq.[1]

قال ابن شاذان: أخبرنا أحمد بن محمد بن سعيد، عن الحسين بن محفوظ، قال: حدثنا أحمد بن إسحاق، قال: حدثني الغطريف بن عبد السلام بصنعاء اليمن، قال: حدثني عبد الرزاق، عن معمر، عن الزهري، قال: حدثني أبو بكر عبد الله بن عبد الرحمن، قال: سمعت عثمان بن عفان، قال: سمعت عمر بن الخطاب، قال: سمعت أبا بكر بن أبي قحافة يقول: سمعت رسول الله صلى الله عليه وآله يقول: إن الله تبارك وتعالى خلق من نور وجه علي بن أبي طالب عليه السلام ملائكة يسبحون ويقدسون ويكتبون ثواب ذلك لمحبيه ومحبي ولده عليهم السلام.

In the aforementioned tradition, we observe a Twelver source quoting Ibn ʿUqda with three intermediaries between him and ʿAbdurrazzāq. From the report's text and isnād, it is apparent that it is quite a preposterously embellished Shīʿite forgery, and it hence is quite clear that some of Ibn ʿUqda's purported intermediaries between him and ʿAbdurrazzāq were unreliable. This finding raises concerns with the other contemporaneous figures' transmission, which was cited by al-Nuʿmānī alongside that of Ibn ʿUqda', assuming they were all not transmitting the book from the same source(s).

What is additionally noteworthy is that Muḥammad b. Hammām b. Suhayl, one of the sources cited by al-Nuʿmānī, is quoted elsewhere transmitting *Kitāb Sulaym* with a different isnād, route D, as can be seen in figure 1.1.

After citing this severely disconnected chain of transmission for *Kitāb* Sulaym, al-Nuʿmānī cited another isnād. He said:

> And Hārūn b. Muḥammad relayed to us of the book through other than these routes. He said: Aḥmed b. ʿUbaydillāh b. Jaʿfar b. al-Muʿallā al-Hamadānī informed us, he said: Abū al-Ḥasan ʿAmr b. Jāmiʿ b. ʿAmr b. Ḥarb al-Kindī informed us, he said ʿAbdullāh b. al-Mubārak, a reliable Kūfan *sheikh* of ours, informed us, he said: ʿAbdurrazzāq b. Hammām, our *sheikh*, informed us, on the authority of Maʿmar, from, Abān b. Abī ʿAyyāsh, from Sulaym b. Qays al-Hilālī.[2]

1 Mi'at Manqaba min Manāqib Amīr al-Mu'minīn by Ibn Shādhān (p. 160-162)
2 Kitāb al-Ghayba by al-Nuʿmānī (p. 74)

قال النعماني: وأخبرنا به من غير هذه الطرق هارون بن محمد، قال: حدثنى أحمد بن عبيد الله ابن جعفر بن المعلى الهمداني، قال: حدثني أبوالحسن عمرو بن جامع بن عمرو بن حرب الكندى، قال: حدثنا عبد الله بن المبارك - شيخ لنا كوفي ثقة - قال: حدثنا عبدالرزاق بن همام شيخنا، عن معمر، عن أبان بن أبي عياش، عن سليم ابن قيس الهلالي....

This isnād is quite unreliable: all of its transmitters beneath ʿAbdurrazzāq are unknown.

- Al-Nuʿmānī did not identify his informant, Hārūn b. Muḥammad.
- Aḥmed b. ʿUbaydillāh b. Jaʿfar is unknown to Twelver scholarship, let alone Sunnī scholarship.[1]
- ʿAmr b. Jāmiʿ is similarly unknown to Twelver and Sunnī scholarship.[2] Ibn ʿAsākir relayed that he died in the year 330.[3]
- The Kūfan ʿAbdulllāh b. al-Mubārak is an unknown figure, despite his alleged endorsement by the obscure ʿAmr b. Jāmiʿ. This individual is not to be confused with the renowned Sunnī *muḥaddith* who shares the same name.[4]

Āghā Bozorg's Later Manuscripts

In his *magnum opus, al-Dharīʿa ilā Taṣānīf al-Shīʿa*, Āghā Bozorg (d. 1389) cited three manuscripts that reference route A, (1) an old manuscript in the library of Hādī Āl Kāshif al-Ghiṭāʾ (d. 1361), (2) a manuscript written by Muḥammad al-Mūsawī al-Khawānsārī (d. 1313) in 1270, and (3) a manuscript in the possession of Abū ʿAlī al-Ḥāʾirī (d. 1216). Āghā Bozorg noted that all of these manuscripts commenced with the following isnād:

> Abū Ṭālib Muḥammad b. Ṣubayḥ b. Rajāʾ informed us in Damascus in 334, he said: Abū ʿUmar ʿIsma b. Abī ʿIṣma al-Bukhārī informed

1 Mustadarakāt ʿIlm Rijāl al-Ḥadīth by al-Shāhrūdī (1/347-348, 1/361)
2 Mustadarakāt ʿIlm Rijāl al-Ḥadīth (6/29)
3 Tārīkh Dimashq by Ibn ʿAsākir (45/451)
4 The renowned Sunnī ḥadīthist, ʿAbdullāh b. al-Mubārak (d. 181), was not a Kūfan, and he used to directly transmit directly from Maʿmar, bypassing ʿAbdurrazzāq (d. 211). Additionally, it was ʿAbdurrazzāq who used to transmit from Ibn al-Mubārak and not vice versa. Hence, if the forger of this isnād had intended for ʿAbdullāh b. al-Mubārak to be the renowned Sunnī scholar, then he has fallen into an obvious error. Otherwise, this ʿAbdullāh b. al-Mubārak is an unknown figure.

> us, he said Abū Bakr Aḥmed b. Mundhir al-Ṣanʿānī, a pious and trusted *sheikh* and the neighbor of Isḥāq b. Ibrāhīm al-Dabarī, informed us in Sanʿā', he said: ʿAbdurrazzāq b. Hammām b. Nāfiʿ al-Ṣanʿānī al-Ḥimyarī, he said: Abū ʿUrwa Maʿmar b. Rāshid al-Baṣrī informed us, he said: Abān b. Abī ʿAyyāsh invited me....[1]

قال الآغا بزرك: وأما في نسخة عتيقة توجد في مكتبة الشيخ هادي آل كاشف الغطاء وهي إلى نصف الكتاب وكذا نسخة شيخنا العلامة النوري التي هي بخط السيد محمد الموسوي الخوانساري سنة 1270، في ثلاثة آلاف وخمس مئة بيت وهي الآن عند الشيخ ميرزا محمد علي الاردوبادي وكذا في نسخة كانت عند الشيخ أبي علي الحائري الرجالي كما أورد أولها في منتهى المقال ، وفي نسخة نقل مفتتحها في إستقصاء الافحام عند بيان إعتباره، فصدر السند في جميع هذه النسخ هكذا:

حدثني أبو طالب محمد بن صبيح بن رجاء بدمشق سنة 334 قال أخبرني أبو عمر [عمرو] عصمة بن عصمة أبي عصمة البخاري قال حدثنا أبو بكر أحمد بن منذر بن أحمد الصنعاني بصنعاء - شيخ صالح مأمون جار إسحق بن إبراهيم الدبري – قال: حدثنا أبو بكر عبدالرزاق بن همام بن نافع الصنعاني الحميري، قال: حدثنا ابو عروة معمر بن راشد البصري، قال: دعاني أبان بن أبي عياش قبل موته بشهر فقال إني رأيت الليلة رؤيا أني لخليق أن أموت....

It seems as though these three manuscripts are interdependent sources that stem from a common manuscript of the book. None of these later manuscripts cite an isnād back to the first transmitter cited in their isnāds, Muḥammad b. Ṣubayḥ, and the isnād cited within these manuscripts is quite weak.

Muḥammad b. Ṣubayḥ b. Rajā' al-Thaqafī is an obscure figure whose reliability is unknown to both Sunnī and Shīʿite scholarship. Ibn ʿAsākir (d. 571) mentioned that he transmitted in Damascus from a variety of sources, including his purported source for *Kitāb Sulaym*, ʿIṣma b. Abī ʿIṣma.[2]

قال ابن عساكر: محمد بن صبيح بن رجاء أبو طالب الثقفي. حدث بدمشق عن مطين الكوفي وأحمد بن سعيد صاحب الزبير بن بكار وأبي عبد الملك أحمد بن إبراهيم وأبي علي إسماعيل بن محمد بن قيراط العذري وأحمد بن الحسين بن السفر وأبي عبد الله الحسين بن سليمان بن داود النحوي وأبي الحسن أحمد ابن أنس بن مالك

1 Al-Dharīʿa ilā Taṣānīf al-Shīʿa by al-Ṭehrānī (2/156-157)
2 Tārīkh Dimashq by Ibn ʿAsākir (53/274)

وأبي عمرو عصمة بن أبي عصمة – واسمه إسرافيل ويقال إسرائيل – وأبي بكر أحمد بن علي بن سعيد القاضي وإبراهيم بن يونس البصري ومحمد بن سليمان المروزي.

ʿIṣma b. Abī ʿIṣma is ʿIṣma b. Isrāʾīl b. Bajmāk al-Bukhārī, and he was an obscure transmitter.[1] Ibn ʿAdī said, "He resided in Egypt, and he then moved to Damascus."[2]

قال ابن عدي: حَدَّثَنَا عِصْمَةُ بْنُ بَجْمَاكَ – كَانَ مُقِيمًا بِمِصْرَ ثُمَّ تَحَوَّلَ إِلَى دِمَشْقَ.

Nevertheless, it does not seem like he was a Shīʿite nor does it seem like he had any organic connection to *Kitāb Sulaym.* In a variety of instances, he is quoted transmitting traditions and sayings of some prominent Sunnī ḥadīth critics, and Ibn ʿAdī transmitted such material from him in his book, *al-Kāmil fī Ḍuʿafāʾ al-Rijāl.*[3] Judging by the content he had transmitted, it rather seems that he was acquainted with ḥadīth criticism in Sunnī circles, and it would hence be quite odd for such an individual to casually transmit a flamingly Shīʿite text like *Kitāb Sulaym Ibn Qays.*

Aḥmed b. Mundhir b. Aḥmed al-Ṣanʿānī is an unknown individual to both Sunnī and Shīʿite scholarship, despite his alleged endorsement in the isnād. I was not able to find a single instance where this barely existent figure is quoted transmitting anything asides from report in al-Ṭūsī's *Amālī*, a Twelver source. Therein, he is cited transmitting from ʿAbdulWahhāb b. Hammām, ʿAbdurrazzāq's brother, a tradition in ʿAlī's merits.[4]

قال الطوسي: أخبرنا جماعة، عن أبي المفضل، قال: حدثنا أبو الليث محمد بن معاذ بن سعيد الحضرمي بالجار، قال أخبرنا أحمد بن المنذر أبو بكر الصنعاني، قال حدثنا عبد الوهاب بن همام، عن أبيه همام بن نافع، عن همام بن منبه، عن حجر – يعني المدري، قال: قدمت مكة و بها أبو ذر جندب بن جنادة، و قدم في ذلك العام عمر بن الخطاب حاجا، و معه طائفة من المهاجرين و الأنصار فيهم علي بن أبي طالب عليه السلام، فبينا أنا في المسجد الحرام مع أبي ذر جالس إذ مر بنا علي عليه السلام ووقف يصلي بإزائنا، فرماه أبو ذر ببصره، فقلت يرحمك الله يا أبا ذر، إنك لتنظر إلى علي فما تقلع عنه قال إني أفعل ذلك و قد سمعت رسول الله صلى الله عليه

---

1 Tārīkh Dimashq by Ibn ʿAsākir (40/351-352)

2 Al-Kāmil fī Ḍuʿafāʾ al-Rijāl (3/33)

3 See Al-Kāmil fī Ḍuʿafāʾ al-Rijāl (1/300, 1/436, 2/521, 3/33, 3/116, 3/146, 4/63, 6/129, 6/383, 6/483, 8/65, 8/225, 8/514, 9/17)

4 Al-Amālī by al-Ṭūsī (p. 674-675)

و آله يقول النظر إلى علي عبادة، و النظر إلى الوالدين برأفة ورحمة عبادة، و النظر في الصحيفة يعني صحيفة القرآن عبادة، و النظر إلى الكعبة عبادة.

The isnād for this report is blunderous: Abū al-Mufaḍḍal al-Shaybānī was a notorious forger, and his source is unknown. Though this tradition cannot be reliably traced to Aḥmed b. al-Mundhir, it may prove to be valuable, as it demonstrates that later unreliable Shīʿite sources seem to be the source of this alleged relationship between Aḥmed b. al-Mundhir and ʿAbdurrazzāq.

It is difficult to even assume that Ismāʿīl b. Ṣubayḥ, who was cited as a transmitter of this variant of the book, actually transmitted anything from *Kitāb Sulaym*, given the discrepancies exhibited across the text's different manuscripts that give rise to its observably divergent routes. Furthermore, the source cited therein is an obscure source, which, paralleled with the numerous transmittive and textual discrepancies in the book, should be evidence of these manuscripts unreliability. In that case, it would be that one of these manuscripts' anonymous copyists or downstream transmitters after the fourth century forged or fabricated this purported route.

Another Obscure Source from Āghā Bozorg

Āghā Bozorg cited another source that purports to transmit *Kitāb Sulaym* through route A. He noted that one of the manuscripts commenced with the following isnād:

> Ibrāhīm [b. ʿUmar al-Yamānī], from ʿAbdurrazzāq, from Maʿmar b. Rāshid, from Abān, from Sulaym b. Qays."[1]

قال الآغا بزرك: بل في بعض الأسانيد يروي عنه بوسائط كثيرة كما في صدر بعض نسخ أصل سليم هكذا [...]. وأيضا: إبراهيم، عن عبدالرزاق، عن معمر بن راشد، عن أبان، عن سليم بن قيس.

The issue with this claim is similar to those of Āghā Bozorg's past sources. Since Āghā Bozorg referenced later obscure manuscripts that cannot be reliably traced back to their purported sources, they are generally unreliable. What further compounds the unreliability of much of these claims is the fact that there is much discrepant and conflicting transmission about Ibrāhīm b. ʿUmar al-Yamānī and ʿAbdurrazzāq, and several other

1 Al-Dharīʿah ilā Taṣānīf al-Shīʿa (2/154)

sources cite both men transmitting *Kitāb Sulaym* through different sources, as shall be demonstrated shortly.

Route B

Route B cites the aforementioned Ibrāhīm b. ʿUmar al-Yamānī transmitting *Kitāb Sulaym* via ʿAbdurrazzāq → his father → Abān b. Abī ʿAyyāsh → Sulaym b. Qays. This route's source are two later manuscripts: (1) al-Ḥammūʾī al-Khurāsānī's manuscript from the tenth century, and (2) Abū ʿAbdillāh al-Mujtahid al-Mūsawī's (d. 1001) manuscript.[1]

قال محقق كتاب سليم بن قيس: الأسانيد إلى إبراهيم بن عمر اليماني، وهي مذكورة في مفتتح عدد من النسخ كنسخة الحموئي الخراساني وأبي عبد الله المجتهد الموسوي هكذا :الحسن بن أبي يعقوب الدينوري عن إبراهيم بن عمر اليماني عن عمه عبد الرزاق بن همام الصنعاني عن أبيه هلال بن نافع عن أبان بن أبي عياش عن سليم بن قيس الهلالي.

These later manuscripts cite an obscure figure named Abū al-Ḥasan b. Abī Yaʿqūb al-Daynawarī transmitting *Kitāb Sulaym* from Ibrāhīm b. ʿUmar with the aforementioned isnād. Like the previously mentioned manuscripts, this variant quotes an earlier source that predated it by many centuries without citing any intermedies between them. What further compounds the unreliability of this purported variant is the fact that al-Ḥasan b. Abī Yaʿqūb al-Daynawarī is a totally unknown transmitter in Sunnī and Shīʿite sources. Furthermore, this route embodies an instance of conflicting transmission about Ibrāhīm b. ʿUmar al-Yamānī where he is presented transmitting the book from ʿAbdurrazzāq, from his father, as opposed to Route A, where he is presented transmitting the book from ʿAbdurrazzāq, from Maʿmar b. Rāshid.

Route C

This route is the isnād for *Kitāb Sulaym* cited by al-Ṭūsī (d. 460) and Ibn al-Najāshī (d. 450) in their book catalogs (*Fihrists*). They both cited Ibn Abī Jīd transmitting *Kitāb Sulaym* from Muḥammad b. al-Ḥasan b. al-Walīd → Muḥammad b. al-Qāsim Mājīlawayh → Muḥammad b. ʿAlī al-Ṣayrafī → Ḥammād b. ʿĪsā and ʿUthmān b. ʿĪsā. After that point in the isnād, al-Ṭūsī's

1 Kitāb Sulaym b. Qays (p. 91)

isnād cited Ḥammād and ʿUthmān transmitting the book from Abān b. Abī ʿAyyāsh, from Sulaym, while Ibn al-Najāshī's isnād cited Ḥammād and ʿUthmān transmitting the book from Ibrāhīm b. ʿUmar al-Yamnānī, from Sulaym b. Qays.[1]

Either way, this isnād is quite unreliable: Muḥammad b. ʿAlī al-Ṣayrafī is the notorious Abū Samīna, and he was condemned by Twelver authorities as a vile forger. Ibn al-Najāshī (d. 450) described him saying:

> He is very weak, corrupt in his beliefs, and he is not to be relied upon in anything. He had migrated to Qom, and he was known in al-Kūfa for lying. He stayed with Aḥmed b. Muḥammad b. ʿĪsā for a while, but he became known for his *ghuluww*. Aḥmed b. Muḥammad b. ʿĪsā then expelled him from Qom...[2]

قال ابن النجاشي: محمد بن علي بن إبراهيم بن موسى أبو جعفر القرشي مولاهم، صيرفي، ابن أخت خلاد المقرئ، وهو خلاد بن عيسى. وكان يلقب محمد بن علي أبا سمينة، ضعيف جدا، فاسد الاعتقاد، لا يعتمد في شي ء. وكان ورد قم وقد اشتهر بالكذب بالكوفة ونزل على أحمد بن محمد بن عيسى مدة، ثم تشهر بالغلو، فجفا، وأخرجه أحمد بن محمد بن عيسى عن قم، وله قصة.

Ibn al-Ghaḍāʾirī similarly disparaged Muḥammad b. ʿAlī al-Ṣayrafī. He described him saying:

> A Kūfan liar who was extreme. He had entered Qom. His status was exposed in it, and Aḥmed b. Muḥammad b. ʿĪsā Al-Ashʿarī expelled him from the city. He was infamous for his extremist beliefs. He should never be considered, and his ḥadīth should not be transcribed.[3]

وقال ابن الغضائري: مُحَمَّدُ بنُ عليّ بن إبْراهيم بن مُحَمَّد، الصَيْرَفِيُّ ابنُ أُخت خَلاّد المُقْرِئُ أَبُو جَعْفَر، الملقّب بأبي سَمِينة، كُوْفِيٌّ كذّابٌ غالٍ. دَخَلَ قُم واشْتَهَرَ أمْرُهُ بِها، ونَفاهُ أَحْمَدُ بنُ مُحَمَّد بن عِيْسى الأشْعريُّ عنها. وكانَ شَهِيْراً في الارْتِفاع، لا يُلْتَفَتُ إليهِ، ولا يُكْتَبُ حديثُهُ.

1 Rijāl al-Najāshī (p. 10), al-Fihrist by al-Ṭūsī (p. 134-135)
2 Rijāl al-Najāshī (p. 317-318)
3 Al-Rijāl by Ibn al-Ghaḍāʾirī (p. 94)

Al-Kashshī said:

> In one of his books, al-Faḍl [b. Shādhān] said, "The infamous liars are Abū al-Khaṭṭāb, Yūnus b. Ẓabyān, Yazīd al-Ṣāyigh, Muḥammad b. Sinān, and Abū Samīna is the most infamous of them all."[1]

قال الكشي: وذكر الفضل في بعض كتبه: الكذابون المشهورون أبوالخطاب ويونس بن ظبيان ويزيد الصايغ ومحمدبن سنان وأبوسمينة أشهرهم.

Though this isnād cited by al-Ṭūsī and al-Najāshī is of little value, Twelver primary sources contain traditions that ascribe fragments of *Kitāb Sulaym* to Ḥammād b. ʿĪsā al-Juhanī through seemingly independent isnāds. These traditions, however, mostly cite Ḥammād transmitting these fragments through Ibrāhīm b. ʿUmar and/or ʿUmar b. Udhayna, from Abān b. Abī ʿAyyāsh. Hence, it seems as though (at least) some of *Kitāb Sulaym's* contents can be traced to Ḥammād b. ʿĪsāIn that regard, it seems route C is the most representative of *Kitāb Sulaym's* original transmission, though it does not accurately outline Ḥammād's sources in his transmission of the book, and more will come on that later.

Route D

Route D is the seemingly strongest isnād for *Kitāb Sulaym Ibn Qays.* In one manuscript, Al-Ṭūsī is quoted relaying this tradition from Hārūn b. Mūsā al-Talʿukbarī ⟶ Abū ʿAlī Muḥammad b. Hammām b. Suhayl ⟶ ʿAbdullāh b. Jaʿfar al-Ḥimyarī ⟶ Yaʿqūb b. Yazīd, Muḥammad b. al-Ḥusayn b. Abī al-Khaṭṭāb and Aḥmed b. Muḥammad b. ʿĪsā ⟶ Ibn Abī ʿUmayr ⟶ ʿUmar b. Udhayna ⟶ Abān b. Abī ʿAyyāsh ⟶ Sulaym b. Qays al-Hilālī.[2]

قال: قال الشيخ أبو جعفر: وأخبرنا أبو عبد الله الحسين بن عبيد الله الغضائري، قال: أخبرنا أبو محمد هارون بن موسى بن أحمد التلعكبري رحمه الله، قال: أخبرنا أبو علي ابن همام بن سهيل، قال: أخبرنا عبد الله بن جعفر الحميري، عن يعقوب بن يزيد ومحمد بن الحسين بن أبي الخطاب وأحمد بن محمد بن عيسى، عن محمد بن أبي عمير عن عمر بن أذينة عن أبان بن أبي عياش عن سليم بن قيس الهلالي.

This route is apparently authentic according to Twelver standards. However, it is, in fact, far from that. Route D is found at the forefront of a

---

1 Rijāl al-Kashshī (p. 386)
2 Kitāb Sulaym Ibn Qays (p. 124)

manuscript, and it commences with Hibatullāh b. Namā (d. post-580) transmitting the book with four isnāds back to al-Ṭūsī (d. 460), who is then quoted transmitting the book with the aforementioned isnād.[1]

The first issue in this isnād is the anonymity of the sources that cite this isnād from Hibatullāh b. Namā (d. post-580), for the first reference to this manuscript seems to be in al-Majlisī's (d. 1111) aforereferenced *Biḥār al-Anwār.*

Furthermore, the isnād ascribed to al-Ṭūsī seemmay prove to embody some serious damning errors. As an example, ʿAbdullāh b. Jaʿfar al-Ḥimyarī in the isnād is quoted transmitting the book from three transmitters, (1) Yaʿqūb b. Yazīd, (2) Ibn Abī al-Khaṭṭāb and (3) Aḥmed b. Muḥammad b. ʿĪsā, who all are then quoted transmitting the book from Muḥammad b. Abī ʿUmayr. This reference may prove to be grossly inaccurate, for a careful assessment of Twelver primary sources will reveal that these figures transmitted contents of *Kitāb Sulaym* via different sources, namely route C. In fact, ʿAbdullāh b. Jaʿfar al-Ḥimyarī, the source of this alleged isnād is quoted elsewhere relaying the book through different routes.

Ibn Bābawayh Jr. (d. 381), in *Kamāl al-Dīn wa-Tamām al-Niʿma*, relayed from his father and Muḥammad b. al-Ḥasan, from Saʿd b. ʿAbdillāh and ʿAbdullāh b. Jaʿfar al-Ḥimyarī, from Muḥammad b. ʿĪsā, Yaʿqūb b. Yazīd and Ibrāhīm b. Hāshim, all of whom relayed from Ḥammād b. ʿĪsā, from ʿUmar b. Udhayna, from Abān, from Sulaym etc.[2]

قال ابن بابويه في «كمال الدين وتمام النعمة»: حدثنا أبي، ومحمد بن الحسن رضي الله عنهما قالا: حدثنا سعد بن عبد الله، وعبد الله بن جعفر الحميري، جميعا: عن محمد بن عيسى، ويعقوب بن يزيد وإبراهيم بن هاشم، جميعا عن **حماد بن عيسى**، عن عمر بن أذينة عن أبان بن أبي عياش، عن سليم بن قيس الهلالي، أنه سمع من سلمان، ومن أبي ذر، ومن المقداد حديثا عن رسول الله صلى الله عليه وآله أنه قال: من مات وليس له امام، مات ميتة جاهلية. ثم عرضه على جابر وابن عباس، فقالا: صدقوا وبروا، وقد شهدنا ذلك وسمعناه من رسول الله صلى الله عليه وآله، وان سلمان قال: يا رسول الله انك قلت: من مات وليس له إمام، مات ميتة جاهلية، من هذا الامام يا رسول الله؟ قال: من أوصيائي، يا سلمان، فمن مات من امتي وليس له إمام منهم يعرفه فهى ميتة جاهلية، فان جهله وعاداه، فهو مشترك، وان جهله ولم يعاده ولم يوال له عدوا فهو جاهل وليس بمشرك.

1 Biḥār al-Anwār by al-Majlisī (1/77)
2 Kamāl al-Dīn wa-Tamām al-Niʿma by Ibn Bābawayh (p. 380-381)

This tradition indicates that ʿAbdullāh b. Jaʿfar's sources could have been misrepresented in route D. In route D, he is quoted transmitting the text from three figures, (1) Yaʿqūb b. Yazīd, (2) Ibn Abī al-Khaṭṭāb and (3) Aḥmed b. Muḥammad b. ʿĪsā, all of whom are quoted transmitting from Ibn Abī ʿUmayr. However, Ibn Bābawayh's isnād presents ʿAbdullāh b. Jaʿfar transmitting from three sources, (1) Muḥammad b. Īsā b. ʿUbayd, (2) Yaʿqūb b. Yazīd and (3) Ibrāhīm b. Hāshim, all of whom transmitted from Ḥammād b. ʿĪsā, which resembles route C in transmission.[1] It should also be noted that Yaʿqūb b. Yazīd, an alleged source of al-Ḥimyarī in route D, is quoted here transmitting Sulaym b. Qays' tradition from Ḥammād b. Īsā, not Ibn Abī ʿUmayr.

Not only is there evidence which indicates that ʿAbdullāh b. Jaʿfar al-Ḥimyarī's sources for *Kitāb Sulaym* were misrepresented in route D, but it is also not farfetched that his alleged three sources' sources were being misrepresented as well.

Speaking of Yaʿqūb b. Yazīd, two other traditions relayed by Ibn Bābawayh similarly cited him transmitting a fragment of *Kitāb Sulaym* via Ḥammād b. ʿĪsā, not Ibn Abī ʿUmayr.[2]

قال ابن بابويه في «كمال الدين وتمام النعمة»: حدثنا أبي، ومحمدبن الحسن رضي الله عنهما قالا: حدثنا سعد بن عبدالله قال: حدثنا يعقوب بن يزيد، عن حماد بن عيسى، عن عمر بن اذينة، عن أبان بن أبي عياش، عن سليم بن قيس الهلالي قال: رأيت عليا عليه السلام في مسجد رسول الله صلى الله عليه وآله في خلافة عثمان وجماعة يتحدثون ويتذاكرون العلم والفقه فذكر نا قريشا(وشرفها) وفضلها وسوابقها وهجرتها وماقال فيها رسول الله صلى الله عليه وآله من الفضل مثل قوله " الائمة من قريش " وقوله " الناس تبع لقريش " و " قريش أئمة العرب " وقوله " لاتسبوا قريشا " وقوله " إن للقرشي قوة رجلين من غيرهم " وقوله " من أبغض قريشا أبغضه

1 In fact, this entire practice in transmission, where one transmitter proceeds to simultaneously quote multiple sources transmitting the same account from a single shared source of theirs, is significantly more prone to a wide array of errors. The transmitter who relays the traditions of three separate figures as a single account is increasingly susceptible to (1) false attributions, (2) the fusion of different traditions and (3) the improper partitioning of the tradition(s) according to their original variation. These errors tend to be related, and it seems to be the case that something of this nature has occurred with route D.

2 Kamāl al-Dīn wa-Tamām al-Niʿma (p. 260, 380-381), al-Khiṣāl by Ibn Bābawayh (p. 477)

الله." وقوله " من أراد هو ان قريش أهانه الله "..." وذكروا الانصار وفضلها وسوابقها ونصرتها وما أثني الله تبارك وتعالى عليهم في كتابه، وماقال فيهم رسول الله صلى الله عليه وآله من الفضل، و ذكروا ماقال في سعد بن عبادة وغسيل الملائكة، فلن يدعو ا شيئا من فضلهم حتى قال كل حي: منا فلان وفلان....

وقال ابن بابويه في «الخصال»: حدثنا أبي رضي الله عنه قال : حدثنا سعد بن عبد الله ، عن أحمد بن محمد ابن عيسى ، عن محمد بن أبي عمير ، عن عمر بن اذينة ، عن أبان بن أبي عياش، عن سليم بن قيس الهلالي، وحدثنا محمد بن الحسن بن الوليد رضي الله عنه قال : حدثنا محمد بن الحسن الصفار ، عن يعقوب بن يزيد ، وإبراهيم بن هاشم جميعا ، عن حماد بن عيسى ، عن إبراهيم بن عمر اليماني ، عن أبان بن أبي عياش، عن سليم بن قيس الهلالي قال : سمعت عبد الله بن جعفر الطيار يقول : كنا عند معاوية أنا والحسن والحسين وعبد الله بن عباس وعمر بن أبي سلمة ، واسامة بن زيد فجرى بيني وبين معاوية كلام فقلت لمعاوية : سمعت رسول الله صلى الله عليه واله يقول : أنا أولى بالمؤمنين من أنفسهم ثم أخي علي بن أبي طالب عليه السلام أولى بالمؤمنين من أنفسهم ، فإذا استشهد علي فالحسن ابن علي أولى بالمؤمنين من أنفسهم ، ثم ابنه الحسين بعد أولى بالمؤمنين من أنفسهم فاذا استشهد فابنه علي بن الحسين الاكبر أولى بالمؤمنين من أنفسهم ، ثم ابني محمد بن علي الباقر أولى بالمؤمنين من أنفسهم ، وستدركه يا حسين ، ثم تكمله اثنى عشر إماما تسعة من ولد الحسين رضي الله عنه ، قال : عبد الله بن جعفر : ثم استشهدت الحسن والحسين و عبد الله بن عباس وعمر بن أبي سلمة واسامة بن زيد فشهدوا لي عند معاوية ، قال : سليم بن قيس الهلالي : وقد سمعت ذلك من سلمان وأبي ذر والمقداد وذكروا أنهم سمعوا ذلك من رسول الله صلى الله عليه واله .

In al-Ḥasan b. Sulaymān al-Ḥillī's (d. ~806) abridgement of the third century Twelver ḥadīth collection, *Baṣā'ir al-Darajāt*, we find an interesting instance where one of the aforementioned transmitters cited as ʿAbdullāh b. Jaʿfar's informants in route D, Ibn Abī al-Khaṭṭāb, is quoted transmitting a tradition of Sulaym b. Qays through other than Ibn Abī ʿUmayr. Ibn Abī al-Khaṭṭāb is rather quoted transmitting the tradition from ʿUthmān b. ʿĪsā, from Ibn Udhayna, from Abān, from Sulaym, which similarly resembles route C.[1]

قال الحسن بن سليمان الحلي في «مختصر بصائر الدرجات»: وعنه وعلي بن اسماعيل بن عيسى ومحمد بن الحسين بن أبي الخطاب، عن عثمان بن عيسى، عن عمر بن أذينة، عن أبان بن أبي عياش عن سليم بن قيس الهلالي،

1 Mukhtaṣar Baṣā'ir al-Darājāt by al-Ḥillī (p. 104)

قال: سمعت عليا " ع " يقول في شهر رمضان وهو الشهر الذي قتل فيه وهو بين ابنيه الحسن والحسين عليهما السلام وبني عبد الله ابن جعفر بن ابى طالب سمعت عليا عليه السلام يقول في شهر رمضان - وهو الشهر الذي قتل فيه - وهو بين ابنيه الحسن والحسين عليهما السلام وبني عبد الله بن جعفر بن أبي طالب وخاصة شيعته، وهو يقول: دعوا الناس وما رضوا لأنفسهم، وألزموا أنفسكم السكوت ودولة عدوكم، فإنه لا يعدمكم ما ينتحل أمركم وعدو باغ حاسد... الخبر.

Additionally, Aḥmed b. Muḥammad b. ʿĪsā, who is quoted transmitting from Ibn Abī ʿUmayr in 'Route D,' can be similarly found, in several instances, transmitting fragments of *Kitāb Sulaym* from Ḥammād b. ʿĪsā, from Ibrāhīm b. ʿUmar, which would constitute Route C.[1]

روى الكليني في «الكافي» عن محمد بن يحيى، عن أحمد بن محمد بن عيسى، عن حماد بن عيسى، عن عمر بن اذينة، عن أبان بن أبي عياش، عن سليم بن قيس الهلالي قال: سمعت أمير المؤمنين عليه السلام يحدث عن النبي صلى الله عليه وآله أنه قال في كلام له: العلماء رجلان: رجل عالم آخذ بعلمه فهذا ناج وعالم تارك لعلمه فهذا هالك، وإن أهل النار ليتأذون من ريح العالم التارك لعلمه، وإن أشد أهل النار ندامة وحسرة رجل دعا عبدا إلى الله فاستجاب له وقبل منه فأطاع الله فأدخله الله الجنة وأدخل الداعي النار بتركه علمه واتباعه الهوى وطول الامل، أما اتباع الهوى فيصد عن الحق وطول الامل ينسي الآخرة.

وروى كذلك الكليني عن محمد بن يحيى، عن أحمد بن محمد بن عيسى، وعلي بن إبراهيم، عن أبيه جميعا، عن حماد بن عيسى، عن عمر بن اذينة، عن أبان بن أبي عياش، عن سليم بن قيس قال: سمعت أمير المؤمنين عليه السلام يقول: قال رسول الله صلى الله عليه وآله: منهومان لا يشبعان طالب دنيا وطالب علم، فمن اقتصر من الدنيا على ما أحل الله له سلم، ومن تناولها من غير حلها هلك، إلا أن يتوب أو يراجع، ومن أخذ العلم من اهله وعمل بعلمه نجا، ومن أراد به الدنيا فهي حظه.

However, it should also be noted that Aḥmed b. Muḥammad b. ʿĪsā is quoted elsewhere transmitting some fragments of Kitāb Sulaym from Muḥammad b. Abī ʿUmayr as is purported in route D.[2]

---

1 Al-Kāfī by al-Kulaynī (1/25-26)

2 Al-Imāma wa-l-Ṭabṣira by Ibn Bābawayh Sr. (p. 110), ʿUyūn Akhbār al-Riḍā (1/52)

روى ابن بابويه في «الإمامة والتبصرة» – وعنه ابنه في «عيون أخبار الرضا» – عن سعد بن عبدالله، عن أحمد بن محمد بن عيسى، عن محمد بن أبي عمير، عن عمر بن أذينة، عن أبان بن أبي عياش، عن سليم بن قيس الهلالي، قال: سمعت عبدالله بن جعفر الطيار، يقول: كنا عند معاوية والحسن والحسين عليهما السلام، وعبدالله بن عباس، وعمر بن أبي سلمة، وأسامة بن زيد – فذكر حديثا جرى بينه وبينه، أنه قال لمعاوية بن أبي سفيان–: سمعت رسول الله صلى الله عليه وآله، يقول: إني أولى بالمؤمنين من أنفسهم.

All in all, these few examples from ʿAbdullāh b. Jaʿfar and his purported sources indicate that the source of route D likely is an inaccurate presentation of al-Ḥimyarī's (and his sources') transmission of the text. What may further attest to this route's defectiveness is that it was not cited by al-Ṭūsī and Ibn al-Najāshī in their entries for *Kitāb* Sulaym, despite it being the seemingly most authentic Twelver isnād for *Kitāb Sulaym.* Hence, it is possible that this alleged isnād for the entirety of *Kitāb Sulaym* was only forged after al-Ṭūsī's death. It should also be noteworthy that though the extant works of al-Ṭūsī make several references to Sulaym b. Qays, there is not a single reference therein of route D.[1]

It is also possible that al-Ṭūsī claimed to transmit *Kitāb Sulaym* as claimed in route D. In that case, the defectiveness and issue in the isnād would stem from ʿAbdullāh b. Jaʿfar al-Ḥimyarī or one of the downstream transmitters.

Hypotheticcally, if the fragments from *Kitāb Sulaym* ascribed to Ibn Abī ʿUmayr prove to be relayed by him, then it is possible that he had originally acquired them from Ḥammād b. ʿĪsā and then omitted him from the isnād, for Ibn Abī ʿUmayr, after all, was a student of Ḥammad.[2] All in all, several indicators suggest that route D is not independent of route C. Additionally, it cannot be verified that Ibn Abī ʿUmayr relayed the entirety of the extant *Kitāb Sulaym Ibn Qays,* though it may be the case that he relayed a few traditions that can be found in the book.

Route E

Route E is the isnād for *Kitāb Sulaym* cited by al-Kashshī (d. mid-fourth century). Al-Kashshī relayed his copy of *Kitāb Sulaym* via Muḥammad b. al-

1 Tahdhīb al-Aḥkām by al-Ṭūsī (4/163, 6/376, 9/206-209), al-Amālī by al-Ṭūsī (p. 888), al-Fihrist by al-Ṭūsī (p. 134-135), Kitāb al-Ghayba by al-Ṭūsī (p. 209)

2 See Biḥār al-Anwār of al-Majlisī (40/210, 47/351, 63/388, 98/93, 101/10)

Ḥasam al-Barāthī ⟶ al-Ḥasan b. ʿAlī b. Kaysān ⟶ Isḥāq b. Ibrāhīm b. ʿUmar al-Yamānī ⟶ Ibn Udhayna ⟶ Abān b. Abī ʿAyyāsh ⟶ Sulaym b. Qays.[1]

قال الكشي: حدثنى محمد بن الحسن البراثي، قال: حدثنا الحسن بن علي بن كيسان، عن إسحاق بن إبراهيم بن عمر اليماني، عن ابن أذينه، عن أبان بن أبي عياش، قال: هذا نسخة كتاب سليم بن قيس العامري ثم الهلالي، دفعه إلى ابان ابن ابي عياش وقراه، وزعم ابان انه قرأه على علي بن الحسين عليهما السلام قال: صدق سليم رحمة الله عليه هذا حديث نعرفه.

This isnād is weak, for Muḥammad b. al-Ḥasan al-Barāthī and al-Ḥasan b. ʿAlī b. Kaysān were both obscure transmitters according to Twelver scholarship, and nothing is known about them in Sunnī sources.[2] Additionally, there is an error in this isnād where Ibrāhīm b. ʿUmar al-Yamānī's name was erroneously transcribed as Isḥāq b. Ibrāhīm b. ʿUmar. This route is not a separate route for the book's transmission, and it evidently is not independent of Route C.

Pivotal Transmitter Assessment

After amassing the book's purported routes of transmission, it becomes apparent that its transmission ultimately come down to one or two routes. I have arrived at several conclusions regarding the book's isnāds: (1) Route E is not independent of Route C, (2) Route D, as recorded in later Twelver bibliographical sources, embodies errors and is likely interdependent with Route C as well, and (3) Routes A and B are interdependent. These findings leave the book with only one route of transmission or, in the best-case scenario, two routes of transmission.

In these isnāds, we observe that the book's purported transmission revolves around a few pivotal transmitters. A careful assessment of these transmitters' biographical data will prove to be insightful when ascertaining the origins and historicity of *Kitāb Sulaym*. The pivotal transmitters of *Kitāb Sulaym* are:

1. Ḥammād b. ʿĪsā al-Juhanī
2. Ibrāhīm b. ʿUmar al-Yamānī
3. ʿAbdurrazzāq b. Hammām al-Ṣanʿānī
4. ʿUmar b. Udhayna

---

1 Rijāl al-Kashshī (p. 82)
2 Al-Mufīd min Muʿjam Rijāl al-Ḥadīth (p. 148, 512)

5. Abān b. Abī ʿAyyāsh
6. Sulaym b. Qays

Ḥammād b. ʿĪsā al-Juhanī (d. 208)

Ḥammād b. ʿĪsā b. ʿUbayda al-Juhanī was cited as a transmitter of *Kitāb Sulaym* in Route C, and there seem to be good reasons to believe that this figure played a crucial role as a source of the early kernel traditions of *Kitāb Sulaym Ibn Qays.*

Ḥammād b. ʿĪsā was a Kūfan Shīʿite figure who moved to the city of Baṣra,[1] and he was disparaged by the early ḥadīth critics. Abū Ḥātim al-Rāzī (d. 277) said, "He is weak in ḥadīth."[2]

قال أبو حاتم: هو ضعيف الحديث.

Al-Bukhārī (d. 256) said, "Ḥammād b. Saʿīd al-Baṣrī. He transmitted from Ḥanẓala. He is disapproved (*munkar*) in ḥadīth."[3] Abū Zurʿā al-Rāzī (d. 264) and Abū Ḥātim al-Rāzī (d. 277) rightfully noted that al-Bukhārī was referring to Ḥammād b. ʿĪsā.[4]

قال البخاري في «التاريخ الكبير»: حَماد بْن سَعِيد، الْبَصْرِيّ، عَنْ حنظلة. مُنكر الحديث.

قال ابن أبي حاتم عن أبي زرعة, "وانما هو حماد بن عيسى." سمعت أبي يقول, "هو كما قال أبو زرعة، لأن حماد بن عيسى هو واسطي وحماد بن سعيد يقال له البراء هو بصرى."

Abū Dāwūd (d. 275) said, "He is weak."[5]

قال أبو عبيد الآجري: سألت أبا دَاوُد عَن حماد بْن عيسى، فقال, "ضعيف."

Al-Tirmidhī (d. 279), after transmitting an infamous tradition of Ḥammād, said, "He has exclusively transmitted it, and he is sparse in transmission. The people have transmitted from him."[6]

روى له الترمذي حديثه ثم قال, "وَقَدْ تَفَرَّدَ بِهِ وَهُوَ قَلِيلُ الحَدِيثِ، وَقَدْ حَدَّثَ عَنْهُ النَّاسُ."

---

1 Rijāl al-Barqī (p. 145), Rijāl al-Najāshī (p. 139), Rijāl al-Ṭūsī (p. 166)
2 Al-Jarḥ wa-l-Taʿdīl by Ibn Abī Ḥātim (3/145)
3 Al-Tārīkh al-Kabīr by al-Bukhārī (3/19)
4 Bayān Khaṭaʾ al-Bukhārī fī Tarīkhih (p. 24)
5 Suʾālāt Abī ʿUbayd al-Ājurrī li-Abī Dāwūd (p. 238)
6 Al-Jāmiʿ al-Kabīr by al-Tirmidhī (5/328)

Al-Bazzār (d. 292), after transmitting that very same ḥadīth of Ḥammād b. ʿĪsā, said, "It was merely Ḥammād b. ʿĪsā who transmitted it from Ḥanẓala, and he is frail (*layyin*) in transmission. His transmission was weakened because of this ḥadīth."[1]

وقال البزار في مسنده: إِنَّمَا رَوَاهُ عَنْ حَنْظَلَةَ حَمَّادُ بْنُ عِيسَى وَهُوَ لَيِّنُ الْحَدِيثِ، وَإِنَّمَا ضُعِّفَ حَدِيثُهُ بِهَذَا الْحَدِيثِ.

Yaḥyā b. Maʿīn (d. 233) was asked about that a ḥadīth of Ḥammād, and he said, "We did not hear it from anyone, but Ḥammād b. ʿĪsā transmitted it. He is a decent (*ṣāliḥ*) *sheikh*."[2]

قال عباس الدوري: فذاكرنا بهذا يحيى بن معين، فقال ما سمعنا من أحد إلا أن حماد بن عيسى رواه، وهو شيخ صالح.

Zakariyyā b. Yaḥyā al-Sājī (d. 307) said, "It has reached me that Yaḥyā b. Maʿīn or Yaḥyā b. Saʿīd said, '[...] Jaʿfar's transmission is upright and sound when the reliable transmitters transmit from him, but if Ḥammād b. ʿĪsā and his scribe, Mughīth, transmit from him, then it is not sound'," which speaks to Ḥammād's perceived unreliability.[3]

قال مغلطاي: قال أبو يحيى: وبلغني عن ابن معين أو ابن سعيد أنه قيل له: يقدم مجالدا على جعفر بن محمد؟ فقال: كان جعفر أوثق من مجالد، ومن أين كان له أحاديث جعفر بن محمد، حديث جعفر مستقيم صحيح إذا حدث عنه الثقات، وإذا حدث عنه حماد بن عيسى ومغيث كاتبه فلا.

Ibn Ḥibbān (d. 354) described Ḥammād b. ʿĪsā saying, "A *sheikh* who transmits distorted things from Ibn Jurayj and ʿAbdulʿAzīz b. ʿUmar b. ʿAbdilʿAzīz that appear forged to the specialist in ḥadīth. He cannot be relied upon."[4]

قال ابن حبان في «المجروحين»: حَمَّاد بْن عِيسَى الْجُهَنِيّ، شيخ يَرْوِي عَن بن جريج وَعبد الْعَزِيز بْن عُمَر ابْن عبد الْعَزِيز أَشْيَاء مقلوبة تتخايل إِلَى من هَذَا الشَّأْن صناعته أَنَّهَا معمولة، لَا يَجُوز الِاحْتِجَاج بِهِ.

Al-Dāraquṭnī (d. 385) weakened Ḥammād on at least two occasions.[5]

1 Musnad al-Bazzār (1/243)
2 Tārīkh Dimashq by Ibn ʿAsākir (20/49)
3 Ikmāl Tahdhīb al-Kamāl (3/228)
4 Al-Majrūḥīn by Ibn Ḥibbān (1/253-254)
5 Al-Ḍuʿafāʾ wa-l-Matrūkūn by al-Dāraquṭnī (2/149), al-Muʾtalif wa-l-Mukhtalif by al-Dāraquṭnī (3/1515)

ذكره الدارقطني في «الضعفاء والمتروكين» وقال: حماد بن عيسى، غريق الجحفة.

وقال الدارقطني في «المؤتلف والمختلف»: حَمَّاد بن عيسى بن عَبِيدَة بن الطُّفَيْل الجُهَنِي، بَصْريّ يَرْوي عن حَنْظَلة بن أبي سُفْيان وعن الثَّوْرِيّ وغيرهما، ضَعِيف الحَدِيث.

The Shīʿite-leaning ḥadīthist, al-Ḥākim al-Naysābūrī (d. 405), described Ḥammād saying, "A *dajjāl* (severe liar) who transmits fabricated ḥadīths from Ibn Jurayj, Jaʿfar b. Muḥammad and others."[1]

قال الحاكم في «المدخل إلى الصحيح»: حماد بن عيسى الجهني، يقال له الغريق. دجال يروى عن ابن جريج وجعفر بن محمد الصادق وغيرهما أحاديث موضوعة.

Abū Nuʿaym al-Aṣbahānī (d. 430) said, "He transmitted disapproved reports (*manākīr*) from Ibn Jurayj and Jaʿfar b. Muḥammad. He is worthless."[2]

قال أبو نعيم في «الضعفاء»: حماد بن عيسى الجهني، يعرف بغريق الجحفة. روى عن بن جريج وجعفر بن محمد بالمناكير، لا شيء.

As evident, Ḥammād b. ʿĪsā was perceived to be an unreliable transmitter by the ḥadīth critics. However, later Twelver biographical sources after the late fourth and fifth centuries believed that Ḥammād was a reliable transmitter.[3] What is further noteworthy about Ḥammād is that he seems to be the primary source to almost all references to Ibrāhīm b. ʿUmar al-Yamānī in Twelver sources. Hossein Modarresi touched on this phenomenon saying:

> With very few exceptions (Kāfī 1: 86, 112, 4: 168, 5: 143; Ṭūsī, Amālī: 735–6), all quotations from this author in Shīʿite works of ḥadīth are through Ḥammād b. ʿĪsā (see Khu'ī 5: 231–2).[4]

It appears Ḥammād b. ʿĪsā claimed to transmit a number of texts from Ibrāhīm b. ʿUmar. Al-Ṭūsī (d. 460) said regarding Ibrāhīm b. ʿUmar al-Yamānī, "He has *uṣūl* which Ḥammād b. ʿĪsā relayed from him."[5]

---

1 Al-Madkhal ilā al-Ṣaḥīḥ (p. 130)
2 Al-Ḍuʿafā' by Abū Nuʿaym (p. 74)
3 See his entries in Rijāl al-Kashshī (p. 225), Rijāl al-Najāshī (p. 139-140), Rijāl al-Ṭūsī (p. 309), and al-Fihrist of al-Ṭūsī (p. 110)
4 Tradition and Survival: A Bibliographical Survey of Early Shīʿite Literature (1/292)
5 Rijāl al-Ṭūsī (p. 106)

قال أبو جعفر الطوسي: إبراهيم بن عمر الصنعاني اليماني، له أصول رواها عنه حماد بن عيسى.

These observations are important, especially considering that many traditions in Twelver sources that reference Sulaym b. Qays can be traced to Ḥammād b. ʿĪsā. In these numerous instances, it is rather apparent that Ḥammād acquisition or transmission of *Kitāb Sulaym* is via Ibrāhīm b. ʿUmar al-Yamānī ⟶ ʿUmar b. Udhayna ⟶ Abān b. Abī ʿAyyāsh ⟶ Sulaym b. Qays. Ḥammād was not only a pivotal transmitter of *Kitāb Sulaym Ibn Qays'* traditions, but he also was the primary source of information on some of the book's upstream transmitters, such as Ibrāhīm b. ʿUmar al-Yamānī. This is quite a powerful observation that will prove to be insightful later in this book as I date *Kitāb Sulaym's* authorship and assess its origins.

Ibrāhīm b. ʿUmar al-Yamānī

Ibrāhīm b. ʿUmar al-Yamānī is an interesting figure who was a pivotal transmitter of the core text of *Kitāb Sulaym.* I have had suspicions about this figure's identity for quite some time, and I believe I may have arrived at some insightful hypotheses in this regard. One of the manuscripts of *Kitāb Sulaym* stated that ʿAbdurrazzāq b. Hammām was Ibrāhīm b. ʿUmar's uncle.[1]

قال الآغا بزرك: بل في بعض الاسانيد يروي عنه بوسائط كثيرة كما في صدر بعض نسخ أصل سليم هكذا: عن إبراهيم بن عمر اليماني عن عمه عبدالرزاق بن همام الذي توفي سنة 211...

This quote may prove to be groundbreaking, for ʿAbdurrazzāq had a nephew by the name of Ibrāhīm b. ʿAbdillāh who was severely disparaged by the *muhaddithīn* for ascribing dubious traditions to his uncle. Ibn Ḥibbān (d. 354) said:

> "Ibrāhīm b. ʿAbdillāh b. Hammām, ʿAbdurrazzāq's nephew. He transmits many distorted reports from ʿAbdurrazzaq that cannot be relied upon by whomever transmits them."

Ibn Ḥibbān then mentioned some of his dubious traditions.[2]

1 Al-Dharīʿah ilā Taṣānīf al-Shīʿa by Āghā Bozorg al-Ṭehrānī (2/154)
2 Al-Majrūḥīn by Ibn Ḥibbān (1/118)

قال ابن حبان: إِبْرَاهِيمُ بْنُ عَبْدِ اللَّهِ بْنِ همام بن أَخِي عَبْد الرَّزَّاق يروي عَن عَبْد الرَّزَّاق المقلوبات الْكَثِيرَة الَّتِي لَا يَجُوز الِاحْتِجَاج لمن يَرْوِيهَا.

Ibn ʿAdī stated that Ibrāhīm was disapproved (*munkar*) in ḥadīth, and he stated that most of what he transmitted consists of disapproved reports (*manākīr*).[1]

قال ابن عدي: إبراهيم بن عَبد الله بْنِ هَمَّامٍ، ابْنُ أَخِي عَبد الرَّزَّاق. منكر الحديث.

وساق له ابن عدي أحاديث ثم قال: وَهَذِهِ الأَحَادِيثُ مَنَاكِيرُ مَعَ سَائِرِ مَا يَرْوِي ابْنُ أَخِي عَبد الرَّزَّاق هَذَا.

Abū al-Fatḥ al-Azdī (d. 369) said, "He is abandoned in ḥadīth, a liar. His ḥadīth should not be transcribed."[2]

وقال الأزدي: متروك الحديث كذاب لا يكتب حديثه.

Al-Dāraquṭnī (d. 385) described him saying, "A liar who fabricates ḥadīth."[3]

وقال الدارقطني: إبراهيم بن عبيد الله بن همام بن أخي عبد الرزاق عن عمه كذاب يضع الحديث.

Al-Ḥākim al-Naysābūrī (d. 405) said, "He transmitted fabricated ḥadīths from his uncle, and Muḥammad b. al-Ḥasan b. Qutayba al-ʿAsqalānī transmitted some of them."[4]

وقال الحاكم: إبراهيم بن عبد الله بن همام ابن أخي عبد الرزاق حدث عنه عمه بأحاديث موضوعه وقد روى عنه محمد بن الحسن بن قتيبة العسقلاني أحاديث منها.

Abū Nuʿaym (d. 430) made similar remarks to those of al-Ḥākim.[5]

وقال أبو نعيم: إبراهيم بن عبد الله بن همام بن أخي عبد الرزق حدث بالموضوعات عن عمه روى عنه الشاميون حدثونا عن بن قتيبة عنه.

Asides from Ibrāhīm's unreliability, it seems as though he was an extreme Shīʿite figure. As an example, he relayed from his uncle,

1 Al-Kāmil fī Ḍuʿafāʾ al-Rijāl (1/440-441)
2 Al-Ḍuʿafāʾ wa-l-Matrūkūn by Ibn al-Jawzī (1/41)
3 Al-Ḍuʿafāʾ wa-l-Matrūkūn by al-Dāraquṭnī (1/251)
4 Al-Madkhal ilā al-Ṣaḥīḥ by al-Ḥākim al-Naysābūrī (p. 116)
5 Al-Ḍuʿafāʾ by Abū Nuʿaym (p. 58)

ʿAbdurrazzāq, from Maʿmar, from Muḥammad b. al-Munkadir, from Jābir b. ʿAbdillāh that he said:

> We, the *Anṣār*, used to test our children with the love of ʿAlī b. Abī Ṭālib. If we found them confirming the love, then we would become aware that they were our children. If we saw otherwise, then we would become aware that they were [illegitimately] born within us.[1]

قال أبو الحسن الغساني: حَدَّثَنَا إِبْرَاهِيمُ بْنُ عَبْدِ اللَّهِ بْنِ هَمَّامٍ قَالَ حَدَّثَنَا عَبْدُ الرَّزَّاقِ قَالَ أَخْبَرَنَا مَعْمَرٌ عَنْ مُحَمَّدِ بْنِ الْمُنْكَدِرِ عَنْ جَابِرِ بْنِ عَبْدِ اللَّهِ قَالَ كُنَّا مَعْشَرَ الْأَنْصَارِ نَمْتَحِنُ أَوْلَادَنَا بِحُبِّ عَلِيِّ بْنُ أَبِي طَالِبٍ صَلَوَاتُ اللَّهِ عَلَيْهِ فَإِنْ وَافَيْنَاهُمْ يَصْدُقُونَ الْمَحَبَّةَ لَهُ عَلِمْنَا أَنَّهُمْ مِنَّا وَإِنْ كَانَ غَيْرَ ذَلِكَ عَلِمْنَا أَنَّهُمْ مَدْخُولُونَ.

Ibrāhīm also relayed with the same isnād that Jābir b. ʿAbdillāh said, "We used to recognize the *munafiqīn* during the Messenger of Allah's ﷺ life through their deviation from ʿAlī b. Abī Ṭālib.[2]

وقال: وَبِإِسْنَادِهِ عَنْ جَابِرِ بْنِ عَبْدِ اللَّهِ قَالَ كُنَّا نَعْرِفُ الْمُنَافِقِينَ عَلَى عَهْدِ رَسُولُ اللَّهِ صَلَّى اللَّهُ عَلَيْهِ وَسَلَّمَ بِازْوِرَارِهِمْ عَنْ عَلِيِّ بْنِ أَبِي طَالِبٍ صَلَوَاتُ اللَّهِ عَلَيْهِ.

The first tradition of Ibrāhīm is a fabrication, and none else transmitted it from ʿAbdurrazzāq with this isnād. The second tradition was relayed through other routes; however, Ibrāhīm exclusively transmitted it from ʿAbdurrazzāq with this isnād.

With these observations considered, is it possible that the purported nephew of ʿAbdurrazzāq cited in the aforementioned sources, Ibrāhīm b. ʿUmar, actually is Ibrāhīm b. ʿAbdillāh al-Ṣanʿānī. However, I am yet to come across further evidence that would allow me to definitively conclude this. Otherwise, the identity of Ibrāhīm b. ʿUmar al-Yamānī, the reputed transmitter of *Kitāb Sulaym*, was discussed in some later Twelver biographical sources, as shall be shortly demonstrated.

Oddly enough, there was a Yemenite transmitter from Yemen by the name of Ibrāhīm b. ʿUmar in Sunnī biographical sources whose *kunya*, name and residence match those of the purported transmitter of *Kitāb Sulaym*.[3]

---

1 Akhbār wa-Ḥikāyāt by al-Ghassānī (p. 49)

2 Akhbār wa-Ḥikāyāt by al-Ghassānī (p. 49-50)

3 See the entry of Abū Isḥāq Ibrāhīm b. ʿUmar b. Kaysān al-Ṣanʿānī in al-Bukhārī's al-Tārīkh al-Kabīr (1/307-308), al-Dūlābī's al-Kunā wa-l-Asmāʾ (1/304).

This individual is Abū Isḥāq Ibrāhīm b. ʿUmar b. Kaysān al-Ṣanʿānī. He was described in Sunnī biographical sources as a reliable transmitter and a pious worshipper.[1] What is also noteworthy is that ʿAbdurrazzāq b. Hammām al-Ṣanʿānī transmitted from this Ibrāhīm in his *Muṣannaf*.[2] Hence, if the Ibrāhīm b. ʿUmar al-Yamānī of *Kitāb Sulaym* was intended to be this Ibrāhīm b. ʿUmar b. Kaysān, then the isnāds in figure 1 that present Ibrāhīm as a student of ʿAbdurrazzāq should be even more evidently dubious.

Though Ibrāhīm b. ʿUmar b. Kaysān's transmission primarily is from non-Shīʿite sources, such as his father, ʿAbdullāh b. Wahb b. Munabbih, Wahb b. Maʾnūs, ʿAbdulKarīm b. Abī al-Mukhāriq, and Ḥafṣ b. Maysara, it appears that he did, in fact, have some connections to some Rāfiḍite figures in Yemen. Abū Bakr al-Rāzī (d. 460) said: ʿAlī b. ʿAbdilWārith said:

> I asked Abū Muḥammad al-Kashwarī, "Who was the first person to bring Rāfiḍism to Yemen?"
>
> Muḥammad b. ʿAbdirraḥīm thus answered saying, "The first man to bring it was a man from Kūfa. Ibrāhīm b. ʿUmar b. Kaysān used to sit with him."
>
> Al-Kashwarī said: Sufyān b. ʿUyayna said, "The people of Yemen are well so as long as they are safe from this man," meaning Ibrāhīm b. ʿUmar b. Kaysān.[3]

قال أبو بكر الرازي في «تاريخ مدينة صنعاء»: قال علي بن عبد الوارث: سألت أبا محمد الكشوري: من أول من جاء بالرفض إلى صنعاء؟ قال: فقال محمد بن عبد الرحيم: أول من جاء به رجل من أهل الكوفة، كان إبراهيم بن عمر بن كيسان يختلف إليه. وقال الكشوري: قال سفيان بن عيينة: أهل اليمن لا بأس بهم إن سلموا من هذا الرجل، يعني إبراهيم بن عمر بن كيسان.

Hishām b. Yūsuf described Ibrāhīm b. ʿUmar b. Kaysān saying, "He was from the best of people in prayer, but there was something wrong in his thought."[4]

1 See his entry in Tahdhīb al-Kamāl fī Asmāʾ al-Rijāl (2/157)

2 Muṣannaf ʿAbdirrazzāq (2/164, 3/157, 3/458, 4/276, 4/518, 4/519, 6/20, 6/134, 6/461, 8/7, 8/107, 8/131, 8/222, 8/254, 8/363, 8/392, 8/430, 8/488, 9/122, 8/448, 9/469)

3 Tārīkh Madīnat Ṣanʿāʾ by al-Rāzī (p. 430)

4 Al-Tārīkh al-Kabīr by al-Bukhārī (1/307)

قال البخاري في «التاريخ الكبير»: قال لى ابراهيم ابن موسى، قال ثنا هشام بن يوسف، قال: أخبرني إبراهيم بن عمر – وكان من أحسن الناس صلاة وكان في رأيه شيء [...].

What is also noteworthy is that much of Ibrāhīm b. ʿUmar b. Kaysān's transmission is from the Baṣran Ibn Abī al-Mukhāriq, which mirrors Ibrāhīm b. ʿUmar's transmission from the Baṣran Ibn Udhayna.

The later Twelver Ibn al-Najāshī (d. 450) described Ibrāhīm b. ʿUmar saying, "A *sheikh* from our companions who was a reliable transmitter (*thiqa*). He transmitted from Abū Jaʿfar (as) and Abū ʿAbdillāh (as)."[1]

قال ابن النجاشي: إبراهيم بن عمر اليماني الصنعاني، شيخ من أصحابنا ثقة. روى عن أبي جعفر وأبي عبد الله عليهما السلام، ذكر ذلك أبو العباس وغيره. له كتاب يرويه عنه حماد بن عيسى وغيره.

أخبرنا محمد بن عثمان، قال: حدثنا أبو القاسم جعفر بن محمد، قال حدثنا عبيد الله بن أحمد بن نهيك، قال: حدثنا ابن أبي عمير، عن حماد بن عيسى، عن إبراهيم بن عمر به.

Al-Ṭūsī (d. 460) dedicated an entry for Ibrāhīm in his *Fihrist*, but he did not comment on his reliability. He said, "Ibrāhīm b. ʿUmar al-Yamānī, and he is al-Ṣanʿānī. He has an *Aṣl*." [2] Al-Ṭūsī, like al-Najāshī, listed him as a companion of both Jaʿfar al-Ṣādiq (d. 148) and al-Bāqir (d. 118).[3]

قال الطوسي: إبراهيم بن عمر اليماني و هو الصنعاني، له أصل.

أخبرنا به عدة من أصحابنا، عن أحمد بن محمد بن الحسن بن الوليد، عن أبيه، عن محمد بن الحسن الصفار، عن أحمد بن محمد بن عيسى، عن الحسين بن سعيد، عن حماد بن عيسى عنه، و أخبرنا أحمد بن عبدون عن أبي طالب الأنباري، عن حميد بن زياد، عن ابن نهيك و القاسم بن إسماعيل القرشي جميعا، عنه.

On the other hand, the Twelver critic, Ibn al-Ghaḍāʾirī (d. 5th century), was critical of Ibrāhīm b. ʿUmar. He said, "Ibrāhīm b. ʿUmar al-Ṣanʿānī al-Yamānī. His *kunya* is Abū Isḥāq. He is very weak. He transmitted from Abū ʿAbdillāh [al-Ṣādiq] and Abū Jaʿfar [al-Bāqir]."[4]

---

1 Rijāl al-Najāshī (p. 22)
2 Al-Fihrist by al-Ṭūsī (p. 44-45)
3 Rijāl al-Ṭūsī (p. 106, 137)
4 Al-Rijāl by Ibn al-Ghaḍāʾirī (p. 36)

وقال ابن الغضائري: إبْراهيمُ بنُ عُمَر، الصَنْعانيّ، اليمانيّ، يُكنّى أبا إسْحاق. ضَعِيفٌ جِدّاً. روى عن أبي جَعْفَر، وأبي عَبْدالله.

From the aforementioned quotes, it is rather obvious that Ibrāhīm b. ʿUmar's mention in some isnāds of *Kitāb Sulaym* is discrepant and defective. In routes A and B, Ibrāhīm b. ʿUmar al-Yamānī is presented relaying the book from ʿAbdurrazzāq (d. 211) and is said to be ʿAbdurrazzāq's nephew. It is quite farfetched for a transmitter who transmitted from ʿAbdurrazzāq (d. 211), his alleged uncle, to simultaneously be a companion of al-Bāqir (d. 118) and Jaʿfar al-Ṣādiq (d. 148).

What is additionally noteworthy about Ibrāhīm b. ʿUmar al-Yamānī is that almost all references to him in Twelver sources, as stated earlier, seem to originate from the unreliable Ḥammād b. ʿĪsā al-Juhanī (d. 208), further obfuscating any attempt to make sense of his identity. This reality opens the door to the possibility that an intentional or non-intentional conflation/misidentification could have occurred with his identity as a result of Ḥammād b. ʿĪsā's unreliability.

In light of this observation, it seems most likely to me that the unreliable Ḥammād b. ʿĪsā had intended for Ibrāhīm b. ʿUmar al-Yamānī to be the reliable Yemenite transmitter, Ibrahīm b. ʿUmar b. Kaysān, as the parallels between both figures are numerous, whether it be their name, residence, *kunya*, their connection to some (ʿIrāqī) Rāfiḍite figures or their transmission from Baṣran transmitters. Furthermore, Ibrāhīm b. ʿUmar b. Kaysān can be presented as someone who was contemporaneous to Jaʿfar al-Ṣādiq (d. 148) and Muḥammad al-Bāqir (d. 118), as opposed to the Ibrāhīm who was ʿAbdurrazzāq's (d. 211) nephew and student. This would be further evidence that the isnāds that present Ibrāhīm b. ʿUmar transmitting *Kitāb Sulaym* from ʿAbdurrazzāq (within routes A and B) are mere forgeries. Either way, the isnāds that cite Ibrāhīm b. ʿUmar transmitting the book of Sulaym are unreliable, regardless of whether Ibrāhīm proves to be Ibrāhīm b. ʿAbdillāh, Ibrāhīm b. ʿUmar b. Kaysān or another figure.

ʿAbdurrazzāq b. Hammām al-Ṣanʿānī (d. 211)

The pivotal transmitter cited as the source of *Kitāb Sulaym* in routes A and B is the reliable Shīʿite-leaning *muḥaddith* of Yemen, ʿAbdurrazzāq b. Hammām al-Ṣanʿānī (d. 211). It has been previously demonstrated that each of the isnāds that cite ʿAbdurrazzāq transmitting this text embody various defects that seriously undermine their credibility. There also are other observations pertaining to this figure that would prove to be valuable when ascertaining his purported role in this book's transmission.

ʿAbdurrazzāq's Shīʿite leanings were denoted by several ḥadīthists, such as al-ʿIjlī (d. 261), Ibn Ḥibbān (d. 354), Ibn ʿAdī (d. 365) and others etc.[1] In fact, it is noted in early ḥadīthist sources that ʿAbdurrazzāq used to sometimes transmit ḥadīths from the *mathālib* genre, which are traditions that portrayed the *ṣaḥāba* in negative lights. Yaḥyā b. Maʿīn said:

> Aḥmed [b. Ḥanbal], Khalaf and another man were once with ʿAbdurrazzāq. When the ḥadīths of the *mathālib* came up, Aḥmed b. Ḥanbal plugged his ears with his fingers for a long time until some of the ḥadīths were finished. He then took his fingers out of his ears and then plugged them back until all of the ḥadīths were over.[2]

قال أبو بكر: وأخبرني العباس بن محمد بن إبراهيم، قال: سمعت جعفرا الطيالسي، يقول: سمعت يحيى بن معين، يقول: كانوا عند عبد الرزاق: أحمد، وخلف، ورجل آخر، فلما مرت أحاديث المثالب وضع أحمد بن حنبل إصبعيه في أذنيه طويلا حتى مر بعض الأحاديث، ثم أخرجهما، ثم ردهما حتى مضت الأحاديث كلها - أو كما قال.

Can this tradition be cited to substantiate ʿAbdurrazzāq's purported transmission of *Kitāb Sulaym*? After a careful of analysis of the book's transmission and ʿAbdurrazzāq's biographical data, the answer certainly is in the negative. First and foremost, the *mathālib* genre spans traditions from a wide array of different subjects, most notably the conflicts between the *saḥāba*, such as the battles of al-Jamāl, Ṣiffīn, the murder of ʿUthmān and related events. Secondly, it is apparent that ʿAbdurrazzāq had a relatively favorable perception of Abū Bakr and ʿUmar, who are portrayed as the murderers of Fāṭima in *Kitāb Sulaym*. As an example, ʿAbdurrazzāq is quoted saying:

> I give precedence to the two *sheikhs* (Abū Bakr and ʿUmar) over ʿAlī due to ʿAlī's preference of them over himself. Had he not given them preference, then I would not have given them preference.

1 Tahdhīb al-Kamāl (18/59-62)
2 Al-Sunna by Abū Bakr b. al-Khallāl (3/502)

> Sufficient of a vice for me is that I love ʿAlī and then go against his speech.[1]

قال ابن عدي: حَدَّثَنَا الشرقي، حَدَّثنا أَبُو الأزهر سمعت عَبد الرَّزَّاق يَقُولُ أفضل الشيخين بتفضيل علي إياهما عَلَى نفسه ولو لم يفضلهما لم أفضلهما كفى بي إزراء أن أحب عليا ثُمَّ أخالف قوله.

This is a sentiment that existed within some early Shīʿite communities, and this report provides a glimpse into ʿAbdurrazzāq's Shīʿism, especially considering that he only gave precedence to Abū Bakr and ʿUmar over ʿAlī because of his belief that ʿAlī, himself, did so. Such statements actually appear to embody an implicit belief in ʿAlī b. Abī Ṭālib's superiority, though they, nonetheless, highlight ʿAbdurrazzāq's non-Rāfiḍite attitude towards Abū Bakr and ʿUmar. ʿAbdurrazzāq, in his *Muṣannaf,* also recorded a tradition that quotes ʿAlī acknowledging Abū Bakr and ʿUmar's as "the best of the *Umma.*"[2]

عبد الرزاق عَنْ حُسَيْنِ بْنِ مِهْرَانَ، عَنِ الْمُطَرِّحِ أَبِي الْمُهَلَّبِ، عَنْ عُبَيْدِ اللَّهِ بْنِ زَحْرٍ، عَنْ عَلِيِّ بْنِ يَزِيدَ، عَنِ الْقَاسِمِ، عَنْ أَبِي أُمَامَةَ قَالَ: جَاءَ أَبُو سَعِيدٍ الْخُدْرِيُّ إِلَى عَلِيِّ بْنِ أَبِي طَالِبٍ وَهُوَ جَالِسٌ وَهُوَ مُحْتَبٍ، فَسَلَّمَ عَلَيْهِ فَرَدَّ عَلَيْهِ فَقَالَ: أَبَا حَسَنٍ أَخْبِرْنِي عَنِ الْمَشْيِ أَمَامَ الْجِنَازَةِ إِذَا شَهِدْتُهَا أَيُّ ذَلِكَ أَفْضَلُ أَخَلْفَهَا أَمْ أَمَامَهَا؟ قَالَ: فَقَطَّبَ عَلِيٌّ بَيْنَ عَيْنَيْهِ، ثُمَّ قَالَ: [......] إِنَّ خَيْرَ هَذِهِ الْأُمَّةِ أَبُو بَكْرِ بْنِ أَبِي قُحَافَةَ وَعُمَرُ بْنُ الْخَطَّابِ، ثُمَّ اللَّهُ أَعْلَمُ بِالْخَيْرِ أَيْنَ هُوَ، وَلَئِنْ كُنْتَ رَأَيْتَهُمَا يَفْعَلَانِ ذَلِكَ فَإِنَّهُمَا لَيَعْلَمَانِ أَنَّ فَضْلَ الْمَاشِي خَلْفَهَا عَلَى الْمَاشِي أَمَامَهَا كَفَضْلِ صَلَاةِ الْمَكْتُوبَةِ عَلَى صَلَاةِ التَّطَوُّعِ...

In his *Muṣannaf,* ʿAbdurrazzāq also relayed traditions that positively portrayed Abū Bakr inauguration, including a tradition where ʿAlī affirms his belief in Abū Bakr's suitability for the leadership of the Muslim community.[3]

قال عبد الرزاق: أَخْبَرَنَا ابْنُ مُبَارَكٍ، عَنْ مَالِكِ بْنِ مِغْوَلٍ، عَنِ ابْنِ أَبْجَرَ قَالَ: لَمَّا بُويِعَ لِأَبِي بَكْرٍ رَضِيَ اللَّهُ عَنْهُ جَاءَ أَبُو سُفْيَانَ إِلَى عَلِيٍّ، فَقَالَ: غَلَبَكُمْ عَلَى هَذَا الْأَمْرِ أَذَلُّ أَهْلِ بَيْتٍ فِي قُرَيْشٍ، أَمَا وَاللَّهِ لَأَمْلَأَنَّهَا خَيْلًا وَرِجَالًا. قَالَ: فَقُلْتُ: مَا زِلْتَ عَدُوًّا لِلْإِسْلَامِ وَأَهْلِهِ فَمَا ضَرَّ ذَلِكَ الْإِسْلَامَ وَأَهْلَهُ شَيْئًا، إِنَّا رَأَيْنَا أَبَا بَكْرٍ لَهَا أَهْلًا.

Elsewhere, ʿAbdurrazzāq is authentically quoted saying:

---

1 Al-Kāmil fī Ḍuʿafā' al-Rijāl (6/540)

2 Muṣannaf ʿAbdirrazzāq al-Ṣanʿānī (3/447-449)

3 Muṣannaf ʿAbdirrazzāq al-Ṣanʿānī (5/450)

By Allah, my chest was never content with giving precedence to ʿAlī over Abū Bakr and ʿUmar. May the mercy of Allah be upon Abū Bakr and ʿUmar, and may the mercy of Allah be upon ʿUthmān. May the mercy of Allah be upon ʿAlī. Whoever does not love them is not a believer. The most secure of our actions is our love of them all. May Allah be pleased with them all, and may He not place on our necks any liability in their regard. May He resurrect us in their assembly and company. *Amīn ya rabb al-ʿālamīn.*[1]

قال عبد الله: قثنا سَلَمَةُ بْنُ شَبِيبٍ أَبُو عَبْدِ الرَّحْمَنِ النَّيْسَابُورِيُّ، قَالَ: سَمِعْتُ عَبْدَ الرَّزَّاقِ يَقُولُ: وَاللَّهِ مَا انْشَرَحَ صَدْرِي قَطُّ أَنْ أُفَضِّلَ عَلِيًّا عَلَى أَبِي بَكْرٍ وَعُمَرَ، وَرَحْمَةُ اللَّهِ عَلَى أَبِي بَكْرٍ وَعُمَرَ، وَرَحْمَةُ اللَّهِ عَلَى عُثْمَانَ، رَحْمَةُ اللَّهِ عَلَى عَلِيٍّ، وَمَنْ لَمْ يُحِبَّهُمْ فَمَا هُوَ بِمُؤْمِنٍ، وَإِنَّ أَوْثَقَ أَعْمَالِنَا حُبُّنَا إِيَّاهُمْ أَجْمَعِينَ، رَضِيَ اللَّهُ عَنْهُمْ أَجْمَعِينَ، وَلَا جَعَلَ لِأَحَدٍ مِنْهُمْ فِي أَعْنَاقِنَا تَبِعَةً، وَحَشَرَنَا فِي زُمْرَتِهِمْ وَمَعَهُمْ، آمِينَ رَبَّ الْعَالَمِينَ.

It would be an anachronism to understand ʿAbdurrazzāq's Shīʿism in light of contemporary Twelver Shīʿite theology. Rather, ʿAbdurrazzāq's Shīʿite leanings manifested in his intense affinity to ʿAlī and his hatred of ʿAlī's enemies. As an example, ʿAbdurrazzāq, in one instance, is quoted reviling Muʿāwiya b. Abī Sufyān.[2]

قال العقيلي: حدثني أحمد بن زكير الحضرمي قال: حدثنا محمد بن إسحاق بن يزيد البصري قال: سمعت مخلدا الشعيري يقول: كنت عند عبد الرزاق فذكر رجل عند [عنده] معاوية فقال: لا تقذر مجلسنا بذكر ولد أبي سفيان.

Abdurrazzāq is also quoted casually criticizing ʿUmar b. al-Khaṭṭāb whilst relaying a tradition that involved him, which should be indicative of his Shīʿite tendencies.[3]

قال العقيلي: سمعت علي بن عبد الله بن المبارك الصنعاني يقول: كان زيد بن المبارك لزم عبد الرزاق فأكثر عنه ثم خرق كتبه ولزم محمد بن ثور فقيل له في ذلك فقال: كنا عند عبد الرزاق فحدثنا بحديث معمر، عن الزهري، عن مالك بن أوس بن الحدثان الحديث الطويل، فلما قرأ قول عمر لعلي والعباس: فجئت أنت تطلب ميراثك من ابن أخيك، وجاء هذا يطلب ميراث امرأته من أبيها، قال عبد الرزاق: انظروا إلى الأنوك، يقول: تطلب

1 Faḍā'il al-Ṣaḥāba by Aḥmed b. Ḥanbal (1/146)
2 Al-Ḍuʿafāʾ al-Kabīr by al-ʿUqaylī (3/109)
3 Al-Ḍuʿafāʾ al-Kabīr by al-ʿUqaylī (3/110)

أنت ميراثك من ابن أخيك ويطلب هذا ميراث امرأته من أبيها، ألا يقول رسول الله صلى الله عليه وسلم؟ قال زيد بن المبارك: فقمت فلم أعد إليه ولا أروي عنه حديثا أبدا.

ʿAbdurrazzāq's aforementioned statements regarding Abū Bakr and ʿUmar hence are not to be confused with the Sunnī attitude towards both men, though it may appear, at first glance, similar to it. Nonetheless, it seems that ʿAbdurrazzāq gave Abū Bakr and ʿUmar precedence over ʿAlī in a mere technical sense due to the overflowing amount of traditions that quote ʿAlī b. Abī Ṭālib asserting their superiority. Given that all isnāds for *Kitāb Sulaym* back to ʿAbdurrazzāq are blunderous, these statements of his further demonstrate that the book's ascription to him is nothing short of a forgery. Accordingly, it should not be a surprise to the reader that the Shīʿite ʿAbdurrazzāq is also quoted declaring Rāfiḍites to be disbelievers. Abū Bakr b. Zanjawayh said: I heard ʿAbdurrazzāq say, "The Rāfiḍite is a *kāfir*."[1]

قال ابن عدي: حَدَّثَنَا ابْنُ أَبِي عِصْمَةَ، حَدَّثَنا أَحْمَدُ بْنُ أَبِي يَحْيى، قَالَ: سَمِعْتُ أَبَا بَكْرِ بْنَ زَنْجَوَيْهِ يَقُولُ: سَمعتُ عَبد الرَّزَّاق يَقُولُ: الرافضي كافر.

ʿAbdurrazzāq's excommunication (*takfīr*) of extremist Shīʿites who reviled Abū Bakr and ʿUmar ironically seems to stem from his Shīʿite leanings. Since ʿAbdurrazzāq believed that ʿAlī, himself, had praised Abū Bakr and ʿUmar and viewed them favorably, the extreme Shīʿites who reviled both men were in blatant opposition to ʿAlī b. Abī Ṭālib. This disobedience of ʿAlī by the Rāfiḍites apparently was perceived by ʿAbdurrazzāq to be a greater sin than their revilement of both Abū Bakr and ʿUmar. These observations should cumulatively demonstrate that Routes A and B, which cite ʿAbdurrazzāq transmitting the extant recension of Kitāb Sulaym, were forged in his name.

What I also find noteworthy is the fact ʿAbdurrazzāq's aforementioned declaration of Rāfiḍites to be disbelievers (*kuffār*) was relayed by ʿIṣma b. Abī ʿIṣma, a transmitter who was dubiously presented in some of *Kitāb Sulaym's* purported routes as a transmitter of the book from ʿAbdurrazzāq!

ʿUmar b. Udhayna (d. ~169)

The obscurity in the origins of *Kitāb Sulaym Ibn Qays* commences with the figure known as ʿUmar b. Udhayna, who is said to have ad been a head figure

1 Al-Kāmil fī Ḍuʿafāʾ al-Rijāl (6/540)

of the proto-Twelver community in Baṣra, ʿIrāq. ʿUmar, however, is totally unknown in Sunnī sources.

Routes C, D and E for the book all ultimately converge to ʿUmar b. Udhayna, regardless of their apparent discrepancies, and ʿUmar possibly is the source of *Kitāb Sulaym's* kernel traditions. Later Twelver biographers considered ʿUmar b. Udhayna reliable in transmission. Ibn al-Najāshī (d. 450) said:

> "The *sheikh* of our Baṣran companions and their face. He transmitted from Abū ʿAbdillāh by mail."

Al-Najāshī also listed his lineage back to the ancient patriarch of the Arabs, ʿAdnān, thus demonstrating that al-Najāshī viewed him as an Arab by lineage.[1]

قال ابن النجاشي: عمر بن محمد بن عبد الرحمن بن أذينة بن سلمة بن الحارث بن خالد بن عائذ بن سعد بن ثعلبة بن غنم بن مالك بن بهثة بن جديمة بن الديل بن شن بن أفصى بن عبد القيس بن أفصى بن دعمي بن جديلة بن أسد بن ربيعة بن نزار بن معد بن عدنان. شيخ أصحابنا البصريين ووجههم، روى عن أبي عبد الله عليه السلام بمكاتبة.

ʿUmar's purported lineage, which was cited by al-Najāshī (d. 450), is contested by a claim made by the earlier Shīʿite biographer, Ibn al-Barqī, who stated that ʿUmar b. Udhayna was a client (*mawlā*) of the Arabian tribe, Banī ʿAbdilqays. Ibn al-Barqī further stated that ʿUmar b. Udhayna was not his real name. Rather, his original name was Muḥammad b. ʿUmar b. Udhayna, and his father's name, ʿUmar, merely prevailed over his first name.[2]

وقال ابن البرقي: محمد بن عمر بن أذينة، غلب عليه اسم أبيه وهو مدني مولى عبد القيس.

Al-Kashshī (d. mid-fourth century) said:

> I heard my *sheikhs*, among them al-ʿUbaydī and others, state that Ibn Udhayna was a Kūfan. He had fled from [the caliph] al-Mahdī, and he died in Yemen. It is for that reason that not much has been transmitted from him. It is said that his name is Muḥammad b.

1 Rijāl al-Najāshī (p. 272)
2 Rijāl al-Barqī (p. 142)

> ʿUmar b. Udhayna: his father's name prevailed over his own name. He is a Kūfan and client (*mawlā*) of ʿAbdulqays.[1]

قال أبو عمرو الكشي: حمدويه بن نصير، قال: سمعت أشياخي منهم العبيدي وغيره، ان ابن أذينة كوفي، وكان هرب من المهدي، ومات باليمن، فلذلك لم يرو عنه كثير، ويقال: اسمه محمد بن عمر بن أذينة، غلب عليه اسم أبيه، وهو كوفي مولى لعبد القيس.

Al-Kashshī's entry for Ibn Udhayna further reiterates that he was a *mawlā* (client) of Banī ʿAbdilQays and not an Arab by lineage. Al-Ṭūsī (d. 460) said, "He is reliable (*thiqa*). He has a book."[2]

قال الطوسي:عمر بن أذينة، ثقة له كتاب.

These claims surrounding Ibn Udhayna are quite strange. On one hand, he is claimed to have been a prominent head figure of the Shīʿite community in Baṣra whose prominence eventually resulted in his manhunt by Abbasid authorities, leading to his exile from Baṣra to Yemen. On the other end, he clearly is a totally unknown and irrelevant figure in non-Twelver sources, which one would expect to make note of this presumably significant figure as they did with other notorious historical figures pursued by authorities. Furthermore, Ibn Udhayna's obscurity had an observable effect on his identity in Twelver biographical sources, where his name and origins were obfuscated and his transmission is said to be scarce.

Since all isnāds for *Kitāb Sulaym Ibn Qays* back to Ibn Udhayna are unreliable, Ibn Udhayna's reliability or unreliability does not necessarily have much bearing on the book's authenticity. Nevertheless, al-Kashshī's aforementioned report is fascinating, for Ibn Udhayna's emigration to Yemen may explain the book's dubious ascription to the *muḥaddith* of Yemen, ʿAbdurrazzāq al-Ṣanʿānī (d. 211). In fact, I have come across a tradition that may demonstrate Ibn Udhayna's role in disseminating this text's kernel in Yemen.

---

1 Rijāl al-Kashshī (p. 238)

2 Rijāl al-Ṭūsī (p. 313), al-Fihrist by al-Ṭūsī (p. 175)

The Zaydī scholar, Muḥammad b. Sulaymān al-Kūfī (d. post-320), transmitted a tradition through an obscure chain of Yemenī transmitters who cited Ibn Udhayna transmitting from Abān, from Sulaym. Muḥammad b. Sulaymān said:

> Abū Aḥmed [ʿAbdurrḥmān b. Aḥmed al-Hamadānī] informed us, he said, ʿUbayd [b. Muḥammad b. Ibrāhīm al-Ṣan'ānī] informed us, he said: Muḥammad b. ʿUmar b. Abī Muslim informed us, he said: ʿAbdulQuddūs b. Ibrāhīm b. Mirdās informed us, he said: Muḥammad b. ʿAbdirraḥmān b. Udhayna informed us, on the authority of Abān b. Abī ʿAyyāsh, from Sulaym b. Qays, from Salmān that he said:
>
> When the Messenger of Allah ﷺ fell ill, we entered upon him, and he told the people, "Leave me alone with *Ahlulbait*." Thus, the people left, and I got up with them.
>
> He [the Messenger of Allah] then said, "Sit O Salmān, for you are one of us, *Ahlulbait.*"
>
> He then praised Allah and extolled Him, and then he said, "O children of ʿAbdManāf, worship Allah and do not associate anything with him; for if I were granted permission to prostrate [to someone], I would not have preferred anyone over you. I have seen [in a dream] on this pulpit of mine twelve men, all from Quraysh: two from the descendants of al-Ḥarb b. Umayyah and ten from the descendants of al-ʿĀṣ b. Umayyah, all misguided and misleading. They shall push my Ummah backwards from the straight path!"
>
> Then, he told al-ʿAbbās, "Verily, their destruction is by the hands of your descendants." Then he said, "Fear Allah in my family, the members of my household, for the *Dunyā* has never persisted for anyone before us, and it shall not persist for anyone after us."
>
> Then, he told ʿAlī, "The nation of Truth is the most righteous of states. Verily, you shall rule after them for every day: two days, and for every month: two months, and for every year: two years."
>
> Then he said, "There are six whom Allah has cursed in His Book: (1) One who adds to the Book of Allah, (2) the denier Allah's *Qadar*, (3) one who makes permissible against my family what Allah had forbidden, (4) one who abandons my *Sunnah*, (5) one who robs the Muslims of their spoils of war, and (6) and one who transgresses

with wrath attempting to humiliate those whom Allah had honored and honor those whom Allah has humiliated!"[1]

قال محمد بن سليمان الكوفي في «فضائل أمير المؤمنين»: حدثنا أبو أحمد، قال: حدثنا عبيد، قال: حدثنا محمد بن عمر بن أبي مسلم، قال: حدثنا عبد القدوس بن إبراهيم بن مرداس، قال: أخبرنا محمد بن عبد الرحمان بن أذينة، عن أبان بن أبي عياش، عن سليم بن قيس الهلالي : عن سلمان، قال: لما ثقل رسول الله [صلى الله عليه وآله] دخلنا عليه فقال للناس: اخلوا لي عن أهل البيت. فقام الناس وقمت معهم فقال، اقعد يا سلمان إنك منا أهل البيت فحمد الله واثنى عليه ثم قال: يا بني عبد مناف اعبدوا الله ولا تشركوا به شيئا فإنه لو قد أذن لي بالسجود لم أوثر عليكم أحدا إني رأيت على منبري هذا اثني عشر كلهم من قريش رجلين من ولد الحرب بن أمية وعشرة من ولد العاص بن أمية كلهم ضال مضل يردون أمتي عن الصراط القهقرى! ثم قال للعباس أما إن هلكتهم على يدي ولدك. ثم قال : فاتقوا الله في عترتي أهل بيتي فإن الدنيا لم تدم لاحد قبلنا ولا تبقى لنا ولا تدوم لاحد بعدنا. ثم قال لعلي: دولة الحق أبر الدول أما إنكم ستملكون بعدهم باليوم يومين وبالشهر شهرين وبالسنة سنتين. ثم قال: ستة لعنهم الله في كتابه: الزائد في كتاب الله والمكذب بقدر الله والمستحل من عترتي ما حرم الله والتارك لسنتي والمستأثر على المسلمين بفيئهم والمتسلط بالجبروت ليذل من أعز الله ويعز من أذل الله.

Some of this tradition relayed by Muḥammad b. Sulaymān can be found in *Kitāb Sulayn* today, albeit it is mentioned with a different context.[2]

أبان عن سليم، قال: حدثني عبد الله بن جعفر بن أبي طالب قال: كنت عند معاوية ومعنا الحسن والحسين وعنده عبد الله بن العباس والفضل بن العباس، فالتفت إلي معاوية فقال: يا عبد الله بن جعفر، ما أشد تعظيمك للحسن والحسين والله ما هما بخير منك ولا أبوهما خير من أبيك، ولولا أن فاطمة بنت رسول الله أمهما لقلت: ما أمك أسماء بنت عميس دونها!

فغضبت من مقالته وأخذني ما لم أملك معه نفسي، فقلت: والله إنك لقليل المعرفة بهما وبأبيهما وبأمهما. بل والله لهما خير مني ولأبوهما خير من أبي ولأمهما خير من أمي. يا معاوية، إنك لغافل عما سمعته أنا من رسول الله صلى الله عليه وآله يقول فيهما وفي أبيهما وفي أمهما، قد حفظته ووعيته ورويته.

1 Manāqib al-Imām Amīr al-Muʿminīn by Muḥammad b. Sulaymān (2/171-172)
2 Kitāb Sulaym b. Qays (P. 361-362)

قال معاوية: هات ما سمعت – وفي مجلسه الحسن والحسين وعبد الله بن عباس والفضل بن عباس وابن أبي لهب – فوالله ما أنت بكذاب ولا متهم. فقلت: إنه أعظم مما في نفسك. قال: وإن كان أعظم من أحد وحراء جميعا، فلست أبالي إذا لم يكن في المجلس أحد من أهل الشام وإذ قتل الله صاحبك وفرق جمعكم وصار الأمر في أهله ومعدنه فحدثنا فإنا لا نبالي ما قلتم ولا ما ادعيتم.

قلت: سمعت رسول الله صلى الله عليه وآله – وقد سئل عن هذه الآية: (وما جعلنا الرؤيا التي أريناك إلا فتنة للناس والشجرة الملعونة في القرآن)، فقال: إني رأيت اثني عشر رجلا من أئمة الضلالة يصعدون منبري وينزلون، يردون أمتي على أدبارهم القهقرى.

فيهم رجلان من حيين من قريش مختلفين تيم وعدي، وثلاثة من بني أمية، وسبعة من ولد الحكم بن أبي العاص. وسمعته يقول: (إن بني أبي العاص إذا بلغوا ثلاثين رجلا جعلوا كتاب الله دخلا وعباد الله خولا ومال الله دولا...

Abū Jaʿfar Muḥammad b. Sulaymān al-Kūfī was a Kūfan Zaydī traditionist who eventually moved to Ṣaʿda, Yemen, where he became the judge of the Zaydī Imām, Yaḥyā b. al-Ḥusayn b. al-Qāsim al-Rassī (d. 298).[1] Muḥammad b. Sulaymān's isnād for this tradition consists of Yemenite transmitters all the way back to Ibn Udhayna.[2] All in all, the existence of

1 Tārīkh Dimashq by Ibn ʿAsākir (41/292), Ṭabaqāt al-Zaydiyya al-Kubrā by al-Shihārī (p. 971-972)

2 Muḥammad b. Sulaymān transmitted the tradition from the Abū Aḥmed ʿAbdurraḥmān b. Aḥmed al-Hamadānī, who was praised by Aḥmed b. ʿAlī ʿArashānī (d. 590). See Qulādat al-Naḥr fī Wafayāt Aʿyān al-Dahr by Bāmakhrama (2/672).

قال الطيب بامخرمة في «قلادة النحر»: قال القاضي العرشاني: عبد الرحمن بن أحمد الهمداني أبو أحمد، كان فقيها فاضلا محدثا، قدم صنعاء، وسمع من الدبري كما مر، وسمع منه– أعني: عبد الرحمن المذكور–مشايخ صنعاء: الحسن بن عبد الأعلى، والكشوري وغيره.

Abū Aḥmed transmitted this tradition from ʿUbayd b. Muḥammad b. Ibrāhīm al-Kashwarī (d. 288 or 248), a *ḥāfiẓ* from Ṣanʿāʾ, Yemen. Al-Khalīlī (d. 446) described him saying, "He is ʿAbdullāh b. Muḥammad, a scholar and *ḥāfiẓ* who has [authored] works. He died in 288." See Siyar Aʿlām al-Nubalāʾ (13/350).

this Yemenī tradition lends credence to the proposition that Ibn Udhayna played a role in the dissemination of the kernel of *Kitāb Sulaym*, especially considering his reputed exile in Yemen.

Another possibility regarding Ibn Udhayna's true identity is exemplified in a tradition of Sulaym b. Qays relayed by Ibn ʿAsākir (d. 571) in *Tārīkh Dimashq*. Ibn ʿAsākir said: Abū al-Ghanāʾim Muḥammad b. ʿAlī b. al-Ḥasan al-Ḥasanī informed us, al-Qāḍī Muḥammad b. ʿAbdillāh al-Juʿfī informed us, al-Ḥusayn b. Muḥammad b. al-Farazdaq informed us, al-Ḥasan b. ʿAlī b. Bazīʿ informed us, Muḥammad b. ʿUmar informed us, Ibrāhīm b. Isḥāq informed us, ʿAbdullāh b. Udhayna al-Baṣrī informed us, on the authority of Abān b. Abī ʿAyyāsh, from Sulaymān b. Qays al-ʿĀmirī that he said:

> I saw Uways al-Qarnī at Ṣiffīn lyind dead between ʿAmmār and Khuzayma b. Thābit.[1]

قال ابن عساكر في «تاريخ دمشق»: أنبأنا أبو الغنائم محمد بن علية [علي] بن الحسن الحسني، حدثنا القاضي محمد بن عبد الله الجعفي، حدثنا الحسين بن محمد بن الفرزدق، نا الحسن بن علي بن بزيع، حدثنا

قال الذهبي: قَالَ الخليلي: هُوَ عبد الله بن محمد، عالم حافظ لَهُ مصنفات، مات سنة ثمانٍ وثمانين ومائتين.

ʿAbdulquddūs b. Ibrāhīm b. Mirdās was an obscure transmitter from Ṣanʿāʾ, Yemen. See Tafsīr al-Qurʾān al-ʿAẓīm of Ibn Abī Ḥātim (4/1244).

قال ابن أبي حاتم في تفسيره: أَخْبَرَنَا جَعْفَرُ بْنُ عَلِيٍّ الْمَعْرُوفُ بِأَبِي أذك الْحَوَارِيِّ فِيمَا كَتَبَ إلي، ثنا إسماعيل ابن أَبِي أُوَيْسٍ، حَدَّثَنِي أَبُو عَبْدِ اللَّهِ عَبْدُ الْقُدُّوسِ بْنُ إِبْرَاهِيمَ بْنِ عُبَيْدِ اللَّهِ بْنِ مِرْدَاسٍ الْعَبْدَرِيُّ مَوْلَى بَنِي عَبْدِ الدَّارِ الصَّنْعَانِيُّ....

Muḥammad b. ʿUmar b. Abī Muslim was an obscure Yemenite transmitter from Ṣanʿāʾ, Yemen. He was a prominent reciter of the Quran who used to lead prayers in the grand mosque of Ṣanʿā during Ramaḍān. See Tārīkh Madīnat Ṣanʿāʾ of al-Rāzī (p. 345).

قال أحمد بن محمد بن عبد الله الصنعاني الرازي في «تاريخ مدينة صنعاء»: وكان بها محمد بن عمر بن أبي مسلم السمسار، وكان محمود القراءة عند عامة أهل صنعاء والمقدم في مسجد جماعتهم على غيره في شهر رمضان؛ كان قرأ على بكر بن عبد الله بن الشرود.

Hence, it becomes clear that every transmitter in this isnād is from Ṣanʿāʾ, Yemen.

1 Tārīkh Dimashq by Ibn ʿAsākir (9/455)

محمد بن عمر، حدثنا إبراهيم بن إسحاق، حدثنا عبد الله بن أذينة البصري، عن أبان بن أبي عياش، عن سليمان بن قيس العامري، قال: رأيت أويسا القرني بصفين صريعا بين عمار وخزيمة بن ثابت.

This is an interesting isnād that is authentic up till al-Ḥasan b. ʿAlī b. Bazīʿ, who appears to be an unknown Kūfan transmitter.[1] Similarly, Muḥammad b. ʿUmar in the isnād is al-Jurjānī, and his reliability seems unknown.[2] Nonetheless, what is noteworthy in this tradition's isnād is that it presents Ibn Udhayna's name as ʿAbdullāh b. Udhayna al-Baṣrī. ʿAbdullāh b. ʿUṭārid b. Udhayna was an infamous unreliable Baṣran transmitter who was believed to be a forger by several critics.

Ibn ʿAmmār al-Mawṣilī (d. 242) forbade the transcription of his ḥadīths and demonstrated that he was a liar.[3] Ibn ʿAdī (d. 365) described him saying, "He is disapproved in his transmission of ḥadīth (*munkar al-ḥadīth*)," and Ibn ʿAdī criticized several traditions of his whilst also stating that he relayed other uncorroborated things.[4]

قال ابن عدي في «الكامل في ضعفاء الرجال»، "عبد الله بن عطارد بن أذينة الطائي بصري منكر الحديث." وقال، "ولابن أذينة من الحديث غير ما ذكرت مما، لا يتابع عليه ولم أر للمتقدمين فيه كلاما فأذكره."

Ibn Ḥibbān (d. 354) said about him, "He is severely disapproved in ḥadīth. He transmits from Thawr that which is not from his transmission. He cannot be relied upon in any circumstance." Ibn Ḥibbān also described his bundle of traditions saying that it "is impermissible to be mentioned in the books unless it is for the sake of criticizing its transmitter."[5]

قال ابن حبان في «كتاب المجروحين»، "عبد الله بن أذينة، شيخ يروي عن ثور يزيد، روى عنه إسحاق بن عيسى الأبلي، منكر الحديث جدا، يروي عن ثور ما ليس من حديثه لا يجوز الاحتجاج به بحال..." وقال: أخبرنا بالحديثين جميعا حمزة بن داود بن سليمان بن الحكم بن سليمان بن الحجاج بن يوسف بن أبي عقيل الثقفي بالأبلة، قال: حدثنا إسماعيل بن عيسى بن زاذان الأبلي، قال: حدثنا عبد الله بن أذينة، عن ثور بن يزيد في نسخة كتبناها عنه لا يحل ذكرها في الكتب إلا على سبيل القدح في ناقلها."

1 Tārīkh al-Islām by al-Dhahabī (6/314)
2 Tārīkh Jurjān by al-Sahmī (p. 390)
3 Al-Jāmiʿ li-Akhlāq al-Rāwī wa-Ādāb al-Sāmiʿ by al-Khaṭīb al-Baghdādī (1/133)
4 Al-Kāmil fī Ḍuʿafāʾ al-Rijāl (5/358-359)
5 Kitāb al-Majrūḥīn by Ibn Ḥibbān (2/18-19)

This ʿAbdullāh b. Udhayna is also quoted on several occasions transmiting traditions via Jaʿfar al-Ṣādiq, from his father, as can be observed with ʿUmar b. Udhayna in Twelver sources as well.[1]

قال الخطيب في «تلخيص المتشابه في الرسم»: أخبرنا الحسن بن الحسين النعالي، أنا أحمد بن نصر بن عبد الله الذارع، نا هاشم بن القاسم أبو الحسين العصفري، نا عبد الملك بن عبد ربه الطائي، نا عبد الله بن أذينة الطائي، نا جعفر بن محمد، عن أبيه، عن جده، أن علي بن أبي طالب عليه السلام أتي بسحاقيين فضربهما مائة مائة ونفاهما.

وقال ابن شاذان القمي الرافضي في «مائة منقبة من مناقب أمير المؤمنين»: حدثنا جعفر بن محمد بن قولويه رحمه الله، قال حدثني علي بن الحسن النحوي، قال: حدثني أحمد بن محمد، قال: حدثني منصور بن أبي العباس، قال: حدثني علي بن أسباط، عن الحكم بن بهلول، قال: حدثني أبو همام، قال: حدثني عبدالله بن اذينة، عن جعفر بن محمد، عن أبيه، عن علي بن الحسين، عن أبيه قال: قام عمر بن الخطاب إلى النبي صلى الله عليه وآله فقال: إنك لا تزال تقول لعلي: أنت مني بمنزلة هارون من موسى ....

The parallels between both figures revolve around several observations, such as the fact that (1) both men were Baṣran, (2) both men were known by the patronymic, Udhayna, (3) both men seem to be from the same generation, (4) both men relayed traditions from Jaʿfar al-Ṣādiq, and (4) ʿAbdullāh b. Udhayna appears in the place of ʿUmar b. Udhayna in an isnād back to Sulaym b. Qays in Ibn ʿAsākir's *Tārīkh Dimashq*. The challenge with these parallels is that they may prove to be mere coincidences, and the mention of ʿAbdullāh b. Udhayna in an isnād back to Sulaym b. Qays may prove to be a mere typographical error as well. Nonetheless, I found the similarities between both transmitters worthy of consideration when asessing ʿUmar b. Udhayna's identity, though I cannot definitively assert much beyond that. More will come on Ibn Udhayna as the remainder of the pivotal transmitters are assessed.

Abān b. Abī ʿAyyāsh, Sulaym b. Qays or Neither?

All documented routes for *Kitāb Sulaym* converge to Ibn Udhayna, who claimed to transmit the book from Abān b. Abī ʿAyyāsh, from Sulaym b.

1 Talkhīṣ al-Mutashābih fī al-Rasm (2/655), Miʾat Manqaba min Manāqib Amīr al-Muʾminīn by Ibn Shādhān al-Qummī (p. 172-174)

Qays, and the isnāds from ʿAbdurrazzāq that bypassed Ibn Udhayna are all forged routes. The story at the forefront of *Kitāb Sulaym* mentioned that Sulaym made Abān promise that he would not disclose the book with anyone until Sulaym's death.[1]

قال سليم: وإني هممت حين مرضت أن أحرقها، فتأثمت من ذلك وقطعت به. فإن جعلت لي عهد الله عز وجل وميثاقه أن لا تخبر بها أحدا ما دمت حيا، ولا تحدث بشيء منها بعد موتي إلا من تثق به كثقتك بنفسك، وإن حدث بك حدث أن تدفعها إلى من تثق به من شيعة علي بن أبي طالب صلوات الله عليه ممن له دين وحسب.

Aḥmed b. ʿAlī al-ʿAqīqī (d. ~280) said, "[...] so no one transmitted from Sulaym b. Qays except Abān b. Abī ʿAyyāsh."[2]

قال ابن المطهر الحلي في «خلاصة الأقوال»: وقال السيد علي بن احمد العقيقي: [...] فلم يرو عن سليم بن قيس احد من الناس سوى ابان بن ابي عياش.

Ibn al-Nadīm (d. 438) further said, "Abān b. Abī ʿAyyāsh transmitted it, and no one else transmitted it."[3]

قال ابن النديم: رواه أبان بن أبي عياش، لم يروه غيره.

Some contemporary Twelver apologists for *Kitāb Sulaym* cite instances of Ibrāhīm b. ʿUmar al-Yamānī's direct transmission from Sulaym as a corroboration to Abān's transmission from Sulaym. However, a careful examination of figure 1.1 on page 14 will demonstrate that Ibrāhīm's transmission of *Kitāb Sulaym,* in reality, originates from Abān. It thus cannot be said that Ibrāhīm's account is an independent corroboration to Abān's transmission of the book. Rather, Ibrāhīm b. ʿUmar's seemingly direct transmission from Sulaym merely is a byproduct of the occasional omission of the intermediaries between both individuals in some isnāds.

Abān b. Abī ʿAyyāsh was a Baṣran figure who, despite his reputed piety, was severely criticized by the ḥadīth critics due to his continuous lapses and questionable integrity in the transmission of ḥadīth. I have observed several Shīʿite defenders of *Kitāb Sulaym* attempt to dismiss all the criticism Abān had received by Sunnī and Shīʿite critics by characterizing it as some anti-

---

1 Kitāb Sulaym Ibn Qays (p. 126)
2 Khulāṣat al-Aqwāl fī Maʿrifat al-Rijal by al-Ḥillī (p. 162)
3 Al-Fihrist by Ibn al-Nadīm (p. 271)

Shīʿite polemic spearheaded by Shuʿba b. al-Ḥajjāj (d. 160), who supposedly disparaged Abān due to his alleged Shīʿite beliefs. This characterization, however, is multifacetedly inaccurate.

Abān b. Abī ʿAyyāsh's downfall as a transmitter rather commenced with Abū ʿAwāna al-Waḍḍāḥ b. ʿAbdillāh (d. 176). Aḥmed b. Ḥanbal said:

> The first person to perish Abān was Abū ʿAwāna. He compiled most ḥadīths of al-Ḥasan [al-Baṣrī]. He then went to Abān, and he read them to him.[1]

قال عَبد اللَّهِ بْنُ أَحْمَدَ، قَال: قَال أَبِي: قَالَ عفان: أول من أهلك أَبَان بْن أَبِي عياش أَبُو عَوَانة أنه جمع حديث الْحَسَن عامته فجاء به إلى أَبَان فقرأه عَلَيْهِ.

Aḥmed's statement entails that Abān carelessly transmitted to Abū ʿAwāna the ḥadīths of al-Ḥasan al-Baṣrī, not recognizing that he had not heard those traditions. It seems Abū ʿAwāna tested Abān multiple times in this regard. Abū ʿAwāna said:

> When al-Ḥasan died, I desired his speech, so I gathered it from al-Ḥasan's companions. I then went to Abān, and he transmitted it to me from al-Ḥasan, so I do not deem it permissible to transmit from Abān.[2]

قال العقيلي: حَدَّثَنِي آدَمُ بْنُ مُوسَى قَالَ : حَدَّثَنَا مُحَمَّدُ بْنُ إِسْمَاعِيلَ الْبُخَارِيُّ قَالَ : حَدَّثَنَا يَحْيَى بْنُ مَعِينٍ عَنْ عَفَّانَ عَنْ أَبِي عَوَانَةَ قَالَ : لَمَّا مَاتَ الْحَسَنُ اشْتَهَيْتُ كَلاَمَهُ فَجَمَعْتُهُ مِنْ أَصْحَابِ الْحَسَنِ فَأَتَيْتُ أَبَانَ بْنَ أَبِي عَيَّاشٍ فَقَرَأَهُ عَلَيَّ عَنِ الْحَسَنِ , فَلاَ أَسْتَحِلُّ أَنْ أَرْوِيَ عَنْهُ .

ʿAffān said: I heard Abū ʿAwāna say:

> "I used to not hear a ḥadīth from al-Ḥasan in al-Baṣra except that I went with it to Abān b. Abī ʿAyyāsh, and he would transmit it to me from al-Ḥasan. I eventually compiled a book from that." Abū ʿAwāna used to not transmit from Abān.[3]

1 Al-ʿIlal wa-Maʿrifat al-Rijāl – Riwāyat ʿAbdillāh (2/537)
2 Al-Ḍuʿafāʾ al-Kabīr by al-ʿUqaylī (1/40)
3 Tārīkh Ibn Maʿīn – Riwāyat al-Dūrī (4/275)

قال الدوري: سَمِعت يحيى يَقُول: سَمِعت عَفَّان يَقُول: سَمِعت أَبَا عوَانَة يَقُول: كنت لَا أسمع بِالْبَصْرَةِ حَدِيثا عَن الْحسن إِلَّا جِئْت بِهِ إِلَى أبان بن أبي عَيَّاش فيحدثني بِهِ عَن الْحسن حَتَّى جمعت مِنْهُ مُصحفا. قَالَ عَفَّان: وَكَانَ أَبُو عوَانَة لَا يحدث عَن أبان.

Abū ʿAwāna also said:

> I went to Abān with a book that contains ḥadīths from his transmission. At the bottom of the book was the ḥadīth of a man from the people of Wāsiṭ, and Abān recited it all to me [as his own ḥadīths].[1]

قال ابن أبي حاتم: نا عمر بن شبة النميري، نا موسى بن إسماعيل، نا أبو عوانة: قال أتيت أبان بن عياش بكتاب فيه حديث من حديثه وفي أسفل الكتاب حديث رجل من أهل واسط، فقرأه علي أجمع.

Abān's careless transmission of miscellaneous documents presented to him can be observed in various instances. Sulaymān b. Ḥarb (d. 224) said:

> Someone informed me that he saw Ibn Jurayj approach Abān with a book, and Ibn Jurayj told him, "This is your ḥadīth, so give me permission to transmit it." Abān said, "Yes," so Ibn Jurayj took the book and left. [2]

In this context, Yazīd b. Zurayʿ (d. 182) is quoted saying:

> I saw Ibn Jurayj approach Abān with a closed booklet. He then told Abān, "Can I transmit this from you?" Abān said, "yes."[3]

قال الخطيب البغدادي في «الكفاية»: أَخْبَرَنَا ابْنُ الْفَضْلِ، أنا عَبْدُ اللَّهِ بْنُ جَعْفَرٍ، ثنا يَعْقُوبُ بْنُ سُفْيَانَ، ثنا سُلَيْمَانُ بْنُ حَرْبٍ , قَالَ: حَدَّثَنِي مَنْ رَأَى ابْنَ جُرَيْجٍ جَاءَ إِلَى أَبَانَ بْنِ أَبِي عَيَّاشٍ بِكِتَابٍ فَقَالَ: هَذَا حَدِيثُكَ فَأَجِزْهُ لِي , قَالَ: نَعَمْ، قَالَ: فَأَخَذَ الْكِتَابَ وَذَهَبَ.

ويروى عن يزيد بن زريع أنه قال: رَأَيْتُ ابْنَ جُرَيْجٍ جَاءَ إِلَى أَبَانَ بْنِ أَبِي عَيَّاشٍ بِكُرَّاسَةٍ مُطَبَّقَةٍ , فَقَالَ: أَرْوِي هَذِهِ عَنْكَ؟ قَالَ: نَعَمْ.

---

1 Al-Jarḥ wa-l-Taʿdīl by Ibn Abī Ḥātim (2/295)
2 Al-Kifāya fī ʿIlm al-Riwāya by al-Khaṭīb al-Baghdādī (p. 320)
3 Al-Kifāya fī ʿIlm al-Riwāya (p. 320)

Ḥammād b. Salama said:

> I distorted Thābit al-Bunānī's ḥadīths [to test him], and they did not pass through. I also distorted Abān b. Abī ʿAyyāsh's ḥadīths, and they passed through.[1]

قال الخطيب: أَنَا أَبُو بَكْرٍ الْبَرْقَانِيُّ، قَالَ: قَرَأْتُ عَلَى مُحَمَّدِ بْنِ مَحْمُودٍ الْمَرْوَزِيِّ، بِهَا، حَدَّثَكُمْ مُحَمَّدُ بْنُ عَلِيٍّ الْحَافِظُ، نَا زِيَادُ بْنُ يَحْيَى، نَا بَهْزُ بْنُ أَسِيدٍ، عَنْ حَمَّادِ بْنِ سَلَمَةَ، قَالَ: قَلَبْتُ أَحَادِيثَ عَلَى ثَابِتٍ الْبُنَانِيِّ فَلَمْ تَنْقَلِبْ، وَقَلَبْتُ عَلَى أَبَانَ بْنِ أَبِي عَيَّاشٍ فَانْقَلَبَتْ.

Elsewhere, Ḥammād clarified how he had tested Thābit al-Bunānī, and that would provide insight about his testing of Abān b. Abī ʿAyyāsh. Ḥammād said:

> I used to distort Thābit al-Bunānī's ḥadīth [to test him], for it used to be said, "storytellers do not memorize [properly]."
>
> I would say to him about a ḥadīth of Anas, "ʿAbdurraḥmān b. Abī Laylā informed you?" He would reply, "No, it was Anas who informed us." I would then say to him about a ḥadīth of ʿAbdurraḥmān b. Abī Laylā, "How did Anas relay it to you?" He would reply, "No, it was ʿAbdurraḥmān b. Abī Laylā who informed us."[2]

قال الخطيب: أَنَا أَبُو الْحُسَيْنِ عَلِيُّ بْنُ مُحَمَّدِ بْنِ عَبْدِ اللَّهِ الْمُعَدَّلُ، أَنَا عُثْمَانُ بْنُ أَحْمَدَ الدَّقَّاقُ، قَالَ: قُرِئَ عَلَى مُحَمَّدِ بْنِ أَحْمَدَ بْنِ الْبَرَاءِ: وَأَنَا حَاضِرٌ، قَالَ: قَالَ عَلِيُّ بْنُ عَبْدِ اللَّهِ الْمَدِينِيُّ عَنْ بَهْزٍ، عَنْ حَمَّادِ بْنِ سَلَمَةَ، قَالَ: كُنْتُ أُقَلِّبُ عَلَى ثَابِتٍ الْبُنَانِيِّ حَدِيثَهُ، وَكَانُوا يَقُولُونَ: الْقُصَّاصَ لا يَحْفَظُونَ، وَكُنْتُ أَقُولُ لِحَدِيثِ أَنَسٍ: حَدَّثَكَ عَبْدُ الرَّحْمَنِ بْنُ أَبِي لَيْلَى؟ فَيَقُولُ لا إِنَّمَا حَدَّثَنَاهُ أَنَسٌ، وَأَقُولُ لِحَدِيثِ عَبْدِ الرَّحْمَنِ بْنِ أَبِي لَيْلَى: كَيْفَ حَدَّثَكَ أَنَسٌ؟ فَيَقُولُ لا إِنَّمَا حَدَّثَنَاهُ عَبْدُ الرَّحْمَنِ بْنُ أَبِي لَيْلَى.

Shuʿba b. al-Ḥajjāj (d. 160) also reportedly tested Abān in this regard. Bahz was once asked by Ḥirmī about Abān, to which Bahz reported that Shuʿba said:

> "I wrote down Anas' ḥadīths as al-Ḥasan's and al-Ḥasan's ḥadīths as Anas'. I then presented both to Abān, and he read them to me."

1 Al-Jāmiʿ li-Akhlāq al-Rāwī wa-Ādāb al-Sāmiʿ (1/135)

2 Al-Jāmiʿ li-Akhlāq al-Rāwī wa-Ādāb al-Sāmiʿ (1/135)

Ḥirmī thus commented, "Wretched is what he had done. Is this even permissible?"[1]

قال العقيلي: حدثنا محمد بن سعيد بن بلج، قال: سمعت عبد الرحمن بن الحكم بن بشير بن سليمان يقول: سمعت بهزا – وسأله حرمي عن أبان بن أبي عياش – فذكر عن شعبة قال: كتبت حديث أنس عن الحسن، وحديث الحسن عن أنس فرفعتهما إليه فقرأهما علي. فقال حرمي: بئس ما صنع، وهذا يحل؟

Some individuals clearly perceived this method of testing a transmitter to be distasteful; nevertheless, this account further demonstrates Abān's carelessness and incompetence in transmission such that he used to readily relay any document or tradition presented to him without ascertaining whether it truly was from his transmission or not. Perhaps it is for such reasons that the volume of Abān's transmission from Anas b. Mālik was grossly inflated when compared to that of Anas' reliable companions. Suwayd b. ʿAbdilʿAzīz said: Shuʿba b. al-Ḥajjāj told me about Abān b. Abī ʿAyyāsh:

> Qatāda merely used to relay 200 ḥadīths from Anas, and Abān relays 2,000 ḥadīths from Anas![2]

قال أبو زرعة: حَدَّثنا إسحاق بن إبراهيم الجُرْجَاني ، وغيره ، قالا : حَدَّثنا هشام بن عمار ، حَدَّثنا سُوَيْد بن عَبد العزيز ، قال : قال لي شعبة بن الحجاج يحدث عن أبان بن أبي عياش ، وإنما كان قَتَادة يروي عن أَنس مئتي حديث ، وأبان يروي عن أَنس ألفي حديث .

Similar criticism of Abān was expounded by other ḥadīth critics. Ibn Abī Ḥātim al-Rāzī said:

> Abū Zurʿa (d. 264) was asked about Abān b. Abī ʿAyyāsh, and he said, "He is a Baṣran whose ḥadīth is abandoned," and he refused to read his ḥadīth to us.
>
> Abū Zurʿa was then asked, "Did he used to intentionally lie?" Abū Zurʿa said, "No. He used to hear ḥadīth from Anas, Shahr b.

---

1 Al-Ḍuʿafāʾ al-Kabīr by al-ʿUqaylī (1/40)

2 Suʾālāt al-Bardhaʿī li-Abī Zurʿa al-Rāzī (p. 201). It should be noted that Suwayd b. ʿAbdilʿAzīz was a weak transmitter. However, the figures cited in his tradition do not seem farfetched from reality, and it is generally similar to what Ibn Ḥibbān had previously said.

> Ḥawshab and al-Ḥasan, and he would not distinguish between them [in transmission]."[1]

قال ابن أبي حاتم: سئل أبو زرعة عن أبان بن أبي عياش فقال: بصرى متروك حديثه. ولم يقرأ علينا حديثه، فقيل له كان يتعمد الكذب؟ قال لا، كان يسمع الحديث من أنس وشهر بن حوشب ومن الحسن فلا يميز بينهم.

Ibn Ḥibbān (d. 354) said about Abān:

> He was among the worshippers who used to stay up at night in prayer and fold the days by fasting. He heard some ḥadīths from Anas b. Mālik. He sat with al-Ḥasan, and he would hear his speech and memorize it. When transmitting, he would sometimes unknowingly confuse the speech he had heard from al-Ḥasan to be a prophetic tradition relayed from Anas. He perhaps transmitted more than 1,500 ḥadīths from Anas much of which have no basis.[2]

قال ابن حبان: وَكَانَ من الْعِبَاد الَّذِينَ يسهر اللَّيْل بِالْقيام ويطوي النَّهَار بالصيام سمع عَن أَنَس بْن مَالِك أَحَادِيث وجالس الْحَسَن فَكَانَ يسمع كَلَامه ويحفظه فَإِذَا حدث رُبَّمَا جعل كَلام الْحَسَن الَّذِي سَمعه من قَوْله عَن أنس عَن النَّبِي صَلَّى اللَّهُ عَلَيْهِ وَسَلَّمَ وَهُوَ لَا يعلم وَلَعَلَّه روى عَن أَنَس أَكْثَر من ألف وَخَمْسمِائَة حَدِيث مَا لكبير شَيْء مِنْهَا أصل يرجع إِلَيْهِ.

Some critics noted that Abān, despite his apparent piety, was an unreliable transmitter. Abū Ḥātim al-Rāzī (d. 275) said, "Abān b. Abī ʿAyyāsh is abandoned (*matrūk*) in ḥadīth. He was a pious man, but he was afflicted with poor retention."[3]

قال ابن أبي حاتم: سمعت أبي يقول: أبان بن أبي عياش متروك الحديث وكان رجلا صالحا لكن بلى بسوء الحفظ.

ʿAmr b. ʿAlī al-Fallās (d. 249) said, "He is abandoned (*matrūk*) in ḥadīth, and he is a pious man..."[4]

---

1 Al-Jarḥ wa-l-Taʿdīl by Ibn Abī Ḥātim (2/296)
2 Al-Majrūḥīn by Ibn Ḥibbān (1/96)
3 Al-Jarḥ wa-l-Taʿdīl by Ibn Abī Ḥātim (2/296)
4 Al-Kāmil fī Ḍuʿafāʾ al-Rijāl (2/57)

قال ابن عدي: حدَّثَنَا خالد بْن النضر، حَدَّثَنَا عَمْرو بْن عَلِيّ قَالَ أَبَان بْن أَبِي عياش هُوَ أَبَان بْن فيروز مولى لأنس مولى لعبد القيس وفي رواية غير خالد متروك الْحَدِيث، وَهو رجل صَالِح، يُكَنَّى أبا إسماعيل.

Zakariyyā b. Yaḥyā al-Sājī (d. 307) said:

> He was a pious and generous man who had some negligence. He confuses and errs in ḥadīth. The people transmitted from him. His ḥadīth was abandoned due to negligence that was in him....[1]

قال مغلطاي: وقال الساجي في كتاب «الجرح والتعديل» تأليفه: كان رجلا صالحا سخيا كريما، فيه غفلة، يهم في الحديث ويخطئ فيه، روى عنه الناس، ترك حديثه لغفلة كانت فيه لم يحدث عنه شعبة، ولا عبد الرحمن، ولا يحيى، وقيل لشعبة: ما تقول في يونس عن الحسن؟ قال: سمن وعسل، قيل: فعون عن الحسن؟ قال: خل وزيت، قيل: فأبان قال: إن تركتني وإلا تقيأت. وفي رواية: بول حمار منتن.

In this context, Mālik b. Dīnār (d. 123) is quoted describing Abān as the peacock of reciters (*ṭāwūs al-qurrā'*).[2] It should be noted, however, that Mālik did not witness the later period of Abān's life, for he died around two decades prior to Abān b. Abī ʿAyyāsh's death.

قال ابن عدي: حَدَّثَنَا مُحَمد بْن جعفر الإمام، قَال: قِيل لإسحاق بْن أَبِي إسرائيل حدثكم سفيان بْن عُيَينة، قَال: كَانَ مَالِك بْن دينار يَقُولُ لأبان بن أبي عياش طاووس القراء.

After verifying Abān's incompetence, carelessness and unreliability as a transmitter, Shuʿba (d. 160) was one of the most vocal critics of Abān. He is reported to have said:

> Drinking my donkey's urine till I am quenched is more preferable to me than saying, "Abān b. Abī ʿAyyāsh informed me."[3]

قال العقيلي: حدثني أحمد بن محمد بن منصور القوهستاني قال: حدثنا عبد الله بن أبي الحارث قال: سمعت شعيب بن حرب يقول: سمعت شعبة يقول: لأن أشرب من بول حماري حتى أروى أحب إلي من أن أقول: حدثني أبان بن أبي عياش.

1 Ikmāl Tahdhīb al-Kamāl (1/168)
2 Al-Kāmil fī Ḍuʿafā' al-Rijāl (2/60)
3 Al-Ḍuʿafā' al-Kabīr by al-ʿUqaylī (1/38)

Other similar hyperbolic statements were relayed from Shuʿba. Shuʿba is recorded saying, "I would rather be a highway bandit than transmit ḥadīth from Abān."[1]

قال ابن شاهين: وفي رواية النضر بن شميل، عن شعبة، قال: لئن أقطع الطريق أحب إلي أن أروي عن أبان.

Additionally, Shuʿba is authentically quoted saying, "For a man to commit *zinā* is better for him than transmitting ḥadīth from Abān b. Abī ʿAyyāsh."[2]

قال شعبة: لأن يزني الرجل ، خير له من أن يروى عن أبان بن أبي عياش .

Shuʿba's active disparagement of Abān became so intense at one point to the extent that some people asked Shuʿba to cease his criticism of Abān out of respect to his age and status. Ibn Abī Ḥātim said: Muḥammad b. Muslim [b. Wāra] informed us, he said: one of Ḥammād b. Zayd's companions informed me, on the authority of Ḥammād b. Zayd that he said:

> ʿAbbād b. ʿAbbād and I once approached Shuʿba b. al-Ḥajjāj, and we asked him to desist from disparaging Abān b. Abī ʿAyyāsh. On the next day, we went to the *masjid* of *al-Jāmiʿ*, and he saw us there.
>
> He called out to us saying, "O Abū Muʿāwiya, I have thought about what you have discussed with me, and I have found that I cannot remain silent about it!"
>
> Ḥammād said, "Shuʿba used to engage in this [criticism of transmitters] out of a sense of duty [to enforce good and forbid evil]."[3]

قال ابن أبي حاتم: نا محمد بن مسلم، قال: حدثني بعض أصحاب حماد بن زيد، عن حماد بن زيد، قال: أتيت أنا وعباد بن عباد إلى شعبة بن الحجاج فسألناه أن يكف عن أبان بن أبي عياش ويسكت عنه، فلما كان من الغد خرجنا إلى مسجد الجامع فبصر بنا فنادانا، فقال: يا أبا معاوية، نظرت فيما كلمتموني فوجدت لا يسعني السكوت، قال حماد: وكان شعبة يتكلم في هذا حسبة.

---

1 Tārīkh Asmāʾ al-Ḍuʿafāʾ wa-l-Kadhdhābīn wa-l-Matrūkīn by Ibn Shāhīn (p. 158)

2 Suʾālāt al-Bardhaʿī li-Abī Zurʿa al-Rāzī (p. 200)

3 Al-Jarḥ wa-l-Taʿdīl by Ibn Abī Ḥātim (1/171). Similar accounts are relayed about this incident via other isnāds.

Ultimately, Shuʿba even said, "Had it not been for my embarrassment from the people, I would not have even prayed for Abān [at his funeral prayer.]"[1]

قال شعبة: لَوْلَا الْحَيَاءُ مِنَ النَّاسِ مَا صَلَّيْتُ عَلَى أَبَانَ.

Ibn ʿAdī (d. 365) described Abān saying:

> Abān b. Abī ʿAyyāsh has traditions asides from what I had mentioned, and he is not corroborated in most of what he transmits. His weakness is apparent, and al-Thawrī, Maʿmar, Ibn Jurayj, Isrāʾīl, Ḥammād b. Salama and others transmitted from him as I had mentioned. I hope that he was among those who did not intentionally lie but rather used to undergo confusion and err [in transmission]. Most of what Abān had been implicated with stems from the transmitters from him, for unknown transmitters transmitted from him due to his weakness. He is closer to weakness than he is to truthfulness as was stated by Shuʿba.[2]

قال ابن عدي: وَأَبَانُ بْنُ أَبِي عَيَّاشٍ لَهُ رِوَايَاتٌ غَيْرَ مَا ذَكَرْتُ وَعَامَّةُ مَا يَرْوِيهِ، لاَ يُتَابعُ عليه، وَهو بَيِّنُ الأَمْرِ فِي الضَّعْفِ وَقَدْ حَدَّثَ عَنْهُ كَمَا ذَكَرْتُهُ الثَّوْرِيّ وَمَعْمَرٌ، وَابْنُ جُرَيج وَإِسْرَائِيلُ وَحَمَّادُ بْنُ سَلَمَةَ وَغَيْرُهُمْ مِمَّنْ لَمْ نَذْكُرْهُمْ وَأَرْجُو أَنَّهُ مِمَّنْ لا يَتَعَمَّدُ الْكَذِبَ إِلا أَنْ يُشَبَّهَ عليه ويغلط وعامة ما أتاني أَبَان مِنْ جِهَةِ الرُّوَاةِ لا مِنْ جِهَتِهِ لأَنَّ أَبَان رَوَوْا عنه قوم مجهولين لما أَنَّهُ فِيهِ ضَعْفٌ، وَهو إِلَى الضعف أقرب منه إلى الصدق كما قال شُعْبَة.

Though al-Thawrī relayed some traditions from Abān, as was stated by Ibn ʿAdī, he reportedly criticized him on some occasions. ʿAbdurraḥmān b. al-Ḥakam b. Bashīr said: I heard a *sheikh* tell my father:

> I told Sufyān al-Thawrī, "Why do you not transmit from Abān b. Abī ʿAyyāsh?" or "Why are you sparse in your transmission from Abān?" He said, "Abān was forgetful of ḥadīth."[3]

قال ابن أبي حاتم: نا محمد بن سعيد المقرئ الرازي: ثنا عبد الرحمن ابن الحكم بن بشير، يقول: سمعت شيخا يحدث أبي، قال: قلت لسفيان الثوري: ما لك لا تحدث عن أبان بن أبي عياش؟ أو مالك قليل الحديث عن أبان؟ قال: كان أبان نسيا للحديث.

1 Al-Ḍuʿafāʾ al-Kabīr by al-ʿUqaylī (1/39)
2 Al-Kāmil fī Ḍuʿafāʾ al-Rijāl (2/67)
3 Al-Jarḥ wa-l-Taʿdīl by Ibn Abī Ḥātim (1/77)

Other contemporaries of Abān had unfavorable perceptions of his reliability as a transmitter. ʿAmr b. ʿAlī said, "Yaḥyā [b. Saʿīd] and ʿAbdurraḥmān [b. Mahdī] used to not transmit from Abān b. Abī ʿAyyāsh."[1]

قال ابن أبي حاتم: نا علي بن الحسين قال: سمعت أبا حفص – يعني عمرو بن علي الصيرفي – يقول: كان يحيى وعبد الرحمن لا يحدثان عن أبان بن أبي عياش.

Aḥmed b. Ḥanbal (d. 241) said, "He is abandoned (*matrūk*) in ḥadīth. The people have abandoned his ḥadīth since a while."[2]

قال عبد الله: سألته عن أبان بن أبي عياش، فقال: متروك الحديث، ترك الناس حديثه مذ دهر من الدهر.

Ibn ʿAwn (d. 151), the renowned Baṣran scholar, reportedly refused to shake Abān's hand upon meeting him.[3]

قال أبو زرعة: حَدَّثنا فهد بن سُلَيْمان المصري ، حَدَّثنا أبو مسعود ، حَدَّثنا عباد بن عباد الخَوَّاص ، عن ابن عَوْن ، وذكرت له أبان بن أبي عياش ، قال : لقيني فبسط يده إِلَيَّ ، فقلت : ما إلى ذاك من سبيل.

The renowned Kūfan *muḥaddith*, Wakīʿ b. al-Jarrāḥ (d. 196), when coming across Abān's transmission, would conceal his identity and say "a man" instead of "Abān" due to his reputed weakness.[4]

قال أحمد بن حنبل: كان وكيع إذا أتى على حديث أبان بن أبي عياش يقول "رجل" لا يسميه استضعاف له.

Other critics severely criticized Abān and even deemed him a forger. Ibn Miḥriz quoted Yaḥyā b. Maʿīn (d. 233) stating that Abān used to lie.[5] Yaḥyā, in a story involving him and Aḥmed b. Ḥanbal, also described Maʿmar's *nuskha* from Abān as forged (*mawḍūʿ*), and Aḥmed concurred with Yaḥyā that it was forged.[6] Ibn Maʿīn also described Abān's transmission as worthless (*laysa ḥadīthuhu bi-shayʾ*).[7]

قال ابن محرز: وسمعت يحيى – وقيل له أبان بن أبي عياش – فقال: كان يكذب.

---

1 Al-Jarḥ wa-l-Taʿdīl by Ibn Abī Ḥātim (2/296)
2 Al-ʿIlal wa-Maʿrifat al-Rijāl – Riwāyat ʿAbdillāh (1/412)
3 Suʾālāt al-Bardhaʿī li-Abī Zurʿa al-Rāzī (p. 200)
4 Al-ʿIlal wa-Maʿrifat al-Rijāl – Riwāyat ʿAbdillāh (2/525)
5 Tārīkh Ibn Maʿīn – Riwāyat Ibn Miḥriz (1/64)
6 Al-Madkhal ilā Kitāb al-Iklīl by al-Ḥākim (p. 32)
7 Al-Jarḥ wa-l-Taʿdīl by Ibn Abī Ḥātim (2/296)

قال الحاكم: أخبرني أَبُو عِمْرَانَ مُوسَى بْنُ سَعِيدٍ الْحَنْظَلِيُّ الْحَافِظُ بِهَمَذَانَ، قَالَ: حدثني أَحْمَدُ بْنُ إِسْحَاقَ الْقَاضِي بِالدِّينَوَرِ، قَالَ: سَمِعْتُ أَبَا بَكْرٍ الأَثْرَمَ يَقُولُ: رَأَى أَحْمَدُ بْنُ حَنْبَلٍ يَحْيَى بْنَ مَعِينٍ رَحِمَهُمَا اللَّهُ بِصَنْعَاءَ فِي زَاوِيَةٍ وَهُوَ يَكْتُبُ صَحِيفَةَ مَعْمَرٍ عَنْ أَبَانٍ عَنْ أَنَسٍ فَإِذَا اطَّلَعَ عَلَيْهِ إِنْسَانٌ كَتَمَهُ فَقَالَ لَهُ أَحْمَدُ تَكْتُبُ صَحِيفَةَ مَعْمَرٍ عَنْ أَبَانٍ عَنْ أَنَسٍ وَتَعْلَمُ أَنَّهَا مَوْضُوعَةٌ فَلَوْ قَالَ لَكَ قَائِلٌ أَنْتَ تَتَكَلَّمُ فِي أَبَانٍ ثُمَّ تَكْتُبُ حَدِيثَهُ عَلَى الْوَجْهِ فَقَالَ رَحِمَكَ اللَّهُ يَا أَبَا عَبْدِ اللَّهِ أَكْتُبُ هَذِهِ الصَّحِيفَةَ عَنْ عَبْدِ الرَّزَّاقِ عَنْ مَعْمَرٍ عَلَى الْوَجْهِ فَأَحْفَظُهَا كُلَّهَا وَأَعْلَمُ انها موضوعة حتى لا يجيء بَعْدَهُ إِنْسَانٌ فَيَجْعَلُ بَدَلَ أَبَانٍ ثَابِتًا وَيَرْوِيهَا عَنْ مَعْمَرٍ عَنْ ثَابِتٍ عَنْ أَنَسٍ فَأَقُولُ لَهُ كَذِبْتَ إِنَّمَا هِيَ عَنْ أَبَانٍ لَا عَنْ ثَابِتٍ.

قال ابن أبي حاتم: أنا ابن أبي خيثمة فيما كتب إلي، قال سمعت يحيى ابن معين يقول: أبان بن أبي عياش ليس حديثه بشيء.

Shuʿba b. al-Ḥajjāj (d. 160), when discussing a specific tradition relayed by Abān, said:

> "My cloak and donkey are charity if Abān was not lying in this ḥadīth."
>
> Yazīd b. Hārūn then told him, "Then why did you hear from him?" Shuʿba replied, "Who has patience [to abstain] from this ḥadīth?!" referring to Abān's ḥadīth from Ibrāhīm b. ʿAlqama from ʿAbdullāh on *qunūṭ*.[1]

قال العقيلي: حَدَّثَنَا أَحْمَدُ بْنُ صَدَقَةَ قَالَ: حَدَّثَنَا مُحَمَّدُ بْنُ حَرْبٍ الْوَاسِطِيُّ قَالَ: سَمِعْتُ يَزِيدَ بْنَ هَارُونَ يَقُولُ: قَالَ شُعْبَةُ: رِدَائِي وَحِمَارِي فِي الْمَسَاكِينِ صَدَقَةٌ إِنْ لَمْ يَكُنْ أَبَانُ بْنُ أَبِي عَيَّاشٍ يَكْذِبُ فِي هَذَا الْحَدِيثِ قَالَ: قُلْتُ لَهُ: فَلِمَ سَمِعْتَ مِنْهُ؟ قَالَ: وَمَنْ يَصْبِرُ عَلَى ذَا الْحَدِيثِ، يَعْنِي حَدِيثَ أَبَانَ , عَنْ إِبْرَاهِيمَ عَنْ عَلْقَمَةَ , عَنْ عَبْدِ اللَّهِ فِي الْقُنُوتِ.

Some later critics, however, refrained from accusing Abān of intentional forgery, despite his severe weakness. Al-Bazzār is quoted saying, "I feel shy before Allah to say that Abān b. Abī ʿAyyāsh and Ṣāliḥ al-Murrī were both liars."[2]

---

1 Al-Ḍuʿafāʾ al-Kabīr by al-ʿUqaylī (1/38)
2 Ikmāl Tahdhīb al-Kamāl (1/169)

قال مغلطاي: وفي «إيضاح الإشكال» لابن سعيد حافظ مصر: قال البزار: إني لأستحيي من الله عز وجل أن أقول إن أبان بن أبي عياش وصالحا المري كذابان، قال عبد الغني: وهو أبان بن فيروز، وهو أبو الأغر الذي يروي عنه الثوري.

Aḥmed b. Ḥanbal (d. 241), Abū Dāwūd (d. 275) and al-Nasāʾī (d. 303) prohibited the transcription of Abān's ḥadīth.[1]

قال ابن أبي حاتم: نا محمد بن حمويه بن الحسن، قال: سمعت أبا طالب قال قال أحمد - يعني ابن حنبل: لا تكتب عن ابان بن عياش شيئا.

قال أبو عبيد: قُلْت لأبي داود: أبان بن أبي عَيَّاش، يُكتب حَدِيثه؟ قَالَ: لا يُكتب حديث أبان.

قال النسائي: ليس بثقة، ولا يُكتب حديثه.

Sallām b. Abī Muṭīʿ (d. 164) is also quoted prohibiting an individual from transmitting anything from Abān.[2]

قال مغلطاي: وقال الأنصاري: قال لي سلام ابن أبي مطيع: لا تحدث عن أبان شيئا.

ʿAlī b. al-Madīnī (d. 234) said, "He was very weak in our opinion."[3]

قال محمد بن عثمان بن أبي شيبة: وسَألتُ عَلِيًّا عن أَبَان بن أبي عَيَّاش، فَقَالَ: كان ضَعِيْفًا ضَعِيْفًا عِنْدَنَا.

Asides from the aforementioned criticisms, Abān was described as an abandoned (*matrūk*) transmitter by Ibn Saʿd (d. 230), Ibn al-Barqī (d. 249), Ibn al-Jārūd (d. 307), al-Dāraquṭnī (d. 385), and al-Jawraqānī (d. 543) etc.[4]

Criticism and disparagement of Abān was not solely championed by Sunnī ḥadīth critics. Rather, his criticism can also be observed in Twelver biographical sources. Al-Ṭūsī (d. 460) described Abān, saying, "A weak *tabiʿī*."[5]

قال الطوسي: أبان بن أبي عياش فيروز، تابعي ضعيف.

---

1 Al-Jarḥ wa-l-Taʿdīl by Ibn Abī Ḥātim (2/296), Suʾālāt Abī ʿUbayd al-Ājurrī (p. 319), Tahdhīb al-Kamāl (2/22),

2 Ikmāl Tahdhīb al-Kamāl (1/168)

3 Suʾālāt Muḥammad b. ʿUthmān b. Abī Shayba li-ʿAlī b. al-Madīnī (p. 33)

4 Al-Ṭabaqāt al-Kabīr by Ibn Saʿd (9/253), al-Ḍuʿafāʾ wa-l-Matrūkūn by al-Dāraquṭnī (1/258), Ikmāl Tahdhīb al-Kamāl (1/169)

5 Rijāl al-Ṭūsī (p. 108)

Ibn al-Ghaḍā'irī said, "He was weak, and he should not even be considered. Our companions ascribed to him the forgery of *Kitāb Sulaym Ibn Qays.*"[1]

قال ابن الغضائري: أبانُ بنُ أبي عيّاش، واسمُ أبي عيّاش: فَيْرُوز، تابعيٌّ روى عن أنس بن مالك. وروى عن عليّ بن الحُسَيْن. ضَعِيفٌ، لا يُلْتَفَتُ إليه. وَيَنسِبُ أصحابُنا وَضْعَ كتاب سُلَيْم بن قَيْسٍ.

Given the inauthenticity of all of *Kitāb Sulaym's* isnāds back to Abān and Abān's unreliability as a transmitter, the book evidently is inauthentic. However, did Abān have an actual role in the forgery and/or dissemination of this text? I believe there are sufficient reasons to conclude that Abān has little connection to most of the extant text known as *Kitāb Sulaym*, as will be further expounded.

I have come across some Shīʿites, starting with the Shīʿite cleric, Muḥsin al-Amīn (d. 1371), cite a quote from Aḥmed b. Ḥanbal as evidence of Abān's espousal of Shīʿite beliefs.[2] The quote comes from a secondary biographical source, Ibn Ḥajar's *Tahdhīb al-Tahdhīb*. In it, Aḥmed is quoted saying:

قال ابن حجر: وقال أيضا: لا يكتب عنه قيل كان له هوى قال كان منكر الحديث.

Moḥsen al-Amīn understood from this quote that Aḥmed was describing Abān as an individual who had whims (*hawā*), hence a Shīʿite according to his understanding. Asides from the numerous issues with that conclusion, al-Amīn actually misunderstood the quote from Ibn Ḥanbal. In the tradition, Aḥmed did not state that Abān had a whim (*hawā*), but he was merely being asked whether Abān had whims or not. This is evident in the primary source being quoted by Ibn Ḥajar where Abū Ṭālib, Aḥmed b. Ḥanbal's companion, said:

> Aḥmed said, "Do not write anything from Abān b. Abī ʿAyyāsh."
>
> **I asked, "Did he have a whim (*hawā*)?"** He replied, "He was disapproved (*munkar*) in ḥadīth."[3]

قال ابن أبي حاتم: نا محمد بن حمويه بن الحسن، قال: سمعت أبا طالب قال قال أحمد - يعني ابن حنبل -: لا تكتب عن ابان بن عياش شيئا. **قلت: كان له هوى؟** قال: كان منكر الحديث.

---

1 Al-Rijāl by Ibn al-Ghaḍā'irī (p. 36)
2 Aʿyān al-Shīʿa by Mohsen Al-Amin (2/103)
3 Al-Jarḥ wa-l-Taʿdīl by Ibn Abī Ḥātim (2/296)

I am yet to come across a tradition in Abān's verified corpus that would indicate his espousal of beliefs particularly aligned with those of *Kitāb Sulaym Ibn Qays.* Out of all the criticism directed at Abān, his theological beliefs and leanings were rather spared, and his critics occasionally even made note of his piety. Had the criticism of Abān stemmed from some theological deviance, then one would expect to come across references to his beliefs, as is the case with many contemporaneous and later Shīʿite transmitters. In summary, Abān's unreliability as a transmitter is rather obvious, and it, alone, would be sufficient of a reason to challenge and dismiss the book's authenticity. However, I believe Abān's (un)reliability is actually inconsequential to the text's authenticity and origins, since much of it was developed and dubiously ascribed to him after his death.[1]

Above Abān in the isnād is Sulaym b. Qays, the book's alleged author. Sulaym was quite an obscure figure in early Sunnī and Shīʿite biographical sources.

Despite *Kitāb Sulaym Ibn Qays'* significant status within many contemporary Shīʿite circles, Sulaym b. Qays' biographical data in early Twelver sources is quite meager. The Twelver biographer, Ibn al-Najāshī (d. 450), listed him among the "pious predecessors who authored works," and he said, "Sulaym Ibn Qays al-Hilālī. He has a book. He is nicknamed Abū Ṣādiq."[2]

قال ابن النجاشي: سليم بن قيس الهلالي، له كتاب، يكنى أبا صادق.

Al-Ṭūsī (d. 460) similarly said:

> "Sulaym Ibn Qays al-Hilālī. He is nicknamed Abū Ṣādiq. He has a book."[3]

قال أبو جعفر الطوسي: سليم بن قيس الهلالي، يكنى أبا صادق، له كتاب.

1 More shall come later in this book on why I do not believe Abān has a substantive relationship to (at least most of) the extant recension of *Kitāb Sulaym Ibn Qays.*

2 Rijāl al-Najāshī (p. 10)

3 Al-Fihrist by al-Ṭūsī (p. 134)

Al-Ṭūsī also listed Sulaym as a companion of ʿAlī, al-Ḥasan, al-Ḥusayn, ʿAlī b. al-Ḥusayn and al-Bāqir.[1] Ibn al-Barqī listed Sulaym among the close, select companions (*awliyāʾ*) of ʿAlī b. Abī Ṭālib.[2]

قال ابن البرقي: و من أصحاب أمير المؤمنين عليه السلام: [...] قال: و من الأولياء: [...] وذكر سليم بن قيس الهلالي.

Hossein Modarressi stated that the aforementioned Twelver biographical sources relied on the introductory note at the beginning of *Kitāb Sulaym* for Sulaym b. Qays' biographical data.[3] This seems to be the case, for Sulaym is otherwise an obscure figure to Shīʿite scholarship. As an example, the fifth century Twelver rijālist, Ibn al-Ghaḍāʾirī, said:

> Sulaym b. Qays al-Hilālī al-ʿĀmirī. He transmitted from the Commander of the Faithful, al-Ḥasan, al-Ḥusayn and ʿAlī b. al-Ḥusayn. This famous book is ascribed to him. Our companions used to say, "Sulaym is not known, and he was not mentioned in any report."
>
> I have found him mentioned in other instances outside his book and independently of Abān b. Abī ʿAyyāsh. Ibn ʿUqda mentioned some ḥadīths from him in *Rijāl Amīr al-Muʾminīn*."[4]

قال ابن الغضائري: سُلَيْمُ بنُ قَيْس، الهِلاليّ، العامِريّ. روى عن أميرالمُؤْمنين ، والحَسَنِ، والحُسَيْنِ، وعليّ بن الحُسَيْن (ع). ويُنْسَبُ إليه هذا الكتابُ المَشْهُورُ. وكانَ أصحابُنا يقُولُون: إنّ سُلَيْماً لا يُعْرَفُ، ولا ذُكِرَ في خَبَرٍ. وقد وجدتُ ذِكْرَهُ في مواضعَ من غير جِهَةِ كتابِهِ، ولا من روايةِ أبان ابن أبي عيّاش عنهُ. وقد ذَكَرَ لهُ ابنُ عُقْدة في «رجال أمير المؤمنين (ع)» أحاديثَ عنهُ.

Ibn al-Ghaḍāʾirī's statement is indicative of Sulaym's obscurity in certain Twelver scholarly circles at the time. The Muʿtazilite Ibn Abī al-Ḥadīd (d. 656), author of the renowned commentary on *Nahj al-Balāgha* reiterated this theme. He said:

---

1 Rijāl al-Ṭūsī (p. 62, 84, 88, 99, 119)

2 Rijāl al-Barqī (p. 39)

3 Tradition and Survival: A Bibliographical Survey of Early Shīʾite Literature (1/83)

4 Al-Rijāl by Ibn al-Ghaḍāʾirī (p. 63)

> Regarding Sulaym b. Qays' al-Hilālī's report, it is worthless. Sulaym's *madhhab* is known, and his book among them (the Shīʿa), which is named *Kitāb Sulaym*, is sufficient of a reason to reject his report. However, I have heard some of them stating that this name did not denote an actual person; and that there never was anyone in the world known as Sulaym b. Qays al-Hilālī; and that the book ascribed to him is spurious, fabricated and of no basis, though some do list him among the transmitters.[1]

قال ابن أبي الحديد: فأما رواية سليم بن قيس الهلالي فليست بشيء، وسليم معروف المذهب ويكفي في رد روايته كتابه المعروف بينهم المسمى «كتاب سليم»، على أني قد سمعت من بعضهم من يذكر أن هذا الاسم على غير مسمى، وأنه لم يكن في الدنيا أحد يعرف بسليم بن قيس الهلالي وأن الكتاب المنسوب إليه منحول موضوع لا أصل له، وإن كان بعضهم يذكره في اسم الرجال.

Hossein Modarresi echoes this sentiment regarding the nonexistence of Sulaym b. Qays. He said, "It is, however, obvious that such a person never existed and that the name is only a pen name used for the sole purpose of launching an anti-Umayyad polemic in the troublesome later years of that dynasty."[2]

These claims regarding Sulaym's nonexistence are inaccurate and lacking, given that they disregard Sunnī primary and biographical sources to further explore that proposition. In a few Sunnī sources, there is sufficient mention of Sulaym to conclude that an individual by this name likely existed, albeit he was quite different in character and status than the figure purported in *Kitāb Sulaym*, which is nothing short of a pro-Rāfiḍite caricature of his identity. As an example, the renowned Sunnī ḥadīthist, Abū Ḥātim al-Rāzī (d. 277), made note of a transmitter by this name. He said:

> Sulaym b. Qays al-ʿĀmirī. He transmitted from Suḥaym b. Nawfal, and Abān transmitted from him.[3]

قال ابن أبي حاتم: سليم بن قيس العامري. روى عن سحيم بن نوفل، روى عنه أبان. سمعت أبي يقول ذلك.

This biographical entry is concise; however, Abū Ḥātim noted that Abān transmitted from this Sulaym, which makes it reasonable to conclude that

1 Sharḥ Nahj al-Balāgha by Ibn Abī al-Ḥadīd (12/216-217)

2 Tradition and Survival: A Bibliographical Survey of Early Shī'ite Literature (1/82-83)

3 Al-Jarḥ wa-l-Taʿdīl by Ibn Abī Ḥātim (4/214)

this figure likely is the Sulaym b. Qays in question today. Abū Ḥātim additionally noted that Sulaym transmitted from the Kūfan *tābiʿī*, Suḥaym b. Nawfal, and this may later prove to be a noteworthy observation.

Other than Sulaym's mention in Ibn Abī Ḥātim's *al-Jarḥ wa-l-Taʿdīl*, I came across several instances of Sulaym b. Qays' transmission in Sunnī sources. The first of them is Sulaym's transmission from Suḥaym b. Nawfal.

Ibn Abī Shayba said: Muḥammad b. al-Ḥasan al-Asadī informed us, on the authority of Ibrāhīm b. Ṭahmān, from Sulaym b. Qays, from Suḥaym b Nawfal that he said:

> ʿAbdullāh b. Masʿūd told me, "How will you be when the worshippers combat each other?" I said, "And that will take place?" He said, "Yes, [between] Muḥammad's companions."
>
> I then said, "And what should I do?" He said, "Withhold your tongue and conceal your location. Stick with what you know, and do not discard what you know in exchange for you do not recognize."[1]

قال ابن أبي شيبة: حَدَّثَنَا مُحَمَّدُ بْنُ الْحَسَنِ الأَسَدِيُّ ، عَنْ إِبْرَاهِيمَ بْنِ طَهْمَانَ ، عَنْ سُلَيْمِ بْنِ قَيْسٍ الْعَامِرِيِّ ، عَنْ سُحَيْمِ بْنِ نَوْفَلٍ ، قَالَ : قَالَ لِي عَبْدُ اللهِ بْنُ مَسْعُودٍ : كَيْفَ أَنْتُمْ إِذَا اقْتَتَلَ الْمُصَلُّونَ قُلْتُ : وَيَكُونُ ذَلِكَ ؟ قَالَ : نَعَمْ ، أَصْحَابُ مُحَمَّدٍ صَلَّى الله عَلَيْهِ وَسَلَّمَ ، قُلْتُ : وَكَيْفَ أَصْنَعُ ، قَالَ : كُفَّ لِسَانَك وَأَخِفَّ مَكَانَك ، وَعَلَيْك بِمَا تَعْرِفُ ، وَلاَ تَدَعْ مَا تَعْرِفُ لِمَا تُنْكِرُ.

It should be noted that this isnād back to Sulaym is not the strongest, since it was transmitted by Muḥammad b. al-Ḥasan al-Asadī, a criticized transmitter. Nevertheless, this tradition may prove to be insightful in multiple regards. It presents Sulaym trasnmitting from ʿAbdullāh b. Masʿūd (d. 63) via an intermediary, Suḥaym b. Nawfal. Additionally, the transmitter from Sulaym is Ibrāhīm b. Ṭaḥmān (d. 163). Perhaps this may indicate that the historical Sulaym b. Qays comes from a later generation than that of the Sulaym purported in *Kitāb Sulaym*, who allegedly was born two years before the *hijra* and directly learned from senior companions, such as Muʿādh b. Jabal (d. 17), ʿAlī (d. 40), Salmān (d. 34), al-Miqdād (d. 33) and Abū Dharr (d. 32).[2]

1 Muṣannaf Ibn Abī Shayba (21/184)
2 Kitāb Sulaym Ibn Qays (p. 69, 126)

Another potential instance of Sulaym's recorded transmission from a *tābiʿī* can be seen in a tradition relayed by Abān, from Sulaymān b. Qays al-ʿĀmirī, from Masrūq b. al-Ajdaʿ that he said:

> I entered upon ʿĀʾisha, and she said, "What has Yazīd b. Qays al-Arḥabī done, may Allah curse him (*laʿanahu Allāh*)!" I said, "O mother of the believers, he has died."
>
> She thus said, "I seek the forgiveness of Allah," twice. I said, "O mother of the believers, for what reason did you justify cursing him, and you then sought forgiveness [from that]?"
>
> She replied, "I cursed him because he was an ambassador between me and ʿAlī b. Abī Ṭālib, and he relayed from me things I did not say. As to my seeking of forgiveness, the Messenger of Allah ﷺ prohibited us from cursing the dead."[1]

قال الخطيب البغدادي: أَخْبَرَنَا الْحَسَنُ بْنُ أَبِي بَكْرٍ، أَخْبَرَنَا عَبْدُ الصَّمَدِ بْنُ عَلِيٍّ الطَّسْتِيُّ، أَخْبَرَنَا السَّرِيُّ بْنُ سهل الجنديسابوري، حَدَّثَنَا عَبْدُ اللَّهِ بْنُ رَشِيدٍ، أَخْبَرَنَا أَبُو عُبَيْدَةَ مُجَاعَةُ بْنُ الزُّبَيْرِ عَنْ أَبَانٍ عَنْ سُلَيْمَانَ بْنِ قَيْسٍ الْعَامِرِيِّ عَنْ مَسْرُوقِ بْنِ الأَجْدَعِ قَالَ: دَخَلْتُ عَلَى عَائِشَةَ فَقَالَتْ: مَا فَعَلَ يَزِيدُ بْنُ قَيْسٍ الرَّحْبِيُّ – لَعَنَهُ اللَّهُ؟ قَالَ: قُلْتُ: يَا أُمَّ الْمُؤْمِنِينَ مَاتَ {قَالَتْ: أَسْتَغْفِرُ اللَّهَ – مَرَّتَيْنِ. قُلْتُ: يَا أُمَّ الْمُؤْمِنِينَ بِمَ اسْتَحْلَلْتِ لَعْنَتَهُ ثُمَّ اسْتَغْفَرْتِ؟ قَالَتِ: اسْتَحْلَلْتُ لَعْنَتَهُ لأَنَّهُ كَانَ سَفِيرًا بَيْنِي وَبَيْنَ عَلِيِّ بْنِ أَبِي طالب فبلغ عني مالم أَقُلْ} وَأَمَّا اسْتِغْفَارِي فَإِنَّ رَسُولَ اللَّهِ – صَلَّى اللَّهُ عَلَيْهِ وَسَلَّمَ – نَهَانَا أَنْ نَلْعَنَ الأَمْوَاتَ – أَوْ قال: موتانا!

This tradition cannot be reliably traced to Abān, and it hence cannot be taken at face value. Nevertheless, Sulaym in this report is presented transmitting from ʿĀʾisha (d. 57) via the *tābiʿī*, Masrūq (d. 62), as an intermediary between them, and Sulaym's position in the isnād is similar to that of the previous tradition.

There are other traditions from Sulaym b. Qays that are quite insightful. Maʿmar b. Rāshid narrated on the authority of Abān, from Sulaym b. Qays al-Ḥanẓalī that he said:

> ʿUmar once gave a sermon and he said, "The thing I fear the most for you after me is that an innocent man is taken and sawn just as a camel is slaughtered; and his meat is exposed to fire just as a

---

1 Al-Asmāʾ al-Mubhama fī al-Anbāʾ al-Muḥkama by al-Khaṭīb al-Baghdādī (p. 338)

camel's meat is; and it would be said, 'he is a disobeyer,' and he actually is not a disobeyer."

ʿAlī, while under the pulpit, thus said, "And when is that O commander of the faithful? Or when does the affliction become severe, pride appears, progeny is enslaved, *fitan* strike them just as a stone mill strikes the sediments in it and a fire strikes lumber?"

ʿUmar said, "And when is that, ʿAlī?" He said, "If *fiqh* is sought for other than the faith, knowledge is sought for other than [its] implementation, and the *Dunyā* is sought through the actions of the *Ākhira.*"[1]

معمر بن راشد، عَنْ أَبَانَ، عَنْ سُلَيْمِ بْنِ قَيْسٍ الْحَنْظَلِيِّ، قَالَ: خَطَبَ عُمَرُ، فَقَالَ, " إِنَّ أَخْوَفَ مَا أَتَخَوَّفُ عَلَيْكُمْ بَعْدِي أَنْ يُؤْخَذَ الرَّجُلُ مِنْكُمُ الْبَرِيءُ، فَيُؤْشَرُ كَمَا يُؤْشَرُ الْجَزُورُ، وَيُشَاطُ لَحْمُهُ كَمَا يُشَاطُ لَحْمُهَا، وَيُقَالُ: عَاصٍ وَلَيْسَ بِعَاصٍ "، قَالَ: فَقَالَ عَلِيٌّ وَهُوَ تَحْتَ الْمِنْبَرِ, " وَمَتَى ذَلِكَ يَا أَمِيرَ الْمُؤْمِنِينَ؟ أَوْ: بِمَا تَشْتَدُّ الْبَلِيَّةُ، وَتَظْهَرُ الْحَمِيَّةُ، وَتُسْبَى الذُّرِّيَّةُ، وَتَدُقُّهُمُ الْفِتَنُ كَمَا تَدُقُّ الرَّحَا ثُفْلَهَا، وَكَمَا تَدُقُّ النَّارُ الْحَطَبَ؟ "، قَالَ, " وَمَتَى ذَلِكَ يَا عَلِيُّ؟ "، قَالَ, " إِذَا تُفُقِّهَ لِغَيْرِ الدِّينِ، وَتُعُلِّمَ لِغَيْرِ الْعَمَلِ، وَالْتُمِسَتِ الدُّنْيَا بِعَمَلِ الآخِرَةِ "

In this tradition, Sulaym does not mention being present in the gathering. From Sulaym's transmission in the past sources, it appears that his transmission of this account is disconnected. A later source that references Maʿmar b. Rāshid's tradition, however, presents Sulaym claiming to had witnessed the sermon. This later accretion, however, is worthy of discretion and scrutiny, given that the tradition in Maʿmar's book makes no mention of Sulaym's presence at the sermon.[2] Either way, this tradition is quite valuable, for it quotes ʿAlī b. Abī Ṭālib referring to ʿUmar as the commander of the faithful (*amīr a-muʾminīn*), which is strange when considering *Kitāb Sulaym's* characterization of ʿUmar b. al-Khaṭṭāb. This tradition similarly presents ʿUmar and ʿAlī amicably conversing with each other, though it seems to hint at ʿAlī's superior knowledge. Later in history, a significantly distorted variant of this tradition makes its way into *Kitāb Sulaym*, and more will come on it later in this book.

1 Al-Jāmiʿ by Maʿmar b. Rāshid al-Azdī (11/36)

2 Al-Mustadrak ʿalā al-Ṣaḥīḥayn by al-Ḥākim (4/498). It should additionally be noted that al-Ḥākim's informant in this tradition is as an obscure transmitter, which would question any addition relayed by him that cannot be found in Maʿmar's actual book.

Another tradition that cites Sulaym b. Qays is what was recorded by ʿAbdurrazzāq in his *Muṣannaf,* on the authority of Maʿmar, from Abān, from Sulaym b. Qays, from ʿAnbasa b. Abī Sufyān from Umm Ḥabība that the Prophet ﷺ said:

> "Whosoever prays twelve *rakʿāt*, then Allah shall build for him a house in heaven. Whosoever builds a mosque, then Allah shall build for him a house more spacious than it."[1]

عبد الرزاق، عَنْ مَعْمَرٍ، عَنْ أَبَانَ، عَنْ سُلَيْمَانَ بْنِ قَيْسٍ ، عَنْ عَنْبَسَةَ بْنِ أَبِي سُفْيَانَ، عَنْ أُمِّ حَبِيبَةَ، أَنّ النَّبِيَّ قَالَ: مَنْ صَلَّى فِي يَوْمٍ اثْنَتَيْ عَشْرَةَ رَكْعَةً، بَنَى اللَّهُ لَهُ بَيْتًا فِي الْجَنَّةِ، وَمَنْ بَنَى مَسْجِدًا، بَنَى اللَّهُ لَهُ أَوْسَعَ مِنْهُ.

I fear that Abān may had originally acquired this tradition from Shahr b. Ḥawshab and then misattributed it to Sulaym b. Qays. It is relayed elsewhere from Shahr, from ʿAnbasa, and one of the criticisms directed at Abān was that he used to confuse Shahr's transmission with others' transmission, as was mentioned earlier.[2] Either way, ʿAnbasa technically was a *tābiʿī*, and he was alive in the year 47.[3]

Al-Dāraquṭnī (d. 385) relayed a tradition via Ṣāliḥ b. Abī al-Aswad, from Abān b. Abī ʿAyyāsh, from Sulaym b. Qays, from his father that the Prophet ﷺ said, "These two sons of mine are the masters of the youth of this *Umma.*"[4]

قال ابن طاهر في «أطراف الغراب والأفراد»: حديث : قال رسول الله صلى الله عليه وسلم للحسن والحسين: إن ابنيَّ هذين سيدا هذه الأمة... الحديث. تفرد به صالح بن أبي الأسود، عن أبان بن أبي عياش، عن سليم بن قيس، عن أبيه.

Since Ṣāliḥ b. Abī al-Aswad was a weak transmitter, it is difficult to ascertain the utility and accuracy of the claims in this isnād. Nonetheless, what is interesting is that Sulaym b. Qays' father is identified therein as Qays b. Kaʿb. This tradition is quite popular, and it unsurprisingly was

---

1 Al-Muṣannaf of ʿAbdurrazzāq al-Ṣanʿānī (3/75)

2 See ʿAnbasa b. Abī Sufyān's entry in al-Bukhārī's al-Tārīkh al-Kabīr (7/36)

3 Tārīkh al-Islām by al-Dhahabī (2/434)

4 Aṭrāf al-Gharāʾib wa-l-Afrād of Ibn al-Qaysarānī (2/116). The referenced text of al-Dāraquṭnī has mostly been lost; however, parts of it survive through Ibn Ṭāhir's book, *Aṭrāf al-Gharāʾib wa-l-Afrād.* I was unable to ascertain al-Dāraquṭnī's isnād back to Ṣāliḥ b. Abī al-Aswad, though it was noted by al-Dāraquṭnī that it was exclusively relayed by Ṣāliḥ [with this isnād in this form].

referenced in *Kitāb Sulaym* in several different contexts, though it may be a sheer coincidence due to the popularity of this tradition in Shīʿite circles.[1]

From the aforementioned traditions, it can be demonstrated that a figure by the name of Sulaym b. Qays, who was referenced as a source of traditions by Abān b. Abī ʿAyyāsh, likely existed, though there seem to be disparities between this historical Sulaym and the Sulaym of *Kitāb Sulaym.*

Kitāb Sulaym mentioned that Sulaym b. Qays fled from ʿIrāq following al-Ḥajjāj b. Yūsuf al-Thaqafī's appointment as its governor, which was in the year 95.[2] At the time, Abān is said to be 14 years old. Hence, according to *Kitāb Sulaym,* Abān would have been born sometime around the years 61 and 62. Abān's death date was in 138, and his age during his death according to *Kitāb Sulaym* hence would be around 76-77 years old.[3]

قال أبو محمد الفاكهي في فوائده: سَمِعْتُ يَعْقُوبَ يَقُولُ: مَاتَ حُمَيْدٌ الطَّوِيلُ فِي جُمَادَى الْأُولَى سَنَةَ أَرْبَعِينَ وَمِائَةٍ، قَالَ: وَمَاتَ أَبَانُ بْنُ أَبِي عَيَّاشٍ فِي أَوَّلِ رَجَبٍ سَنَةَ ثَمَانٍ وَثَلَاثِينَ وَمِائَةٍ.

This claim is interesting, for historical sources make no note of a figure by the name of Sulaym b. Qays who was pursued by al-Ḥajjāj into exile. Certainly, being an eminent pro-Alid figure who was particularly sought and pursued by Umayyad authorities should entail that the pursued individual was of prominence, yet we oddly find no mention of a figure that matches this description in any sources, including historical sources that compiled the names of notable people who had went into hiding out of fear of al-Ḥajjāj.[4]

Sulaym b. Qays is rather a quite obscure figure, and almost everything that may be discerned about him was exclusively relayed by the weak Abān b. Abī ʿAyyāsh, further complicating any serious attempt to discern his identity. In this regard, Amir-Moezzi posited a noteworthy objection to those who denied Sulaym's very existence and/or prominence. He said:

> It is difficult to accept this assertion, which radically rejects a rich bibliographical and prosopographical tradition; moreover, even if

---

1 Kitāb Sulaym Ibn Qays (p. 132, 197, 236, 275, 323)

2 Kitāb Sulaym Ibn Qays (p. 125), Tārīkh al-Rusul wa-l-Mulūk by al-Ṭabarī (6/202)

3 Fawāʾid Abī Muḥammad al-Fākihī (p. 375)

4 As an example, the noble ḥadīthist, ʿAbdulGhanī b. Saʿīd al-Azdī (d. 409), authored a book that compiled the names of individuals who had fled from al-Ḥajjāj, *Kitāb al-Mutawārīn Alladhīna Ikhtafaw min al-Ḥajjāj Ibn Yūsuf al-Thaqafī,* and he made no mention of Sulaym b. Qays.

> the attribution is problematic, the putative author must have really existed and been respected by the Alids, otherwise what legitimacy could a writing ascribed to a fictitious person have possessed?[1]

This objection, *ceterus paribus*, seems reasonable. However, it misrepresents the issue at hand: the author (forger) of *Kitāb Sulaym* presented this text as a document compiled by a direct companion of ʿAlī b. Abī Ṭālib, Sulaym b. Qays. Regardless of Sulaym's true standing, convincing the medieval Shīʿite (or Sunnī) reader of *Kitāb Sulaym* that it was authored by a direct companion of ʿAlī certainly would, by default, grant this text greater significance, authority and relevance in the eyes of the reader than if it were authored by some third or fourth century Shīʿte partisan. If a later Shīʿite forger was able to convince his audience that his forgeries originated from a companion of ʿAlī, albeit an obscure one, then that would nonetheless lend weight to those otherwise insignificant texts.

Furthermore, the author of this text clearly was not content with the mere reliance on Sulaym b. Qays as an anchor for the book's authenticity and credibility. He hence fabricated various endorsements of the book which he ascribed to several prominent figures, such as al-Ḥasan al-Baṣrī, Abū al-Ṭufayl, ʿUmar b. Abī Salama, and ʿAlī b. al-Ḥusayn, in an attempt to further bolster the book's authority and perceived authenticity.[2] Such endorsements were fabricated precisely to grant more credibility to a text that was attributed to a generally obscure and unknown historical figure. The forger of *Kitāb Sulaym*, however, likely recognized that this lionization of the obscure Sulaym b. Qays as some eminent, pursued companion of ʿAlī and an author of an early foundational text would warrant serious concern about how such a seemingly significant figure was widely unknown and obscure in earlier literature. For this reason, the author of *Kitāb Sulaym* fabricated an entire narrative at the forefront of the book that conveniently explains away any objection surrounding Sulaym's contradictory prominence and obscurity: he actually was a renowned figure, but he is obscure because he had fled into exile, where he secretly disseminated this seminal text!

In this regard, the forger of *Kitāb Sulaym* had effectively had his cake and eaten it. On one hand, he reaped the benefits of ascribing his forgery to an obscure and unknown figure, preventing contemporaneous and later critics from cross-referencing its claims with otherwise available and

---

1 The Silent Qu'an and the Speaking Qur'an (p. 16-17)

2 Kitāb Sulaym Ibn Qays (p. 127-129

accessible information about that figure. On the other hand, the forger of this text compensated for its pseudepigraphical author's obscurity by claiming that the text was endorsed by several eminent *tābiʿīn*, including ʿAlī b. al-Ḥusayn b. ʿAlī b. Abī Ṭālib, and by creating a narrative that conveniently explains away Sulaym's obscurity.

Asides from the aforementioned points, Amir-Moezzi's contention presumes that the sole objective behind the forgery of this book and similar texts was to grant legitimacy to the text being forged. Forgers, however, were often constrained by other concerns and variables, such as fear of being identified and/or discredited, which would be almost inevitable if the forger were to directly ascribe unknown traditions to a popular figure whose identity and traditions were known and accessed by many. Many forgers hence used to attribute their dubious traditions through unreliable and obscure sources.[1]

1 See for, example, al-Ḥasan b. ʿAlī b. Ṣāliḥ al-ʿAdawī's entry in Ibn ʿAdī's *al-Kāmil fī Ḍuʿafāʾ al-Rijāl.* Ibn ʿAdī described him saying, "He fabricates ḥadīth, steals it [from some sources] and then ascribes it to other people. He transmits from people that are not known, and he is suspect in their regards that Allah never created them." See al-Kāmil fī Ḍuʿafāʾ al-Rijāl (3/195).

Additionally, refer to Yaḥyā b. Maʿīn's comment on al-Wāqidī in Ibn Abī Ḥātim al-Jarḥ wa-l-Taʿdīl (8/21).

These are but a few examples of this phenomenon: forgers used to occasionally claim to relay their spurious traditions through obscure and unknown sources. The rationale behind such behavior is multifaceted, and it is not an inexplicable phenomenon as is insinuated by Amir-Moezzi.

CHAPTER 2: TEXTUAL ANALYSIS

To further understand or contextualize the origins of *Kitāb Sulaym Ibn Qays'*, one must explore its contents alongside its tangled transmission. My textual analysis of the book revolves around multiple noteworthy observations I have made while reading the text:

1. The discovery narrative at the beginning of the book
2. The presence of numerous historical errors throughout the book
3. The presence of anachronisms within the text
4. The occurrence of falsifications throughout the text

These observations would contextualize and further confirm the transmitive issues that plague the text's purported isnāds, which were expounded in the past chapter.

The Discovery Narrative

A common theme that has been recurrently observed in forged texts is a phenomenon known as a "discovery narrative." Wheeler describes this phenomenon saying:

> A person claims to have discovered an older, previously hidden text containing sacred knowledge, and he then duly circulates that knowledge to the world. The term "discovery narrative" may be used to describe this phenomenon, although other terms can also be found in the literature, such as "find story," "Fundbericht," and "pseudo-documentarism."[1]

Ehrman elaborated on this phenomenon saying:

> One final technique used by some forgers involves a "discovery narrative." If a book shows up this week claiming to have been

1 G. J. Wheeler, "The Finding of Hidden Texts in Esoteric and -Other Religious Traditions: Some Notes on 'Discovery Narratives.'" Correspondences: Journal for the Study of Esotericism, no. 2 (2019): 339.

> written two hundred years ago, one might well wonder where it has been all this time. Forgers sometimes begin or end their writing by describing what has led to the book's disappearance and discovery. For example, an author might begin a book by explaining that he had a dream, and in this dream he was told to dig a deep hole on the south side of the oak tree in the field across the stream from his farm. When he dug the hole, he found an ancient wooden box. Inside the box was a deteriorating manuscript. He has now copied this manuscript out by hand, and this is it, a revelation given directly by Christ to the apostle James and hidden from the world until now.
>
> The book then claims to have been written by James, as "copied" by the discoverer of the manuscript. The book is not widely known, because it has been hidden all these years. But now it has come to light, and here it is. Except it's not really here. What is here is a book not written by James, but by a forger claiming to be James, who has conveniently included an explanation for why no one has ever heard of this book before.[1]

As evident, the purpose of these anecdotes that occasionally accompanied past forgeries was to justify and explain away their obscurity and lend credence to the mysteriously "discovered" text.[2] As put by Wheeler:

> A discovery narrative works, in essence, by harnessing this prerational force for the purpose of increasing the value of the text to which it is attached. The basic purpose of a discovery narrative is to substitute the text's true but mundane origin for a false but more valuable one. The psychological motivation is no doubt a conviction that the text's contents are so important that they deserve to be validated in a suitably out-of-the-ordinary manner. From this point of view, inventing a discovery narrative is not so much an act of deceit as a means of communicating a higher truth.[3]

---

1 Forged: Writing in the Name of God—Why the Bible's Authors Are Not Who We Think They Are (p. 35)

2 Forgers and Critics: Creativity and Duplicity in Western Scholarship (p. 57-58)

3 Wheeler, "The Finding of Hidden Texts in Esoteric and -Other Religious Traditions," 355.

Wheeler further elaborates:

> Discovery narratives are seductive things. Even when we do not believe them, we may feel that we wish that we could do so. They are exciting and mysterious. They announce the disclosure of hidden secrets. In some cases, the drama is heightened by the presence of overtly supernatural elements. In any event, they offer us the irresistible chance of accessing a past that is otherwise lost, and the "thrill of making a fragile connection with something distant and unusual."[1]

Kitāb Sulaym, in this regard, is no exception. The book commences with a long anecdote from one of the book's purported transmitters, Abān, where he is quoted providing a detailed story that explains his (exclusive) acquisition of the book. That anecdote commences with commentary from Ibn Udhayna, the alleged transmitter of this text from Abān. Ibn Udhayna reportedly said:

> Abān b. Abī ʿAyyāsh once invited me around a month prior to his death. He told me, "I saw a dream yesterday [which hinted to] the imminence of my death. I then saw you next morning, and I was happy to see you. I saw Sulaym in a dream last night, and he told me, 'O Abān, you shall die in these coming days, so fear Allah with regards to my trust, and do not lose it. Conceal it as you have promised, and only share it with a man from the Shīʿa of ʿAlī b. Abī Ṭālib who is of piety and status.'
>
> When I saw you this morning, I was happy to see you, and I remembered my dream of Sulaym b. Qays."[2]

قال عمر بن أذينة: دعاني أبان بن أبي عياش قبل موته بنحو شهر فقال لي: رأيت البارحة رؤيا، أني خليق أن أموت سريعا. إني رأيتك الغداة ففرحت بك. إني رأيت الليلة سليم بن قيس الهلالي فقال لي: يا أبان، إنك ميت في أيامك هذه. فاتق الله في وديعتي ولا تضيعها، وف لي بما ضمنت من كتمانها. ولا تضعها إلا عند رجل من شيعة علي بن أبي طالب صلوات الله عليه له دين وحسب. فلما بصرت بك الغداة فرحت برؤيتك وذكرت رؤياي سليم بن قيس.

1 Wheeler, "The Finding of Hidden Texts in Esoteric and -Other Religious Traditions," 355.

2 Kitāb Sulaym Ibn Qays (p. 125)

Abān is then quoted providing an anecdote which explains his clandestine acquisition of Kitāb Sulaym. He is quoted saying:

> When al-Ḥajjāj arrived to Iraq, he inquired about Sulaym b. Qays. Sulaym thus fled from him, and he came to us in Nawbandajan while hiding; and he stayed at our house. I have never seen a man who was more honorable, diligent, prolongedly sorrowful, reclusive and resentful of fame than him. I was 14 years old at the time, and I had recited the Quran. I used to ask him, and he would tell me about the people of Badr.
>
> I heard many ḥadīths from him which he had transmitted from ʿUmar b. Abī Salama, the son of Umm Salama the Prophet's ﷺ wife, Mu'ādh b. Jabal, Salmān al-Fārisī, ʿAlī b. Abī Tālib, Abū Dharr, al-Miqdād, ʿAmmār and al-Barāʾ b. ʿĀzib. He then asked me to conceal them, but he did not make me swear an oath to that.
>
> When he was dying, he invited me and spoke to me privately. He said, "O Abān, I have lived by you, and I have only seen from you that which I liked. I possess some writings that I had heard from the reliable transmitters and transcribed with my own hands. In them are ḥadīths which I do not want exposed to the public, since the people would object to them and be outraged by them. These writings are true, and I have taken them from the people of truth, understanding, patience and piety: ʿAlī b. Abī Tālīb, Salmān al-Fārisī, Abū Dharr al-Ghifārī, al-Miqdād b. al-Aswad.
>
> There is not a single ḥadīth in them that I had heard from one of them except that I had asked another about it until they would eventually all agree upon it, so I followed them on it. They also contain things I later heard from other people among the people of truth. When I fell ill, I initially intended to burn them, but I then felt bad about that, so I refrained from doing so.
>
> Shall you swear to me, [O Abān], an oath by Allah to not inform anyone of it so as long as I am alive and to not transmit anything from it to anyone after my death asides except those who you trust as you trust yourself; and if anything were to happen to you, then you shall hand it over to whom you trust from the Shīʿa of ʿAlī b. Abī Ṭālib, who are of piety and status."

> I then promised him that, so he handed me the writings and recited them all to me. Sulaym died soon after that...[1]

لما قدم الحجاج العراق سأل عن سليم بن قيس، فهرب منه فوقع إلينا بالنوبندجان متواريا، فنزل معنا في الدار. فلم أر رجلا كان أشد إجلالا لنفسه ولا أشد اجتهادا ولا أطول حزنا منه، ولا أشد خمولا لنفسه ولا أشد بغضا لشهرة نفسه منه. وأنا يومئذ ابن أربع عشرة سنة، وقد قرأت القرآن، وكنت أسأله فيحدثني عن أهل بدر. فسمعت منه أحاديث كثيرة عن عمر بن أبي سلمة ابن أم سلمة زوجة النبي صلى الله عليه وآله، وعن معاذ بن جبل وعن سلمان الفارسي وعن علي بن أبي طالب عليه السلام وأبي ذر والمقداد وعمار والبراء بن عازب. ثم استكتمنيها ولم يأخذ علي فيها يمينا.

فلم ألبث أن حضرته الوفاة، فدعاني وخلا بي وقال: يا أبان، إني قد جاورتك فلم أر منك إلا ما أحب. وإن عندي كتبا سمعتها عن الثقات وكتبتها بيدي، فيها أحاديث لا أحب أن تظهر للناس، لأن الناس ينكرونها ويعظمونها. وهي حق أخذتها من أهل الحق والفقه والصدق والبر، عن علي بن أبي طالب صلوات الله عليه وسلمان الفارسي وأبي ذر الغفاري والمقداد بن الأسود رضي الله عنهم.

وليس منها حديث أسمعه من أحدهم إلا سألت عنه الآخر حتى اجتمعوا عليه جميعا، فتبعتهم عليه، وأشياء بعد سمعتها من غيرهم من أهل الحق. وإني هممت حين مرضت أن أحرقها، فتأثمت من ذلك وقطعت به. فإن جعلت لي عهد الله عز وجل وميثاقه أن لا تخبر بها أحدا ما دمت حيا، ولا تحدث بشئ منها بعد موتي إلا من تثق به كثقتك بنفسك، وإن حدث بك حدث أن تدفعها إلى من تثق به من شيعة علي بن أبي طالب صلوات الله عليه ممن له دين وحسب.

فضمنت ذلك له، فدفعها إلي وقرأها كلها علي. فلم يلبث سليم أن هلك، رحمه الله.

This anecdote, which is ascribed to Abān, is a textbook example of a "discovery narrative." It is to be understood in light of the fact that this text was allegedly authored by companion of ʿAlī in the first century, yet it only came to public light in the third and fourth centuries. Hence, we find that the earliest reference to *Kitāb Sulaym* as a separate book occurs in the fourth century. Prior to that, we can only observe a few fragmented traditions from it in a few Twelver ḥadīth collections.

The discovery narrative, however, does not end there. The author of this text further attempted to grant his work legitimacy by claiming that the

---

1 Kitāb Sulaym Ibn Qays (p. 125-126)

book was then endorsed by ʿAlī b. al-Husayn.[1] The author, however, was not satisfied with an individual endorsement by the fourth Twelver *imām*, so he additionally claimed that the book was endorsed by al-Ḥasan al-Baṣrī, ʿUmar b. Abī Salama and Abū Al- Ṭufayl.[2]

It is unclear who the exact author of this anecdote really is, though I do not believe Abān is to be credited with its authorship. All-in-all, it seems that there are three main individuals who are candidate authors of this story, (1) ʿUmar b. Udhayna, (2) Ibrāhīm b. ʿUmar al-Yamānī or (3) Ḥammād b. ʿĪsā al-Juhanī, since the book's isnāds mostly revolve around these figures who transmitted the text from each other. Nevertheless, I am yet to come across any conclusive evidence that would allow me to champion a particular stance in this regard.

Historical Errors

The presence of blatant historical errors in *Kitāb Sulaym Ibn Qays* is a noteworthy phenomenon that provides valuable context behind the book's authorship and origins. Though many historical errors exist in the text today, I have opted to shed light on a few notable ones I had noted and studied.

Muḥammad b. Abī Bakr at His Father's Deathbed

In the 37th report of *Kitāb Sulaym*, Muḥammad b. Abī Bakr is quoted elaborating on his father's death and describing it as an eyewitness. Sulaym is quoted saying:

> I then met Muḥammad b. Abī Bakr, and I asked him, "Has anyone asides from your brother, ʿAbdurraḥmān, ʿĀʾisha and ʿUmar witness your father's death?" He said, "No."
>
> I asked, "Did they hear from him what you had heard?" He said, "They heard parts of it, and they cried and said, 'he has gone insane!', but they did not hear everything I had heard."[3]

---

1 Kitāb Sulaym Ibn Qays (p. 125-126)

2 Kitāb Sulaym Ibn Qays (p. 127-128)

3 Kitāb Sulaym Ibn Qays (p. 348)

قال سليم: فلقيت محمد بن أبي بكر فقلت: هل شهد موت أبيك غير أخيك عبد الرحمن وعائشة وعمر؟ قال: لا. قلت: وهل سمعوا منه ما سمعت؟ قال: سمعوا منه طرفا فبكوا وقالوا: يهجر. فأما كل ما سمعت أنا فلا.

Muḥammad b. Abī Bakr is then quoted saying:

> When I was alone with him [Abū Bakr], I told him, "O father, say, *la ilaha illa Allah.*" He replied, "I shall never say it nor am I capable of saying it until I am admitted into Hellfire and I enter the coffin!"
>
> When he mentioned the coffin. I initially thought he had gone insane, so I asked him, "What coffin?" He said, "A coffin made of fire, locked with a lock of fire. It contains twelve men, me and my companion!"
>
> I asked, "ʿUmar?" He replied, "Yes. Who else could I be referring to?! Along with ten other men in a pit in *Jahannam* covered by a boulder! Whenever Allah wants to inflame the Hellfire, He would lift that boulder!"[1]

فقلت له لما خلوت به: يا أبه، قل: لا إله إلا الله. قال: لا أقولها أبدا ولا أقدر عليها حتى أرد النار فأدخل التابوت. فلما ذكر التابوت ظننت أنه يهجر. فقلت له: أي تابوت؟ فقال: تابوت من نار مقفل بقفل من نار، فيه اثنا عشر رجلا، أنا وصاحبي هذا. قلت: عمر؟ قال: نعم، فمن أعني؟ وعشرة في جب في جهنم عليه صخرة إذا أراد الله أن يسعر جهنم رفع الصخرة.

Though this account may sound like a summary of a plausible conversation that may have taken place at a deathbed between a dying father and his son, it is, in fact, fictitious. Muḥammad b. Abī Bakr was only three years old when his 60+ year old father died. He could not have conversed with his father in this manner, let alone recollected this purported conversation many years later as an adult. Alas, the later Shīʿte fabricator of this account, not recognizing its sheer impossibility, probably supposed Muḥammad b. Abī Bakr was a suitable character in the scene due to his reputed pro-Alid inclinations as a son of Abū Bakr.

One of the earliest figures to draw attention to this historical error was the fifth century Shīʿite critic, Ibn al-Ghaḍāʾirī. In his book, *al-Rijāl,* he said:

> The book is fabricated without a doubt, and in it are several indicators which demonstrate this. One of them is what is

1 Kitāb Sulaym Ibn Qays (p. 349)

> mentioned in it regarding Muḥammad b. Abī Bakr giving his father a reminder when he was dying.[1]

قال ابن الغضائري: والكتابُ موضُوعٌ، لا مِرْيَةَ فيهِ، وعلى ذلك علاماتٌ فيهِ تَدُلُّ على ما ذكرناهُ. منها: ما ذَكَرَ أَنَّ مُحَمَّدَ بنَ أبي بَكْرٍ وَعَظَ أباهُ عندَ مَوْتِهِ، ومنها: أَنَّ الأئمّةَ ثلاثةَ عَشَر، وغيرُ ذلك.

Al-Khoei attempted to bypass Ibn al-Ghaḍāʾirī's criticism by repeatedly claiming that Ibn Al-Ghaḍā'irī's book is inauthentically ascribed to him; however, that is irrelevant, since the point still stands regardless of whether it was made by Ibn Al-Ghaḍā'irī or not.[2] Al-Khoei then proceeds to quote al-Mirzā al-Astarābādī (d. 1028) claiming that his manuscript of the book mentions that it was ʿAbdullāh b. ʿUmar who addressed his father, ʿUmar, while he was in his deathbed, not Muḥammad b. Abī Bakr. Al-Khoei also quoted al-Tafrīshī (d. post-1030) stating that a "virtuous individual" (perhaps referring to al-Mirzā al-Astarābādī) mentioned that he had a copy that quoted ʿAbdullāh b. ʿUmar admonishing his father and that it did not quote Muḥammad b. Abī Bakr doing so. Al-Khoei also quoted al-Ḥurr al-ʿĀmilī (d. 1104) stating that the errors cited by Ibn al-Ghaḍāʾirī are not present in the manuscript he possessed.[3]

The references to al-Astarābādī and al-Tifrishī demonstrate that there were some manuscripts of the book being circulated in the eleventh century that appropriated this criticized passage by replacing Muḥammad b. Abī Bakr with ʿAbdullāh b. ʿUmar. Nevertheless, the published edition of Kitāb Sulaym today, which the editor based on 14 surviving manuscripts of the book, contains this ahistorical excerpt that was problematized by Ibn al-Ghaḍāʾirī.

Al-Khoei later said:

> As for Muḥammad b. Abī Bakr giving his father a reminder as he was dying, if it is authentic, then it is plausible as a *karāma* or supernatural event, though it is impossible according to the norms."[4]

---

1 Al-Rijāl by Ibn al-Ghaḍāʾirī (p. 63)

2 That generally is the case, unless al-Khoei's argument is that this claim surrounding *Kitāb Sulaym* exclusively comes via Ibn al-Ghaḍāʾirī's book. In that case, challenging the book's ascription would be understandable, though, in our case, it is inconsequential.

3 Muʿjam Rijāl al-Ḥadīth (9/230-231)

4 Muʿjam Rijāl al-Ḥadīth (9/234)

قال الخوئي: وأما وعظ محمد بن أبي بكر أباه عند موته ، فلو صح فهو – وإن لم يمكن عادة – إلا أنه يمكن أن يكون على نحو الكرامة وخرق العادة.

It is telling how al-Khoei, despite the innumerable issues in the book, was willing to utilize some *ad hoc* appeal to the supernatural to provide an explanation to this obviously problematic passage. It goes without saying that most Sunnī and Shīʿite Muslims who problematize this excerpt in *Kitāb Sulaym*, such as Ibn al-Ghaḍāʾirī, myself and other critics, do not contest the existence of miracles and supernatural events. Rather, the issue with al-Khoei's appeal is multifaceted: when a dubious text or report that is plagued with trasnmittive and textual defects embodies a claim that is, at face value, erroneous and ahistorical, the more plausible explanation is that the claim simply is an error. Otherwise, such convenient *ad hoc* appeals effectively undermine the foundations of textual criticism.

What is additionally noteworthy in this regard is that *Kitāb Sulaym* does not hint to the special or miraculous nature of this incident. Rather, it seems to present it as a normal memory of Muḥammad b. Abī Bakr that was casually discussed between him and Sulaym. Shīʿite appeals that project supernatural explanations onto Muḥammad b. Abī Bakr's recollection of this event simply are attempts at salvaging this evidently problematic passage in the book.

Al-Ḥasan al-Baṣrī's Alleged Audition (*samāʿ*) from Abū Dharr and Others

In *Kitāb Sulaym*, ʿAlī b. al-Ḥusayn is quoted asking Abān b. Abī ʿAyyāsh whether he had heard of a certain ḥadīth or not, and he then proceeded to ask him about his sources. Abān mentioned that al-Ḥasan al-Baṣrī had informed him that he heard of the ḥadīth from Abū Dharr, al-Miqdād, and ʿAlī b. Abī Ṭālib.[1]

قال علي بن الحسين: وممن؟ فقلت: ومن الحسن بن أبي الحسن البصري أنه سمعه من أبي ذر ومن المقداد بن الأسود الكندي ومن علي بن أبي طالب صلوات الله عليه.

There are good reasons to believe that this entire passage in *Kitāb* Sulaym is a blatant forgery and historical error. Abū Dharr al-Ghifārī, one of al-Ḥasan al-Baṣrī's alleged informants in the aforementioned passage died in the year 32, when al-Ḥasan was around 10-11 years old. Additionally,

1 Kitāb Sulaym Ibn Qays (p. 129)

Abū Dharr had primarily resided in al-Shām, and he only returned to Medīna in the year 30 where the 8-9 year old al-Ḥasan resided. Abū Dharr then departed from Medīna shortly after that, and he resided in al-Rabdha till his death.[1] Hence, al-Ḥasan could have only met Abū Dharr during a small window of time when he was less than ten years old during Abū Dharr's brief return to Medīna, which is a quite narrow and highly unlikely possibility. When that is taken into account, alongside the fact that al-Ḥasan used to transmit from Abū Dharr via an intermediary, it becomes evident that al-Ḥasan's transmission from Abū Dharr is disconnected and that the claim in *Kitāb Sulaym* is a later forgery.[2]

Abū al-Dardā' at Ṣiffīn

The 25th report in *Kitāb Sulaym* revolves around certain events that took place prior to the battle of Ṣiffīn. Sulaym is quoted saying:

> Muʿāwiya called Abū al-Dardā' and Abū Hurayra, while we were with the commander of the faithful (ʿAlī), and he told them, "Go to ʿAlī, and convey to him my *salam*. Tell him..."
>
> The report then states that Abū al-Dardā' and Abū Hurayra eventually conveyed the message to ʿAlī, and they then returned to Muʿāwiya.[3]

قال: إن معاوية دعا أبا الدرداء ونحن مع أمير المؤمنين عليه السلام بصفين ودعا أبا هريرة فقال لهما: انطلقا إلى علي فاقرآه مني السلام وقولا له.... الخبر.

The battle of Ṣiffīn occurred in 37, two years after the murder of ʿUthmān in 35.[4] Abū al-Dardā', however, died in Damascus during the reign of ʿUthmān, and he was not alive during the battle of Ṣiffīn, let alone an envoy

1 Tārīkh al-Rusul wa-l-Mulūk by al-Ṭabarī (4/283-285), Tārīkh al-Madīna by Ibn Shabba (3/1034, 3/1037)

2 Al-Mujtabā min al-Sunan by al-Nasā'ī (4/24, 6/48). Al-Ḥasan al-Baṣrī relayed traditions from Abū Dharr via an intermediary, Ṣaʿṣaʿa b. Muʿāwiya. Elsewhere, al-Ḥasan al-Baṣrī never explicitly mentioned meeting Abū Dharr and directly acquiring traditions from him.

3 Kitāb Sulaym Ibn Qays (p. 288-291)

4 Tārīkh Khalīfa Ibn Khayyāṭ (p. 191), al-Tārīkh al-Awsaṭ by al-Bukhārī (1/77), Tārīkh Abī Zurʿa al-Dimashqī (p. 187-188), al-Tārīkh al-Kabīr - al-Sifr al-Thālith by Ibn Abī Khaythama (2/47), Tārīkh al-Rusul wa-l-Mulūk by al-Ṭabarī (5/57)

during the conflict. Various earlier Damascene authorities made note of Abū al-Dardā''s death during 'Uthmān's reign.

Sa'īd b. 'Abdul'Azīz al-Dimashqī (d. 167) said, "Abū al-Dardā' and Ka'b al-Aḥbār both died two years before the end 'Uthmān's reign."[1]

قال أبو زرعة: وَسَمِعْتُ أَبَا مُسْهِرٍ يَقُولُ: حَدَّثَنَا سَعِيدُ بْنُ عَبْدِ الْعَزِيزِ قَالَ: مَاتَ أَبُو الدَّرْدَاءِ، وَكَعْبُ الأحبار فِي خِلاَفَةِ عُثْمَانَ لِسَنَتَيْنِ بَقِيَتَا من خلافته.

Al-Awzā'ī (d. 157) said, "Abū al-Dardā' died 2 years prior to the murder of 'Uthmān."[2]

قال أبو زرعة: فَحَدَّثَنِي عَبْدُ الرَّحْمَنِ بْنُ إِبْرَاهِيمَ قال: حَدَّثَنَا سُوَيْدُ بْنُ عَبْدِ الْعَزِيزِ عَنِ الْأَوْزَاعِيِّ قَالَ: مَاتَ أَبُو الدَّرْدَاءِ قَبْلَ قَتْلِ عُثْمَانَ بِسَنَتَيْنِ.

The claim was formerly relayed by Abū al-Dardā''s scribe, Muslim b. Mishkam. Yazīd b. Abī Maryam narrated a prophetic tradition on the authority of Abū 'Ubaydillāh Muslim b. Mishkam, from Abū al-Dardā', and it concluded stating that Abū al-Dardā' died two years prior to 'Uthmān's murder.[3]

روى يَزِيدُ بْنُ أَبِي مَرْيَمَ، عن أَبِي عُبَيْدِ اللَّهِ مُسْلِم بْنِ مِشْكَمٍ، عَنْ أَبِي الدَّرْدَاءِ ، قَالَ: قَالَ رَسُولُ اللَّهِ, " أَنَا فَرَطُكُمْ عَلَى الْحَوْضِ، فَلأَلْفَيَنَّ مَا نُوزِعْتُ فِي أَحَدِكُمْ، فَأَقُولُ: هَذَا مِنِّي، فَيُقَالُ: إِنَّكَ لا تَدْرِي مَا أَحْدَثُوا بَعْدَكَ "، فَقُلْتُ: يَا رَسُولَ اللَّهِ، ادْعُ اللَّهَ أَنْ لا يَجْعَلَنِي مِنْهُمْ، قَالَ, " لَسْتَ مِنْهُمْ "، فَمَاتَ قَبْلَ عُثْمَانَ بِسَنَتَيْنِ.

Al-Wāqidī (d. 207), al-Haytham b. 'Adī (d. 207), al-Madā'inī (d. 224), Muḥammad b. 'Abdillāh b. Numayr (d. 234), al-Fallās (d. 249), Abū Mūsā Muḥammad b. al-Muthannā (d. 252) and others further stated that Abū al-Dardā' died in 32.[4]

Al-Haytham b. 'Adī also claimed to transmit a report that quotes Khālid b. Ma'dān stating that Abū al-Dardā' died in 32.[5] However, it is countered

---

1 Tārīkh Abī Zur'a al-Dimashqī (p. 220)

2 Tārīkh Abī Zur'a al-Dimashqī (p. 689)

3 Musnad al-Shāmiyyīn by al-Ṭabarānī (2/311), al-Istī'āb fī Ma'rifat al-Aṣḥāb (3/1229). Other related traditions similarly conclude stating that Abū al-Dardā' simply died prior to 'Uthmān's murder. See al-Tārīkh al-Awsaṭ of al-Bukhārī (1/60) and al-Āḥād wa-l-Mathānī by Ibn Abī 'Āṣim (1/129).

4 Al-Ṭabaqāt al-Kabīr by Ibn Sa'd (4/357), Kitāb al-Tārīkh by al-Fallās (p. 279), Tārīkh Mawlid al-'Ulamā' wa-Wafayātihim (1/117-119)

5 Tārīkh Mawlid al-'Ulamā' wa-Wafayātihim (1/121)

by a report from Ibn Saʿd where Khālid is quoted stating that Abū al-Dardāʾ died in the year 31.[1]

قال ابن زبر: قَالَ الْهَيْثَم وَسمعت الْأَحْوَص يذكر عَن خَالِد بن معدان أَن أَبَا الدَّرْدَاء توفّي سنة اثْنَتَيْنِ وَثَلَاثِينَ.

وقال ابن سعد: وأخبرني غير محمد بن عمر، عن ثور بن يزيد، عن خالد بن معدان قال: توفي أبو الدرداء بالشام سنة إحدى وثلاثين.

Khalīfa b. Khayyāṭ (d. 240) stated that Abū al-Dardāʾ either died in the year 31 or 32.[2] Ismāʾīl b. ʿAyyāsh (d. 181) reportedly stated that Abū al-Dardāʾ died one year prior to the ʿUthmān's death, whose murder was in 35.[3]

Despite the minor disagreements among the aforementioned sources regarding Abū al-Dardāʾ's exact death date, they all agreed that he had died prior to ʿUthmān's death. Hence, it is evident that *Kitāb Sulaym's* claim surrounding Abū al-Dardāʾ's attendance of the battle of Ṣiffīn in 37 is an ahistorical claim made by an incompetent forger who was unacquainted with Abū al-Dardāʾ's biographical data. This error in *Kitāb Sulaym* is an early error in the text, and it can be observed in a tradition relayed by the fourth century Twelver scholar, al-Nuʿmānī, via Sulaym b. Qays.[4] Perhaps the inclusion of Abū al-Dardāʾ in the aforementioned passage stemmed from the fact that Abū al-Dardāʾ was the most prominent companion of the Prophet ﷺ to reside in Damascus, hence a seemingly ideal character to serve as an envoy of Muʿāwiya in this fictitious account.

Exaggerations Surrounding the Battle of al-Jamal:

Eighth century Muslim sociologist and historian, Ibn Khaldūn (d. 808), was one of the earliest figures to address the issue of exaggeration in historical sources, specifically in the context of military history. In his *Muqaddima*, he noted that sources often sensationalized different events by exaggerating the sizes of armies, volume of wealth and taxes etc.[5]

Shīʿite historian, al-Masʿūdī (d. 345), specifically made note of the exaggerations and understatements he had observed in the casualty

1 Al-Ṭabaqāt al-Kabīr by Ibn Saʿd (4/358)
2 Ṭabaqāt Khalīfa b. Khayyāṭ (p. 165)
3 Muwaḍḍiḥ Awhām al-Jamʿ wa-l-Tafrīq Bayn al-Ruwāt (1/359)
4 Kitāb al-Ghayba by al-Nuʿmānī (p. 74)
5 Muqaddimat Ibn Khaldūn (p. 18)

counts/estimates for the Battle of al-Jamal. He similarly noted that these inaccurate figures were the byproduct of their sources' theological biases.[1]

قال المسعودي: وقد تنازع الناس في مقدار من قُتل من الفريقين: فمن مقلل ومكثر، فالمقلل يقول: قتل منهم سبعة آلاف، والمكثر يقول: عشرة آلاف، على حسب ميل الناس وأهوائهم الى كل فريق منهم، وكانت وقعة واحدة في يوم واحد.

Unsurprisingly, this phenomenon mentioned by al-Masʿūdī is observable in *Kitāb Sulaym*. In the 27th report in the book, Sulaym is quoted saying, "I witnessed the day of al-Jamal with ʿAlī, and we were 12,000 in number. The partisans of the camel were more than 120,000 in number."[2]

قال أبان: سمعت سليم بن قيس يقول: شهدت يوم الجمل عليا عليه السلام، وكنا اثني عشر ألفا وكان أصحاب الجمل زيادة على عشرين ومائة ألف.

This is a quite prepostrous exaggeration of the number of combatants in ʿĀʾisha's camp. Let us list the figures cited in a few primary/secondary sources and compare them to the figure mentioned in *Kitāb Sulaym*, as seen in Table 2.1 below.

Source:	ʿĀʾisha's Camp	ʿAlī's Camp
Kitāb Sulaym	**120,000**	12,000
Sayf b. ʿUmar[3]	30,000	20,000
Al-Wāqidī[4]	15,000	20,000
Al-Haytham b. ʿAdī[5]	8,000	12,000
Hishām Ibn al-Kalbī[6]	-	30,000
Hishām Ibn al-Kalbī ⟶ Abū Mikhnaf[7]	3,000+	-

1 Murūj al-Dhahab wa-Maʿādin al-Jawhar (2/275)
2 Kitāb Sulaym Ibn Qays (p. 325)
3 Tārīkh al-Rusul wa-l-Mulūk by al-Ṭabarī (4/505)
4 Mirʾāt al-Zamān fī Tawārīkh al-Aʿyān (6/175)
5 Mirʾāt al-Zamān fī Tawārīkh al-Aʿyān (6/175)
6 Mirʾāt al-Zamān fī Tawārīkh al-Aʿyān (6/175)
7 Jumalun min Ansāb al-Ashrāf (2/224-229)

Salama b. Kuhayl[1]	-	10,000+
Fiṭr b. Khalīfa → Mundhir al-Thawrī → Ibn al-Ḥanafiyya[2]	-	11,900

Table 2.1 A collation of the different estimates pertaining to the number of combatants at the battle of al-Jamal

Though the exact number of combatants at the Battle of al-Jamal may not be precisely discernible, it is evident that the figure cited in *Kitāb Sulaym* is a severely inflated figure that bypasses any reasonable range of estimates. Perhaps this exaggeration was meant to further exaggerate and signify ʿAlī's victory at the Battle of al-Jamal, where his forces would have defeated an enemy force that outnumbered them ten to one.[3]

Al-Faḍl b. al-ʿAbbās' Gathering with Muʿāwiya in 41

One noteworthy tradition in *Kitāb Sulaym* presents a detailed dialogue between Muʿāwiya b. Abī Sufyān and ʿAbdullāh b. Jaʿfar b. Abī Ṭālib that was also witnessed by ʿAbdullāh b. ʿAbbās, al-Faḍl b. al-ʿAbbās, al-Ḥasan and al-Ḥusayn. This gathering is said to have taken place in the year when al-Ḥasan conceded his power to Muʿāwiya, which was the year 41.[4]

أبان عن سليم، قال: حدثني عبد الله بن جعفر بن أبي طالب قال: كنت عند معاوية ومعنا الحسن والحسين وعنده عبد الله بن العباس والفضل بن العباس.... فالتفت إلي معاوية فقال: يا عبد الله بن جعفر، وكان هذا بالمدينة أول سنة جمعت الأمة على معاوية.

The problem with this claim is that virtually all historians and primary sources, despite their disagreement on al-Faḍl's exact death date, agreed that he died many years before 41 AH. Al-Faḍl simply could not have been

1 Tārīkh Khalīfa b. Khayyāṭ (p. 184)
2 Jumalun min Ansāb al-Ashrāf (2/261-262)
3 The researcher and analyst, Tallha Abdulrazaq, graciously provided me with several historical examples where such exaggerations in army counts were made, often to lionize one of the belligerents for attaining unexpected and rather impossible victories. As an example, the Spartan victory at Thermopylae is often characterized by various exaggerations, such as the claim that the defeated Persian army consisted of 1,000,000 men, which is recognized today as an impossible and severely exaggerated claim.
4 Kitāb Sulaym Ibn Qays (p. 361-363)

present at this purported gathering (unless it is to be assumed that his corpse was exhumed from his grave and miraculously brought back to life to witness this rather mundane event).

Muḥammad b. al-Muthannā (d. 252) stated that al-Faḍl died in the year 13.[1] Muḥammad b. al-Sā'ib al-Kalbī (d. 146), ʿAlī b. Abī Sayf al-Madā'inī (d. 224), Khalīfa b. Khayyāṭ (d. 240), Abū Aḥmed al-Ḥākim (d. 378), and Ibn al-Sakan (d. 353) stated that al-Faḍl was martyred at the battle of Ajnādayn, which was in the year 13.[2] Ibn Isḥāq (d. 151) stated that al-Faḍl was killed when he was with Khālid b. al-Walīd during Abū Bakr's reign, which presumably is a reference to the battle of Ajnādayn.[3] Al-Bukhārī (d. 256) stated that al-Faḍl died during Abū Bakr's reign, which was between the years 11 and 13.[4]

Yaḥyā b. Maʿīn (d. 233), Ibn Ḥibbān (d. 354) and Ibn Manda (d. 470) stated that al-Faḍl was killed at the battle of al-Yarmūk, which was in the year 15.[5]

Ibn Saʿd (d. 230) and then al-Balādhurī (d. ~279) both cited unnamed authorities stating that al-Faḍl died during the plague of ʿAmawās in the year 18.[6] This position was claimed by al-Wāqidī (d. 207), Muṣʿab b. ʿAbdillāh al-Zubayrī (d. 236), al-Zubayr b. Bakkār (d. 256), Aḥmed b. ʿAbdillāh al-Barqī (d. 270), Abū Ḥātim al-Rāzī (d. 277), and Yaʿqūb b. Sufyān (d. 277).[7] Abū ʿUbayd al-Qāsim b. Sallām (d. 224) is also quoted adopting this position.[8] Among later scholarship, Ibn ʿAsākir (d. 571), al-Dhahabī (d. 748), Ibn Kathīr (d. 774) and Ibn Ḥajar (d. 852) adopted this position as well.[9]

---

1 Tārīkh Mawlid al-ʿUlamā' wa-Wafayātihim (1/92)

2 Tārīkh Khalīfa b. Khayyāṭ (p. 120), Ṭabaqāt Khalīfa b. Khayyāṭ (p. 547), al-Asāmī wa-l-Kunā by Abū Aḥmed al-Ḥākim (5/50), al-Iṣāba fī Tamyīz al-Ṣaḥāba (5/288)

3 Tārīkh Dimashq by Ibn ʿAsākir (48/333)

4 Al-Tārīkh al-Kabīr by al-Bukhārī (7/114)

5 Tārīkh Ibn Maʿīn – Riwāyat al-Dūrī (3/27), al-Thiqāt by Ibn Ḥibbān (3/329), al-Mustakhraj min Kutub al-Nās li-l-Tadhkira wa-l-Mustaṭraf min Aḥwāl al-Rijāl li-l-Maʿrifa by Ibn Manda (2/407, 2/429)

6 Al-Ṭabaqāt al-Kabīr by Ibn Saʿd (4/51), Jumalun min Ansāb al-Ashrāf (4/26)

7 Nasab Quraysh by Muṣʿab b. ʿAbdillāh al-Zubayrī (p. 25), Al-Jarḥ wa-l-Taḍīl by Ibn Abī Ḥātim (7/63), Tārīkh Dimashq by Ibn ʿAsākir (48/327, 48/329, 48/331, 48/335)

8 Tārīkh Dimashq by Ibn ʿAsākir (48/334)

9 Tārīkh Dimashq by Ibn ʿAsākir (48/320), Tārīkh al-Islām by al-Dhahabī (2/58), al-Bidāya wa-l-Nihāya by Ibn Kathīr (9/611), al-Iṣāba fī Tamyīz al-Ṣaḥāba (5/288)

Al-Haytham b. ʿAdī (d. 207) claimed that al-Faḍl died in the year 28.[1] The aforereferenced Yaʿqūb b. Sufyān (d. 277) is elsewhere quoted stating that al-Faḍl died in Medīna during ʿUthmān's reign, and Ibn ʿAsākir stated that that claim was an error.[2]

Despite the past sources' disagreement regarding al-Faḍl's exact death date, they all agreed that he died multiple years before 41 AH. The latest figure cited was al-Haytham b. ʿAdī's claim, which places al-Faḍl's death around 13 years before the purported gathering in *Kitāb Sulaym* took place. Nonetheless, the two most prominent positions regarding al-Faḍl's death dates was that he either died in the year 13 or 18. This tradition in *Kitāb Sulaym* is but another example of its forger's incompetence and failed attempt at verisimilitude when composing his fictitious accounts.

Al-Muḥassin: Born, Miscarried or Non-Existent?

In some recensions of *Kitāb Sulaym*, it is claimed that Fāṭima suffered a miscarriage as a result of the purported blows dealt to her by the assailants that had stormed her house.[3] In many past and present Shīʿite sources and circles, the miscarried fetus is identified al-Muḥassin, as shall be further expounded in the next chapter under the analysis of Passage 8.

In this regard, it is crucial to perform a thorough survey about this alleged son of ʿAlī and Fāṭima, as that certainly would be insightful and informative when attempting to understand the authorship of *Kitāb Sulaym*, the claims made within it, and the potential sources deployed throughout its composition.

As far as I know, the earliest source to make note of a son of Fāṭima named al-Muḥassin is an obscure *tābiʿī*, named Hāniʾ b. Hāniʾ, who relayed a prophetic tradition in this regad. Abū Isḥāq al-Sabīʿī (d. 126) narrated on the authority of Hāniʾ b. Hāniʾ, from ʿAlī b. Abī Ṭālib that he said:

> When al-Ḥasan was born, I named him Ḥarb. The Messenger of Allah then came and said, "Show me my son. What have you named him?" I said, "Ḥarb." He said, "Rather, he is Ḥasan."

1 Maʿrifat al-Ṣaḥāba li-Abī Nuʿym (4/2278), Tārīkh Dimashq by Ibn ʿAsākir (48/335)
2 Tārīkh Dimashq by Ibn ʿAsākir (48/335)
3 Kitāb Sulaym Ibn Qays (p. 149), Biḥār al-Anwār of al-Majlisī (28/283)

> When al-Ḥusayn was born, I named him Ḥarb. The Messenger of Allah then came and said, "Show me my son. What have you named him?" I said, "Ḥarb." He said, "Rather, he is Ḥusayn."
>
> When the third one was born, I named him Ḥarb. The Messenger of Allah then came and said, "Show me my son. What have you named him?" I said, "Ḥarb." He said, "Rather, he is Muḥassin."
>
> He (the Prophet) then said, "I named them after the names of Aaron's son's: Shabbar, Shubayr and Mushabbir."[1]

عَنْ أَبِي إِسْحَاقَ، عَنْ هَانِئِ بْنِ هَانِئٍ، عَنْ عَلِيٍّ رَضِيَ اللَّهُ عَنْهُ، قَالَ: لَمَّا وُلِدَ الْحَسَنُ سميته حربا، فجاء رَسُولُ اللَّهِ فَقَالَ " أَرُونِي ابْنِي، مَا سَمَّيْتُمُوهُ؟ "، قَالَ: قُلْتُ: حَرْبًا، قَالَ, " بَلْ هُوَ حَسَنٌ "، فَلَمَّا وُلِدَ الْحُسَيْنُ سَمَّيْتُهُ حَرْبًا، فَجَاءَ رَسُولُ اللَّهِ فَقَالَ, " أَرُونِي ابْنِي، مَا سَمَّيْتُمُوهُ؟ "، قَالَ: قُلْتُ: حَرْبًا، قَالَ, " بَلْ هُوَ حُسَيْنٌ "، فَلَمَّا وُلِدَ الثَّالِثُ سَمَّيْتُهُ حَرْبًا، فَجَاءَ النَّبِيُّ فَقَالَ, " أَرُونِي ابْنِي، مَا سَمَّيْتُمُوهُ؟ "، قُلْتُ: حَرْبًا، قَالَ, " بَلْ هُوَ مُحَسِّنٌ "، ثُمَّ قَالَ, " سَمَّيْتُهُمْ بِأَسْمَاءِ وَلَدِ هَارُونَ: شَبَّرُ، وَشَبِيرُ، وَمُشَبِّرٌ ".

Those who authenticated this tradition, such as Ibn Ḥibbān (d. 354),[2] al-Ḥākim (d. 405),[3] Ibn Ḥajar (d. 852)[4] and others, consequently believed that Fāṭima had given birth to a child named al-Muḥassin during the Prophet's life, contrary to the claims that he was miscarried after the Prophet's death.

A ninth century Ismāʿīlī Shīʿite *dāʿī* of the Ṭayyibī sect, Idrīs ʿImād al-Dīn al-Qurashī (d. 872), recognized that this tradition conflicted with the narrative adopted in later Shīʿite circles in this regard. He maintainted, however, that the more popular position that is a matter of consensus is that Fāṭima miscarried Muḥassin as a result of ʿUmar's assault against her.[5] It goes without saying that the consensus referenced in his statement is referring to some consensus within the Ismāʿīlī sect or among later Shīʿite scholarship in general.

There are some considerably weaker later traditions that mention al-Muḥassin, but they cannot be deemed independent of Hāniʾ's tradition due to the severe weakness of their isnāds. In fact, it appears that Hāniʾ's tradition was a primary source of information on ʿAlī's purported son, Muḥassin, who was otherwise a generally obscure and unknown figure.

1 Musnad Aḥmed (2/264), al-Adab al-Mufrad by al-Bukhārī (p. 378)
2 Ṣaḥīḥ Ibn Ḥibbān (4/209), Kitāb al-Thiqāt by Ibn Ḥibbān (2/304)
3 Al-Mustadrak ʿala al-Ṣaḥīḥayn by al-Ḥākim al-Naysābūrī (3/180)
4 Al-Iṣāba fī Tamyīz al-Ṣaḥāba by Ibn Ḥajar (6/192)
5 Al-Muḥassin al-Sibṭ Mawlūd am Siqṭ by al-Kharsān (p. 35-46)

Ibn Qudāma (d. 620), in his genealogical book, *al-Tabyīn fī Ansāb al-Qurashiyyīn*, said regarding al-Muḥassin b. ʿAlī b. Abī Ṭālib, "We do not know of him except from the ḥadīth relayed by Hāniʾ b. Hāniʾ from ʿAlī b. Abī Ṭālib [...]. It appears that he died as a child."[1]

قال ابن قدامة في «التبيين في أنساب القرشيين»: محسن بن علي بن أبي طالب، لا نعرفه إلا في الحديث الذي يرويه هانئ بن هانئ، عن علي بن أبي طالب رضي الله عنه [....]. والظاهر أنه مات طفلا.

Given that Hāniʾ's tradition appears to be pivotal to the discussion surrounding al-Muḥassin's identity, I believe it is worthy of analysis and scrutiny. Early ḥadīthist authorities were of varying positions on Hāniʾ's status, as often is the case with generally obscure *tābiʿīn* who were not prolific transmitters of ḥadīth.

As stated earlier, some ḥadīthists may had implicitly endorsed his reliability by authenticating his tradition. Others, such as al-Nasāʾī (d. 303)[2] and al-ʿIjlī (d. 261),[3] endorsed his reliability as well. Some, however, such as al-Shāfiʿī (d. 204)[4] and Ibn al-Madīnī (d. 234),[5] deemed him unknown (*majhūl*), effectively weakening whatever is exclusively relayed through him. Al-Ṭabarī (d. 310), despite his acceptance of another tradition relayed by Hāniʾ, acknowledged that Hāniʾ is unknown (*majhūl*) to the ḥadīthists.[6] On the other hand, some, such as Ibn Saʿd (d. 230), deemed Hāniʾ an unreliable Shīʿite who was disapproved in his transmission (*munkar al-ḥadīth*).[7]

Barring Hāniʾ's evident obscurity, there are other reasons to question his tradition's authenticity. As an example, other accounts of this event relayed by some *tābiʿīn*, such as Sālim b. Abī al-Jaʿad (d. 97)[8] and ʿAbdullāh b. Muḥammad b. ʿAqīl b. Abī Ṭālib (d. 141),[9] make no mention of a third son named Muḥassin. What is also noteworthy is that some *tābiʿīn*, such as Muḥammad b. ʿAlī b. al-Ḥusayn b. ʿAlī b. Abī Ṭālib (d. 118)[10] and ʿIkrima (d.

1 Al-Tabyīn fī Ansāb al-Qurashiyyīn by Ibn Qudāma (p. 111), Mirʾāt al-Zamān Fī Tawārīkh al-Aʿyān by Sibṭ Ibn al-Jawzī (6/475)
2 Tahdhīb al-Kamāl fī Asmāʾ al-Rijāl by al-Mizzī (30/145)
3 Tārīkh al-Thiqāt by al-ʿIjlī (p. 455)
4 Al-Sunan al-Kubrā of al-Bayhaqī (7/370)
5 Tahdhīb al-Tahdhīb by Ibn Ḥajar (4/262)
6 Tahdhīb al-Āthār by al-Ṭabarī (4/157)
7 Al-Ṭabaqāt al-Kabīr by Ibn Saʿd (8/342)
8 Muṣannaf Ibn Abī Shayba (17/166)
9 Musnad Aḥmed (2/464-465), Musnad al-Bazzār (2/251)
10 Muṣannaf ʿAbdirrazzāq (4/335)

~104),[1] relayed that the Prophet derived al-Ḥusayn's name from al-Ḥasan's name, which may conflict with the tradition that their names were derived from the names of Aaron's children. For such reasons and other possible arguments, I believe that Hāniʾ b. Hāniʾ's tradition, especially the portion exclusively relayed by him, cannot be taken at face value in the absence of a sufficient corroboration.

Some have claimed that another tradition may be cited as evidence of al-Muḥassin's existence. The tradition was relayed via Ismāʿīl b. Muslim, on the authority of ʿUmāra b. al-Qaʿqāʿ, from Abū Zurʿa, from Abū Hurayra that he said where it is stated that a son of Fāṭima fell ill and then later died before the Prophet.[2]

قال البزار في مسنده: حدثنا محمد بن بشار بندار قال: أخبرنا أبو بحر عبد الرحمن بن عثمان قال: حدثنا إسماعيل بن مسلم , عن عمارة بن القعقاع , عن أبي زرعة , عن أبي هريرة رضي الله عنه , قال ثقل ابن لفاطمة رضي الله عنها فبعثت إلى رسول الله صلى الله عليه وسلم تدعوه فقال رسول الله صلى الله عليه وسلم: ارجع فإن له ما أخذ وله ما أبقى وكل لأجل بمقدار فلما احتضر بعثت إليه وقال لنا قوموا فلما جلس جعل يقرأ {فلولا إذا بلغت الحلقوم وأنتم حينئذ تنظرون} حتى قبض فدمعت عينا رسول الله صلى الله عليه وسلم قال سعد يا رسول الله تبكي وتنهى عن البكاء قال إنما هي رحمة وإنما يرحم الله من عباه الرحماء.

قال البزار: وهذا الحديث لا نعلم رواه عن عمارة عن أبي زرعة إلا إسماعيل بن مسلم، وإسماعيل قد روى عنه الأعمش والثوري وجماعة على أنه ليس بالحافظ.

What is noteworthy in this regard is that other accounts mention this incident without identifying the daughter or grandchild of the Prophet involved. Barring the issues in the account's isnād, which were alluded to by al-Bazzar,[3] Ibn Ḥajar cited al-Bazzār's tradition, arguing that it would entail that the deceased child was al-Muḥassin. Ibn Ḥajar, however, concluded that the correct position is that the daughter of the Prophet mentioned in the ḥadīth was Zaynab, not Fāṭima, which would necessarily entail that the child mentioned therein was not al-Muḥassin.[4]

A variety of sources that came after Hāniʾ b. Hāniʾ affirmed that Fāṭima gave birth to a child named al-Muḥassin who had died young. This was

---

1 Muṣannaf ʿAbdirrazzāq (4/335)
2 Musnad al-Bazzār (17/179)
3 Ismāʿīl b. Muslim was a weak transmitter. See his entry in Tahdhīb al-Kamāl of al-Mizzī (3/198-205)
4 Fatḥ al-Bārī Sharḥ Sharḥ Ṣaḥīḥ al-Bukhārī by Ibn Ḥajar (3/156)

stated by Ibn Isḥāq (d. 151),[1] al-Zubayr b. Bakkār (d. 256),[2] Ibn Qutayba (d. 276),[3] al-Balādhurī (d. 279),[4] al-Yaʿqūbī (d. 284),[5] al-Muṭahhar b. Ṭāhir al-Maqdisī (d. ~355),[6] Ibn Ḥazm (d. 456),[7] Abū al-Qāsim ibn Manda (d. 470),[8] al-Qurṭubī (d. 600),[9] Abū al-Fidāʾ (d. 732),[10] Ibn Sayyid al-Nās (d. 734) and others. The Zaydī Imām, Yaḥyā b. al-Ḥusayn al-Hārūnī (d. 424), similarly claimed that al-Muḥassin died young.[11]

It appears that some sources, such as Ibn al-Athīr (d. 630) and others, were uncertain about the existence of al-Muḥassin.[12] The renowned historian, al-Ṭabarī (d. 310), when listing out Fāṭima's children, said, "It is said that she had another son from ʿAlī named al-Muḥassin who died young."[13]

قال الطبري في تاريخه: فأول زوجة تزوجها فاطمه بنت رسول الله ص، ولم يتزوج عَلَيْهَا حَتَّى توفيت عنده، وَكَانَ لها مِنْهُ من الولد: الْحَسَن والحسين، ويذكر أنه كَانَ لها مِنْهُ ابن آخر يسمى محسنا توفي صغيرا، وزينب الكبرى، وأم كلثوم الكبرى.

The Sunnī historian, Ibn Kathīr (d. 774), said, "As for Fāṭima, her cousin, ʿAlī b. Abī Ṭālib, married her in Ṣafar in year 2. She birthed for him al-Ḥasan and al-Ḥusayn. It is said that she birthed Muḥassin as well. She also birthed for him Umm Kulthūm and Zaynab."[14]

قال ابن كثير في «البداية والنهاية»: وأما فاطمة فتزوجها ابن عمها علي بن أبي طالب في صفر سنة اثنتين، فولدت له الحسن والحسين، ويقال ومحسن، وولدت له أم كلثوم وزينب.

---

1 Al-Siyar wa-l-Maghāzī by Ibn Isḥāq (p. 247)
2 Tadhkirat al-Khawāṣṣ by Sibṭ Ibn al-Jawzī (p. 54)
3 Al-Maʿārif by Ibn Qutayba (p. 211)
4 Jumalun min Ansāb al-Ashrāf by al-Balādhurī (2/189)
5 Tārīkh al-Yaʿqūbī (p. 203)
6 Al-Badʾ wa-l-Tārīkh by al-Maqdisī (5/75)
7 Jamharat Ansāb al-ʿArab by Ibn Ḥazm (p. 16, 38)
8 Al-Mustakhraj min Kutub al-Nās by Ibn Manda (1/38)
9 Al-Taʿrīf bi-l-Ansāb wa-l-Tanwīh bi-Dhawī al-Aḥsāb by al-Qurṭubī (p. 42)
10 Al-Mukhtaṣar fī Akhbār al-Bashar by Abū al-Fidāʾ al-Ḥamawī (1/181)
11 Al-Ifāda fī Tārīkh al-Aʾimma al-Sāda by al-Hārūnī (p. 23)
12 Al-Kāmil fī al-Tārīkh by Ibn al-Athīr (2/747)
13 Tārīkh al-Rusul wa-l-Mulūk by al-Ṭabarī (5/153)
14 Al-Bidāya wa-l-Nihāya by Ibn Kathīr (11/25)

Some sources, such as the Shīʿite al-Masʿūdī (d. 346), vaguely listed al-Muḥassin as a child of ʿAlī b. Abī Ṭālib without saying anything about his aftermath.[1]

A plethora of sources, when listing out ʿAlī and Fāṭima's children, did not mention a child named al-Muḥassin. Ibn Saʿd (d. 230), after listing out ʿAlī's children and making no mention of al-Muḥassin, said, "It is only these who have been verified to us as ʿAlī's children."[2]

قال ابن سعد في «الطبقات الكبير»: لم يصح لنا من ولد علي رضي الله عنه غير هؤلاء.

This statement of Ibn Saʿd is insightful, as Ibn Saʿd was aware of Hāniʾ b. Hāniʾ's aforementioned tradition since he had relayed it in his *Ṭabaqāt.* This would mean that he deemed the contents of Hāniʾ's tradition ahistorical and insufficient to conclude the existence of a child named al-Muḥassin. Others, such as Ibn Shihāb (d. 124)[3] and Muṣʿab b. ʿAbdillāh al-Zubayrī (d. 236),[4] when listing out ʿAlī and Fāṭima's children, similarly did not mention al-Muḥassin.

Some later Sunnī sources, such as al-Mizzī (d. 742),[5] al-Suyūṭī (d. 911)[6] and others, mentioned that al-Muḥassin was miscarried during his mother's pregnancy. A few later sources, such as Muḥib al-Dīn al-Ṭabarī (d. 694), al-Ṣāliḥī (d. 942),[7] and al-ʿIṣāmī (d. 1111), quoted al-Layth b. Saʿd (d. 175) listing al-Muḥassin among Fāṭima's children. Al-Ṣāliḥī further added that al-Muḥassin died from a miscarriage, and this appears to be his own comment on al-Layth's cited statement.

Regarding al-Layth b. Saʿd's aforementioned quote, it is noteworthy to point out that an earlier sound reference to al-Layth in al-Dūlābī's (d. 310) *al-Dhurriyya al-Ṭāhira*, when citing al-Layth in this regard, makes no mention of al-Muḥassin as a son of Fāṭima.

---

1 Murūj al-Dhahab wa-Maʿādin al-Jawhar by al-Masʿūdī (3/58)
2 Al-Ṭabaqāt al-Kabīr by Ibn Saʿd (3/18)
3 Al-Sunan al-Kubrā of al-Bayhaqī (7/111-113)
4 Nasab Quraysh by Muṣʿab b. ʿAbdillāh al-Zubayrī (p. 40-44)
5 Tahdhīb al-Kamāl fī Asmāʾ al-Rijāl by al-Mizzī (20/479)
6 Al-Ṣuyūṭī mentioned this in his concise work, al-ʿUjāja al-Zarnabiyya fī al-Sulāla al-Zaynabiyya.
7 Subul al-Hudā wa-l-Rashād fī Sīrat Khayr al-ʿIbād by al-Ṣāliḥī (11/51)

قال الدولابي في «الذرية الطاهرة»: حدثني أحمد بن عبد الله بن عبد الرحيم، نا عبد الله بن صالح، حدثني الليث بن سعد، قال: تزوج علي بن ابي طالب فاطمة بنت رسول الله صلى الله عليه وآله وسلم، فولدت له: حسنا وحسينا وزينب وأمّ كلثوم ورقية، فماتت رقية ولم تبلغ.

Ibn al-Jawzī, when outlining the names of Fāṭima's children, mentioned that Ibn Isḥāq (d. 150) added al-Muḥassin amongst Fāṭima's children, while al-Layth b. Saʿd added Ruqayya.[1]All in all, it seems possible, if not likely, that the later references to al-Layth b. Saʿd that cite him listing al-Muḥassin among Fāṭima's children may simply embody interpolations that are not reflective of al-Layth's original statement.

In Shīʿite literature, there are references to a miscarried child named al-Muḥassin. A tradition relayed by al-Kulaynī (d. 329) and Ibn Bābawayh (d. 381) via al-Qāsim b. Yaḥyā, on the authority of his grandfather al-Ḥasan b. Rāshid, on the authority of Abū Baṣīr, from Jaʿfar al-Ṣādiq, from his father, from his grandfather that ʿAlī said:

> [...] Name your children before they are born. If you do not know whether they are male of female, then give them names that could be for a male or a female. If you meet your miscarried children on the Day of Resurrection and you had not named them prior to that, the miscarried child will say to his father, "Should you have not given me a name since the Messenger of Allah named Muḥassin before he was born?!"[2]

عن القاسم بن يحيى، عن جده الحسن ابن راشد، عن أبي بصير، عن أبي عبد الله عليه السلام قال: حدثني أبي عن جدي قال: قال أمير المؤمنين عليه السلام: سمو أولادكم قبل أن يولدوا فأن لم تدروا أذكر أم أنثى فسموهم بالأسماء التي تكون للذكر والأنثى فإن أسقاطكم إذا لقوكم يوم القيامة ولم تسموهم يقول السقط لأبيه: ألا سميتني وقد سمى رسول الله صلى الله عليه وآله محسنا قبل أن يولد.

اللفظ لفظ الكليني، وهو مقتطع من خطبة طويلة رواها ابن بابويه بتمامها.

This tradition is an excerpt from a lengthy sermon ascribed to ʿAlī b. Abī Ṭālib, and it is inauthentic. Al-Qāsim b. Yaḥyā and his grandfather, al-Ḥasan b. Rāshid, were weakened by the Twelver critic, Ibn al-Ghaḍāʾirī (d. fifth century).[3] The inauthenticity of this tradition transcends the narrow debate

1 Talqīḥ Fuhūm Ahl Al-Athar by Ibn al-Jawzī (p. 30)
2 Al-Kāfī by al-Kulaynī (6/14), Al-Khiṣāl by Ibn Bābawayh (p. 634)
3 Al-Rijāl by Ibn al-Ghaḍāʾirī (p. 49, 86)

on the status of al-Qāsim b. Yaḥya and his grandfather according to Twelver biographical sources, and Abū Baṣīr is also to be suspected as a possibly compromised and unreliable transmitter in this isnād. Either way, his lengthy tradition is an embellished and extremely detailed fabrication that is dubiously ascribed to ʿAlī b. Abī Ṭālib. Nonetheless, this tradition affirms the existence of a miscarried child named al-Muḥassin, though it makes no mention of an assault on Fāṭima. Contrary to Hāniʾ b. Hāniʾʾs earlier tradition, this Shīʿite report claims that the Prophet named al-Muḥassin prior to his birth and that al-Muḥassin then died before he was born, which could further be evidence of its dubiousness.

It appears that the Twelver scholar, al-Mufīd (d. 413), expressed uncertainty towards the existence and consequent miscarriage of al-Muḥassin. In *al-Irshād*, he said, "The children of the Commander of the Faithful are 27 in number, including males and females." After listing out their names, al-Mufīd said, "Among the Shīʿa are some who say that Fāṭima miscarried a boy after the Prophet's death who he had named al-Muḥassin as he was in the womb. According to the opinion of this group of the Shīʿa, the children of the Commander of the Faithful are 28 in number..."[1]

قال المفيد في «الإرشاد»: فأولاد أمير المؤمنين سبعة وعشرون ولدا ذكرا وأنثى. [...] وفي الشيعة من يذكر أن فاطمة (صلوات الله عليها) أسقطت بعد النبي ذكرا كان سماه رسول الله صلى الله عليه وسلم وهو حمل محسنا. فعلى قول هذه الطائفة: أولاد أمير المؤمنين ثمانية وعشرون (عليه السلام) ولدا، والله أعلم وأحكم.

A fifth century Twelver geneologist, ʿAlī b. Abī al-Ghanāʾim al-ʿUmarī al-ʿAlawī, when listing out ʿAlī b. Abī Ṭālib's children, said something similar to what was stated by al-Mufīd. He said:

> They did not count Muḥassin, since he was born dead. The Shīʿa have relayed the story of al-Muḥassin and the kick. I found some book of geneology mentioning al-Muḥassin, but it did not mention the kick from a source that I rely upon.[2]

قال علي بن أبي الغنائم العلوي في «المجدي في أنساب الطالبيين»: ولم يحتسبوا بمحسن لأنه ولد ميتا، وقد روت الشيعة خبر المحسن والرفسة. ووجدت في بعض كتب أهل النسب يحتوي على ذكر المحسن، ولم يذكر الرفسة من جهة أعول عليها.

---

1 Al-Irshād by al-Mufīd (p. 233)

2 Al-Majdī fī Ansāb al-Ṭālibiyyīn by al-ʿAlawī (p. 193)

The later Twelver scholar, Ibn Shahr ʾĀshūb (d. 588), clearly is more confident in this narrative, for he listed al-Muḥassin as a miscarried son of Fāṭima. He then proceeded to reference an earlier source, *al-Maʿārif* of Ibn Qutayba (d. 276), claiming that al-Muḥassin's miscarriage resulted from Qunfudh's assault on Fāṭima.[1]

قال ابن شهر آشوب في «مناقب آل أبي طالب»: وأولادها: الحسن، والحسين، والمحسن سقط، وفي معارف القتيبي: ان محسنا فسد من زخم قنفذ العدوي، وزينب، وأم كلثوم.

It goes without saying that no such quote exists in Ibn Qutayba's *al-Maʿārif.* To the contrary, Ibn Qutayba merely stated that al-Muḥassin had died as when he was young, as mentioned earlier. Ibn Shahr ʾĀshūb's reference to Ibn Qutayba is a misquotation, and perhaps Ibn Shahr ʾĀshūb was referencing the pseudepigraphical source attributed to Ibn Qutayba, *al-Imāma wa-l-Siyāsa,* which mentions Qunfudh. More will come on that later in the assessment of passage 8 in chapter 3.

All in all, this is the majority of the substantive evidence regarding al-Muḥassin, and it appears to be quite subpar. The numerous non-Shīʿite sources cited in this chapter that affirmed al-Muḥassin's status as a son of Fāṭima often were not independent of each other. Rather, many, if not most, simply are quoting the earlier sources that were cited. Furthermore, it seems possible, if not liely, that the claims made in these sources revolve entirely on Hāniʾ b. Hāniʾ's obscure ḥadīth, which would further undermine this narrative. The Shīʿite claims that al-Muḥassin was named by the Prophet as he was in his mother's womb would hence be a later development in this narrative, and the claim that he was consequently miscarried is yet another development or inference. Furthermore, the claim that his miscarriage was caused by a physical assault on his pregnant mother is but another development in the series of accretions that were inserted into this narrative. Chapter 3 will contain a detailed synopsis of the Twelver narrative pertaining to the purported assault on Fāṭima.

The Death Date of Fāṭima

In *Kitāb Sulaym Ibn Qays,* Sulaym is quoted saying, "[...] Fāṭima hence remained alive for forty days following her father's death."[2]

1 Manāqib Āl Abī Ṭālib by Ibn Shahr ʾĀshūb (3/407)
2 Kitāb Sulaym Ibn Qays (p. 392)

أبان بن أبي عياش، عن سليم بن قيس، قال: كنت عند عبد الله بن عباس في بيته وعنا جماعة من شيعة علي، فحدثنا فكان فيما حدثنا أن قال: [...] فبقيت فاطمة عليها السلام بعد وفاة أبيها رسول الله صلى الله عليه وآله أربعين ليلة.

Though it is not uncommon for classical sources to disagree on the death dates of historical figures, it is noteworthy that Kitāb Sulaym's dating of Fāṭima's death is virtually opposed to all Sunnī, Twelver and Zaydī authorities in this regard. The only source, according to my knowledge, who adopted the position found in *Kitāb Sulaym* was the Kūfan historian, al-Haytham b. ʿAdī (d. 207),[1] which may, in fact, be quite telling about the book's author and the sources he utilized whilst composing the book.

The *tābiʿī*, ʿAbdullāh b. Burayda (d. 115), stated that Fāṭima lived seventy days after her father's death.[2] The Twelver scholars, al-Ṣaffār (d. 290) and al-Kulaynī (d. 329) relayed a tradition via Ibn Maḥbūb, on the authority of ʿAlī b. Riʾāb, from Abū ʿUbayda Ziyād b. ʿĪsā that Jaʿfar al-Ṣādiq (d. 148) stated that Fāṭima lived for 75 days after the Prophet's ﷺ death.[3] Al-Kulaynī similarly relayed another tradition from Jaʿfar al-Ṣādiq which states that Fāṭima died 75 days after the Prophet's ﷺ death.[4] These two traditions are authentic according to Twelver standards, and al-Kulaynī elsewhere adopted this position regarding Faṭima's death as well.[5]

روى الكليني في «الكافي» والصفار في «بصائر الدرجات» من طريق ابن محبوب، عن ابن رئاب، عن أبي عبيدة قال: سأل أبا عبد الله عليه السلام بعض أصحابنا عن الجفر فقال: هو جلد ثور مملوء علما، قال: له فالجامعة؟ قال: تلك صحيفة طولها سبعون ذراعا في عرض الأديم مثل فخذ الفالج، فيها كل ما يحتاج الناس إليه، وليس من قضية إلا وهي فيها، حتى أرش الخدش. قال: فمصحف فاطمة عليها السلام؟ قال، فسكت طويلا ثم

1 Mirʾāt al-Zamān fī Tawārīkh al-Aʿyān by Sibṭ Ibn al-Jawzī (5/60)

2 Tārīkh Khalīfa b. Khayyāṭ (p. 96), Tārīkh al-Madīna by Ibn Shabba (1/108), al-Maṣābīḥ by Abū al-ʿAbbās al-Ḥasanī (p. 267)

3 Baṣāʾir al-Darajāt by al-Ṣaffār (p. 188), al-Kāfī by al-Kulaynī (1/142)

4 Al-Kāfī by al-Kulaynī (3/128). A noteworthy point about this tradition brought to my attention by Farīd Al-Baḥrainī is that it quotes Jaʿfar al-Ṣādiq stating that Fāṭima used to visit the martyrs' graves [at Uḥud] twice a week following her Father's death, a bizarre and unexpected feat for a woman who was purportedly beaten until she suffered a miscarriage, fractured ribs and a severely bruised body as a result of a vicious assault. In this context, it should be noted that Mt. Uḥud is about 10 km away from the Prophet's ﷺ mosque in Medīna.

5 Al-Kāfī by al-Kulaynī (1/291)

قال: إنكم لتبحثون عما تريدون وعما لا تريدون إن فاطمة مكثت بعد رسول الله صلى الله عليه وآله خمسة وسبعين يوما وكان دخلها حزن شديد على أبيها وكان جبرئيل عليه السلام يأتيها فيحسن عزاء ها على أبيها، ويطيب نفسها، ويخبرها عن أبيها ومكانه، ويخبرها بما يكون بعدها في ذريتها، وكان علي عليه السلام يكتب ذلك، فهذا مصحف فاطمة عليها السلام.

قال الكليني في «الكافي»: عدة من أصحابنا، عن أحمد بن محمد، عن الحسين بن سعيد، عن النضر بن سويد، عن هشام بن سالم، عن أبي عبدالله عليه السلام قال: سمعته يقول: عاشت فاطمة سلام الله عليها بعد رسول الله صلى الله عليه وآله خمسة وسبعين يوما لم تركا شره ولاضاحكة تأتي قبور الشهداء في كل جمعة مرتين الاثنين والخميس فتقول: ههنا كل رسول الله صلى الله عليه وآله وههنا كان المشركون.

وقال الكليني: علي بن إبراهيم، عن أبيه، عن ابن أبي عمير، عن هشام بن سالم، عن أبي عبدالله (عليه السلام) قال: سمعته يقول: عاشت فاطمة (عه) بعد أبيها خمسة وسبعين يوما لم تر كاشرة ولا ضاحكة. تأتي قبور الشهداء في كل جمعة مرتين: الاثنين والخميس فتقول: ههنا كان رسول الله (صلى الله عليه وآله) ههنا كان المشركون.

وقال الكليني في «الكافي»: ولدت فاطمة عليها وعلى بعلها السلام بعد مبعث رسول الله صلى الله عليه وآله بخمس سنين، وتوفيت عليها السلام ولها ثمان عشرة سنة وخمسة وسبعون يوما، وبقيت بعد أبيها صلى الله عليه وآله خمسة وسبعين يوما.

This position was also ascribed to Jaʿfar al-Ṣādiq by the anonymous fifth century Twelver author of *Dalāʾil al-Imāma*, pseudo-Ibn Rustum. He relayed this position via his own dubious isnād.[1]

قال مصنف كتاب «دلائل الإمامة»: حدثني محمد بن هارون التلعكبري، قال: حدثني أبي، قال: حدثني أبو علي محمد بن همام بن سهيل (رضي الله عنه)، قال: روى أحمد ابن محمد بن البرقي، عن أحمد بن محمد الأشعري القمي، عن عبد الرحمن بن أبي نجران، عن عبد الله بن سنان، عن ابن مسكان، عن أبي بصير، عن أبي عبد الله جعفر بن محمد (عليه السلام)، قال: ولدت فاطمة (عليها السلام) في جمادى الآخرة، يوم العشرين منه، سنة خمس وأربعين من مولد النبي (صلى الله عليه وآله). وأقامت بمكة ثمان سنين، وبالمدينة عشر سنين، وبعد وفاة

1 Dalāʾil al-Imāma (p.45-46)

أبيها خمسة وسبعين يوما. وقبضت في جمادي الآخرة يوم الثلاثاء لثلاث خلون منه، سنة إحدى عشرة من الهجرة...

ʿAbdullāh b. al-Muʾammal (d. 169) relayed a tradition through Abū al-Zubayr → Jābir and through Ibn Abī Mulayka →ʿĀʾisha that Fāṭima died two months after her father's death,[1] but ʿAbdullāh b. al-Muʾammal was an unreliable transmitter.[2] Furthermore, this tradition conflicts with what seems to be authentically established from ʿĀʾisha elsewhere, as shall be demonstrated.

ʿAmr b. Dīnār authentically quoted Abū Jaʿfar al-Bāqir (d. 114) stating that Fāṭima died three months following the Messenger of Allah's ﷺ death.[3] Another tradition relayed by al-Dūlābī (d. 310) quotes al-Bāqir stating that Fāṭima died 95 days following the Messenger of Allah's ﷺ death.[4] Al-Muṭahhar b. Ṭāhir al-Maqdisī (d. ~355) reiterated this position,[5] and Abū al-Qāsim Ibn Manda (d. 470) similarly stated that Fāṭima lived for 100 days following her father's death.[6] The position that Fāṭima died three months following her father's death was deemed the correct position by al-Ḥākim (d. 405), and he claimed that Ibn Ḥanbal (d. 241) adopted it as well.[7]

The Zaydī Imām, Abū Ṭālib al-Hārūnī (d. 424) relayed a tradition via his own isnād that quotes Abū Jaʿfar al-Bāqir (d. 114) stating that Fāṭima died four months after the Prophet's ﷺ death.[8] This tradition is inauthentic, as its isnād contains Jābir b. Yazīd al-Juʿfī and ʿAmr b. Abī al-Miqdām, and it conflicts with what is authentically relayed from al-Bāqir that Fāṭima died three months following the Prophet's ﷺ death.

قال أبو طالب: أَخْبَرَنَا أبو العَبَّاسِ أَحْمَدُ بن إِبْرَاهِيمَ الحَسَنِي رحمه الله تعالى، قَالَ: حَدَّثَنَا عَلِيُّ بن الحَسَنِ بن سُلَيْمَانَ البَجَلِي، قَالَ: أَخْبَرَنَا مُحَمَّدُ بن عَبْدِالْعَزِيزِ، قَالَ: حَدَّثَنَا إِسْمَاعِيلُ بن أَبَانَ العَامِرِيُّ، عَنْ عَمْرِو بن أَبِي الْمِقْدَامِ، عَنْ جَابِرِ بن يَزِيدَ الجُعْفِي، عَنْ أَبِي جَعْفَرٍ مُحَمَّدِ بن عَلِيٍّ (عَلَيْهِمَا السَّلامُ) أَنَّهُ سُئِلَ كَمْ عَاشَتْ فَاطِمَةُ عَلَيْهَا السَّلاَمُ بَعْدَ رَسُولِ الله صلى الله عليه وآله وسلم؟، قَالَ: أَرْبَعَةَ أَشْهُرٍ وَتُوُفِّيَتْ وَلَهَا ثَلاثٌ وَعِشْرُونَ سَنَةً.

---

1 Al-Mustadrak ʿAlā al-Ṣaḥīḥayn by al-Ḥākim (3/178)
2 See ʿAbdullāh's entry in Mīzān al-ʿItidāl (p. 840).
3 Al-Ṭabaqāt al-Kabīr by Ibn Saʿd (10/29), al-Muʿjam al-Kabīr by al-Ṭabarānī (22/399)
4 Al-Dhurriyya al-Ṭāhira (p. 110)
5 Al-Badʾ wa-l-Tārīkh by al-Maqdisī (5/20)
6 Al-Mustakhraj min Kutub al-Nās by Ibn Manda (1/38)
7 Faḍāʾil Fāṭima al-Zahrāʾ by al-Ḥākim (p. 78)
8 Taysīr al-Maṭālib fī Amālī Abī Ṭālib (p. 138-139)

Ibn Shihāb (d. 124) narrated on the authority of ʿUrwa b. al-Zubayr from ʿĀʾisha, the Prophet's ﷺ wife, that Fāṭima lived for six months following the Prophet's ﷺ death.[1] Ibn Isḥāq (d. 151) is quoted relaying this claim from Yaḥyā b. ʿAbbād b. ʿAbdillāh b. al-Zubayr, from his father, from ʿĀʾisha;[2] however, the isnād unto Ibn Isḥāq is unreliable since it includes Muḥammad b. Ḥumayd. Elsewhere, Ibn Isḥāq adopted this position.[3] If this position is the claim of ʿĀʾisha herself and not an interpolation of al-Zuhrī or ʿUrwa, then it would be the strongest position out of all claims pertaining to Fāṭima's death date since ʿĀʾisha was an eyewitness and contemporary of Fāṭima. The second century Medinite historian, Abū Maʿshar al-Sindī (d. 170), said, "it has reached us that she lived for six months after him ﷺ."[4] This position was also adopted by Abū al-Ḥasan al-Madāʾinī (d. 225),[5] Saʿīd b. Kathīr b. ʿUfayr (d. 226),[6] al-ʿIjlī (d. 261),[7] Ibn Ḥibbān (d. 354),[8] and Ibn Zabr (d. 379),[9] and it was deemed the correct or strongest position by al-Wāqidī (d. 207),[10] al-Bayhaqī (d. 458),[11] Ibn al-Athīr (d. 630),[12] Sibṭ Ibn a-Jawzī (d. 654)[13] and Muḥib al-Dīn al-Ṭabarī (d. 694)[14] etc.

Yazīd b. Abī Ziyād (d. 137) relayed on the authority of ʿAbdullāh b. al-Ḥārith b. Nawfal b. al-Ḥārith b. ʿAbdilMuṭṭalib (d. 84) that Fāṭima died eight months after her father's death; however, Yazīd was a weak transmitter.[15] Khalīfa b. Khayyāṭ (d. 240) quoted ʿAmr b. Dīnār (d. 126) via a descent isnād similarly stating that Fāṭima died eight months following the Messenger of Allah's ﷺ death.[16]

The point of this section is not particularly to debate the correct position regarding Fāṭima's death date. Rather, it is to demonstrate the stark obscurity of the claim made within *Kitāb Sulaym Ibn Qays* about Fāṭima's

---

1 Ṣaḥīḥ al-Bukhārī (4/79), Ṣaḥīḥ Muslim (3/1380)
2 Al-Muʿjam al-Kabīr by al-Ṭabarānī (22/398)
3 Tārīkh al-Islām by al-Dhāhabī (2/10)
4 Al-Tārīkh al-Kabīr - al-Sifr al-Thālith by Ibn Abī Khaythama (2/41)
5 Al-Istīʿāb fī Maʿrifat al-Aṣḥāb by Ibn ʿAbdilBarr (4/1899)
6 Tārīkh al-Islām by al-Dhahabī (2/29)
7 Tārīkh al-Thiqāt by al-ʿIjlī (p. 523)
8 Al-Thiqāt by Ibn Ḥibbān (2/170)
9 Tārīkh Mawlid al-ʿUlamāʾ wa-Wafayātihim by Ibn Zabr (1/85)
10 Al-Ṭabaqāt al-Kabīr by Ibn Saʿd (10/29)
11 Dalāʾil al-Nubuwwa by al-Bayhaqī (6/365)
12 Usd al-Ghāba fī Maʿrifat al-Ṣaḥāba by Ibn al-Athīr (6/225)
13 Mirʾāt al-Zamān fī Tawārīkh al-Aʿyān by Sibṭ Ibn al-Jawzī (5/60)
14 Dhakhāʾir al-ʿUqbā fī Manāqib Dhawī al-Qurbā by Muḥib al-Dīn (p. 52)
15 Tārīkh Dimashq by Ibn ʿAsākir (3/160)
16 Tārīkh Khalīfa b. Khayyāṭ (p. 96)

death such that it explicitly conflicts with what is deemed authentic by Sunnī, Zaydī and even Twelver scholarship. The claim that Fāṭima died 45 days after her father's death is quite an outlier position that is not substantiated by much data, if any. Furthermore, it conflicts with what was authentically recorded from more reliable sources according to Sunnī and Shīʿite scholarship. This error is yet another example of a blatant historical error embodied within *Kitāb Sulaym Ibn Qays*. Such minute errors alone would not necessarily be sufficient to condemn the text as a forgery; however, their abundance in the text, paralleled with a variety of other observable textual and transmittive defects within it, should further attest to *Kitāb Sulaym's* problematic nature.

Qunfudh: The Fictional Villain

A figure by the name of Qunfudh is mentioned more than 22 times throughout *Kitāb Sulaym Ibn Qays*. He is described as "a blunt, vulgar, and uncouth man from among the *Ṭulaqā'* from the clan of Banī ʿAdī."[1]

قال: فقال عمر: نرسل إليه قنفذا، وهو رجل فظ غليظ جاف من الطلقاء أحد بني عدي بن كعب.

This figure is hence claimed to be a figure from ʿUmar's clan, Banī ʿAdī, and his mention among the *Ṭulaqā'* entails that he only accepted Islam after the conquest of Mecca in year 8. Later in the book, Qunfudh is said to be a paternal cousin of ʿUmar b. al-Khaṭṭāb.[2]

قال سليم: فبعث إليه ابن عم لعمر يقال له: قنفذ، فقال له: يا قنفذ انطلق إلى علي فقل له: أجب خليفة رسول الله، فبعثا مرارا وأبى علي (عليه السلام) أن يأتيهم...

Qunfudh is also described as a governor who was later appointed by ʿUmar b. al-Khattāb, and he is given the patronymic, "al-ʿAdawī," reiterating his belonging to the clan of Banī ʿAdī.[3]

قال سليم: فأغرم عمر بن الخطاب تلك السنة جميع عماله أنصاف أموالهم لشعر أبي المختار، ولم يغرم قنفذ العدوي شيئا – وقد كان من عماله – ورد عليه ما أخذ منه – وهو عشرون ألف درهم – ولم يأخذ منه عشره ولا نصف عشره»

1 Kitāb Sulaym Ibn Qays (p. 149)
2 Kitāb Sulaym Ibn Qays (p. 385)
3 Kitāb Sulaym Ibn Qays (p. 223)

In *Kitāb Sulaym*, Qunfudh is presented as one of the main assailants in the alleged attack on Fāṭima's house, and he is portrayed as ʿUmar's righthand and executive. In the fourth report in the book, Abū Bakr and ʿUmar are quoted conspiring to force ʿAlī to pledge his allegiance to Abū Bakr. Sulaym relayed from Salmān that he said:

> Abū Bakr asked, "Who shall we send to him?" ʿUmar replied, "We shall send Qunfudh, as he is a blunt, vulgar, and uncouth man from among the *Ṭulaqā'* from the clan of Banī ʿAdī bin Kaʿb."
>
> So he sent Qunfudh to him along with a group of aides. He asked ʿAlī for permission [to enter his house], but ʿAlī refused to grant them permission. The companions of Qunfudh thus returned to Abū Bakr and ʿUmar where they were seated in the mosque, surrounded by the masses. They said, "We were not given permission [to enter]."
>
> ʿUmar said, "Go. If he does not give you permission, then enter his house without permission!"
>
> They then returned and asked for permission, and Fāṭima said, "I prohibit you from entering my house without permission." Hence, they left the scene, and Qunfudh – the damned - stayed put.[1]

فقال أبو بكر: من نرسل إليه؟ فقال عمر: نرسل إليه قنفذا، وهو رجل فظ غليظ جاف من الطلقاء أحد بني عدي بن كعب. فأرسله إليه وأرسل معه أعوانا وانطلق فاستأذن على علي عليه السلام، فأبى أن يأذن لهم. فرجع أصحاب قنفذ إلى أبي بكر وعمر – وهما جالسان في المسجد والناس حولهما – فقالوا: لم يؤذن لنا. فقال عمر: اذهبوا، فإن أذن لكم وإلا فادخلوا عليه بغير إذن! فانطلقوا فاستأذنوا، فقالت فاطمة عليها السلام: أحرج عليكم أن تدخلوا على بيتي بغير إذن. فرجعوا وثبت قنفذ الملعون.

Qunfudh's role in the attack becomes more apparent after ʿAlī's alleged strangling of ʿUmar. Sulaym relayed from Salmān that he said:

> ʿUmar sent out yearning for support, so the people approached until they entered the house. ʿAlī leaped to his sword, and Qunfudh thus returned to Abū Bakr fearing that ʿAlī would confront him with his sword, since he was aware of ʿAli's strength and sternness. Abū Bakr told Qunfudh, "Go back. If he does not come outside, break into his house. If he refrains, then burn his house with fire!"

1 Kitāb Sulaym Ibn Qays (p. 149)

> Qunfudh - the damned - thus went alongside his companions, and they barged into the house without permission. ʿAlī leaped to his sword, but they outnumbered him as they were many. Some of them drew their swords, outnumbered him, pinned him down and tied a rope around his neck.
>
> Fāṭima stood as a barrier between him and them at the house entrance, so Qunfudh - the damned - struck her with his whip. When she died, there was a bruise on her shoulder that resembled a bracelet as a result of his strike, may Allah curse him and those who sent him.[1]

قال سليم: قال سلمان: [...] فأرسل عمر يستغيث، فأقبل الناس حتى دخلوا الدار وثار علي عليه السلام إلى سيفه فرجع قنفذ إلى أبي بكر وهو يتخوف أن يخرج علي عليه السلام إليه بسيفه، لما قد عرف من بأسه وشدته. فقال أبو بكر لقنفذ: إرجع، فإن خرج وإلا فاقتحم عليه بيته، فإن امتنع فاضرم عليهم بيتهم النار. فانطلق قنفذ الملعون فاقتحم هو وأصحابه بغير إذن، وثار علي عليه السلام إلى سيفه فسبقوه إليه وكاثروه وهم كثيرون، فتناول بعضهم سيوفهم فكاثروه وضبطوه فألقوا في عنقه حبلا! وحالت بينهم وبينه فاطمة عليها السلام عند باب البيت، فضربها قنفذ الملعون بالسوط فماتت حين ماتت وإن في عضدها كمثل الدملج من ضربته، لعنه الله ولعن من بعث به.

Later in the book, Sulaym is quoted criticizing ʿUmar for his decision to fine all of his deputies and confiscate half of their wealth, and he proceeds to mention Qunfudh in this context as well. He said:

> ʿUmar bin al-Khaṭṭāb fined all of his governors half of their wealth that year, as a result of Abū al-Mukhtar's poem. He, however, did not fine Qunfudh anything, and he was one of his governors. He returned to him what he had initially taken from him, and it amounted to 20,000 Dirhams, yet he did not confiscate a tenth of it nor half of that![2]

قال سليم: فأغرم عمر بن الخطاب تلك السنة جميع عماله أنصاف أموالهم لشعر أبي المختار، ولم يغرم قنفذ العدوي شيئا - وقد كان من عماله - ورد عليه ما أخذ منه - وهو عشرون ألف درهم - ولم يأخذ منه عشره ولا نصف عشره.

---

1 Kitāb Sulaym Ibn Qays (p. 150-151)

2 Kitāb Sulaym Ibn Qays (p. 222-223)

Sulaym is then quoted saying:

> I met ʿAlī and I asked him about what ʿUmar had done. He said, "Do you know why ʿUmar refrained from fining Qunfudh?" I said, "No."
>
> He said, "It is because Qunfudh was the one who struck Fāṭima with a whip when she attempted to stand as a barrier between me and them. She died – may the blessings of Allah be upon her – with a bruise on her shoulder from that strike, which resembled a bracelet![1]

قال أبان: قال سليم: فلقيت عليا صلوات الله عليه وآله فسألته عما صنع عمر؟ فقال: هل تدري لم كف عن قنفذ ولم يغرمه شيئا؟!. قلت: لا. قال: لأنه هو الذي ضرب فاطمة صلوات الله عليها بالسوط حين جاءت لتحول بيني وبينهم، فماتت صلوات الله عليها، وإن أثر السوط لفي عضدها مثل الدملج.

Hence, we see that this Qunfudh figure in *Kitāb Sulaym* is said to be (1) a man from the *Ṭulaqā'*, (2) from the tribe of Banī ʿAdī, (3) a cousin of ʿUmar, (4) one of the key assailants against Fāṭima and (5) a later deputy of ʿUmar.

The issue with these claims, however, is that no such figure exists. Rather, the closest semblance of a match to this description is a companion of the Prophet ﷺ known as Qunfudh b. ʿUmayr b. Judʿān, who actually was from the clan of Banī al-Taym, Abū Bakr's clan. Ibn Ḥajar (d. 852) dedicated an entry to this figure in his biographical compendium pertaining to the Prophet's ﷺ companions. He said:

> Qunfudh b. ʿUmayr b. Judʿān al-Taymī, the father of al-Muhājir. He has companionship. This was stated by Abū ʿUmar [Ibn ʿAbdilBarr]. He said, "ʿUmar appointed him as governor of Mecca, and he then dismissed him. He then appointed Nāfiʿ b. ʿAbdilḤārith instead."[2]

قال ابن حجر: قنفذ بن عمير بن جدعان التيمي، والد المهاجر. له صحبة، قاله أبو عمر، قال: وولاه عمر مكة ثم صرفه، واستعمل نافع بن عبد الحارث.

Ibn Ḥajar further expounded Qunfudh's lineage when addressing his son, al-Muhājir b. Qunfudh. He said, "al-Muhājir b. Qunfudh b. ʿUmayr b. Judʿān b. Kaʿb b. Saʿd b. Taym b. Murra al-Qurashī al-Taymī."[3]

---

1 Kitāb Sulaym Ibn Qays (p. 222-223)

2 Al-Iṣāba fī Tamyīz al-Ṣaḥāba (5/346)

3 Al-Iṣāba fī Tamyīz al-Ṣaḥāba (6/181)

قال ابن حجر: المهاجر بن قنفذ بن عمير بن جدعان بن كعب بن سعد بن تيم بن مرة القرشيّ التيميّ.

It hence becomes apparent that this figure actually is the second cousin of Abū Bakr's father, ʿUthmān b. ʿĀmir b. ʿAmr b. Kaʿb b. Saʿd b. Taym b. Murra.

Al-Balādhurī (d. ~279) stated that Qunfudh used to harm the Prophet, and his statement is referring to the Meccan period of Islam prior the emigration to Medīna and Qunfudh's conversion.[1]

قال البلاذري: فأما عمير بْن جدعان فولد: قنفذ بْن عمير، أدرك النَّبِيّ صَلَّى اللَّهُ عَلَيْهِ وَسَلَّمَ، فكان مؤذيا له.

Asides from that, not much is known about Qunfudh. Due to Qunfudh's obscurity and general irrelevance, later Shīʿite sources often contradicted each other when addressing this figure.

The anonymous fifth century Shīʿite author of *Dalāʾil al-Imāmah* relayed a dubious tradition back to Jaʿfar al-Ṣādiq (d. 148) where he is quoted describing Qunfudh as the *mawlā* (client) of ʿUmar b. al-Khaṭṭāb.[2]

روى صاحب «دلائل الإمامة» بإسناده إلى جعفر الصادق، قال: وكان سبب وفاتها أن قنفذا مولى عمر لكزها بنعل السيف بأمره، فأسقطت محسنا ومرضت من ذلك مرضا شديدا، ولم تدع أحدا ممن آذاها يدخل عليها.

The claim that Qunfudh was a client (*mawlā*) of ʿUmar not only contradicts the biographical data on Qunfudh, but it also contradicts the claim in *Kitāb Sulaym* as well. Other Shīʿite sources, such as al-Khuṣaybī (d. 334) and pseudo-Ibn Qutayba in *al-Imāma wa-l-Siyāsa*, described Qunfudh as the client (*mawlā*) of Abū Bakr.[3]

---

1 Jumalun min Ansāb al-Ashrāf (10/155)

2 Dalāʾil al-Imāma by pseudo-Ibn Rustum (p. 45-46). Many today believe that *Dalāʾil al-Imāma* was authored by the Shīʿite author, Ibn Rustum al-Ṭabarī. However, there are ample reasons to believe that the actually was not the author of this text. Rather, its author is an anonymous fifth century figure. See al-Akhbār al-Dakhīla of al-Tustarī (p. 43-48).

Furthermore, the isnād of this tradition is weak, and it will be dissected during the analysis of Passage 8 in Chapter 3.

3 Al-Hidāya al-Kubrā by al-Khuṣaybī (p. 179), al-Imāma wa-l-Siyāsa by pseudo-Ibn Qutayba (p. 22)

Ibn Qutayba was a prominent Sunnī scholar; however, there are various reasons to question the validity of *al-Imāma wa-l-Siyāsa's* ascription to him. Many academics hence refer to the author of this text as pseudo-Ibn Qutayba. Furthermore, the isnād cited for this account by this book's anonymous author is weak. It should also be noted that pseudo-Ibn Qutayba's account makes no mention of a physical assault on Fāṭima, let

قال الخصيبي: فأخذ عمر السوط من قنفذ مولى أبي بكر...

وقال منتحل كتاب الإمامة والسياسة المنسوب إلى ابن قتيبة: فقال أبو بكر لقنفد – وهو مولى له – اذهب فادع لي عليا...

Evidently, there never was a figure called Qunfudh who was ʿUmar's paternal cousin, ʿUmar's client (*mawlā*), or Abū Bakr's client (*mawlā*). Rather, the only individual that matches some of the descriptions in *Kitāb Sulaym* is a figure who was the second-cousin of Abū Bakr's father.

Khalīfa b. Khayyāṭ (d. 240) stated that Qunfudh b. ʿUmayr was ʿUmar's second governor in Mecca. ʿUmar eventually dismissed him of his duties and appointed Nāfiʿ b. ʿAbdilḤārith in his place.[1]

قال خليفة بن خياط: تَسْمِيَة عُمَّال عُمَر بْن الْخطاب عَلَى مَكَّة مُحرز بْن حَارِثَة بْن ربيعَة بْن عَبْد الْعُزَّى بْن عَبْد شمس ثمَّ عَزله وَولى قنفذ بْن عُمَيْر بْن جدعَان التَّيْمِيّ ثمَّ عَزله وَولى نَافِع بْن عَبْد الْحَارِث الْخُزَاعِيّ.

Al-Balādhurī (d. ~279) further stated that ʿUmar b. al-Khaṭṭab had flogged Qunfudh's son, al-Muhājir b. Qunfudh, alongside his wife for the consumption of intoxicants, which may further undermine *Kitāb Sulaym's* claim that Qunfudh was given preferential and exceptional treatment by ʿUmar (given the other inaccuracies embodied in the book surrounding Qunfudh).[2]

قال البلاذري: وَكَانَ المهاجر بْن قنفذ بْن عمير بْن جدعان عَلَى شرط عُثْمَان بْن عَفَّان، وَكَانَ عمر جلده وامرأته ثمانين ثمانين فِي شراب.

All in all, this figure, as portrayed in *Kitāb Sulaym*, is a fictional figure that only emerged in later Shīʿite circles as the narrative surrounding Fāṭima's purported murder continued to develop and proliferate with the progression of time. He is only mentioned as an assailant in the purported attack on Fāṭima in later unreliable Shīʿite sources, and it appears that this figure is a post-third century Shīʿite caricature of an otherwise insignificant historical figure known as Qunfidh b. ʿUmayr. According to my findings, the earliest source to introduce this Qunfudh as a belligerent in the attack on Fāṭima's house is *al-Mustarshid* of the late third and early fourth century

---

alone an assault led by Qunfudh. Later, in this book, I expound some of the serious issues and flaws in pseudo-Ibn Qutayba's account.

1 Tārīkh Khalīfa b. Khayyāṭ (p. 153)

2 Jumalun min Ansāb al-Ashrāf (10/155)

Twelver author, Ibn Rustum al-Ṭabarī. In it, *al-Ṭabarī* relayed an unreliable tradition via a dubious isnād that mentions Qunfudh in this context.[1] All else, Qunfudh is quite sparsely mentioned in later Twelver sources in the context of this event.

Anachronisms in Kitāb Sulaym

An anachronism is defined as a "a thing belonging or appropriate to a period other than that in which it exists, especially a thing that is conspicuously old-fashioned."[2] The presence of anachronisms in a historical text often is indicative of the text's unreliable transmission or its dubious origins. Jeremy Bentham elaborated on this phenomenon saying:

> In a living language there are always variations in words, in the meaning of words, in the construction of phrases, in the manner of spelling, which may detect the age of a writing, and lead to legitimate suspicions of forgery.[3]

Joe Nickell said:

> Anachronistic word usage, however, especially combined with other suspicious elements, can provide evidence that underscores the word questioned in the case of a questioned historical document, and in some cases the evidence can be decisive.[4]

Various academics have made note of the presence of anachronisms in Kitāb Sulaym. In his paper, *Violence and Scripture in the Book of Sulaym Ibn Qays*, Amīr-Moezzi said:

> The pseudographical character of the *Kitāb Sulaym b. Qays* is obvious. The presence in its midst of data at times originating several centuries later than the period of its presumed author—and especially the many passages on the Abbasid Revolution or even the number twelve of the Imāms—permits the historian no doubt in this regard.[5]

---

1 Al-Mustarshid fī Imāmat Amīr al-Mu'minīn (p. 376-378). I discuss this tradition in more detail in chapter 3 of this book under my analysis of passage 8.

2 Oxford Dictionary 2019

3 A Treatise On Judicial Evidence (p. 140)

4 Detecting Forgery: Forensic Investigation of Documents (p. 104)

5 The Silent Qur'an and the Speaking Qur'an (p. 18)

Robert Gleave made note of the collective usage of some advanced hermeneutical terms in Kitāb Sulaym, which he argued emerged after the death of its alleged author. In his paper, *Early Shiite hermeneutics and the dating of Kitāb Sulaym Ibn Qays*, he shed light on the following passage from the book, where Sulaym is quoted saying

> [ʿAlī] came over and said to me, "You have asked, so understand the answer. In the hands of the people there is both valid and invalid (*ḥaqqan wa-bāṭilan*), truthfulness and falsity (*ṣidqan wa-kiḏban*), abrogating and abrogated (*nāsikhan wa-mansūkhan*), general and particular (*ʿāmman wa-khāṣṣan*), decisive and ambiguous (*muḥkaman wa-mutashābihan*), preservation and whimsy (*ḥifzan wa-wahman*)."[1]

قال سليم: فأقبل علي فقال لي: يا سليم، قد سألت فافهم الجواب. إن في أيدي الناس حقا وباطلا، وصدقا وكذبا، وناسخا ومنسوخا، وخاصا وعاما، ومحكما ومتشابها، وحفظا ووهما.

Gleave comments on this passage saying:

> Turning to the report's text in detail, the listings of category pairs are a common means of presenting the findings of hermeneutic reflection. Most of the pairings given here were taken up within the later hermeneutic tradition and given technical definitions: *ṣidq/kiḏb*, *nāsikh/mansūkh*, *ʿāmm/khāṣṣ* and *muḥkam/mutashābih*. They are well known and regularly found located together (often with supplements, such as *ẓāhir/bāṭin*, *ḥaqīqa/majāz* and *muṭlaq/muqayyad*) in later *tafsīr* and *uṣūl* works. The *muḥkam*/*mutashābih* pairing is, of course Quranic (Q. 3:7); the notion of *naskh* is less explicitly (or easily) traced within the Quran; and while the other terms exist within the Quran, they do not appear as hermeneutic categories, either individually or in pairs. I would argue that the collocation of the categories here, as a list of pairings into which revelatory material can be placed, probably reflects a mature hermeneutic science, rather than any rudimentary exegetical theory of the first century AH. This apparent anachronism hints at the report being considerably later than the period of "Sulaym". An examination of whether the terms (either individually or in pairs) are used in a manner congruent with later conceptions of (say) abrogation and particularization also indicate

1 Kitāb Sulaym Ibn Qays (p. 181)

> a point of formulation sometime after the turn of the second century AH (late eighth century CE).[1]

Gleave concludes his analysis of the passage saying:

> The content of the first section of the tenth report appears, then, as a rather audacious attempt to attribute to ʿAlī knowledge and mastery of exegetical techniques and a level of hermeneutic sophistication which came into existence in the late eighth/early ninth century. Having said that, there are points in the text where the fit between the use of technical terminology and concepts within later Muslim hermeneutic understanding and those found in the report is not perfect. This perhaps indicates that the appropriate context in which to view the report is the early formative period of hermeneutic thinking in the Muslim religious sciences (namely the late eighth and early ninth century CE), rather than the fully flourished theoretical awareness one finds in tenth-century works of tafsīr and uṣūl al-fiqh.[2]

He also concluded his paper saying:

> My argument is that the listing of these hermeneutic categories together, as a sort of "tool box" for the exegete, shows a level of interpretative self-awareness that is most likely to have emerged contemporary with (and arguably after the impact of) the work of al-Shafiʿī.[3]

As evident, Gleave dates this report to a period between the late second and early third centuries AH, which is more than a century after Sulaym's purported death in 76. When I initially read Gleave's paper more than one year ago, I found his dating of this passage compelling. Recently, however, I came across some evidence that may undermine some of his conclusions. In the *Tafsīr* of Muqātil b. Sulaymān (d. 150), one comes across a passage that collectively embodies much of the jargon referenced in Sulaym's tradition among other related terms as well.[4]

---

1 Robert Gleave (2015). Early Shiite hermeneutics and the dating of Kitāb Sulaym Ibn Qays. Bulletin of the School of Oriental and African Studies, 78, pp 89.

2 Ibid., 78, 99.

3 Ibid., 78, 102.

4 Tafsīr Muqātil Ibn Sulaymān al-Azdī (1/22)

قال عبد الخالق بن الحسن: حدثنا عبيد الله ، قال : وحدثنا أبي ، عن الهذيل ، عن مقاتل ، أنه قال : في القرآن خاص وعام ، خاص للمسلمين ، وخاص في المشركين ، وعام لجميع الناس ، ومتشابه ، ومحكم ، ومفسر ، ومبهم ، وإضمار ، وتمام ، وصلات في الكلام مع ناسخ ومنسوخ، وتقديم وتأخير ، وأشباه مع وجوه كثيرة ، وجواب في سورة أخرى ، وأمثال ضربها الله عز وجل لنفسه ، وأمثال ضربها للكافر والصنم ، وأمثال ضربها للدنيا ، والبعث ، والآخرة ، وخبر الأولين ، وخبر ما في الجنة والنار ، وخاص لمشرك واحد ، وفرائض، وأحكام ، وحدود ، وخبر ما في قلوب المؤمنين ، وخبر ما في قلوب الكافرين ، وخصومة مشركي العرب ، وتفسير ، وللتفسير تفسير.

If this tradition can be dated to Muqātil b. Sulaymān (d. 150), then Gleave's dating of these terms (and their respective utilizations) to al-Shāfiʿī's (d. 204) epoch and its aftermaths is off by at least half a century. Rather, such jargon usage, utilization and paring is more appropriately dated to the early/mid second century, near the end of the *tābiʿin's* era when hermeneutical debates and discussions were on the rise. Additionally, I would note that some of these terms are not anachronistic per se in an early first century setting. Rather, the collective utilization of these terms to explain the existence of conflicting prophetic traditions precisely is the anachronism at play in this passage.

A variety of other anachronisms can be observed dispersed throughout *Kitāb Sulaym.* The third report in *Kitāb Sulaym* contains a poem supposedly composed by al-ʿAbbās (d. 32) where he is presented lamenting the fact that rulership had been taken away from Banī Hāshim and ʿAlī b. Abī Ṭālib. He is quoted saying:

> "Is he [ʿAli] not the first to pray towards your *qibla*,
>
> and the most knowledgeable of people in the *āthār* and *sunan*?"[1]

قال: فخرجوا من عنده وأنشأ العباس يقول:

ما كنت أحسب هذا الأمر منحرفا — عن هاشم ثم منهم عن أبي حسن
أليس أول من صلى لقبلتكم — وأعلم الناس بالآثار والسنن
وأقرب الناس عهدا بالنبي ومن — جبريل عون له في الغسل والكفن
من فيه ما في جميع الناس كلهم — وليس في الناس ما فيه من الحسن

1 Kitāb Sulaym Ibn Qays (p. 142)

من ذا الذي ردكم عنه فنعرفه   ها إن بيعتكم من أول الفتن

The interchangeable and complementary usage of the terms, *āthār* and *sunan*, to denote Prophetic traditions is an anachronism that arose around one century after the death of al-ʿAbbās (d. 32). The terms, in this context, generally are characteristic of 2nd century hermeneutics. Outside *Kitāb Sulaym*, there is no sound refence to a contemporaneous companion of the Prophet ﷺ utilizing both terms in this manner, and this text was composed after the first century.

What further supports this assertion is the fact that this poem is ascribed to a later figure that died after al-ʿAbbās in other independent sources. The Medinite historian, al-Zubayr b. Bakkār (d. 256) ascribed this exact poem to a descendent of Abū Lahab bin ʿAbdulmuttalib.[1]

قال الزبير بن بكار: وَقَالَ بَعْضُ وَلَدِ أَبِي لَهَبِ بْنِ عَبْدِ الْمُطَّلِبِ بْنِ هَاشِمٍ شِعْرًا:

مَا كُنْتُ أَحْسَبُ أَنَّ الأَمْرَ مُنْصَرِفٌ   عَنْ هَاشِمٍ ثُمَّ مِنْهَا عَنْ أَبِي حَسَنِ

أَلَيْسَ أَوَّلَ منْ صَلَّى لِقِبْلَتِكُمْ   وَأَعْلَمَ النَّاسِ بِالْقُرْآنِ وَالسُّنَنِ

وَأَقْرَبَ النَّاسِ عَهْدًا بِالنَّبِيِّ وَمَنْ   جِبْرِيلُ عَوْنٌ لَهُ فِي الْغُسْلِ وَالْكَفَنِ

مَا فِيهِ مَا فِيهِمُ لا يَمْتَرُونَ بِهِ   وَلَيْسَ فِي الْقَوْمِ مَا فِيهِ مِنَ الْحَسَنِ

مَاذَا الَّذِي رَدَّهُمْ عَنْهُ فَتَعْلَمُهُ   هَا إِنَّ ذَا غَبْنُنَا مِنْ أَعْظَمَ الْغَبَنِ

Ibn ʿAbdilBarr identified this descendent of Abū Lahab as al-Faḍl b. al-ʿAbbās b. ʿUtbah b. Abī Lahab.[2] Al-Fadl's death date is unknown, but he, however, was a contemporary of al-Farazdaq (d. 114). His death date probably is sometime within the early 2nd century. This poem would be more appropriately ascribed to al-Faḍl than al-ʿAbbās b. ʿAbdilMuṭṭalib (d. 32), though it is also dubiously ascribed to a few other companions of the Prophet.

Interestingly, the Twelver scholar, al-Mufīd (d. 413), attributed this poem to someone else, ʿAbdullāh b. al-Mughīra b. al-Ḥārith b. ʿAbdilMuṭṭalib, whose companionship with the Prophet ﷺ is contested.[3]

---

1 Al-Akhbār Al-Muwaffaqiyyāt by al-Zubayr b. Bakkār al-Asadī (p. 221)

2 Al-Istīʿāb fī Maʿrifat al-Aṣḥāb (3/1133)

3 Al-Jamal by al-Mufīd al-ʿUkbarī (p. 58)

قال المفيد في «كتاب الجمل»: وكان عبد الله بن أبي سفيان بن الحرث بن عبد المطلب خارجا عن المدينة فدخلها وقد بايع الناس أبا بكر، فوقف في وسط المسجد وأنشأ يقول:

ما كنت أحسب هذا الأمر منتقلا عن هاشم ثم منها عن أبي حسن

أليس أول من صلى لقبلتهم وأعرف الناس بالآثار والسنن

وآخر الناس عهدا بالنبي ومن جبريل عون له بالغسل والكفن

من فيه ما فيهم لا يمترون به وليس في القوم ما فيه من الحسن

فما الذي ردكم عنه فنعلمه ها إن بيعتكم في أول الفتن

The indicators of forgery in this passage from *Kitāb Sulaym* are hence twofold: (1) the presence of anachronisms in the text and (2) the contested attribution of this poetry to al-ʿAbbās, especially its attribution to a more suitable later historical figure.

In the book exist other anachronisms worthy of exposition. On at least two occasions in *Kitāb Sulaym*, Abū Bakr is addressed as the commander of the faithful (*Amīr al-Muʾminīn*).[1] This utilization of the title, however, is an anachronism, for ʿUmar b. al-Khaṭṭāb reputedly was the first caliph to assume that title. Yaʿqūb b. ʿAbdirraḥmān narrated on the authority of Mūsā b. ʿUqba, from Ibn Shihāb that he said:

> ʿUmar b. ʿAbdilʿAzīz asked Abū Bakr b. Sulaymān b. Abī Ḥathma, "Why was Abū Bakr's signature, Abū Bakr, the successor of the Prophet? And after him ʿUmar's signature, ʿUmar the successor of Abū Bakr? Who first referred to himself as commander of the faithful?"
>
> Ibn Abī Ḥathma responded saying, "My grandmother, al-Shifaʾ, who was among the first woman emigrants (*al-muhājirāt*), informed me that whenever ʿUmar b. al-Khaṭṭāb entered the market, he would visit her."
>
> She said, "ʿUmar once asked the governor of the two ʿIrāqs to dispatch to him two noble men so that he may inquire them about the status of ʿIrāq and its inhabitants. The governor of the two ʿIrāqs thus sent Labīd b. Rabīʿah and ʿAdī b. Ḥātim. They arrived to Medīna and then tied their mounts in the courtyard of the mosque. They then entered the mosque and found ʿAmr b. al-ʿĀṣ. They told

1 Kitāb Sulaym Ibn Qays (p. 148, 386)

him, 'O ʿAmr, seek permission from the commander of the faithful, so that we may enter upon him.'

ʿAmr thus got up and entered upon ʿUmar saying, 'Peace be upon you O commander of the faithful!'

ʿUmar replied to him saying, 'What made you utter this title, O son of al-ʿĀṣ? You shall inform me."

ʿAmr said, 'Yes. Labīd b. Rabīʿa and ʿAdī b. Hatim came, and they told me: Seek permission from the commander of the believers so that we may enter upon him. So I said: Indeed you have got his name right. He is the commander and we are the believers.'

The signature was used since then."[1]

يَعْقُوبُ بْنُ عَبْدِ الرَّحْمَنِ، عَنْ مُوسَى بْنِ عُقْبَةَ، عَنِ ابْنِ شِهَابٍ، أَنَّ عُمَرَ بْنَ عَبْدِ الْعَزِيزِ، " سَأَلَ أَبَا بَكْرِ بْنَ سُلَيْمَانَ بْنِ أَبِي حَثْمَةَ: لِمَ كَانَ أَبُو بَكْرٍ يَكْتُبُ: مِنْ أَبِي بَكْرٍ خَلِيفَةِ رَسُولِ اللَّهِ، ثُمَّ كَانَ عُمَرُ يَكْتُبُ بَعْدَهُ: مِنْ عُمَرَ بْنِ الْخَطَّابِ خَلِيفَةِ أَبِي بَكْرٍ، مَنْ أَوَّلُ مَنْ كَتَبَ: أَمِيرَ الْمُؤْمِنِينَ؟

فَقَالَ: حَدَّثَتْنِي جَدَّتِي الشِّفَاءُ وَكَانَتْ مِنَ الْمُهَاجِرَاتِ الأُوَلِ، وَكَانَ عُمَرُ بْنُ الْخَطَّابِ رَضِيَ اللَّهُ عَنْهُ إِذَا هُوَ دَخَلَ السُّوقَ دَخَلَ عَلَيْهَا، قَالَتْ: كَتَبَ عُمَرُ بْنُ الْخَطَّابِ إِلَى عَامِلِ الْعِرَاقَيْنِ: أَنِ ابْعَثْ إِلَيَّ بِرَجُلَيْنِ جَلْدَيْنِ نَبِيلَيْنِ، أَسْأَلُهُمَا عَنِ الْعِرَاقِ وَأَهْلِهِ، فَبَعَثَ إِلَيْهِ صَاحِبُ الْعِرَاقَيْنِ بِلَبِيدِ بْنِ رَبِيعَةَ، وَعَدِيِّ بْنِ حَاتِمٍ، فَقَدِمَا الْمَدِينَةَ فَأَنَاخَا رَاحِلَتَيْهِمَا بِفِنَاءِ الْمَسْجِدِ، ثُمَّ دَخَلا الْمَسْجِدَ فَوَجَدَا عَمْرَو بْنَ الْعَاصِ، فَقَالا لَهُ: يَا عَمْرُو، اسْتَأْذِنْ لَنَا عَلَى أَمِيرِ الْمُؤْمِنِينَ عُمَرَ، فَوَثَبَ عَمْرٌو فَدَخَلَ عَلَى عُمَرَ، فَقَالَ: السَّلامُ عَلَيْكَ يَا أَمِيرَ الْمُؤْمِنِينَ، فَقَالَ لَهُ عُمَرُ: مَا بَدَا لَكَ فِي هَذَا الاسْمِ يَا ابْنَ الْعَاصِ؟ لَتَخْرُجَنَّ مِمَّا قُلْتَ، قَالَ: نَعَمْ، قَدِمَ لَبِيدُ بْنُ رَبِيعَةَ، وَعَدِيُّ بْنُ حَاتِمٍ، فَقَالا لِي: اسْتَأْذِنْ لَنَا عَلَى أَمِيرِ الْمُؤْمِنِينَ، فَقُلْتُ: أَنْتُمَا وَاللَّهِ أَصَبْتُمَا اسْمَهُ، وَإِنَّهُ الأَمِيرُ، وَنَحْنُ الْمُؤْمِنُونَ، فَجَرَى الْكِتَابُ مِنْ ذَلِكَ الْيَوْمِ.

This tradition is authentic. Additionally, the Medinite historian, Ibn Shabbah, dedicated an entire chapter in *Tārīkh al-Madīna* for reports pertaining to ʿUmar's unprecedented assumption of that title.[2]

---

1 Al-Adab al-Mufrad by al-Bukhārī (p. 464), al-Muʿjam al-Kabīr by al-Ṭabarānī (1/64)

2 Tārīkh al-Madīna by Ibn Shabba (2/677-680)

Al-Ṭabarī (d. 310) said, "The first person to be addressed as the commander of the faithful was 'Umar b. al-Khaṭṭāb. It then became the norm, and the caliphs have been using this title till this day." [1]

قَالَ أَبُو جَعْفَر الطبري: أَوَّلُ مَنْ دُعِيَ أَمِيرَ الْمُؤْمِنِينَ عُمَرُ بْنُ الْخَطَّابِ، ثُمَّ جَرَتْ بِذَلِكَ السُّنَّةُ، وَاسْتَعْمَلَهُ الْخُلَفَاءُ إِلَى الْيَوْمِ.

This claim was reiterated by later historians, and it hence becomes evident that Abū Bakr was not addressed nor known as the commander of the faithful. Rather, *Kitāb Sulaym's* utilization of this term for that era is an anachronism that is indicative of the text's dubious origins or corrupted transmission. The text's author, assuming the title was the normative title of all caliphs, probably thought it was a good idea to cite it as a title of Abū Bakr, not realizing it was only used after his death.

Falsifications

Falsification is a deceptive literary tactic that occurs whenever someone copies an author's text by hand, but alters it in some way, omitting something, adding something, or just changing the wording.[2] These alterations, in many instances, are mere scribal errors; however, they can also be the result of malicious tampering with a text. Ehrman says:

> In the vast majority of the cases, the changes that copyists made were simply an accident: the slip of a pen, the misspelling of a word, the accidental omission of a word or a line. Sometimes, though, scribes changed their texts because they wanted to do so, either because they thought their scribal predecessors made a mistake that needed to be corrected or because they wanted to add something to the text (or take away something or change something). As I've indicated, this kind of falsification is close to forgery; it is one author passing off his own words as the words of a respected authority. [3]

1 Tārīkh al-Rusul wa-l-Mulūk (4/208)

2 Forged: Writing in the Name of God—Why the Bible's Authors Are Not Who We Think They Are (p. 240)

3 Forged: Writing in the Name of God—Why the Bible's Authors Are Not Who We Think They Are (p. 242)

The problem with this phenomenon should be clear: when later copyists and scribes intentionally altered past texts, the reliability of those texts is jeopardized as their original authors are potentially misrepresented and/or misquoted. Furthermore, the reader of those texts is made to believe that these emergent alterations actually are the words of the text's original author when they actually originate from a later copyist.

There are sound reasons to believe that the early recensions of *Kitāb Sulaym* were further tampered with and distorted by later scribes at multiple phases in history. Hossein Modarresi noted that the insertions and constant accretions gradually incorporated into the book eventually gave rise to the variation in the different manuscripts of the book we possess today. He said:

> Owing to the fact that a number of insertions were made in the book, there are variations among its different manuscripts, as described by Agha Buzurg 2: 152–9.8 Fortunately, later accretions seem always to have been in the form of insertions and additions rather than replacements and alterations. The old core is therefore preserved in most of the manuscripts, even at the cost of obvious contradictions. Some of these variations are noted in the editions of the book: a number of Najaf editions; Beirut, 1407; Qum, 1415 (the one used here is Najaf: Haydariyya, n.d., 236 pp.).[1]

One of the earliest figures to make note of the presence of falsifications in *Kitāb Sulaym* was the Twelver scholar, al-Mufīd (d. 413). In *Taṣḥīḥ Iʿtiqādāt al-Imāmiyya*, al-Mufīd commented on the book saying:

> [...] This book, however, is not trusted, and most of it cannot be acted upon. Muddling and deception have occurred within its contents. The religious one must thus refrain from acting upon all that is in it, and he must not depend on most of it nor should he rely on its transmitters. He must leap to the scholars so that they may clarify to him the truth from the falsehood in it.[2]

قال المفيد: وأمّا ما تعلّق به أبو جعفر من حديث سُليم الذي رجع فيه إلى الكتاب المضاف إليه برواية أبان بن أبي عيّاش؛ فالمعنى فيه صحيح، غير أنّ هذا الكتاب غير موثوق به، وقد حصل فيه تخليط وتدليس؛ فينبغي

1 Tradition and Survival: A Bibliographical Survey of early Shī'ite Literature (1/86)

2 Taṣḥīḥ Iʿtiqādāt al-Imāmiyya by al-Mufīd (p. 149-150)

للمتديِّن أن يجتنب العمل بكلّ ما فيه، ولا يُعَوِّل على جملته والتقليد لروايته، ولْيَفزع إلى العلماء فيما تَضَمَّنه من الأحاديث لِيُوقفوه على الصحيح منها والفاسد.

Several early Twelver critics, for example, made note of the fact that the book stated the *imāms* were thirteen in number, contrary to orthodox Twelver theology, which places the number of *imams* at twelve. This was one of Ibn al-Ghaḍā'irī's objections to the book's authenticity.[1]

قال ابن الغضائري: والكتابُ موضُوعٌ، لا مِرْيَةَ فيهِ، وعلى ذلك علاماتٌ فيهِ تَدُلُّ على ما ذكرناهُ. منها: ما ذَكَرَ أَنَّ مُحَمَّدَ بنَ أبي بَكْرٍ وَعَظَ أباهُ عندَ مَوْتِهِ، ومنها: أَنَّ الأئمّةَ ثلاثةَ عَشَر، وغيرُ ذلك.

The mentioning of thirteen imāms in Kitāb Sulaym was not exclusively noted by Ibn al-Ghaḍā'irī. Ibn al-Najāshī, in his *Fihrist*, described a Shī'ite scholar by the name of Hibatullāh b. Aḥmed saying:

> He heard much ḥadīth, and used to engage in *kalam*. He used to attend the gathering of Abū al-Ḥusayn b. al-Shabīh al-'Alawī, who was Zaydī in his *madhhab*. He compiled a book for him, and he mentioned in it that the imāms were thirteen in number including Zayd b. 'Alī b. al-Ḥusayn. He appealed to a ḥadīth in *Kitāb Sulaym* which stated that the imāms were twelve descendants of the Commander of the Faithful.[2]

قال ابن النجاشي: هبة الله بن أحمد بن محمد الكاتب أبو نصر، المعروف بابن برنية. كان يذكر أن أمه أم كلثوم بنت أبي جعفر محمد بن عثمان العمري. سمع حديثا كثيرا، وكان يتعاطى الكلام، ويحضر مجلس أبي الحسين بن الشبيه العلوي الزيدي المذهب، فعمل له كتابا، وذكر أن الأئمة ثلاثة عشر مع زيد بن علي بن الحسين، واحتج بحديث في كتاب سليم بن قيس الهلالي أن الأئمة اثنا عشر من ولد أمير المؤمنين عليه السلام. له كتاب في الإمامة، وكتاب في أخبار أبي عمرو وأبي جعفر العمريين ورأيت أبا العباس بن نوح قد عول عليه في الحكاية في كتابه أخبار الوكلاء. وكان هذا الرجل كثير الزيارات، وآخر زيارة حضرها معنا يوم الغدير سنة أربعمائة بمشهد أمير المؤمنين عليه السلام.

This controversial aspect of the book seemed to have been quite notable in the past, for the Shī'ite historian, al-Mas'ūdī (d. 345), similarly made note

1 Al-Rijāl by Ibn al-Ghaḍā'irī (p. 63)

2 Rijāl al-Najāshī (p. 421)

of *Kitāb Sulaym's* unique mention of twelve imams from the descendants of ʿAlī b. Abī Ṭālib.[1]

قال المسعودي في «التنبيه والإشراف»: وفرق الزيدية والقطعية بالإمامة الاثنا عشرية منهم الذين أصلهم في حصر العدد ما ذكره سليم بن قيس الهلالي في كتابه الّذي رواه عنه أبان بن أبى عياش أن النبي صلّى الله عليه وسلّم قال لأمير المؤمنين على بن أبى طالب عليه السلام: أنت واثنا عشر من ولدك أئمة الحق؛ ولم يرو هذا الخبر غير سليم بن قيس.

It is hence evident that earlier manuscripts of the book denoted that the Imāms were thirteen in number, not twelve. It seems, however, that such passages in the book were later theologically appropriated by Twelver scribes and copyists. Hossein Modarressi expounds this specific example saying:

> There is also a reference to twelve (sic) Imāms from among the descendants of ʿAlī who would succeed him (ibid.: 217–18). The relevant passage is inserted in a paragraph that describes how God looked at the people of the earth and selected from among them the Prophet and ʿAlī as his chosen ones. (This follows the statement about the masters of Paradise noted above). The passage then continues by asserting that God then took a second glance (at the earth) and chose, after the Prophet and ʿAlī, twelve legatees of the descendants of the Prophet to be the elect of his community in each generation. The style itself identifies this last line as a later insertion, obviously added after the number of the Imāms was finally determined early in the fourth century. This addition was of course a careless slip as the contributor had failed to note that it would raise the number of the Imāms, when we include ʿAlī himself, to thirteen. Najāshī: 330 reports that a fourth century Shīʾite author, in a book he wrote for a Zaydi patron and in order to please him, used this passage to argue that Zayd b. ʿAlī, the eponym of Zaydi Shiʿism, was also an Imām, adding his name to the list of the Imāmites' twelve Imāms. This was the only report on the number of the Imāms in the version of the Kitāb Sulaym available to the historian Masʿudi in the early fourth century (see his Tanbih: 198–9) However, soon after that when Nuʿmani wrote his Kitāb al-ghayba around 340, there was at least one copy of the Kitāb Sulaym with many further references inserted here and there on the final

1 Al-Tanbīh wa-l-Ishrāf by al-Masʿūdī (198-199)

> number of the Imāms. The sentences were now more carefully drafted to avoid the problems caused by the former passage. These appear in the printed versions of the work too (Kitāb Sulaym: 62, 109, 125, 136, 151, 166, 167, 168, 201, 207). These references made the book a major source for the Imāmites' argument that the Twelfth Imām lived in occultation (see Nu'mani: 101–102).[1]

Tamima Bayhom-Daou analyzed an individual report in the book and concluded that it reflected the early stages of development of the Imāmī doctrine of the imāmate and legal theory. She also stated that the report contained evidence of chronological updating, which may indicate that the report had gone through multiple stages of redaction before assuming its final form in *Kitāb Sulaym*.[2]

Patricia Crone, in her analysis of the 23rd report of Kitāb Sulaym, similarly noted the existence of portions that were later added to the text in various epochs in accord with the needs of each epoch.[3]

An example of a quite obvious falsification in *Kitāb Sulaym*, among many, is in a tradition relayed by al-Kulaynī (d. 329) in *al-Kāfī* and al-Ṣaffār (d. 290) in *Baṣā'ir al-Darajāt* with their their isnāds to Ḥammād b. 'Īsā ⟶ Ibrāhīm b. 'Umar ⟶ Sulaym b. Qays ⟶ 'Alī b. Abī Ṭālib, as can be seen in figure 2.1 below.

1 Tradition and Survival: A Bibliographical Survey of early Shī'ite Literature (1/84-85)

2 Tamima Bayhom-Daou (2015). Kitāb Sulaym Ibn Qays revisited. Bulletin of the School of Oriental and African Studies, 78, pp 118.

3 The Silent Qur'an and the Speaking Qur'an (p. 19)

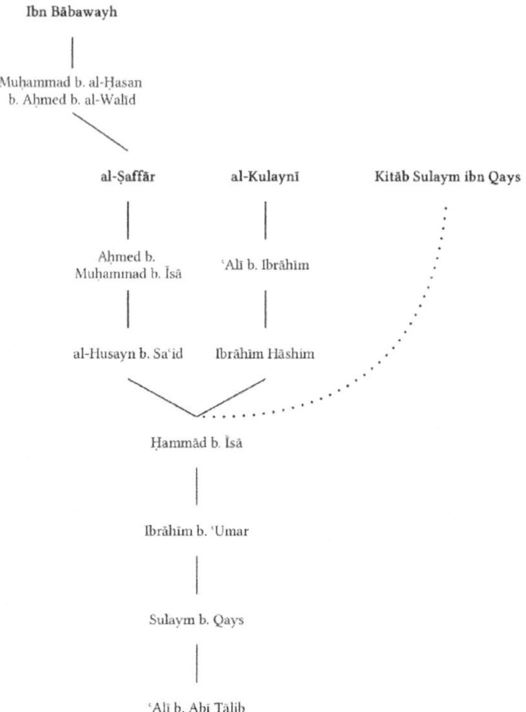

Figure 2.1 A schematic of the isnāds for the tradition at hand

Both al-Ṣaffār (d. 290) and al-Kulaynī (d. 329) quoted ʿAlī b. Abī Ṭālib saying:

> "Allah has purified us and protected us [from sin], and He made us witnesses unto his creation and His proof in His land. He made us with the Quran, and He made the Quran with us: we do not depart from it nor does it depart from us."[1]

حماد بن عيسى، عن ابراهيم بن عمر اليمانى، عن سليم بن قيس الهلالى، عن امير المؤمنين صلوات الله ع قال: ان الله طهرنا وعصمنا وجعلنا شهداء على خلقه وحجته في ارضه وجعلنا مع القران وجعل القران معنا لانفارقه ولايفارقنا.

Interestingly, this passage made its way into *Kitāb Sulaym*, albeit with three significant accretions. In *Kitāb Sulaym*, ʿAlī is quoted saying:

> **I, alongside my legatees after me until the day of Resurrection, are guided guiders who Allah had paired with Himself and His prophet**

1 Baṣāʾir al-Darajāt of al-Ṣaffār (p. 114), al-Kāfī by al-Kulaynī (1/112)

in many verses of the Quran. Allah has purified us and protected us [from sin], and He made us witnesses unto his creation, His proof in His land, **the treasures of His knowledge, the mines of His wisdom, and the interpreters of His revelation**. He made us with the Quran, and He made the Quran with us: we do not depart from it nor does it depart from us **till we meet the Messenger of Allah ﷺ at his pond (*ḥawḍ*) [on the day of Resurrection]**.[1]

قال أبان: قال سليم: سمعت علي بن أبي طالب عليه السلام يقول: [...] **إني أنا وأوصيائي بعدي إلى يوم القيامة هداة مهتدون، الذين قرنهم الله بنفسه ونبيه في آي من الكتاب كثيرة**، وطهرنا وعصمنا وجعلنا شهداء على خلقه وحجته في أرضه **وخزانه على علمه ومعادن حكمه وتراجمة وحيه** وجعلنا مع القرآن والقرآن معنا لا نفارقه ولا يفارقنا **حتى نرد على رسول الله صلى الله عليه وآله حوضه كما قال.**

One hence observes three insertions that have been added to the beginning, middle and ending of the original tradition. This instance is but one example of many falsifications that have taken place in *Kitāb Sulaym Ibn Qays* for various plausible reasons and interests held by the text's later copyist(s) and redactor(s). In this case, it seems as though the final redactor of this passage in *Kitāb Sulaym* desired to increase and exaggerate the praise of ʿAlī and the subsequent Imāms by adding more clauses to the original text. I have further discussed this passage in the upcoming chapter alongside other noteworthy excerpts from the book when attempting to date *Kitāb Sulaym Ibn Qays.*

These examples cumulatively indicate that the integrity of the forged *Kitāb Sulaym* has not been maintained across the centuries. Its contents have been tampered with and appropriated alongside the gradual development of Twelver Shīʿite dogma and hermeneutics. Such findings are concerning, for they entail that the contents of *Kitāb Sulaym* were not authored in unison. Rather, the final rendition of the book today is the byproduct of regulat accretions and modifications that have further obfuscated its origins and kernel text.

1 Kitāb Sulaym Ibn Qays (p. 169)

CHAPTER 3: DATING KITĀB SULAYM

Given *Kitāb Sulaym Ibn Qays'* evident inauthenticity, which is demonstrable in its defective transmission and problematic contents, some questions that can (and should) be asked is: who is the author of the extant text that is found amidst contemporary Twelver Shīʿite circles? What are its origins? The logical possibilities behind its authorship are as follows:

1. It was authored/fabricated by Sulaym b. Qays.
2. It was forged by Abān b. Abī ʿAyyāsh.
3. It was forged by ʿUmar b. Udhayna.
4. It was forged after Ibn Udhayna by one of the downstream transmitters who claimed to transmit the book.

I find the first option highly unlikely, given the past observations pertaining to Sulaym b. Qays. Indeed, there likely was a historical figure by the name of Sulaym b. Qays; however, this figure seems to differ from the Sulaym presented in *Kitāb Sulaym* in multiple regards. Additionally, much of *Kitāb Sulaym's* language is quite flimsy, unsophisticated and quite alien to first century Arabic. Hossein Modarresi described its text saying:

> The book is one written by commoners for commoners. It is a display of primitive, unsophisticated beliefs among the rank and file of the Shī'ites of Kufa during the late Umayyad period with clear residues of the usual Kaysani exaggerations on the virtues of the House of the Prophet.[1]

The historical Sulaym b. Qays, however, is recorded transmitting several eschatological reports, albeit quite mild traditions when compared to the radically more extreme content of *Kitāb Sulaym*. Additionally, Abān's verified transmission from Sulaym, in one instance, presents ʿAlī b. Abī Ṭālib casually addressing ʿUmar as the commander of the faithful (*amīr al-muʾminīn*), a quite noteworthy occurrence when considering *Kitāb Sulaym's* portrayal of ʿUmar and the term's implications in Twelver theology. I find it possible that the predecessor to *Kitāb Sulaym* originally consisted of a few

1 Tradition and Survival: A Bibliographical Survey of early Shī'ite Literature (1/85)

relatively benign traditions relayed by Abān, which were then embellished, expounded, exaggerated and meshed with fabricated accretions by later Shīʿite forgers.

As for the second possibility behind the authorship of *Kitāb Sulaym* which states that it was forged by Abān b. Abī ʿAyyāsh, this is the position that is often adopted by Shīʿite critics of the book and some Sunnī critics. I find this option highly unlikely. Indeed, Abān was an unreliable transmitter whose integrity may even be put to question; however, I am yet to come across any reasonable link between him and most of the book's contents. In fact, I am yet to come across any semblance of data regarding his purported Shīʿite beliefs, despite some contemporary Shīʿite attempts to discredit the criticism he received as an anti-Shīʿite conspiracy. Rather, one finds Abān being praised by numerous Sunnī authorities for his reputed piety, and none make note of any theological deviance espoused on his part. The very same critics of Abān criticized a plethora of contemporaneous Shīʿites for their heretical beliefs, and their silence on Abān's beliefs and their praise of his piety, despite their disparagement of his transmission, should indicate that he was not a Shīʿite, at least not in the extreme sense of the word manifested in *Kitāb Sulaym Ibn Qays.*

Indeed, Abān's reputed unreliability in Sunnī and Shīʿite literature would render *Kitāb Sulaym* inauthentic according both traditions; however, Abān does not seem to have a substantial relationship to most of the book's contents. To reiterate, it is possible that Abān may had originally claimed to transmit a few relatively mild traditions from Sulaym that were later developed and incorporated into this book; however, the unreliability of Abān and the sources that claimed to transmit the book from him, paralleled with the falsification the text clearly had undergone with the progression of time, make it difficult to discern the small kernel of the book relayed by Abān. In this regard, Abān's unreliability is, for the most part, inconsequential to the book's status: much of the book clearly was fabricated after his life, as has been and will continue to be illustrated in this book.

As for the third option, I believe that there are sufficient reasons to believe that ʿUmar b. Udhayna played a significant role in the forgery and/or circulation of some of this book's contents. His reputed exile from Baṣra to Yemen perhaps allowed him to effectively disseminate the text in a distant and alien setting where his relative anonymity would have allowed him to do so without rousing any unwelcomed attention and suspicion. The fact that a small fragment of this book was transmitted independently of *Kitāb*

Sulaym back to Ibn Udhayna via a Yemenī isnād further indicates that the book (or some parts of it) was being disseminated by this figure in Yemen. Additionally, the later ascription of this book to the *muḥaddith* of Yemen, ʿAbdurrazzāq al-Ṣanʿānī, through a variety of dubious isnāds may be a further testimony to the dissemination of this book in Yemen at some point in history. Given that the Baṣran Ibn Udhayna was mentioned in the book's introductory story and that he reportedly was a head Shīʿite figure, alongside the fact that the book was dubiously ascribed to early Baṣran sources, Ibn Udhayna likely played a role in the development and authorship of *Kitāb Sulaym*. What is further noteworthy is that ʿUmar b. Udhayna and Abān b. Abī ʿAyyāsh share a connection to the Baṣran tribe of Banī ʿAbdilqays, which may explain Ibn Udhayna's attribution of this book to none other than the infamous Abān. Furthermore, the renowned ḥadīth critic, Ibn ʿAdī (d. 365), stated that many of the dubious traditions relayed via Abān originated from obscure transmitters who particularly chose to ascribe their dubious traditions to Abān due to his reputed weakness.[1]

قال ابن عدي في «الكامل في ضعفاء الرجال»: [...] وعامة ما أتاني [أتى] أَبَان مِنْ جِهَةِ الرُّوَاةِ لا مِنْ جِهَتِهِ لأَنَّ أَبَان رَوَوْا عنه قوم مجهولين لما أَنَّهُ فِيهِ ضَعْفٌ، وَهو إِلَى الضعف أقرب منه إلى الصدق كما قال شُعْبَة.

Hence, it is apparent that the ascription of the dubious traditions of *Kitāb Sulaym Ibn Qays* to Abān b. Abī ʿAyyāsh is but a manifestation of this phenomenon where unreliable transmitters decided to take advantage of Abān's unreliability by ascribing their traditions to him. In this context, Ibn Udhayna would be one of the many obscure transmitters who engaged in these deceptive practices.

The fourth option, which entails that the book was forged after Ibn Udhayna, is somewhat inevitable, since the book clearly underwent various accretions, developments and falsifications later in history. Hence, it can be said that some of the extant book's contents were incorporated into it after Ibn Udhayna's redaction; however, the extent to which this took place is unclear. In this scenario, the culprit must be one of two men, Ibrāhīm b. ʿUmar al-Yamānī and/or Ḥammād b. ʿĪsā al-Juhanī, for these two figures, alongside Ibn Udhayna, constitute the common link isnād for the book and most fragmented traditions of Sulaym b. Qays in third, fourth and fifth century Twelver primary sources.

---

1 Al-Kāmil fī Ḍuʿafāʾ al-Rijāl (2/67)

Asides from the four aforementioned possibilities behind the authorship of *Kitāb Sulaym*, there is a fifth possibility which I did not mention, which is that *Kitāb Sulaym* (or much of its contents) was forged by an unknown figure who was not listed in the book's isnād. The book then would have been acquired by a downstream transmitter who then decided to falsely back-project it onto Abān or one of the transmitters between Ḥammād b. ʿĪsā and and Abān. Though this option is logically plausible, it is quite difficult to prove, and I believe the available data on the book steers us to a different conclusion.

In the upcoming section, I have dissected multiple relevant passages inside and outside *Kitāb Sulaym Ibn Qays* to further contextualize the past discussion and understand the book's dating and authorship.

Sample Passages

Passage 1

In one report in *Kitāb Sulaym*, an account is mentioned where ʿAlī b. Abī Ṭālib is presented walking alongside the Prophet ﷺ in Medīna. While walking, they both come across a garden, to which ʿAlī expresses his impressment by its beauty. ʿAlī is then promised by the Prophet ﷺ that he shall be granted a better garden in Heaven. After passing seven gardens where ʿAlī similarly expresses his impressment and the Prophet ﷺ promises him even better gardens in Heaven, the Prophet ﷺ then embraces ʿAlī and informs him of the concealed hatred many will display to ʿAlī after the Prophet's ﷺ death.[1]

قال سليم: وحدثني علي بن أبي طالب عليه السلام قال: كنت أمشي مع رسول الله صلى الله عليه وآله في بعض طرق المدينة. فأتينا على حديقة فقلت: يا رسول الله، ما أحسنها من حديقة قال: ما أحسنها ولك في الجنة أحسن منها. ثم أتينا على حديقة أخرى، فقلت: يا رسول الله، ما أحسنها من حديقة قال: ما أحسنها ولك في الجنة أحسن منها. حتى أتينا على سبع حدائق، أقول: يا رسول الله، ما أحسنها ويقول: لك في الجنة أحسن منها. علي عليه السلام الشهيد الوحيد الفريد فلما خلا له الطريق اعتنقني، ثم أجهش باكيا فقال: بأبي الوحيد

1 Kitāb Sulaym Ibn Qays (p. 136)

الشهيد فقلت: يا رسول الله، ما يبكيك؟ فقال: ضغائن في صدور أقوام لا يبدونها لك إلا من بعدي، أحقاد بدر وترات أحد. قلت: في سلامة من ديني؟ قال: في سلامة من دينك.

Interestingly, similar traditions can be found in a few non-Twelver sources, such as Ibn Abī Shayba (d. 217), al-Ṭabarānī (d. 360) and al-Ḥākim (d. 405), and they are all different variants of the same purported event.[1]

قال ابن أبي شيبة في «المصنف» : حَدَّثَنَا أَبُو أُسَامَةَ، قَالَ: حَدَّثَنِي مُحَمَّدُ بْنُ طَلْحَةَ، عَنْ أَبِي عُبَيْدَةَ بْنِ الْحَكَمِ الْأَزْدِيِّ يَرْفَعُ حَدِيثَهُ، أَنّ النَّبِيَّ قَالَ لِعَلِيٍّ, " إِنَّكَ سَتَلْقَى بَعْدِي جَهْدًا "، قَالَ: يَا رَسُولَ اللَّهِ، فِي سَلَامَةٍ مِنْ دِينِي ؟، قَالَ, " نَعَمْ، فِي سَلَامَةٍ مِنْ دِينِكَ. "

وقال الطبراني في «المعجم الكبير»: حَدَّثَنَا الْحَسَنُ بْنُ عَلَوَيْهِ الْقَطَّانُ، ثنا أَحْمَدُ بْنُ مُحَمَّدٍ السُّكَّرِيُّ، ثنا مُوسَى بْنُ أَبِي سُلَيْمٍ الْبَصْرِيُّ، ثنا مِنْدَلٌ، ثنا الأَعْمَشُ، عَنْ مُجَاهِدٍ، عَنِ ابْنِ عَبَّاسٍ رَضِيَ اللَّهُ تَعَالَى عَنْهُمَا، قَالَ: خَرَجْتُ أَنَا وَالنَّبِيُّ وَعَلِيٌّ رَضِيَ اللَّهُ تَعَالَى عَنْهُ، فِي حشانِ الْمَدِينَةِ فَمَرَرْنَا بِحَدِيقَةٍ، فَقَالَ عَلِيٌّ رَضِيَ اللَّهُ تَعَالَى عَنْهُ: مَا أَحْسَنَ هَذِهِ الْحَدِيقَةَ ! يَا رَسُولَ اللَّهِ، فَقَالَ, " حَدِيقَتُكَ فِي الْجَنَّةِ أَحْسَنُ مِنْهَا "، ثُمَّ أَوْمَأَ بِيَدِهِ إِلَى رَأْسِهِ، وَلِحْيَتِهِ ثُمَّ بَكَى حَتَّى عَلا بُكَاؤُهُ، قِيلَ مَا يُبْكِيكَ؟ قَالَ, " ضَغَائِنُ فِي صُدُورِ قَوْمٍ لا يُبْدونها لَكَ حَتَّى يَفْقِدُونِي. "

وقال الحاكم في «المستدرك»: أَخْبَرَنَا أَحْمَدُ بْنُ سَهْلٍ الْفَقِيهُ بِبُخَارَى، ثنا سَهْلُ بْنُ الْمُتَوَكِّلِ، ثنا أَحْمَدُ بْنُ يُونُسَ، ثنا مُحَمَّدُ بْنُ فُضَيْلٍ، عَنْ أَبِي حَيَّانَ التَّيْمِيِّ، عَنْ سَعِيدِ بْنِ جُبَيْرٍ، عَنِ ابْنِ عَبَّاسٍ رَضِيَ اللَّهُ عَنْهُمَا، قَالَ: قَالَ النَّبِيُّ صَلَّى اللَّهُ عَلَيْهِ وَآلِهِ وَسَلَّمَ لِعَلِيٍّ, " أَمَا إِنَّكَ سَتَلْقَى بَعْدِي جَهْدًا ". قَالَ: فِي سَلَامَةٍ مِنْ دِينِي ؟ قَالَ, " فِي سَلَامَةٍ مِنْ دِينِكَ ".

These traditions were relayed through different isnāds, and there hence is understandable and expected variation between them. Asides from these traditions, one comes across another variant of this ḥadīth that is much more similar to *Kitāb Sulaym's* account. It can be found relayed by al-Ājurrī (d. 275), al-Bazzār (d. 292) and al-Khaṭīb al-Baghdādī (d. 463) etc.[2]

قال البزار في مسنده: حَدَّثَنَا عَمْرُو بْنُ عَلِيٍّ، وَمُحَمَّدُ بْنُ مَعْمَرٍ، قَالا: نا حِرْمِيُّ بْنُ عُمَارَةَ بْنِ أَبِي حَفْصَةَ، قَالَ: نا الْفَضْلُ بْنُ عَمِيرَةَ، قَالَ: حَدَّثَنِي مَيْمُونُ الْكُرْدِيُّ، عَنْ أَبِي عُثْمَانَ النَّهْدِيِّ، عَنْ عَلِيٍّ، قَالَ: كُنْتُ أَمْشِي مَعَ رَسُولِ

1 Muṣannaf Ibn Abī Shayba (17/127), al-Muʿjam al-Kabīr by al-Ṭabarānī (11/73), al-Mustadrak ʿalā al-Ṣaḥīḥayn by al-Ḥākim (3/151)

2 Musnad al-Bazzār (2/293), al-Sharīʿa by al-Ājurrī (4/2086), Tārīkh Baghdād (14/384)

اللهِ وَهُوَ آخِذٌ بِيَدِي، فَمَرَرْنَا بِحَدِيقَةٍ، فَقُلْتُ: يَا رَسُولَ اللهِ، مَا أَحْسَنَهَا مِنْ حَدِيقَةٍ، فقالَ, "لَكَ فِي الْجَنَّةِ أَحْسَنُ مِنْهَا " ثُمَّ مَرَرْنَا بِأُخْرَى، فَقُلْتُ: يَا رَسُولَ اللهِ مَا أَحْسَنَهَا مِنْ حَدِيقَةٍ، قَالَ, "لَكَ فِي الْجَنَّةِ أَحْسَنُ مِنْهَا " حَتَّى مَرَرْنَا بِسَبْعِ حَدَائِقَ، كُلُّ ذَلِكَ أَقُولُ مَا أَحْسَنَهَا، وَهُوَ يَقُولُ, "لَكَ فِي الْجَنَّةِ أَحْسَنُ مِنْهَا " فَلَمَّا خَلا لَهُ الطَّرِيقُ اعْتَنَقَنِي، ثُمَّ أَجْهَشَ بَاكِيًا، فَقُلْتُ: يَا رَسُولَ اللهِ مَا يُبْكِيكَ؟ قَالَ, "ضَغَائِنُ فِي صُدُورِ قَوْمٍ لا يُبْدُونَهَا لَكَ إِلا مِنْ بَعْدِي "، قُلْتُ: فِي سَلامَةٍ مِنْ دِينِي ؟ قَالَ, "فِي سَلامَةٍ مِنْ دِينِكَ. "

وقال الآجري في «الشريعة»: حَدَّثَنَا أَبُو بَكْرِ بْنُ أَبِي دَاوُدَ، قَالَ: حَدَّثَنَا إِسْحَاقُ بْنُ مَنْصُورٍ الْكَوْسَجُ، قَالَ: أَنْبَأَنَا حَرَمِيُّ بْنُ عُمَارَةَ بْنِ أَبِي حَفْصٍ، عَنِ الْفَضْلِ بْنِ عَمِيرَةَ الطُّفَاوِيُّ، قَالَ: حَدَّثَنِي مَيْمُونٌ الْكُرْدِيُّ، قَالَ: حَدَّثَنَا أَبُو عُثْمَانَ النَّهْدِيُّ، قَالَ: قَالَ عَلِيٌّ رَضِيَ اللَّهُ عَنْهُ: بَيْنَا رَسُولُ اللَّهِ آخِذٌ بِيَدِي وَنَحْنُ نَمْشِي فِي سِكَكِ الْمَدِينَةِ، إِذْ مَرَرْنَا بِحَدِيقَةٍ، فَقُلْتُ: يَا رَسُولَ اللَّهِ، مَا أَحْسَنَهَا، فَقَالَ, "إِنَّ لَكَ فِي الْجَنَّةِ أَحْسَنَ مِنْهَا " ثُمَّ مَرَرْنَا بِأُخْرَى فَقُلْتُ: يَا رَسُولَ اللَّهِ، مَا أَحْسَنَهَا فَقَالَ, "إِنَّ لَكَ فِي الْجَنَّةِ أَحْسَنَ مِنْهَا " حَتَّى مَرَرْنَا بِتِسْعِ حَدَائِقَ، كُلُّهَا أَقُولُ: يَا رَسُولَ اللَّهِ مَا أَحْسَنَهَا، فَيَقُولُ, "إِنَّ لَكَ فِي الْجَنَّةِ أَحْسَنَ مِنْهَا. "

وقال الخطيب في «تاريخ بغداد»: أَخْبَرَنَا الْحَسَنُ بْنُ أَبِي بَكْرٍ، قَالَ: أَخْبَرَنَا عَبْدُ اللَّهِ بْنُ إِسْحَاقَ بْنِ إِبْرَاهِيمَ الْبَغَوِيُّ، قَالَ: حَدَّثَنَا عَبْدُ اللَّهِ بْنُ أَحْمَدَ بْنِ كَثِيرٍ الدَّوْرَقِيُّ أَبُو الْعَبَّاسِ، وَأَحْمَدُ بْنُ زُهَيْرٍ، قَالا: حَدَّثَنَا الْفَيْضُ بْنُ وَثِيقِ بْنِ يُوسُفَ بْنِ عَبْدِ اللَّهِ بْنِ عُثْمَانَ بْنِ أَبِي الْعَاصِ، قَالَ: أَحْمَدُ بْنُ زُهَيْرٍ قَدِمَ عَلَيْنَا سَنَةَ أَرْبَعٍ وَعِشْرِينَ وَمِائَتَيْنِ، قَالَ: حَدَّثَنَا الْفَضْلُ بْنُ عُمَيْرَةَ، قَالَ: حَدَّثَنِي مَيْمُونُ الْكُرْدِيُّ مَوْلَى عَبْدِ اللَّهِ بْنِ عَامِرٍ أَبُو نُصَيْرٍ، عَنْ أَبِي عُثْمَانَ النَّهْدِيِّ، عَنْ عَلِيِّ بْنِ أَبِي طَالِبٍ، قَالَ: مَرَرْتُ مَعَ رَسُولِ اللَّهِ بِحَدِيقَةٍ، فَقُلْتُ: يَا رَسُولَ اللَّهِ، مَا أَحْسَنَهَا، قَالَ, "لَكَ فِي الْجَنَّةِ خَيْرٌ مِنْهَا " حَتَّى مَرَرْتُ بِسَبْعِ حَدَائِقَ، وَقَالَ أَحْمَدُ بْنُ زُهَيْرٍ: بِتِسْعِ حَدَائِقَ، كُلُّ ذَلِكَ أَقُولُ لَهُ، وَيَقُولُ, "لَكَ فِي الْجَنَّةِ خَيْرٌ مِنْهَا "، قَالَ: ثُمَّ جَذَبَنِي رَسُولُ اللَّهِ وَبَكَى، فَقُلْتُ: يَا رَسُولَ اللَّهِ، مَا يُبْكِيكَ، قَالَ, "ضَغَائِنُ فِي صُدُورِ رِجَالٍ عَلَيْكَ لَنْ يُبْدُوهَا لَكَ إِلا مِنْ بَعْدِي "، فَقُلْتُ: بِسَلامَةٍ مِنْ دِينِي، قَالَ, "نَعَمْ، بِسَلامَةٍ مِنْ دِينِكَ. "

When compared to the past variants of the ḥadīth, this cluster of traditions clearly is more closely related to the variant in *Kitāb Sulaym*, and they are all relayed via al-Faḍl b. ʿUmayra ⟶ Maymūn al-Kurdī ⟶ Abū ʿUthmān al-Nahdī ⟶ ʿAlī. It is hence evident that the aforementioned excerpt from *Kitāb Sulaym* is related to this variant of the tradition.

A more careful review of this tradition's variants will additionally reveal a quite damning finding: the variant relayed by ʿAbdullāh b. Aḥmed b.

Ḥanbal (d. 290) in *Faḍā'il al-Ṣaḥāba* is almost identical to the tradition in *Kitāb Sulaym Ibn Qays.*[1]

قال عبد الله بن أحمد في «فضائل الصحابة»: قثنا عُبَيْدُ اللَّهِ بْنُ عُمَرَ، نا حَرَمِيُّ بْنُ عُمَارَةَ، نا الْفَضْلُ بْنُ عَمِيرَةَ أَبُو قُتَيْبَةَ الْقَيْسِيُّ، قَالَ: حَدَّثَنِي مَيْمُونٌ الْكُرْدِيُّ أَبُو نُصَيْرٍ، عَنْ أَبِي عُثْمَانَ النَّهْدِيِّ، عَنْ عَلِيِّ بْنِ أَبِي طَالِبٍ عَلَيْهِ السَّلامُ، قَالَ: كُنْتُ أَمْشِي مَعَ النَّبِيِّ فِي بَعْضِ طُرُقِ الْمَدِينَةِ، فَأَتَيْنَا عَلَى حَدِيقَةٍ، فَقُلْتُ: يَا رَسُولَ اللَّهِ، مَا أَحْسَنَ هَذِهِ الْحَدِيقَةَ؟ فَقَالَ, " مَا أَحْسَنَهَا؟ وَلَكَ فِي الْجَنَّةِ أَحْسَنُ مِنْهَا "، ثُمَّ أَتَيْنَا عَلَى حَدِيقَةٍ أُخْرَى، فَقُلْتُ: يَا رَسُولَ اللَّهِ، مَا أَحْسَنَهَا مِنْ حَدِيقَةٍ، فَقَالَ, " لَكَ فِي الْجَنَّةِ أَحْسَنُ مِنْهَا "، حَتَّى أَتَيْنَا عَلَى سَبْعِ حَدَائِقَ، أَقُولُ: يَا رَسُولَ اللَّهِ، مَا أَحْسَنَهَا؟ وَيَقُولُ, " لَكَ فِي الْجَنَّةِ أَحْسَنُ مِنْهَا. "

Up till the point where ʿAbdullāh's tradition ends, the report in *Kitāb Sulaym* almost matches it word-for-word. After that, the passage from *Kitāb Sulaym b. Qays* incorporates the ending from Abū Yaʿlā''s (d. 307) variant of this tradition in his *Musnad* with one accretion.[2]

قال أبو يعلى في مسنده: حَدَّثَنَا عَمْرُو بْنُ عَلِيٍّ، وَمُحَمَّدُ بْنُ مَعْمَرٍ، قَالا: نا حِرْمِيُّ بْنُ عُمَارَةَ بْنِ أَبِي حَفْصَةَ، قَالَ: نا الْفَضْلُ بْنُ عَمِيرَةَ، قَالَ: حَدَّثَنِي مَيْمُونُ الْكُرْدِيُّ، عَنْ أَبِي عُثْمَانَ النَّهْدِيِّ، عَنْ عَلِيٍّ، قَالَ: كُنْتُ أَمْشِي مَعَ رَسُولِ اللَّهِ وَهُوَ آخِذٌ بِيَدِي، فَمَرَرْنَا بِحَدِيقَةٍ، فَقُلْتُ: يَا رَسُولَ اللَّهِ، مَا أَحْسَنَهَا مِنْ حَدِيقَةٍ، فقَالَ, " لَكَ فِي الْجَنَّةِ أَحْسَنُ مِنْهَا " ثُمَّ مَرَرْنَا بِأُخْرَى، فَقُلْتُ: يَا رَسُولَ اللَّهِ مَا أَحْسَنَهَا مِنْ حَدِيقَةٍ، قَالَ, " لَكَ فِي الْجَنَّةِ أَحْسَنُ مِنْهَا " حَتَّى مَرَرْنَا بِسَبْعِ حَدَائِقَ، كُلُّ ذَلِكَ أَقُولُ مَا أَحْسَنَهَا، وَهُوَ يَقُولُ, " لَكَ فِي الْجَنَّةِ أَحْسَنُ مِنْهَا " فَلَمَّا خَلا لَهُ الطَّرِيقُ اعْتَنَقَنِي، ثُمَّ أَجْهَشَ بَاكِيًا، فَقُلْتُ: يَا رَسُولَ اللَّهِ مَا يُبْكِيكَ؟ قَالَ, " ضَغَائِنُ فِي صُدُورِ قَوْمٍ لا يُبْدُونَهَا لَكَ إِلا مِنْ بَعْدِي "، قُلْتُ: فِي سَلامَةٍ مِنْ دِينِي؟ قَالَ, " فِي سَلامَةٍ مِنْ دِينِكَ. "

To clarify and demonstrate the striking and uncoincidental similarities between both texts, I have fragmented the three traditions sentence-by-sentence and juxtaposed them to each other in Table 3.1 bellow.

1 Faḍā'il al-Ṣaḥāba of Aḥmed b. Ḥanbal (2/651)
2 Musnad Abī Yaʿlā al-Mawṣilī (1/426)

Kitāb Sulaym Ibn Qays	ʿAbdullāh b. Aḥmed's Tradition	Abū Yaʿlā al-Mawṣilī's Tradition
علي بن أبي طالب عليه السلام قال: كنت أمشي مع رسول الله صلى الله عليه وآله في بعض طرق المدينة،	علي بن أبي طالب عليه السلام قال: كنت أمشي مع النبي صلى الله عليه وسلم في بعض طرق المدينة،	علي بن أبي طالب، قال: بينما رسول الله آخذ بيدي، ونحن نمشي في بعض سكك المدينة،
فأتينا على حديقة فقلت: يا رسول الله، ما أحسنها من حديقة.	فأتينا على حديقة فقلت: يا رسول الله، ما أحسن هذه الحديقة.	إذ أتينا على حديقة، فقلت: يا رسول الله ما أحسنها من حديقة.
قال: ما أحسنها ولك في الجنة أحسن منها،	فقال: ما أحسنها ولك في الجنة أحسن منها،	قال: لك في الجنة أحسن منها،
ثم أتينا على حديقة أخرى، فقلت: يا رسول الله، ما أحسنها من حديقة، قال: ما أحسنها ولك في الجنة أحسن منها.	ثم أتينا على حديقة أخرى، فقلت: يا رسول الله، ما أحسنها من حديقة، فقال: لك في الجنة أحسن منها،	ثم مررنا بأخرى، فقلت: يا رسول الله ما أحسنها من حديقة، قال: لك في الجنة أحسن منها.
حتى أتينا على سبع حدائق، أقول: يا رسول الله، ما أحسنها ويقول: لك في الجنة أحسن منها.	حتى أتينا على سبع حدائق، أقول: يا رسول الله، ما أحسنها ويقول: لك في الجنة أحسن منها.	حتى مررنا بسبع حدائق، كل ذلك أقول ما أحسنها ويقول: لك في الجنة أحسن منها.
فلما خلا له الطريق اعتنقني، ثم أجهش باكيا فقال: **بأبي الوحيد الشهيد.**	-	فلما خلا له الطريق اعتنقني ثم أجهش باكيا،
فقلت: يا رسول الله، ما يبكيك؟ فقال: ضغائن في صدور أقوام لا يبدونها لك إلا	-	قال: قلت: يا رسول الله ما يبكيك؟ قال: ضغائن في

من بعدي، **أحقاد بدر وترات أحد.**		صدور أقوام لا يبدونها لك إلا من بعدي.
قلت: في سلامة من ديني؟ قال: في سلامة من دينك.	-	قال: قلت: يا رسول الله في سلامة من ديني؟، قال: في سلامة من دينك.

Table 3.1 A juxtaposition of ʿAbdullāh b. Aḥmed and Abū Yaʿla's tradition alongside the tradition of *Kitāb Sulaym Ibn Qays*. Barring two accretions in Sulaym's tradition, their similarities are striking.

In table 3.1, we see that Sulaym's account, barring two accretions, is nearly identical to the first portion of ʿAbdullāh b. Aḥmed's variant and the last portion of Abū Yaʿlā's variant. The final portion of Sulaym's account, which is parallel to that of Abū Yaʿlā, embodies two accretions: (1) a clause where the Prophet ﷺ tells ʿAlī, "بأبي الوحيد الشهيد" and (2) a clause where the Prophet ﷺ further described the grudges against ʿAlī as the Pagan grudges from Badr and Uḥud.

As for the first accretion, it should not come as a surprise, at this point, that an identical clause is relayed in a different ḥadīth in none else than Abū Yaʿlā's *Musnad*![1]

قال أبو يعلى في مسنده: حدثنا سويد بن سعيد، حدثنا محمد بن عبد الرحيم بن شروس الحلبي، عن ابن ميناء، عن أبيه، عن عائشة قالت: رأيت النبي صلى الله عليه وسلم " التزم عليا وقبله ويقول, "بأبي الوحيد الشهيد! بأبي الوحيد الشهيد! "

Yes, this clause can also be found in the *Amālī* of the Twelver scholar, al-Mufīd (d. 413), relayed through Abū Yaʿlā's source. His redaction, however, unlike that of Abū Yaʿlā (and *Kitāb Sulaym Ibn Qays*) adds a different story and context to the Prophet's ﷺ purported statement.[2]

قال المفيد في أماليه: أخبرني الشريف أبو عبد الله محمد بن الحسن الجواني، قال: أخبرني المظفر بن جعفر العلوي العمري، قال: حدثنا جعفر بن محمد بن مسعود، عن أبيه، عن محمد بن حاتم، قال: حدثنا سويد بن سعيد، قال: حدثني محمد بن عبد الرحيم اليماني، عن ابن ميناء، عن أبيه، عن عائشة قالت: جاء علي بن أبي طالب ع

1 Musnad Abī Yaʿlā al-Mawṣilī (8/55)
2 Amālī al-Mufīd (p. 69)

يستأذن على النبي ص فلم يأذن له، فاستأذن دفعة أخرى فقال النبي ص: ادخل يا علي، فلما دخل قام إليه رسول الله ص فاعتنقه و قبل بين عينيه و قال: بأبي الشهيد بأبي الوحيد الشهيد!

As for the second accretion in *Kitāb Sulaym's* tradition where the Prophet ﷺ is quoted describing the grudges against ʿAlī as the Pagan grudges from the battles of Badr and Uḥud, it is a Rāfiḍite sentiment that was incorporated into the report by a later redactor (forger) of the book.

Hence, it becomes rather clear that the author of this passage in *Kitāb Sulaym* likely drew material from the *Musnad* of Abū Yaʿlā, ʿAbdullāh b. Aḥmed's tradition in *Faḍāʾil al-Ṣaḥāba*, some secondary source that aggregated both redactions of the tradition, or a related source that relayed the tradition via the same isnād as Abū Yaʿlā and ʿAbdullāh b. Aḥmed. It is noteworthy how these sources, which were seemingly utilized by the author of this passage from *Kitāb Sulaym*, were authored by contemporaneous figures from the late third century, and this may further shed some light on this passage's true author. Additionally, one can appreciate the striking similarities between these accounts by comparing them to the other aforementioned variants of the ḥadīth that differ from each other and the account in *Kitāb Sulaym*, as one would expect with different redactions of a tradition relayed via different sources. All in all, this passage in *Kitāb Sulaym* was incorporated into the book during or after the fourth century, and what further exemplifies this fact is that none of the third, fourth and fifth century Twelver collections that referenced fragments from *Kitāb Sulaym* relayed this tradition via Sulaym b Qays. In fact, this entire tradition about ʿAlī is quite obscure in Twelver sources, and it is more readily recorded in Sunnī literature.

Passage 2

In the two Twelver ḥadīth collections, *al-Kāfī* of al-Kulaynī (d. 329) and *Baṣāʾir al-Darajāt* of al-Ṣaffār (d. 290), is a tradition that is ascribed to Sulaym b. Qays with the isnād(s) presented in figure 3.1.

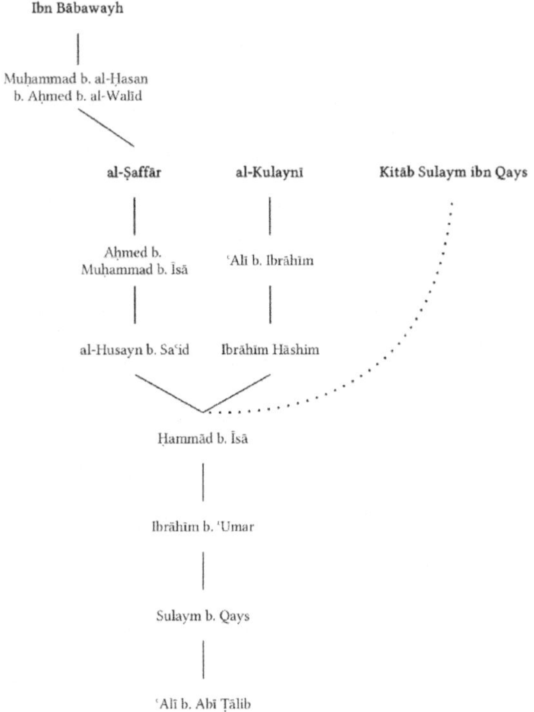

Figure 3.1 A schematic of the isnāds for the tradition at hand

Both reports are nearly identical in their wording, which may indicate their sound attribution to Ḥammād b. ʿĪsā, the pivotal transmitter of *Kitāb Sulaym*. They quote ʿAlī saying:

> Allah has purified us and protected us [from sin], and He made us witnesses unto his creation and His proof in His land. He made us with the Quran, and He made the Quran with us: we do not depart from it nor does it depart from us.[1]

1 Baṣāʾir al-Darajāt (p. 114), al-Kāfī by al-Kulaynī (1/112). Ibn Bābawayh

حماد بن عيسى، عن ابراهيم بن عمر اليماني، عن سليم بن قيس الهلالي، عن امير المؤمنين صلوات الله ع قال: ان الله طهرنا وعصمنا وجعلنا شهداء على خلقه وحجته في ارضه وجعلنا مع القران وجعل القران معنا لانفارقه ولايفارقنا.

This passage made its way into *Kitāb Sulaym*, albeit with three significant accretions in the beginning, middle and end added to the report. In *Kitāb Sulaym*, ʿAlī is quoted saying:

> **I, alongside my legatees after me until the day of Resurrection, are guided guiders who Allah had paired with Himself and His prophet in many verses of the Quran.** Allah has purified us and protected us [from sin], and He made us witnesses unto his creation, His proof in His land, **the treasures of His knowledge, the mines of His wisdom, and the interpreters of His revelation**. He made us with the Quran, and He made the Quran with us: we do not depart from it nor does it depart from us **till we meet the Messenger of Allah ﷺ at his pond (*ḥawḍ*) [on the day of Resurrection]**.[1]

قال أبان: قال سليم: سمعت علي بن أبي طالب عليه السلام يقول: [...] **إني أنا وأوصيائي بعدي إلى يوم القيامة هداة مهتدون، الذين قرنهم الله بنفسه ونبيه في آي من الكتاب كثيرة**، وطهرنا وعصمنا وجعلنا شهداء على خلقه وحجته في أرضه **وخزانه على علمه ومعادن حكمه وتراجمة وحيه** وجعلنا مع القرآن والقرآن معنا لا نفارقه ولا يفارقنا **حتى نرد على رسول الله صلى الله عليه وآله حوضه كما قال.**

This text can also be found in *Kitāb Sulaym*, is indicative that this tradition is perhaps from the kernel traditions of *Kitāb Sulaym*. The text in *Kitāb Sulaym*, however, embodies clear accretions and embellishments, which is evidence that the text was tampered with after Ḥammād b. ʿĪsā (d. 208), and perhaps after al-Kulaynī (d. 329) and al-Ṣaffār (d. 290) as well.

---

also relayed this tradition via al-Ṣaffār in Kamāl al-Dīn wa-Tamām al-Niʿma (p. 230).

1 Kitāb Sulaym Ibn Qays (p. 169)

Al-Kulaynī (d. 329)	Al-Ṣaffār (d. 290)	Kitāb Sulaym Ibn Qays
–	–	**إني أنا وأوصيائي بعدي إلى يوم القيامة هداة مهتدون ، الذين قرنهم الله بنفسه ونبيه في آي من الكتاب كثيرة**
إن الله تبارك وتعالى طهرنا وعصمنا وجعلنا شهداء على خلقه، وحجته في أرضه	ان الله طهرنا وعصمنا وجعلنا شهداء على خلقه وحجته في ارضه	وطهرنا وعصمنا وجعلنا شهداء على خلقه وحجته في أرضه
–	–	**وخزانه على علمه ومعادن حكمه وتراجمة وحيه**
و جعلنا مع القرآن وجعل القران معنا، لا نفارقه ولا يفارقنا.	وجعلنا مع القران وجعل القران معنا، لا نفارقه ولايفارقنا.	وجعلنا مع القرآن والقرآن معنا، لا نفارقه ولا يفارقنا
–	–	**حتى نرد على رسول الله صلى الله عليه وآله حوضه**

Table 3.2 A juxtaposition of al-Kulaynī and al-Ṣaffār's traditions alongside the tradition of *Kitāb Sulaym Ibn Qays*, demonstrating the accretions that have been incorporated into the report in *Kitāb Sulaym*.

As seen in table 3.2, the reports of al-Kulaynī and al-Ṣaffār formulate the core of the tradition that can be found *Kitāb Sulaym*. However, the text in *Kitāb Sulaym* embodies three significant accretions. The first accretion is the clause where ʿAlī is quoted saying, "I, alongside my legatees after me until the day of Resurrection, are guided guiders who Allah had paired with Himself and His prophet in many verses of the Quran." The second accretion is the clause where ʿAlī is quoted saying, "[and we are] the treasures of His knowledge and the mines of His wisdom, and the interpreter of His revelation." The third accretion is the final clause where it is further added that the Quran shall not depart from the legatees till the day of Resurrection when they meet the Messenger of Allah ﷺ.

These accretions effectively embellish the tradition cited by al-Kulaynī and al-Ṣaffār, and they generally tend to add and expound the praise of *Ahlulbayt*. The core of this text relayed by al-Ṣaffār and al-Kulaynī may be dated to Ḥammād b. ʿĪsā's era in the late second and early third century while the accretions in *Kitāb Sulaym* clearly were incorporated into the text later in time. This example further demonstrates that the extant recension of *Kitāb Sulaym* experienced developments and redactions after the third century.

Passage 3

The third passage in question today is a long and extensive tradition relayed by al-Kulaynī (d. 329) in *al-Kāfī* through Sulaym b. Qays. What is noteworthy about this tradition, however, is that is has no mention in *Kitāb Sulaym* today. [1]

قال الكليني في «الكافي»: علي بن إبراهيم، عن أبيه، عن حماد بن عيسى، عن إبراهيم بن عمر اليماني، عن عمربن اذينة، عن أبان بن أبي عياش، عن سليم بن قيس الهلالي، عن أميرالمؤمنين صلوات الله عليه قال: بني الكفر على أربع دعائم: الفسق والغلو، والشك، والشبهة.

والفسق على أربع شعب: على الجفاء والعمى، والغفلة، والعتو، فمن جفا احتقر الحق، ومقت الفقهاء، وأصر على الحنث.

العظيم، ومن عمي نسي الذكر، واتبع الظن، وبارزخالقه، وألح عليه الشيطان، وطلب المغفرة بلا توبة ولا استكانة ولا غفلة ; ومن غفل جنى على نفسه; وانقلب على ظهره وحسب غيه رشدا ; وغرته الاماني ; وأخذته الحسرة والندامة إذا قضي الامر وانكشف عنه الغطاء وبداله ما لم يكن يحتسب ومن عتا عن أمرالله شك ومن شك تعالى الله عليه فأذله بسلطانه وصغره بجلاله كما اغتر بربه الكريم وفرط في أمره والغلو على أربع شعب: على التعمق بالرأي، والتنازع فيه، والزيغ، و الشقاق، فمن تعمق لم ينب إلى الحق ولم يزدد إلا غرقا في الغمرات ولم تنحسر عنه فتنة إلا غشيته اخرى، وانخرق دينه فهو يهوى في أمر مريج، ومن نازع في الرأي وخاصم شهر بالعثل من طول اللجاج، ومن زاغ قبحت عنده الحسنة و حسنت عند السيئة ومن شاق أعورت عليه طرقه واعترض عليه أمره، فضاق عليه مخرجه إذا لم يتبع سبيل المؤمنين.

1 Al-Kāfī by al-Kulaynī (2/220-221)

والشك على أربع شعب: على المرية، والهوى، والتردد، والاستسلام وهو قول الله عزوجل: فبأي آلاء ربك تتمارى"

وفي رواية اخرى: على المرية، والهول من الحق، والتردد، والاستسلام للجهل وأهله.

فمن هاله ما بين يديه نكص على عقبيه، ومن امترى في الدين تردد في الريب، وسبقه الاولون من المؤمنين، وأدركه الآخرون، ووطئته سنابك الشيطان، ومن استسلم لهلكة الدنيا والآخرة هلك فيما بينهما، ومن نجا من ذلك فمن فضل اليقين، ولم يخلق الله خلقا أقل من اليقين.

والشبهة على أربع شعب: إعجاب بالزينة، وتسويل النفس، وتأول العوج ولبس الحق بالباطل، وذلك بأن الزينة تصدف عن البينة وأن تسويل النفس تفحم على الشهوة، وأن العوج يميل بصاحبه ميلا عظيما، وأن اللبس ظلمات بعضها فوق بعض فذلك الكفر ودعائمه وشعبه. قال: والنفاق على أربع دعائم: على الهوى، والهوينا، والحفيظة، والطمع.

فالهوى على أربع شعب: على البغي، والعدوان، والشهوة، والطغيان، فمن بغى كثرت غوائله وتخلى منه وقصر عليه ومن اعتدى لم يؤمن بوائقه ولم يسلم قلبه ولم يملك نفسه عن الشهوات ومن لم يعدل نفسه في الشهوات خاض في الخبيثات ومن طغى ضل على عمد بلا حجة.

والهوينا على أربع شعب: على الغرة، والامل، والهيبة، والمماطلة، وذلك بأن الهيبة ترد عن الحق، والمطاطلة تفرط في العمل حتى يقدم عليه الاجل، ولولا الامل علم الانسان حسب ماهو فيه ولو علم حسب ماهو فيه مات خفاتا من الهول والوجل، والغرة تقصر بالمرء عن العمل.

والحفيظة على أربع شعب: على الكبر والفخر والحمية والعصبية، فمن استكبر أدبر عن الحق ومن فخر فجر ومن حمى أصر على الذنوب ومن أخذته العصبية جار، فبئس الامر أمر بين إدبار وفجور وإصرار وجور على الصراط والطمع على أربع شعب: الفرح، والمرح، واللجاجة، والتكاثر، فالفرح مكروه عند الله، والمرح خيلاء، واللجاجة بلاء لمن اضطرته إلى حمل الآثام، والتكاثر لهو ولعب وشغل واستبدال الذي هو أدنى بالذي هو خير.

فذلك النفاق ودعائمه وشعبه.

والله قاهر فوق عباده تعالى ذكره وجل وجهه وأحسن كل شئ خلقه وانبسطت يداه ووسعت كل شئ رحمته وظهر أمره وأشرق نوره وفاضت بركته واستضاء ت حكمته وهيمن كتابه وفلجت حجته وخلص دينه واستظهر سلطانه وحقت كلمته وأقسطت موازينه وبلغت رسله، فجعل السيئة ذنبا والذنب فتنة والفتنة دنسا وجعل الحسنى عتبى والعتبى توبة والتوبة طهورا، فمن تاب اهتدى، ومن افتتن غوى، ما لم يتب إلى الله ويعترف بذنبه ولا يهلك على الله إلا هالك.

Despite the absence of this tradition from *Kitāb Sulaym Ibn Qays*, it mirrors a tradition in *Kitāb Sulaym* where ʿAlī is quoted speaking about four pillars of *īmān*.[1]

The fact that some references to Sulaym in Twelver sources can be found in the extant *Kitāb Sulaym* while others are totally absent from the book should be indicative that third/fourth century Twelver traditionists, when referencing traditions via Sulaym b. Qays, were not necessarily referencing the text we possess today. Rather, it seems that they were quoting a kernel of traditions that also functioned as source material for the extant recension of the book. This conclusion complements the past observation on how certain traditions in early Twelver sources were later plagued with accretions and modifications once redacted into the extant recension of *Kitāb Sulaym Ibn Qays.*

1 Kitāb Sulaym Ibn Qays (p. 176)

Passage 4

Some Twelver and Zaydī sources transmit a report via Sulaym b. Qays, and their isnāds are as follows:

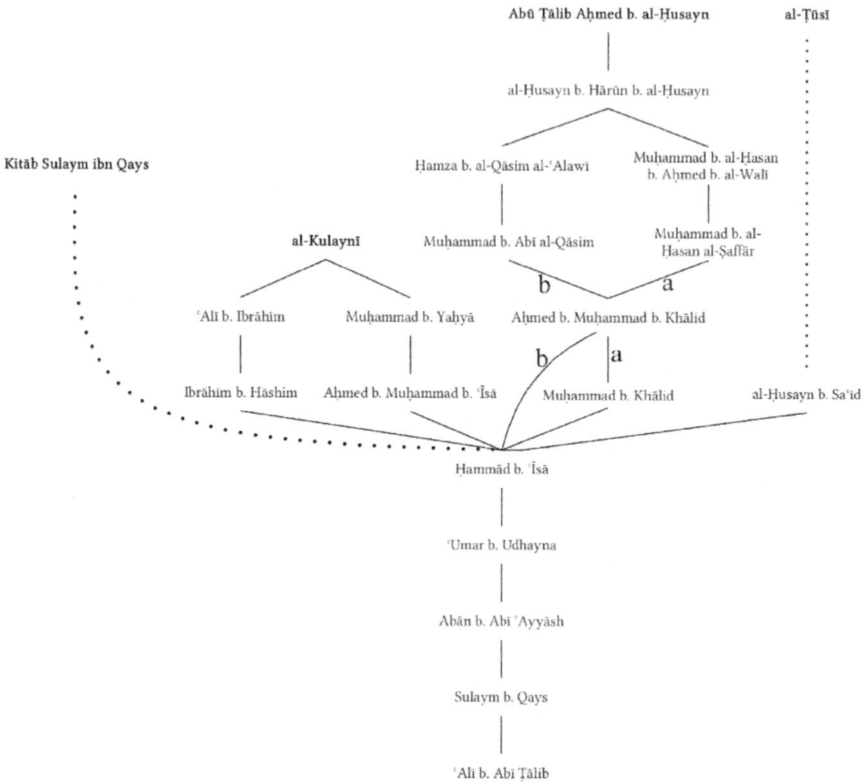

Figure 3.2 A schematic of the isnāds for the tradition at hand

These sources quote ʿAlī b. Abī Ṭālib relaying from the Messenger of Allah ﷺ that he said:

> There are two pursuers who are never satisfied: a pursuer of *Dunyā* and a pursuer of knowledge. Whosoever constrains himself to what Allah had deemed permissible from the *Dunyā*, then he shall be safe. Whosoever takes from what is impermissible from it, then he shall perish, unless he is to repent and return. Whosoever takes knowledge from its people and acts upon his knowledge, then he

> shall be saved. Whosoever pursues it for the *Dunyā*, then that shall be his attainment [from his knowledge.][1]

حماد بن عيسى، عن عمر بن اذينة، عن أبان بن أبي عياش، عن سليم بن قيس قال: سمعت أمير المؤمنين عليه السلام يقول: قال رسول الله صلى الله عليه وآله, "منهومان لا يشبعان طالب دنيا وطالب علم، فمن اقتصر من الدنيا على ما أحل الله له سلم، ومن تناولها من غير حلها هلك، إلا أن يتوب أو يراجع، ومن أخذ العلم من اهله وعمل بعلمه نجا، ومن أراد به الدنيا فهي حظه." اللفظ لفظ الكليني.

This tradition can be found in the extant recension of *Kitāb Sulaym Ibn Qays*.[2] In it, Sulaym is quoted saying:

قال سليم بن قيس: سمعت أبا الحسن عليه السلام يحدثني ويقول: إن النبي صلى الله عليه وآله قال:منهومان لا يشبعان: منهوم في الدنيا لا يشبع منها، ومنهوم في العلم لا يشبع منه. فمن اقتصر من الدنيا على ما أحل الله له سلم، ومن تناولها من غير حلها هلك إلا أن يتوب ويراجع. ومن أخذ العلم من أهله وعمل به نجا، ومن أراد به الدنيا هلك وهو حظه.

I believe this is one of the few texts in *Kitāb Sulaym* that can be traced to the kernel of traditions relayed by Ḥammād b. ʿĪsā (d. 208), which formed the early recension of *Kitāb Sulaym Ibn Qays* that predated the later recensions of the book and their accretions.

Passage 5

One of the few and very interesting texts that can be traced back to Abān b. Abī ʿAyyāsh, which he claimed to relay from Sulaym b. Qays, is a tradition found in the *Jāmiʿ* of the renowned Sunnī traditionist, Maʿmar b. Rāshid (d. 154). What is noteworthy in this tradition, however, is that it had undergone significant changes and developments before being eventually incorporated into *Kitāb Sulaym Ibn Qays*.

Maʿmar b. Rāshid narrated on the authority of Abān, from Sulaym b. Qays al-Ḥanẓalī that he said:

> ʿUmar once gave a sermon and he said, "The thing I fear the most for you after me is that an innocent man is taken and sawn just as

1 Al-Kāfī by al-Kulaynī (1/26), Taysīr al-Maṭālib fī Amālī Abī Ṭālib (p. 205-206, 223-224), Tahdhīb al-Aḥkām by al-Ṭūsī (6/376)

2 Kitāb Sulaym Ibn Qays (p. 261)

> a camel is slaughtered; and his meat is exposed to fire just as a camel's meat is; and it would be said, 'He is a disobeyer,' and he actually is not a disobeyer."
>
> ʿAlī, while under the pulpit, thus said, "And when is that O commander of the faithful?" Or "when does the affliction become severe, pride becomes manifest, progeny is enslaved, *fitan* strike them just as a stone mill strikes the sediments in it and as a fire strikes lumber?"
>
> ʿUmar said, "And when is that, ʿAlī?" He said, "When knowledge is sought for other than the faith; when knowledge is sought for other than [its] implementation; and when the *Dunyā* is sought through the actions of the *Ākhira*."[1]

روى معمر بن راشد – كما في جامعه – عَنْ أَبَانَ، عَنْ سُلَيْمِ بْنِ قَيْسٍ الْحَنْظَلِيِّ، قَالَ: خَطَبَ عُمَرُ، فَقَالَ, "إِنَّ أَخْوَفَ مَا أَتَخَوَّفُ عَلَيْكُمْ بَعْدِي أَنْ يُؤْخَذَ الرَّجُلُ مِنْكُمُ الْبَرِيءُ، فَيُؤْشَرُ كَمَا يُؤْشَرُ الْجَزُورُ، وَيُشَاطُ لَحْمُهُ كَمَا يُشَاطُ لَحْمُهَا، وَيُقَالُ: عَاصٍ وَلَيْسَ بِعَاصٍ "، قَالَ: فَقَالَ عَلِيٌّ وَهُوَ تَحْتَ الْمِنْبَرِ، " وَمَتَى ذَلِكَ يَا أَمِيرَ الْمُؤْمِنِينَ؟ أَوْ: بِمَا تَشْتَدُّ الْبَلِيَّةُ، وَتَظْهَرُ الْحَمِيَّةُ، وَتُسْبَى الذُّرِّيَّةُ، وَتَدُقُّهُمُ الْفِتَنُ كَمَا تَدُقُّ الرَّحَا ثُفْلَهَا، وَكَمَا تَدُقُّ النَّارُ الْحَطَبَ؟ "، قَالَ, " وَمَتَى ذَلِكَ يَا عَلِيُّ؟ "، قَالَ, " إِذَا تُفُقِّهَ لِغَيْرِ الدِّينِ، وَتُعُلِّمَ لِغَيْرِ الْعَمَلِ، وَالْتُمِسَتِ الدُّنْيَا بِعَمَلِ الآخِرَةِ. "

The core of this tradition is found in a report in the Twelver source, *al-Kāfī* of al-Kulaynī (d. 329). Nonetheless, the tradition therein was totally altered and removed from its original context.

Al-Kulaynī narrated on the authority of ʿAlī b. Ibrāhīm, from his father, from Ḥammād b. ʿĪsā, from Ibrāhīm b. ʿUthmān [ʿUmar], from Sulaym b. Qays al-Hilālī that he said:

> The Commander of the Faithful (ʿAlī) once gave a sermon. He praised Allah, extolled Him and then prayed for the Prophet.
>
> He then said, "[...] I heard the Messenger of Allah ﷺ say, 'How shall you be when you are clothed with a *fitna* in which the young shall grow and the old shall age? The people shall embark upon it and make it a *Sunna*. Hence, if something in it is changed, it is said, 'you have changed the *Sunna*!.'

---

1 Al-Jāmiʿ of Maʿmar b. Rāshid (11/360)

> Then, the affliction shall become severe, the progeny will be enslaved, and *fitan* will strike them just as a fire strikes lumber and as a stone mill strikes the sediments in it. They shall seek knowledge for other than the religion, learn for other than [its] implementation and pursue the *Dunyā* with the deeds of the *Ākhira*'."[1]

وروى الكليني في «الكافي» عن علي بن إبراهيم، عن أبيه، عن حماد بن عيسى، عن إبراهيم بن عثمان [عمر]، عن سليم بن قيس الهلالي قال: خطب أمير المؤمنين (ع) فحمد الله وأثنى عليه ثم صلى على النبي صلى الله عليه وآله، ثم قال: [...] إني سمعت رسول الله صلى الله عليه وآله يقول: كيف أنتم إذا لبستم فتنة يربو فيها الصغير ويهرم فيها الكبير، يجري الناس عليها ويتخذونها سنة فإذا غير منها شئ قيل: قد غيرت السنة وقد أتى الناس منكرا! ثم تشتد البلية وتسبى الذرية وتدقهم الفتنة كما تدق النار الحطب وكما تدق الرحا بثفالها ويتفقهون لغير الله ويتعلمون لغير العمل ويطلبون الدنيا بأعمال الآخرة.

This later redaction of the tradition can be found in *Kitāb Sulaym* as well, albeit with a slightly different wording in several instances.[2]

قال سليم بن قيس: سمعت أبا الحسن عليه السلام يحدثني ويقول: [...] إني سمعت رسول الله صلى الله عليه وآله يقول: كيف بكم إذا لبستكم فتنة يربو فيها الوليد ويزيد فيها الكبير، يجري الناس عليها فيتخذونها سنة، فإذا غير منها شئ قيل: إن الناس قد أتوا منكرا! ثم يشتد البلاء وتسبى الذرية وتدقهم الفتن كما تدق النار الحطب وكما تدق الرحى بثفالها، يتفقه الناس لغير الدين ويتعلمون لغير العمل ويطلبون الدنيا بعمل الآخرة.

Evidently, this tradition experienced serious changes between Maʿmar's death in 154 and al-Kulaynī's death in 329. Its initial context in Maʿmar's tradition presents ʿUmar b. al-Khaṭṭāb on the pulpit speaking of a potential *fitna* he feared and briefly describing its tribulations. ʿAlī, who was beneath the pulpit, then further describes its tribulations and precursors. In the later Shīʿite redaction of the report found in *al-Kāfī* and *Kitāb Sulaym*, ʿUmar is entirely removed from the picture. Rather, ʿAlī is presented as the figure giving a sermon, and he proceeds to quote the entire text, which originally was an exchange between ʿUmar and ʿAlī, as a Prophetic tradition.

What is additionally noteworthy is that this report is recorded elsewhere by ʿAbdullāh b. Ayyūb al-Mukhramī (d. 265) via a different Baṣran isnād as

1 Al-Kāfī by al-Kulaynī (8/36-37)
2 Kitāb Sulaym Ibn Qays (p. 262)

a tradition relayed by al-Ḥasan al-Baṣrī (d. 110), and it matches the original tradition relayed by Maʿmar b. Rāshid.[1]

قال عبد الله بن أيوب المخرمي: حدثنا موسى بنُ هلالٍ: حدثنا موسى بنُ سعيدٍ الراسبيُّ، عن الحسنِ، وعونِ بنِ شِبْرَق، عن أبي بكرٍ الهُذَلي، عن الحسنِ قالَ: خطبَ عمرُ الناسَ فقالَ: إنَّ أخوفَ ما أخافُ عليكم أنْ يُؤخذَ المسلمُ البريءُ عندَ اللهِ عزَّ وجلَّ فيُشاطَ لحمُهُ كما يُشاطُ لحمُ الجزورِ، فيقالَ: عاصي وليسَ بعاصي، فقامَ عليٌّ مِن تحتِ المنبرِ قالَ: ومِمَ ذاكَ يا أميرَ المؤمنينَ ولمَّا تشتدَّ البليةُ، وتظهر الحميةُ، وتُسبى الذريةُ، وتدقّهم الفتنُ كما تدقُّ الرَّحا ثفلَها وكما تأكلُ النارُ الحطبَ؟ فقالَ له عمرُ: ومَتى يكونُ ذلكَ ياعليُّ؟ قالَ: إذا تفقَّهوا لغيرِ الدِّينِ، وتعلَّموا لغيرِ العملِ، وطَلَبوا الدُّنيا بعملِ الآخرةِ.

Ibn Qutayba (d. 276) also relayed this tradition via another isnād that ends with ʿUmar, and it matches Maʿmar b. Rāshid and ʿAbdullāh b. Ayyūb's tradition. However, it must be noted that one of the transmitters in the isnād cannot be deemed reliable.[2]

قال ابن قتيبة في «غريب الحديث»: وَقَالَ فِي حَدِيث عمر أَنه خطب النَّاس فقَالَ إِن أخوف مَا أَخَاف عَلَيْكُم أَن يُؤْخَذ الرجل الْمُسلم البريء عِنْد الله فيدسر كَمَا يدسر الْجَزُور ويشاط لَحْمه كَمَا يشاط لحم الْجَزُور يُقَال عَاص وَلَيْسَ بعاص فَقَالَ عَليّ وَكَيف ذَاك وَلما تشتد البلية وَتظهر الحمية وتسب الذُّرِّيَّة وتدقهم الْفِتَن دق الرَّحى بثفالها.

يرويهِ سعيد بن مُحَمَّد الجَرْمِي، عَن أبي ثميلة - وَهُوَ يحيى بن وَاضح، عَن رُمَيْح بن هِلاَل، عَن عبد الله بن بُرَيْدَة، عَن أَبِيه، عَن عمر.

I cite these traditions as supplementary data to what is reported by Maʿmar. Otherwise, the traditions of Maʿmar and al-Kulaynī are sufficient to demonstrate that serious distortion has taken place in Sulaym's report in these later Shīʿte sources, including *Kitāb Sulaym Ibn Qays*. It is evident that this passage in *Kitāb Sulaym*, in its current form, was developed after the death of Maʿmar b. Rāshid, sometime between the mid second century and before the year 329.

---

1 Majmūʿ fīh Muṣannafāt Abī al-Ḥasan Ibn al-Ḥammāmī wa-Ajzāʾ Ḥadīthiyya Ukhrā (p. 234)

2 Gharīb al-Ḥadīth by Ibn Qutayba (1/582)

Passage 6

In Twelver primary sources, we find a tradition relayed through multiple isnāds that converge back to Abān b. Abī ʿAyyāsh → Sulaym b. Qays. This tradition can also be found in *Kitāb Sulaym Ibn Qays*, and its redaction in the book will prove to be noteworthy when its contents are cross-referenced with those of Twelver primary sources. In figure 3.3 below, we can observe the isnāds for the said tradition.

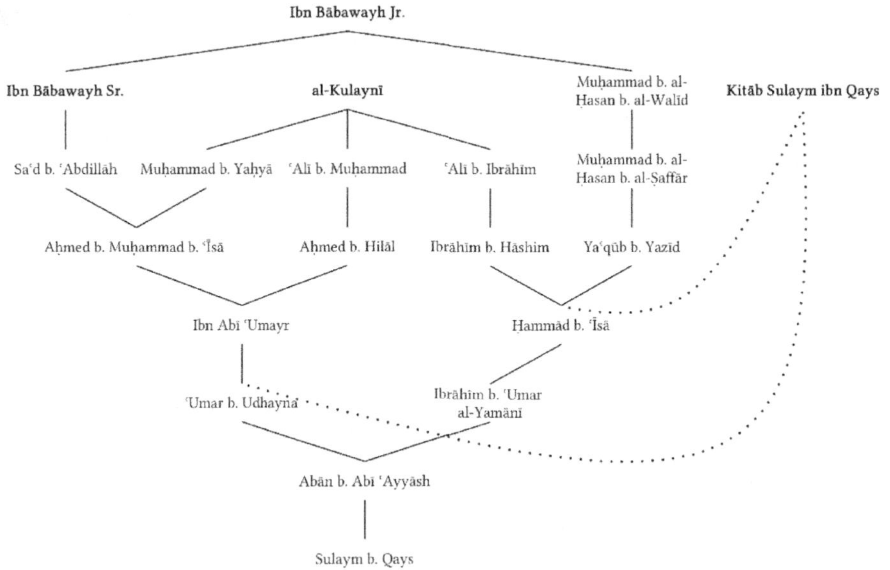

Figure 3.3 An isnād schematic for passage 7 in *Kitāb Sulaym Ibn Qays.*

Before dissecting these accounts in detail, I must note that the two isnāds that converge back to Abān b. Abī ʿAyyāsh are not independent of each other. Rather, Ibrāhīm b. ʿUmar al-Yamānī's transmission originates from ʿUmar b. Udhayna. The illusion of independence given by this diagram merely is due to the omission of some intermediaries from the isnād. In this case Ibrāhīm b. ʿUmar al-Yamānī's actual source for this tradition, ʿUmar b. Udhayna, was omitted in some of the isnāds.

Nonetheless, al-Kulaynī (d. 329), Ibn Bābawayh Sr. (d. 329) and Ibn Bābawayh Jr. (d. 381) all quoted Sulaym b. Qays saying: I heard ʿAbdullāh b. Jaʿfar say:

> Al-Ḥasan, al-Ḥusayn, ʿAbdullāh b. ʿAbbās, ʿUmar b. Abī Salama and Usāma b. Zayd and I were once in the presence of Muʿāwiya. A conversation took place between me and Muʿāwiya, so I told him, "I heard the Messenger of Allah ﷺ say, 'I am more worthy of the believers than themselves. Then my brother, ʿAlī, is more worthy of the believers than themselves. When he is martyred, al-Ḥasan is more worthy of the believers than themselves. Then, my son al-Ḥusayn is more worthy of the believers than themselves. When he is martyred, his son, ʿAlī b. al-Ḥusayn, is more worthy if the believers than themselves, and you shall meet him, O ʿAlī [b. Abī Ṭālib]. Then his son, Muḥammad b. ʿAlī is more worthy of the believers than themselves, and you shall meet him, O Ḥusayn. He then listed the remainder of the twelve imams, nine of whom descend from al-Ḥusayn'."
>
> ʿAbdullāh b. Jaʿfar then said, "I asked al-Ḥasan, al-Ḥusayn, ʿAbdullāh b. ʿAbbās, ʿUmar b. Umm Salama and Usāma b. Zayd to testify [to what I had narrated], and they testified to its veracity before Muʿāwiya.
>
> Sulaym said, "I have heard that as well from Salmān, Abū Dharr, and al-Miqdād, and they mentioned that they heard it from the Messenger of Allah."[1]

عن أبان بن أبي عياش، عن سليم بن قيس قال: سمعت عبدالله بن جعفر الطيار يقول: كنا عند معاوية، أنا والحسن والحسين وعبدالله بن عباس وعمر بن ام سلمة واسامة بن زيد، فجرى بيني وبين معاوية كلام فقلت لمعاوية: سمعت رسول الله صلى الله عليه وآله يقول: أنا أولى بالمؤمنين من أنفسهم، ثم أخي علي بن أبي طالب أولى بالمؤمنين من أنفسهم، فإذا استشهد علي فالحسن بن علي أولى بالمؤمنين من أنفسهم ثم ابني الحسين من بعده أولى بالمؤمنين من أنفسهم، فإذا استشهد فابنه علي بن الحسين أولى بالمؤمنين من أنفسهم وستدركه يا علي، ثم ابنه محمد بن علي أولى بالمؤمنين من أنفسهم وستدركه يا حسين، ثم تكمله اثني عشر إماما تسعة من ولد

---

1 Al-Kāfī by al-Kulaynī (1/339-340), al-Imāma wa-l-Ṭabṣira by Ibn Bābawayh Sr. (p. 110-111), al-Khiṣāl by Ibn Bābawayh Jr. (p. 477)

Ibn Bābawayh Jr. also relayed this tradition from his father in several sources. See ʿUyūn Akhbār al-Riḍā (1/52-53) and Kamāl al-Dīn wa-Tamām al-Niʿma (p. 256-257).

Also refer to al-Nuʿmānī's Kitāb al-Ghayba (p. 96-97) and al-Karājikī's al-Istinṣār (p. 9-10), where it appears al-Kulaynī's report in *al-Kāfī* was being referenced.

الحسين، قال عبدالله بن جعفر: واستشهدت الحسن والحسين وعبدالله بن عباس وعمر بن ام سلمة واسامة بن زيد، فشهدوا لي عند معاوية، قال سليم: وقد سمعت ذلك من سلمان وأبي ذر والمقداد وذكروا أنهم سمعوا ذلك من رسول الله صلى عليه وآله.

The reports of al-Kulaynī, Ibn Bābawayh Sr. and Ibn Bābawayh Jr. are very similar with only minute and negligible differences between them. However, *Kitāb Sulaym*'s redaction of this account is quite different in structure and detail, and it has significantly altered and developed the report in multiple regards. In *Kitāb Sulaym*, Abān is quoted narrating on the authority of Sulaym that he said: ʿAbdullāh b. Jaʿfar informed me, he said:

> I was once in the presence of Muʿāwiya, and with us were al-Ḥasan and al-Ḥusayn. With him were ʿAbdullāh b. ʿAbbās and al-Faḍl b. al-ʿAbbās [as well]. Muʿāwiya then turned to me and said, "How much is your veneration of al-Ḥasan and al-Ḥusayn, yet they – by Allah – are not better than you; nor is their father better than your father! Had Fāṭima not been the Messenger of Allah's ﷺ daughter, then your mother, Asmāʾ bt. ʿUmays would not have been less than her!"
>
> I was angered by what he had said, and I was overtaken [by anger] such that I was not able to hold myself. I told him, "By Allah, you know little about them, their father and their mother! Rather, by Allah, they are both better than me! Their father is better than my father! Their mother is better than my mother! O Muʿāwiya, you are oblivious to what I had heard from the Messenger of Allah ﷺ regarding them both, their father and their mother, which I had memorized, understood and relayed."
>
> Muʿāwiya thus said, "bring forth what you had heard, for by Allah you are not a liar nor are you suspect," while al-Ḥasan, al-Ḥusayn, ʿAbdullāh b. ʿAbbās, al-Faḍl b. al-ʿAbbās and Ibn Abī Lahab were present in his gathering.
>
> I replied, "it is greater than you think." He replied, "I do not mind so as long as no one from the people of al-Shām is present in this gathering, even if it is greater than the mountains of Uḥud and Ḥirāʾ. Now that God had slain your leader dispersed your congregation, and rule has been instilled within its rightful people, inform us, for we do not care about what you say and claim."

I said, "I heard the Messenger of Allah ﷺ say, as he was asked about the verse (And in We made the vision that We had showed you nothing but a *fitna* to mankind, and likewise we made the tree that is cursed in the Qur'an), say, 'I have seen a dream where twelve men from the heads of misguidance ascend and descend my pulpit. They shall cast my *Umma* backwards in regression. Among them were two men from two different clans of Quraysh, Taym and ʿAdī, three from the descendents of Umayya, and seven from the descendants of al-Ḥakam b. Abī al-ʿĀṣ.'

I also heard him say, 'if the descendants of Abū al-ʿĀṣ amount to thirty men, then they shall make the Quran null; the slaves of Allah as property; and the wealth of Allah as circulated possessions [among themselves].'

O Muʿāwiya, I heard the Messenger of Allah ﷺ say, while he was on the pulpit and I was before him with ʿUmar b. Abī Salama, Usāma b. Zayd, Saʿd b. Abī Waqqāṣ, Salmān al-Fārisī, Abū Dharr, al-Miqdād, al-Zubayr b. al-ʿAwwām. He was saying, 'am I not more worthy of the believers than themselves?' We replied, 'yes, O Messenger of Allah.' He then said, 'are my wives not your mothers?' We said, 'Yes, O Messenger of Allah.' He then said, 'Whoever I am his *mawlā*, then ʿAlī is his *mawlā*.' He then placed his hand on ʿAlī's shoulders, and he said, 'O Allah take as a *mawlā* whoever takes him as a *mawlā* and take as an enemy whoever takes him as an enemy.'

He then said, 'O people, I am more worthy of the believers than themselves; they have no authority with me. After me, ʿAlī is more worthy of the believes than themselves; they have no authority with him. After his father, my son al-Ḥasan is more worthy of the believers after his father; they have no authority with him. After his brother, my son al-Ḥusayn is more worthy of the believers; they have no authority with him.'

The Messenger of Allah ﷺ then reiterated, 'O people, when I am martyred, then ʿAlī is more worthy of you then yourselves. When ʿAlī is martyred, then my son al-Ḥasan is more worthy of the believers than themselves. When my son al-Ḥasan is martyred, then my son al-Ḥusayn is more worthy of the believers than themselves. When my son al-Ḥusayn is martyred, then my son ʿAlī b. al-Ḥusayn is more worthy of the believers than themselves; they have no authority with him.'

The Prophet ﷺ then faced ʿAlī and said, 'O ʿAlī, you shall meet him, so convey my *salām* to him. When he is martyred, then his son Muḥammad is more worthy of the believers than themselves. You shall meet him, O Ḥusayn, so convey my *salām* to him. Then, there shall be from the descendants of Muḥammad [b. ʿAlī b. al-Ḥusayn] men, one after another, with whom the people will have no authority.'

He repeated it thrice and then said, 'There is not one of them except that he is more worthy of the believers than themselves; and the people will have no authority with them. All of them are guiding and guided, nine from the descendants of al-Ḥusayn.'

ʿAlī b. Abī Ṭālib then went to the Prophet ﷺ crying, and he said, 'may my father and more be your ransom, will you by killed?!' He replied, 'yes, I will be martyred by poisoning. You will be killed with the strike of a sword, and your beard shall be dyed with the blood of your head. My son al-Ḥasan will die with poisoning. My son al-Ḥusayn will die by the sword; he will be killed by a tyrant who is a son of a tyrant, an illegitimate and son of an illegitimate, a hypocrite son of a hypocrite'."

Muʿāwiya thus said, "O son of Jaʿfar, you have uttered something severe. If what you say is true, then I, the three before me and all those who have taken them as associates have perished! The *Umma* of Muḥammad and the companions of Muḥammad from the *Muhājirīn* and the *Anṣār* would have perished, asides from you, *Ahlulbayt*, your associates and your supporters!"

I said, "By Allah, what I had said is true. I heard it from the Messenger of Allah." Muʿāwiya then said, "O Ḥasan, Ḥusayn and Ibn ʿAbbās, what is Ibn Jaʿfar saying?!" Ibn ʿAbbās replied, "If you do not believe what he said, then send for those who he named, and ask them about it."

Muʿāwiya thus sent for ʿUmar b. Abī Salama and Usāma b. Zayd, and he asked them. They testified that they had heard from the Messenger of Allah ﷺ what ʿAbdullāh b. Jaʿfar had said.

This was in Medīna in the first year when the *Umma* coalesced around Muʿāwiya [as caliph].

Sulaym said, "I heard Ibn Jaʿfar transmit this ḥadīth during the reign of ʿUmar b. al-Khaṭṭāb."[1]

أبان عن سليم، قال: حدثني عبد الله بن جعفر بن أبي طالب قال: كنت عند معاوية ومعنا الحسن والحسين وعنده عبد الله بن العباس والفضل بن العباس. فالتفت إلي معاوية فقال: يا عبد الله بن جعفر، ما أشد تعظيمك للحسن والحسين والله ما هما بخير منك ولا أبوهما خير من أبيك، ولولا أن فاطمة بنت رسول الله أمهما لقلت: ما أمك أسماء بنت عميس دونها! فغضبت من مقالته وأخذني ما لم أملك معه نفسي، فقلت: والله إنك لقليل المعرفة بهما وبأبيهما وبأمهما. بل والله لهما خير مني ولأبوهما خير من أبي ولأمهما خير من أمي. يا معاوية، إنك لغافل عما سمعته أنا من رسول الله صلى الله عليه وآله يقول فيهما وفي أبيهما وفي أمهما، قد حفظته ووعيته ورويته.

قال معاوية: هات ما سمعت – وفي مجلسه الحسن والحسين وعبد الله بن عباس والفضل بن عباس وابن أبي لهب – فوالله ما أنت بكذاب ولا متهم. فقلت: إنه أعظم مما في نفسك. قال: وإن كان أعظم من أحد وحراء جميعا، فلست أبالي إذا لم يكن في المجلس أحد من أهل الشام وإذ قتل الله صاحبك وفرق جمعكم وصار الأمر في أهله ومعدنه فحدثنا فإنا لا نبالي ما قلتم ولا ما ادعيتم.

قلت: سمعت رسول الله صلى الله عليه وآله – وقد سئل عن هذه الآية: (وما جعلنا الرؤيا التي أريناك إلا فتنة للناس والشجرة الملعونة في القرآن)– فقال: إني رأيت اثني عشر رجلا من أئمة الضلالة يصعدون منبري وينزلون، يردون أمتي على أدبارهم القهقرى.

فيهم رجلان من حيين من قريش مختلفين تيم وعدي، وثلاثة من بني أمية، وسبعة من ولد الحكم بن أبي العاص. وسمعته يقول: إن بني أبي العاص إذا بلغوا ثلاثين رجلا جعلوا كتاب الله دخلا وعباد الله خولا ومال الله دولا. يا معاوية، إني سمعت رسول الله صلى الله عليه وآله يقول – وهو على المنبر وأنا بين يديه وعمر بن أبي سلمة وأسامة بن زيد وسعد بن أبي وقاص وسلمان الفارسي وأبو ذر والمقداد والزبير بن العوام – وهو يقول: ألست أولى بالمؤمنين من أنفسهم؟ فقلنا: بلى، يا رسول الله. قال: أليس أزواجي أمهاتكم؟ قلنا:

1 Kitāb Sulaym Ibn Qays (p. 361-364)

بلى، يا رسول الله. قال: من كنت مولاه فعلي مولاه – وضرب بيديه على منكب علي عليه السلام – اللهم وال من والاه وعاد من عاداه.

أيها الناس، أنا أولى بالمؤمنين من أنفسهم، ليس لهم معي أمر. وعلي من بعدي أولى بالمؤمنين من أنفسهم، ليس لهم معه أمر. ثم ابني الحسن من بعد أبيه أولى بالمؤمنين من أنفسهم ليس لهم معه أمر. ثم ابني الحسين من بعد أخيه أولى بالمؤمنين من أنفسهم ليس لهم معه أمر.

ثم عاد صلى الله عليه وآله فقال: أيها الناس، إذا أنا استشهدت فعلي أولى بكم من أنفسكم، فإذا استشهد علي فابني الحسن أولى بالمؤمنين منهم بأنفسهم، فإذا استشهد ابني الحسن فابني الحسين أولى بالمؤمنين منهم بأنفسهم، فإذا استشهد ابني الحسين فابني علي بن الحسين أولى بالمؤمنين منهم بأنفسهم ليس لهم معه أمر. ثم أقبل على علي عليه السلام فقال: يا علي، إنك ستدركه فاقرأه عني السلام. فإذا استشهد فابنه محمد أولى بالمؤمنين منهم بأنفسهم، وستدركه أنت يا حسين فاقرأه مني السلام. ثم يكون في عقب محمد رجال واحد بعد واحد وليس لهم معهم أمر. ثم أعادها ثلاثا ثم قال: وليس منهم أحد إلا وهو أولى بالمؤمنين منهم بأنفسهم ليس معه أمر، كلهم هادون مهتدون تسعة من ولد الحسين.

فقام إليه علي بن أبي طالب عليه السلام وهو يبكي، فقال: بأبي أنت وأمي يا نبي الله، أتقتل؟ قال: نعم، أهلك شهيدا بالسم، وتقتل أنت بالسيف وتخضب لحيتك من دم رأسك، ويقتل ابني الحسن بالسم، ويقتل ابني الحسين بالسيف، يقتله طاغي بن طاغي، دعي بن دعي، منافق بن منافق.

فقال معاوية: يا بن جعفر، لقد تكلمت بعظيم ولئن كان ما تقول حقا لقد هلكت وهلك الثلاثة قبلي وجميع من تولاهم من هذه الأمة، ولقد هلكت أمة محمد وأصحاب محمد من المهاجرين والأنصار غيركم أهل البيت وأوليائكم وأنصاركم.

فقلت: والله إن الذي قلت حق سمعته من رسول الله صلى الله عليه وآله. فقال معاوية: يا حسن ويا حسين ويا بن عباس، ما يقول ابن جعفر؟ فقال ابن عباس: إن لا تؤمن بالذي قال فأرسل إلى الذين سماهم فاسألهم عن ذلك. فأرسل معاوية إلى عمر بن أبي سلمة وإلى أسامة بن زيد فسألهما، فشهدا أن الذي قال عبد الله بن جعفر قد سمعناه من رسول الله صلى الله عليه وآله كما سمعه. وكان هذا بالمدينة أول سنة جمعت الأمة على معاوية. قال سليم: وسمعت ابن جعفر يحدث بهذا الحديث في زمان عمر بن الخطاب.

Hopefully, this passage should be a self-evident example of how early traditions ascribed to Sulaym in Twelver sources were being significantly developed and embellished before their final redaction into *Kitāb Sulaym Ibn Qays*. Take as an example ʿAbdullāh b. Jaʿfar's statement recorded by al-Kulaynī and both Ibn Bābawayhs, "a conversation took place between me and Muʿāwiya." Later in *Kitāb* Sulaym, this concise sentence was exploded into a detailed, multi-paragraph exchange between Muʿāwiya and ʿAbdullāh b. Jaʿfar. Details and information clearly were being added throughout the entire tradition such that what initially was a half-page-long report eventually became around two pages long.

In an attempt to embellish and expand the tradition recorded by al-Kulaynī and both Ibn Bābawayhs (which I will be calling account 1 moving fourth), the author of *Kitāb Sulaym* actually ended up contradicting account 1 in his later redaction (which I will be calling account 2 moving forth). Take for example how al-Ḥasan, al-Ḥusayn, ʿAbdullāh b. ʿAbbās, ʿUmar b. Abī Salama and Usāma b. Zayd were all said to be present in Muʿāwiya's gathering in account 1. In account 2, the gathering commences with al-Ḥasan, al-Ḥusayn, ʿAbdullāh b. al-ʿAbbās and al-Faḍl b. al-ʿAbbās being present in Muʿāwiya's gathering. Hence, the reader is able to observe that Usāma b. Zayd and ʿUmar b. Abī Salama were not initially present in in this assembly according to account 2. Rather, they are only summoned later by Muʿāwiya to testify regarding ʿAbdullāh b. Jaʿfar's claims. In this regard, account 2 diverges from account 1, where all initial attendees of the gathering, al-Ḥasan, al-Ḥusayn, ʿAbdullāh b. ʿAbbās, ʿUmar b. Umm Salama and Usāma b. Zayd, are said to had testified in unison to the veracity of Ibn Jaʿfar's claims upon Ibn Jaʿfar's request.

What is also noteworthy is that the later author of *Kitāb Sulaym* introduced a new character in account 2, al-Faḍl b. al-ʿAbbās, effectively giving rise to an obvious historical error that was not necessarily existent in past redactions of the tradition. This error was discussed in detail in chapter 2 of this book.

I expect some Twelver proponents of *Kitāb Sulaym*, in response to my analysis, to retort by arguing that *Kitāb Sulaym's* voluminous account was neither developed nor embellished from an earlier concise account. Rather, the lengthy variant of this tradition is its original redaction, and the accounts recorded by al-Kulaynī (d. 329), Ibn Bābawayh Sr. (329) and Ibn Bābawayh Jr. (d. 381) merely are abridged versions of that longer tradition. I find it difficult to take this appeal seriously. The four aforementioned sources, al-Kulaynī, Ibn Bābawayh Sr., Ibn Bābawayh Jr. and our extant recension of *Kitāb Sulaym*, claim to relay this tradition through the same route, Ibn Udhayna ⟶ Abān b. Abī ʿAyyāsh ⟶ Sulaym b. Qays. Despite having different routes back to the aforementioned pivot isnād, al-Kulaynī, Ibn Bābawayh Sr. and Ibn Bābawayh Jr.'s accounts have the same structure, so it would be strange to assume that these three accounts were abridged by separate downstream transmitters who "coincidentally" happened to abridge the lengthy tradition at the identical points in the report with nearly identical lexicon. Rather, the more appropriate explanation in such a scenario is that the concise tradition that was redacted similarly by their different sources was the original form of Sulaym b. Qays' account regarding Muʿāwiya and ʿAbdullāh b. Jaʿfar. Later, the tradition was expanded by a forger who compiled/edited the surviving recension of *Kitāb Sulaym Ibn Qays*. This finding is not an isolated incident: it comes as part of a greater trend where such alterations and falsifications to earlier Twelver traditions regarding Sulaym b. Qays are readily observable throughout the extant recension of *Kitāb Sulaym b. Qays*.

Passage 7

In *Kitāb al-Saqīfa* of Abū Bakr al-Jawharī (d. 323), al-Mughīra b. Muḥammad al-Muhallabī (d. 278) and ʿUmar b. Shabba (d. 262) are quoted relaying with an unspecified isnād to Abū Saʿīd al-Khudrī an extensive account pertaining to the pledge of Abū Bakr which he purportedly heard from al-Barāʾ b. ʿĀzib.

This tradition was also cited by al-Ābī (d. 421) as a tradition relayed by Aḥmed b. Abī Ṭāhir (d. 280) in his book, *al-Manthūr wa-l-Manẓūm*, though he similarly did not reference the tradition's isnād.[1]

قال أبو بكر الجوهري: وحدثني المغيرة بن محمد المهلبي من حفظه، وعمر بن شبة من كتابه باسناد رفعه الي أبي سعيد الخدري، قال: سمعت البراء بن عازب يقول: لم أزل لبني هاشم محبا، فلما قبض رسول الله صلى الله عليه وآله خفت أن تتمالأ قريش على اخراج هذا الأمر عنهم، فأخذني ما يأخذ الوالهة العجول، مع ما في نفسي من الحزن لوفاة رسول الله صلى الله عليه وآله فكنت أتردد الى بني هاشم وهم عند النبي صلى الله عليه وآله في الحجرة، وأتفقد وجوه قريش، فإني كذلك إذ فقدت أبا بكر وعمرو وإذ قائل يقول: القوم في سقيفة بني ساعدة، وإذا قائل آخر يقول: قد بويع أبا بكر فلم ألبث وإذا أنا بأبي بكر قد اقبل ومعه عمر وابو عبيدة وجماعة من أصحاب السقيفة وهم محتجزون بالأزر الصنعانية لا يمرون بأحد إلا خبطوه، وقدموه فمدوا يده فمسحوها على يد أبي بكر يبايعه، شاء ذلك أو أبى، فانكرت عقلي وخرجت اشتد حتى انتهيت الى بني هاشم

1 Nathr al-Durr fī al-Muḥāḍarāt by al-Ābī (1/277)

والباب مغلق، فضربت عليهم الباب ضربا عنيفا وقلت: قد بايع الناس لأبي بكر بن أبي قحافة، فقال العباس: تربت أيديكم إلى آخر الدهر، أما اني قد أمرتكم فعصيتموني. فمكثت أكابد ما في نفسي، ورأيت في الليل المقداد، وسلمان وأبا ذر وعبادة بن الصامت، وابا الهيثم بن التميان، وحذيفة وعمارا، وهم يريدون أن يعيدوا الأمر شورى بين المهاجرين.

فلما كان بليل خرجت الى المسجد فلما صرت فيه تذكرت اني كنت اسمع همهمة رسول الله صلى الله عليه وآله، بالقرآن فامتنعت من مكاني فخرجت الى الفضاء، فضاء بني قضاعة، وأجد نفرا يتناجون فلما دنوت منهم سكتوا، فانصرفت عنهم، فعرفوني وما أعرفهم فدعوني إليهم فأتيتهم فأجد المقداد بن الأسود، وعبادة بن الصامت، وسلمان الفارسي، وأبا ذر، وحذيفة، وأبا الهيثم بن التيهان، وإذا حذيفة يقول لهم: والله ليكونن ما أخبرتكم به، والله ما كذبت ولا كذبت، وإذا القوم يريدون ان يعيدوا الأمر شورى بين المهاجرين.

ثم قال ائتوا أُبي بن كعب، فقد علم كما علمت قال: فانطلقنا الى ابي، فضربنا عليه بابه حتى صار خلف الباب، فقال: من أنتم فكلمه المقداد، فقال: ما حاجتكم؟ فقال له: ما أنا بفاتح بابي، وقد عرفت ما جئتم له كأنكم أردتم النظر في هذا العقد فقلنا: نعم، فقال أفيكم حذيفة؟ فقلنا: نعم، قال: فالقول ما قال: وبالله ما افتح عني بابي حتى تجرى على ما هي جارية، ولما يكون بعدها شر منها والى الله المشتكى.

وبلغ الخبر أبا بكر، وعمر، فأرسلا الى أبي عبيدة والمغيرة بن شعبة، فسألاهما عن الرأي، فقال المغيرة: ان تلقوا العباس فتجعلوا له هذا الأمر نصيبا فيكون له ولعقبه، فتقطعوا به من ناحية علي، ويكون لكم حجة عند الناس على علي، إذا مال معكم العباس.

فانطلق أبو بكر، وعمر، وأبو عبيدة، والمغيرة، حتى دخلوا على العباس، وذلك في الليلة الثانية من وفاة رسول الله صلى الله عليه وآله، فحمد أبو بكر الله وأثنى عليه وقال: إن الله ابتعث لكم محمدا صلى الله عليه وآله نبيا، وللمؤمنين وليا، فمن الله عليهم بكونه بين ظهرانيهم، حتى اختار له ما عنده، فخلى على الناس أمورهم ليختاروا لأنفسهم، متفقين غير مختلفين فاختاروني عليهم واليا، ولأمورهم راعيا، فتوليت ذلك، وما أخاف بعون الله وتسديده وهنا ولا حيرة ولا جبنا، وما توفيقي إلا بالله عليه توكلت واليه انيب، وما أنفك يبلغني عن طاعن يقول بخلاف قول عامة المسلمين، يتخذ لكم لجأ فتكونوا حصنه المنيع، وخطبه البديع، فإما دخلتم فيما دخل فيه الناس، أو صرفتموهم عما مالوا إليه، فقد جئناك، ونحن نريد ان نجعل لك في هذا الأمر نصيبا، ولمن بعدك من عقبك إذ كنت عم رسول الله صلى الله عليه وآله، وان كان المسلمون قد رأوا مكانك من

رسول الله صلى الله عليه وآله، ومكان أهلك، ثم عدلوا بهذا الأمر عنكم وعلى رسلكم بني هاشم، فإن رسول الله صلى الله عليه وآله منا ومنكم.

فاعترض كلامه عمر، وخرج الى مذهبه في الخشونة والوعيد واتيان الأمر من أصعب جهاته، فقال: اي والله، واخرى انا لم نأتكم حاجة اليكم، ولكن كرهنا أن يكون الطعن فيما اجتمع عليه المسلمون منكم، فيتفاقم الخطب بكم وبهم فانظروا لأنفسكم وعامتهم، ثم سكت.

فتكلم العباس، فحمد الله وأثنى عليه، ثم قال: ان الله ابتعث محمدا نبيا، كما وصفت، ووليا للمؤمنين، فمن الله به على امته حتى اختار له ما عنده، فخلى الناس على أمرهم ليختاروا لأنفسهم، مصيبين للحق ماثلين عن زيغ الهوى، فان كنت برسول الله طلبت فحقنا أخذت، وان كنت بالمؤمنين فنحن منهم، وما تقدمنا في أمركم فرطا، ولا حللنا وسطا، ولا نزحنا شحطا، فان كان هذا الأمر يجب لك بالمؤمنين، فما وجب إذ كنا كارهين وما أبعد قولك انهم طعنوا من قولك انهم مالوا اليك، وما ما بذلت لنا فان يكن حقك اعطيتناه فامسكه عليك، وان يكن حق المؤمنين فليس لك ان تحكم فيه، وان يكن حقنا لم نرض لك ببعضه دون بعض، وما أقول هذا أروم صرفك عما دخلت فيه، ولكن للحجة نصيبها من البيان، وأما قولك، ان رسول الله صلى الله عليه وآله منا ومنكم، فإن رسول الله صلى الله عليه وآله، ومن شجرة نحن أغصانها وأنتم جيرانها. وأما قولك يا عمر، انك تخاف الناس علينا، فهذا الذي قدمتموه أول ذلك، وبالله المستعان.

After a careful search, I came across a report that may reveal the route of transmission for a portion of the tradition relayed by Abū Bakr al-Jawharī (d. 323) and Aḥmed b. Abī Ṭāhir (d. 280). In *al-Dalāʾil fī Gharīb al-Ḥadīth*, Qāsim al-Saraqusṭī (d. 302) stated that he relayed the tradition, from ʿAlī b. al-Ḥasan b. Khalaf b. Qudayd (d. 312), from ʿUbaydullāh b. Saʿīd b. Kathīr b. ʿUfayr (d. 273), from his father (d. 226).[1]

قال قاسم بن ثابت السرقسطي في «الدلائل في غريب الحديث»: وَقَالَ فِي حَدِيثِ الْعَبَّاسِ رَحِمَهُ اللَّهُ: إِنَّ رَسُولَ اللَّهِ صَلَّى اللَّهُ عَلَيْهِ وَسَلَّمَ لَمَّا تُوُفِّيَ قَالَ عُمَرُ بْنُ الْخَطَّابِ لِأَبِي بَكْرٍ: اذْهَبْ بِنَا إِلَى الْعَبَّاسِ، فَجَعَلَ لَهُ فِي هَذَا الْأَمْرِ نَصِيبًا مِنْ بَعْدِكَ، تَقْطَعُ عَنْكَ نَاحِيَةَ عَلِيِّ بْنِ أَبِي طَالِبٍ وَعَادِيَتَهُ، فَذَهَبُوا إِلَيْهِ لَيْلاً، فَعَرَضُوا ذَلِكَ عَلَيْهِ، فَلَمْ يَرْضَوْا مِنْ جَوَابِهِ، فَقَالَ لَهُ عُمَرُ: عَلَى رِسْلِكُمْ يَا بَنِي هَاشِمٍ، فَإِنَّ رَسُولَ اللَّهِ صَلَّى اللَّهُ عَلَيْهِ وَسَلَّمَ مِنَّا وَمِنْكُمْ، فَقَالَ لَهُ الْعَبَّاسُ، " أَمَّا زَعْمُكَ يَا عُمَرُ أَنَّ رَسُولَ اللَّهِ صَلَّى اللَّهُ عَلَيْهِ وَسَلَّمَ مِنَّا وَمِنْكُمْ، فَإِنَّ رَسُولَ اللَّهِ صَلَّى اللَّهُ عَلَيْهِ

1 Al-Dalāʾil fī Gharīb al-Ḥadīth (2/789)

وَسَلَّمَ مِنْ شَجَرَةٍ، نَحْنُ أَغْصَانُهَا، وَأَنْتُمْ جِيرَانُهَا، فَإِنْ كُنْتَ بِرَسُولِ اللهِ طَلَبْتَ، فَحَقَّنَا أَخَذْتَ، وَإِنْ كَانَ إِنَّمَا يَجِبُ ذَلِكَ بِالْمُؤْمِنِينَ، فَوَاللهِ مَا وَجَبَ إِذْ كُنَّا كَارِهِينَ، وَإِنْ كَانَ حَقُّكَ تَعْرِضُهُ عَلَيْنَا، فَلاَ حَاجَةَ لَنَا فِيهِ، وَإِنْ كَانَ حَقَّ الْمُسْلِمِينَ، فَلَيْسَ لَكَ أَنْ تَحْكُمَ فِيهِ دُونَهُمْ، وَإِنْ كَانَ حَقَّنَا تَعْرِضُهُ عَلَيْنَا، فَإِنَّا لَا نَأْخُذُ بَعْضَهُ دُونَ بَعْضٍ، {وَإِنْ أَدْرِي لَعَلَّهُ فِتْنَةٌ لَكُمْ وَمَتَاعٌ إِلَى حِينٍ} حَدَّثَنَاهُ عَلِيُّ بْنُ الْحَسَنِ، قَالَ: نا عُبَيْدُ اللهِ بْنُ سَعِيدِ بْنِ كَثِيرِ بْنِ عُفَيْرٍ، عَنْ أَبِيهِ.

This is an interesting isnād that is unreliable for multiple reasons: (1) ʿUbaydullāh b. Saʿīd was a severely disparaged transmitter who was particularly criticized for transmitting dubious traditions through his father, and (2) Saʿīd b. Kathīr b. ʿUfayr's (d. 273) transmission of this account clearly is disconnected.[1] Though Saʿīd b. Kathīr's report is similar to the final portions of Ibn Shabba (d. 262) and al-Muhallabī's (d. 278) accounts, it seems that Ibn Shabba and al-Muhallabī's source(s) for their lengthy report cannot be definitively ascertained.

This account is also be found in the *Tārīkh* of al-Yaʿqūbī (d. 284). Al-Yaʿqūbī's account embodies some accretions, including a poem, which was discussed in chapter 2 of this book in the section on anachronisms. In al-Yaʿqūbī's account, the poem is ascribed to ʿUtba b. Abī Lahab.[2]

قال اليعقوبي: وجاء البراء بن عازب، فضرب الباب على بني هاشم وقال: يا معشر بني هاشم، بويع أبو بكر. فقال بعضهم: ما كان المسلمون يحدثون حدثا نغيب عنه، ونحن أولى بمحمد. فقال العباس: فعلوها، ورب الكعبة. وكان المهاجرون والأنصار لا يشكون في علي، فلما خرجوا من الدار قام الفضل بن العباس، وكان لسان قريش، فقال: يا معشر قريش، أنه ما حقت لكم الخلافة بالتمويه، ونحن أهلها دونكم، وصاحبنا أولى بها منكم. وقام عتبة بن أبي لهب فقال:

ما كنت أحسب أن الأمر منصرف عن هاشم ثم منها عن أبي حسن
عن أول الناس إيمانا وسابقة وأعلم الناس بالقرآن والسنن
وآخر الناس عهداً بالنبي ومن جبريل عون له في الغسل والكفن
من فيه ما فيهم لا يمترون به وليس في الناس ما فيه من الحسن
من ذا الذي ردكم عنه فنعرفه وليس في القوم ما فيه من الحسن

1 Lisān al-Mīzān (5/328-329)
2 Tārīkh al-Yaʿqūbī (2/114)

فبعث إليه علي فنهاه. وتخلف عن بيعة أبي بكر قوم من المهاجرين والأنصار، ومالوا مع علي بن أبي طالب، منهم: العباس بن عبد المطلب، والفضل بن العباس، والزبير بن العوام بن العاص، وخالد بن سعيد، والمقداد بن عمرو، وسلمان ألفارسي، وأبو ذر الغفاري، وعمار بن ياسر، والبراء بن عازب، وأبي بن كعب، فأرسل أبو بكر إلى عمر بن الخطاب وأبي عبيدة بن الجراح والمغيرة بن شعبة، فقال: ما الرأي؟ قالوا: الرأي أن تلقى العباس بن عبد المطلب، فتجعل له في هذا الأمر نصيبا يكون له ولعقبه من بعده، فتقطعون به ناحية علي بن أبي طالب حجة لكم على علي، إذا مال معكم، فانطلق أبو بكر وعمر وأبو عبيدة بن الجراح والمغيرة حتى دخلوا على العباس ليلاً، فحمد أبو بكر الله وأثنى عليه، ثم قال: إن الله بعث محمداً نبياً وللمؤمنين وليا، فمن عليهم بكونه بين أظهرهم، حتى اختار له ما عنده، فخلى على الناس أموراً ليختاروا لأنفسهم في مصلحتهم مشفقين، فاختاروني عليهم واليا ولأمورهم راعيا، فوليت ذلك، وما أخاف بعون الله وتشديده وهنا، ولا حيرة، ولا جبنا، وما توفيقي إلا بالله، عليه توكلت، وإليه أنيب، وما أنفك يبلغني عن طاعن يقول الخلاف على عامة المسلمين، يتخذكم لجأ، فتكون حصنه المنيع وخطبة البديع. فإما دخلتم مع الناس فيما اجتمعوا عليه، وإما صرفتموهم عما مالوا إليه، ولقد جئناك ونحن نريد أن لك في هذا الأمر نصيبا يكون لك، ويكون لمن بعدك من عقبك إذ كنت عم رسول الله، وإن كان الناس قد رأوا مكانك ومكان صاحبك... عنكم، وعلى رسلكم بني هاشم، فإن رسول الله صلى الله عليه وسلم منا ومنكم.

فقال عمر بن الخطاب: إي والله وأخرى، إنا لم نأتكم لحاجة إليكم، ولكن كرهاً أن يكون الطعن فيما اجتمع عليه المسلمون منكم، فيتفاقم الخطب بكم وبهم، فانظروا لأنفسكم.

فحمد العباس الله وأثنى عليه وقال: إن الله بعث محمداً كما وصفت نبيا وللمؤمنين ولياً، فمن على أمته به، حتى قبضه الله إليه، واختار له ما عنده، فخلى على المسلمين أمورهم ليختاروا لأنفسهم مصيبين الحق، لا مائلين بزيغ الهوى، فإن كنت برسول الله فحقاً أخذت، وإن كنت بالمؤمنين فنحن منهم، فما تقدمنا في أمرك فرضاً، ولا حللنا وسطاً، ولا برحنا سخطاً، وإن كان هذا الأمر إنما وجب لك بالمؤمنين، فما وجب إذ كنا كارهين. ما أبعد قولك من انهم طعنوا عليك من قولك إنهم اختاروك ومالوا إليك، وما أبعد تسميتك بخليفة رسول الله صلى الله عليه وسلم من قولك خلى على الناس أمورهم ليختاروا فاختاروك، فأما ما قلت إنك تجعله لي، فإن كان حقاً للمؤمنين، فليس لك أن تحكم فيه، وإن كان لنا فلم نرض ببعضه دون بعض، وعلى رسلك، فإن رسول الله صلى الله عليه وسلم من شجرة نحن أغصانها وأنتم جيرانها. فخرجوا من عنده.

My interest in this particular account stems from the fact that a variant of it made its way into *Kitāb Sulaym*. However, unlike the tradition referenced by Abū Bakr al-Jawharī, *Kitāb Sulaym* presents the transmitter of the account from al-Barāʾ b. ʿĀzib as Sulaym b. Qays, not Abū Saʿīd al-Khudrī. It also includes a slight change of order and multiple accretions.

وعن سليم، قال: سمعت البراء بن عازب يقول: كنت أحب بني هاشم حبا شديدا في حياة رسول الله صلى الله عليه وآله وبعد وفاته . فلما قبض رسول الله صلى الله عليه وآله أوصى عليا عليه السلام أن لا يلي غسله غيره، وأنه لا ينبغي لأحد أن يرى عورته غيره، وأنه ليس أحد يرى عورة رسول الله صلى الله عليه وآله إلا ذهب بصره. فقال علي عليه السلام: يا رسول الله، فمن يعينني على غسلك؟ قال: جبرائيل في جنود من الملائكة. فكان علي عليه السلام يغسله، والفضل بن العباس مربوط العينين يصب الماء والملائكة يقلبونه له كيف شاء. ولقد أراد علي عليه السلام أن ينزع قميص رسول الله صلى الله عليه وآله، فصاح به صائح: (لا تنزع قميص نبيك، يا علي). فأدخل يده تحت القميص فغسله ثم حنطه وكفنه، ثم نزع القميص عند تكفينه وتحنيطه. مفاجأة أهل البيت عليهم السلام بعمل أصحاب السقيفة قال البراء بن عازب: فلما قبض رسول الله صلى الله عليه وآله تخوفت أن تتظاهر قريش على إخراج هذا الأمر من بني هاشم. فلما صنع الناس ما صنعوا من بيعة أبي بكر أخذني ما يأخذ الواله الثكول مع ما بي من الحزن لوفاة رسول الله صلى الله عليه وآله. فجعلت أتردد وأرمق وجوه الناس، وقد خلا الهاشميون برسول الله صلى الله عليه وآله لغسله وتحنيطه. وقد بلغني الذي كان من قول سعد بن عبادة ومن اتبعه من جهلة أصحابه، فلم أحفل بهم وعلمت أنه لا يؤول إلى شيء.فجعلت أتردد بينهم وبين المسجد وأتفقد وجوه قريش. فإني لكذلك إذ فقدت أبا بكر وعمر. ثم لم ألبث حتى إذا أنا بأبي بكر وعمر وأبي عبيدة قد أقبلوا في أهل السقيفة وهم محتجزون بالأزر الصنعانية لا يمر بهم أحد إلا خبطوه، فإذا عرفوه مدوا يده فمسحوها على يد أبي بكر، شاء ذلك أم أبى فأنكرت عند ذلك عقلي جزعا منه، مع المصيبة برسول الله صلى الله عليه وآله. فخرجت مسرعا حتى أتيت المسجد، ثم أتيت بني هاشم، والباب مغلق دونهم. فضربت الباب ضربا عنيفا وقلت: يا أهل البيت فخرج إلي الفضل بن العباس، فقلت: قد بايع الناس أبا بكر فقال العباس: (قد تربت أيديكم منها إلى آخر الدهر. أما إني قد أمرتكم فعصيتموني.

فلما كان الليل خرجت إلى المسجد، فلما صرت فيه تذكرت أني كنت أسمع همهمة رسول الله صلى الله عليه وآله بالقرآن. فانبعثت من مكاني فخرجت نحو الفضاء - فضاء بني بياضة -، فوجدت نفرا يتناجون. فلما دنوت منهم سكتوا، فانصرفت عنهم، فعرفوني وما عرفتهم، فدعوني إليهم فأتيتهم فإذا المقداد وأبو ذر وسلمان

وعمار بن ياسر وعبادة بن الصامت وحذيفة بن اليمان والزبير بن العوام، وحذيفة يقول: والله ليفعلن ما أخبرتكم به. فوالله ما كذبت ولا كذبت. وإذا القوم يريدون أن يعيدوا الأمر شورى بين المهاجرين والأنصار.

فقال حذيفة: انطلقوا بنا إلى أبي بن كعب فقد علم مثل ما علمت. فانطلقنا إلى أبي بن كعب فضربنا عليه بابه، فأتى حتى صار خلف الباب، ثم قال: من أنتم؟ فكلمه المقداد. فقال: ما جاء بكم؟ فقال: إفتح بابك، فإن الأمر الذي جئنا فيه أعظم من أن يجري وراء الباب. فقال: ما أنا بفاتح بابي، وقد علمت ما جئتم له. وما أنا بفاتح بابي، كأنكم أردتم النظر في هذا العقد. فقلنا: نعم. فقال: أفيكم حذيفة؟ فقلنا: نعم. قال: القول ما قال حذيفة، فأما أنا فلا أفتح بابي حتى يجري على ما هو جار عليه، ولما يكون بعدها شر منها، وإلى الله جل ثنائه المشتكى.

قال: فرجعوا. ثم دخل أبي بن كعب بيته. وبلغ أبا بكر وعمر الخبر، فأرسلا إلى أبي عبيدة بن الجراح والمغيرة بن شعبة فسألاهما الرأي. فقال المغيرة بن شعبة: أرى أن تلقوا العباس بن عبد المطلب فتطمعوه في أن يكون له في هذا الأمر نصيب يكون له ولعقبه من بعده فتقطعوا عنكم بذلك ناحية علي بن أبي طالب، فإن العباس بن عبد المطلب لو صار معكم كانت الحجة على الناس وهان عليكم أمر علي بن أبي طالب وحده.

قال: فانطلق أبو بكر وعمر وأبو عبيدة بن الجراح والمغيرة بن شعبة حتى دخلوا على العباس بن عبد المطلب في الليلة الثانية من وفاة رسول الله صلى الله عليه وآله. قال: فتكلم أبو بكر فحمد الله جل وعز وأثنى عليه ثم قال: إن الله بعث لكم محمدا نبيا وللمؤمنين وليا، فمن الله عليهم بكونه بين ظهرانيهم، حتى اختار له ما عنده وترك للناس أمرهم ليختاروا لأنفسهم مصلحتهم، متفقين لا مختلفين. فاختاروني عليهم واليا ولأمورهم راعيا، فتوليت ذلك. وما أخاف بعون الله وهنا ولا حيرة ولا جبنا، وما توفيقي إلا بالله. غير أني لا أنفك من طاعن يبلغني فيقول بخلاف قول العامة، فيتخذكم لجأ فتكونون حصنه المنيع وخطبه البديع، فإما دخلتم مع الناس فيما اجتمعوا عليه أو صرفتموهم عما مالوا إليه. فقد جئناك ونحن نريد أن نجعل لك في هذا الأمر نصيبا يكون لك ولعقبك من بعدك، إذ كنت عم رسول الله صلى الله عليه وآله، وإن كان الناس أيضا قد رأوا مكانك ومكان صاحبك فعدلوا بهذا الأمر عنكما.

فقال عمر: أي والله، وأخرى يا بني هاشم على رسلكم، فإن رسول الله صلى الله عليه وآله منا ومنكم، وإنا لم نأتكم لحاجة منا إليكم، ولكن كرهنا أن يكون الطعن فيما اجتمع عليه المسلمون، فيتفاقم الخطب بكم وبهم. فانظروا لأنفسكم وللعامة. ثم سكت.

فتكلم العباس فقال: إن الله تبارك وتعالى ابتعث محمدا صلى الله عليه وآله - كما وصفت - نبيا وللمؤمنين وليا، فإن كنت برسول الله صلى الله عليه وآله طلبت هذا الأمر فحقنا أخذت، وإن كنت بالمؤمنين طلبت فنحن من المؤمنين، ما تقدمنا في أمرك ولا تشاورنا ولا تآمرنا ولا نحب لك ذلك، إذ كنا من المؤمنين وكنا لك من الكارهين. وأما قولك (أن تجعل لي في هذا الأمر نصيبا)، فإن كان هذا الأمر لك خاصة فأمسك عليك فلسنا محتاجين إليك وإن كان حق المؤمنين فليس لك أن تحكم في حقهم دونهم، وإن كان حقنا فإنا لا نرضى منك ببعضه دون بعض. وأما قولك يا عمر (إن رسول الله صلى الله عليه وآله منا ومنكم)، فإن رسول الله شجرة نحن أغصانها وأنتم جيرانها، فنحن أولى به منكم. وأما قولك (إنا نخاف تفاقم الخطب بكم وبنا)، فهذا الذي فعلتموه أوائل ذلك، والله المستعان.

فخرجوا من عنده وأنشأ العباس يقول:

ما كنت أحسب هذا الأمر منحرفا   عن هاشم ثم منهم عن أبي حسن

أليس أول من صلى لقبلتكم   وأعلم الناس بالآثار والسنن

وأقرب الناس عهدا بالنبي ومن   جبريل عون له في الغسل والكفن

من فيه ما في جميع الناس كلهم   وليس في الناس ما فيه من الحسن

من ذا الذي ردكم عنه فنعرفه   ها إن بيعتكم من أول الفتن

What is noteworthy in *Kitāb Sulaym's* account is that it also includes the poem mentioned by al-Yaʿqūbī (d. 284). However, in Sulaym b. Qays' account, this poem is ascribed to al-ʿAbbās b. ʿAbdilMuṭṭalib, not the less relevant ʿUtba b. Abī Lahab, and the poem therein is incorporated into al-ʿAbbās' dialogue with Abū Bakr and ʿUmar. This misattribution of the poem to al-ʿAbbās seems to be a later development in the tradition where the initial partitions within its dialogues were eventually dissolved, intertwined and/or disregarded by later transmitters, and these developments are culminated in the less-partitioned variant of *Kitāb Sulaym Ibn Qays.*

It is difficult to provide a precise dating of this variant of the tradition in *Kitāb Sulaym.* Nevertheless, what is clear is that this entire account exhibited multiple developments throughout its transmission, which culminated in various accretions being incorporated into the text alongside adjustments in its structure/order. In this regard, the variant of this account found in *Kitāb Sulaym* embodies more accretions when compared to the remainder variants.

Passage 8 - Dating the Account of Fāṭima's Murder

Though *Kitāb Sulaym Ibn Qays* is a multivalent theological and historical Twelver Shīʿite text, much of the controversy and discord surrounding its authenticity today stem from its tumultuous account of the attack on Fāṭima. The emphasis on this element of the book is not confined to Sunnī-Shīʿite polemical disputes surrounding the historical aftermaths of the Prophet's ﷺ death, but it has surfaced today, in certain settings, as a controversial intra-Shīʿite dispute as well.[1]

Since *Kitāb Sulaym's* account is the most detailed and controversial account regarding the "Fāṭimid tragedy," understanding the origins and development of this narrative may prove to be crucial to understanding the book's shadowy authorship.

The earliest reports that refer to the commotion at Fāṭima's house following Abū Bakr's pledge of allegiance are quite distinct from the narrative in *Kitāb Sulaym.* Ibn Abī Shayba (d. 235) said: Muḥammad b. Bishr informed us, he said: ʿUbaydullāh b. ʿUmar informed us, he said: Zayd b. Aslam informed us, on the authority of his father that he said:

> When Abū Bakr was pledged allegiance after the Messenger of Allah, ʿAlī and al-Zubayr used to enter upon Fāṭima and consult her and discuss their affairs. When news of that reached ʿUmar b. al-Khaṭṭāb, he set out and entered upon Fāṭima. He said, "O daughter of the Messenger of Allah, none is more beloved to me than your father, and none after him is more beloved to me than you. By Allah, that would not prevent me from commanding that the house is burnt upon them if they congregate with you."
>
> When ʿUmar left, they came to her, and she said, "You are aware that ʿUmar has approached me and swore that he would burn the house upon you! By Allah, he will fulfill what he had sworn to do, so depart in peace! See what you shall do, and do not come back to me!" They thus left her, and they only came back after pledging allegiance to Abū Bakr.[2]

---

1 See, for example, the late Shīʿite cleric, Muḥammad Ḥusayn Faḍlallāh (d. 2010), who ventured to doubt this narrative (or elements of it), only to face severe backlash from Twelver orthodoxy till this day.

2 Muṣannaf Ibn Abī Shayba (20/579)

قال ابن أبي شيبة: حَدَّثَنَا مُحَمَّدُ بْنُ بِشْرٍ، حدثنا عُبَيْدُ اللَّهِ بْنُ عُمَرَ، حَدَّثَنَا زَيْدُ بْنُ أَسْلَمَ، عَنْ أَبِيهِ أَسْلَمَ: أَنَّهُ حِينَ بُويِعَ لِأَبِي بَكْرٍ بَعْدَ رَسُولِ اللَّهِ كَانَ عَلِيٌّ وَالزُّبَيْرُ يَدْخُلَانِ عَلَى فَاطِمَةَ بِنْتِ رَسُولِ اللَّهِ فَيُشَاوِرُونَهَا، وَيَرْتَجِعُونَ فِي أَمْرِهِمْ.

فَلَمَّا بَلَغَ ذَلِكَ عُمَرَ بْنَ الْخَطَّابِ خَرَجَ حَتَّى دَخَلَ عَلَى فَاطِمَةَ، فَقَالَ، "يَا بِنْتَ رَسُولِ اللَّهِ وَاللَّهِ مَا مِنْ أَحَدٍ أَحَبَّ إِلَيْنَا مِنْ أَبِيكِ، وَمَا مِنْ أَحَدٍ أَحَبَّ إِلَيْنَا بَعْدَ أَبِيكِ مِنْكِ، وَايْمُ اللَّهِ مَا ذَاكَ بِمَانِعِي إِنِ اجْتَمَعَ هَؤُلَاءِ النَّفَرُ عِنْدَكِ، أَنْ آمُرَ بِهِمْ أَنْ يُحَرَّقَ عَلَيْهِمُ الْبَيْتُ."

قَالَ: فَلَمَّا خَرَجَ عُمَرُ، جَاءُوهَا فَقَالَتْ: تَعْلَمُونَ أَنَّ عُمَرَ قَدْ جَاءَنِي، وَقَدْ حَلَفَ بِاللَّهِ لَئِنْ عُدْتُمْ لَيُحَرِّقَنَّ عَلَيْكُمُ الْبَيْتَ، وَايْمُ اللَّهِ لَيَمْضِيَنَّ لِمَا حَلَفَ عَلَيْهِ، فَانْصَرِفُوا رَاشِدِينَ، فَرَوْا رَأْيَكُمْ وَلَا تَرْجِعُوا إِلَيَّ. فَانْصَرَفُوا عَنْهَا فَلَمْ يَرْجِعُوا إِلَيْهَا حَتَّى بَايَعُوا لِأَبِي بَكْرٍ."

This tradition's isnād is apparently authentic, but the account is inaccurate in several regards. It interestingly presents Fāṭima as the head figure of this purported Hashemite dissent, not ʿAlī. In fact, ʿAlī's role in this entire account is reduced to that a mere participant who, alongside the other men, used to consult Fāṭima regarding their affairs. ʿAlī's absence from the account is inculcated in ʿUmar's addressal of Fāṭima when attempting to disband the congregation at her residence, not ʿAlī. Asides from that, the tradition misses important details that took place during this event which were covered in other traditions. That, paralleled with the fact that the tradition's isnād embodies potential defects, leads me to conclude that this report is not the most accurate historical description of what took place before Fāṭima's house.[1] Some later isnād-less and embellished redactions of

1 One of his tradition's transmitters is Muḥammad b. Bishr al-ʿAbdī (d. 203), a reliable Kūfan transmitter. He is recorded transmitting the account from ʿUbaydullāh b. ʿUmar al-ʿUmarī (d. 143), a reliable Medinite.

The eminent ḥadīthist, Yaʿqūb b. Shayba (d. 262), noted that the Kūfans' transmission from ʿUbaydullāh tends to generally exhibit more flaws. See Sharḥ ʿIlal al-Tirmidhī of Ibn Rajab (1/129). In fact, a few documented examples exist where Muḥammad b. Bishr can be seen erring in transmission from ʿUbaydullāh; see al-Dāraquṭnī's al-ʿIlal al-Wārida fī al-Aḥādīth al-Nabawiyya (2/160, 13/54).

I have heard someone entertain the possibility that ʿUbaydullāh b. ʿUmar in the isnād may actually be ʿAbdullāh b. ʿUmar al-ʿUmarī, ʿUbaydullāh's unreliable brother. This is possible, considering the aforementioned

this tradition present Aslam claiming to had been a witness to this incident, and they are, for several reasons, inconsequential to my assessment of Aslam's tradition.[1]

There are a few traditions that revolve around the theme of the aforementioned tradition, but all are explicitly inauthentic. Al-Balādhurī reported that Maslama b. Muḥārib narrated on the authority of Sulaymān Al-Taymī and Ibn ʿAwn that [they said]:

> Abū Bakr sent to ʿAlī, requesting his pledge of allegiance, and ʿAlī did not pledge his allegiance to him. ʿUmar thus came with a torch, and Fāṭima met him at the door. She said, "O son of al-Khaṭṭāb, are you going to burn my door upon me?"
>
> He replied, "Yes, that would be better for your father's faith." ʿAlī then came and pledged his allegiance, and he said, "I had intended to not leave my home until I had compiled the Quran."[2]

قال البلاذري: الْمَدَائِنِيُّ، عَنْ مَسْلَمَةَ بْنِ مُحَارِبٍ، عَنْ سُلَيْمَانَ التيمى وعن ابْنِ عَوْنٍ أَنَّ أَبَا بَكْرٍ أَرْسَلَ إِلَى عَلِيٍّ يُرِيدُ الْبَيْعَةَ، فَلَمْ يُبَايِعْ. فَجَاءَ عُمَرُ ومعه فتيلة. فتلقته فاطمة على الباب، فقالت فاطمة: يا ابن الْخَطَّابِ، أَتُرَاكَ مُحَرِّقًا عَلَيَّ بَابِي؟ قَالَ: نَعَمْ، وَذَلِكَ أَقْوَى فِيمَا جَاءَ بِهِ أَبُوكِ. وَجَاءَ عَلِيٌّ فَبَايَعَ وَقَالَ: كُنْتُ عَزَمْتُ أَنْ لا أَخْرُجَ مِنْ مَنْزِلِي حَتَّى أَجْمَعَ الْقُرْآنَ.

This tradition is inauthentic. Maslama b. Muḥārib's reliability is unknown, and the isnād is disconnected after Ibn ʿAwn and Sulaymān al-Taymī. Additionally, the tradition seems to misrepresent ʿAlī's reasoning behind his initial refrainment from pledging his allegiance to Abū Bakr, and more will come on that shortly. It appears that this excuse of ʿAlī only came later following the commotion outside of his house in a somewhat different context.

---

observation and the fact that Muḥammad b. Bishr relayed traditions from both men.

Some critics of the tradition also understandably point out that Aslam al-Madanī was not present in Medīna when the event of al-Saqīfa unfolded, hence opening the door to questions regarding the isnād's connectivity and the possibility of him acquiring it from sources other than ʿUmar b. al-Khaṭṭāb. Either way, this account is not the most accurate account pertaining to the post-Saqīfa commotion that took place at Fāṭima and ʿAlī's house, as shall be demonstrated.

1 Al-Maṣābīḥ by Abū al-ʿAbbās al-Ḥasanī (p. 259-260)

2 Jumalun min Ansāb al-Ashrāf (1/586)

The past two traditions embody a generally similar characterization of the post-Saqīfa events: (1) ʿAlī and his faction initially refrain from pledging allegiance to Abū Bakr, (2) they are threatened by ʿUmar b. al-Khaṭṭab, and (3) they thus pledge allegiance to Abū Bakr without any violence, resistance or commotion. This narrative clearly is not in parallel to that of *Kitāb Sulaym*, which presents a violent and gruesome incursion taking place in Fāṭima's house towards Fāṭima and other partisans of ʿAlī b. Abī Ṭālib.

Another early narrative presents a slightly different spin on the post-Saqīfa events. Muḥammad b. ʿAmr b. ʿAlqama (d. 145) narrated on the authority of Abū Salama b. ʿAbdirraḥmān b. ʿAwf (d. 94) that he said:

> [...] ʿAlī and al-Zubayr entered the house of Fāṭima, the Prophet's ﷺ daughter. ʿUmar thus came, and he said, "Come out for the pledge of allegiance! By Allah, you will come out or I will otherwise burn the house down upon you!"
>
> Al-Zubayr thus came out with his sword drawn, and a man from the Anṣār and Ziyād b. Labīd al-Anṣārī, who was from the clan of Bayāḍa, embraced him. He struck him, and the sword fell out of his hand.
>
> Ziyād thus took the sword, and [Abū Bakr] said, "No! Strike the stone with it!"

This report's transmitter, Muḥammad b. ʿAmr, then said:

> Abū ʿAmr b. Ḥimās, who was from the Laythī clan, informed me, he said, "I witnessed that rock that was struck by the sword."
>
> Abū Bakr then said, "Let them be, for Allah will eventually bring them." They then went out after that and pledged allegiance to Abū Bakr. They said, "There was no one more worthy of the position than you, but we felt that ʿUmar was extorting our matter from us." The people hence pledged allegiance to him on Monday [...].[1]

مُحَمَّدُ بْنُ عَمْرٍو، عَنْ أَبِي سَلَمَةَ قَالَ: [....] وَدَخَلَ عَلِيٌّ وَالزُّبَيْرُ بَيْتَ فَاطِمَةَ بِنْتِ رَسُولِ اللَّهِ صَلَّى اللهُ عَلَيْهِ وَسَلَّمَ، فَجَاءَ عُمَرُ فَقَالَ: اخْرُجُوا لِلْبَيْعَةِ، وَاللَّهِ لَتَخْرُجُنَّ، أَوْ لَأُحَرِّقَنَّهُ عَلَيْكُمْ، فَخَرَجَ الزُّبَيْرُ صَلْتًا بِالسَّيْفِ، فَاعْتَنَقَهُ زِيَادُ بْنُ لَبِيدٍ الْأَنْصَارِيُّ مِنْ بَيَاضَةَ فَدَقَّ بِهِ، وَبَدَرَ السَّيْفَ مِنْ يَدِهِ مِنْهُ، فَأَخَذَهُ زِيَادٌ قَالَ: لَا، وَلَكِنِ اضْرِبْ

1 Ḥadīth Hishām Ibn ʿAmmār (p. 122-125), Sharḥ Nahj al-Balāgha by Ibn Abī al-Ḥadīd (2/56)

بِهِ الْحَجَرَ، قَالَ مُحَمَّدُ بْنُ عَمْرٍو: فَحَدَّثَنِي أَبُو عَمْرِو بْنُ حِمَاسٍ مِنَ اللَّيْثِيِّينَ قَالَ: أَدْرَكْتُ ذَلِكَ الْحَجَرَ الَّذِي فِيهِ ضَرْبَ السَّيْفُ، فَقَالَ أَبُو بَكْرٍ رَضِيَ اللَّهُ عَنْهُ: دَعُوهُمْ فَسَيَأْتِي اللَّهُ بِهِمْ، فَخَرَجُوا بَعْدَ ذَلِكَ فَبَايَعُوهُ، قَالُوا: مَا كَانَ أَحَدٌ أَحَقَّ بِهَا، وَلَا أَوْلَى بِهَا مِنْكَ، وَلَكِنَّا قَدْ عَهِدْنَا مِنْ عُمَرَ يَبْتَزُّنَا أَمْرَنَا، فَبَايَعَهُ النَّاسُ يَوْمَ الاثْنَيْنِ [...].

قلت: وروى نحو هذا الخبر أبو بكر الجوهري في «كتاب السقيفة» بإسناده إلى محمد بن عمرو بن علقمة، وقد أورد ذلك ابن أبي الحديد في شرحه لنهج البلاغة.

This tradition more accurately characterizes the evets that took place at Fāṭima's house. Though Muḥammad b. ʿAmr b. ʿAlqama was criticized in his transmission from Abū Salama and Abū Salama did not witness the events being described in the tradition, this tradition, has a basis. Firstly, Muḥammad b. ʿAmr's quote from Abū ʿAmr b. Ḥimās, where it is stated that he had witnessed the stone on which al-Zubayr's sword was struck, lends credence to the claim being made about al-Zubayr's sword. Secondly, the claim in this tradition is verified in another strong report.

The tradition at hand can be found in the *Maghāzī* of Mūsā b. ʿUqba (d. 141). Mūsā said: Saʿd b. Ibrāhīm informed me, he said: Ibrāhīm b. ʿAbdirraḥmān b. ʿAwf informed me, he said:

> ʿAbdurraḥmān b. ʿAwf was with ʿUmar b. al-Khaṭṭāb on that day, and he was the one who broke al-Zubayr's sword - God knows best as to who actually broke it.
>
> Abū Bakr then got up, gave a sermon before the people, and he apologized to them. He said, "By Allah, I was never eager for leadership in any day or night, nor was I ever interested in it, nor did I ever ask Allah for it in secret or in open. Rather, I was wary of the *fitna*, and I have no respite in leadership. I have been tasked with a grave matter that I cannot bare or withstand except through Allah's assistance. I had wished that the there was someone more suitable for it in my place."
>
> The Muhājirūn thus accepted what he said and what he mentioned as an excuse, and ʿAlī b. Abī Ṭālib and al-Zubayr said, "We were only angered because we were excluded from the council. We see Abū Bakr as the worthiest of it after the Messenger of Allah. He is the companion of the cave where he was the second of two. We

> know his honor and seniority, and the Messenger of Allah ﷺ had commanded him to lead the people in prayer while he was alive."[1]

قال موسى بن عقبة: قَالَ سَعْدُ بْنُ إِبْرَاهِيمَ: حَدَّثَنِي إِبْرَاهِيمُ بْنُ عَبْدِ الرَّحْمَنِ بْنِ عَوْفٍ أَنَّ عَبْدَ الرَّحْمَنِ بْنَ عَوْفٍ رَضِيَ اللَّهُ عَنْهُ كَانَ مَعَ عُمَرَ بْنِ الخطاب رضي الله عنه يومئذ، وَأَنَّهُ هُوَ كَسَرَ سَيْفَ الزُّبَيْرِ، وَاللَّهُ أَعْلَمُ من كَسْرِهِ ، ثُمَّ قَامَ أَبُو بَكْرٍ فَخَطَبَ النَّاسَ وَاعْتَذَرَ إِلَيْهِمْ، فَقَالَ: وَاللَّهِ مَا كُنْتُ حَرِيصًا عَلَى الإِمَارَةِ يَوْمًا قَطُّ وَلا لَيْلَةً، وَلا كُنْتُ فِيهَا رَاغِبًا، وَلا سَأَلْتُهَا اللَّهَ قَطُّ فِي سِرٍّ وَلا عَلانِيَةٍ، وَلَكِنِّي أَشْفَقْتُ مِنَ الْفِتْنَةِ، وَمَا لِي فِي الإِمَارَةِ مِنْ رَاحَةٍ، ولكن قلدت أمرا عظيما ما لي به طاقة ولا يدان إلا بِتَقْوِيَةِ اللَّهِ عَزَّ وَجَلَّ، وَلَوَدِدْتُ أَنَّ أَقْوَى النَّاسِ عَلَيْهَا مَكَانِي، فَقَبِلَ الْمُهَاجِرُونَ - مِنْهُ مَا قَالَ وَمَا اعْتَذَرَ بِهِ، وَقَالَ عَلِيُّ بْنُ أَبِي طَالِبٍ وَالزُّبَيْرُ بْنُ الْعَوَّامِ: مَا غضبنا إلا أنا أخرنا عن المشاورة، وَإِنَّا لَنَرَى أَبَا بَكْرٍ أَحَقَّ النَّاسِ بِهَا بَعْدَ رَسُولِ اللَّهِ صَلَّى اللَّهُ عَلَيْهِ وَسَلَّمَ، إنه لصاحب الغار، ثاني اثنين، وإنا لنعرف لَهُ شَرَفَهُ وَكِبْرَهُ، وَلَقَدْ أَمَرَهُ رَسُولُ اللَّهِ صَلَّى اللَّهُ عَلَيْهِ وَسَلَّمَ بِالصَّلاةِ لِلنَّاسِ وَهُوَ حي.

قال الحاكم في «المستدرك»: صَحِيحٌ عَلَى شَرْطِ الشَّيْخَيْنِ، وَلَمْ يُخَرِّجَاهُ.

This report is the most authentic tradition in this context: Ibrāhīm b. ʿAbdirraḥmān b. ʿAwf was describing an event that involved his father, corroborating what was relayed by his brother, Abū Salama b. ʿAbdirraḥmān b. ʿAwf regarding al-Zubayr and his sword.

Another brief tradition in al-Ṭabarī's *Tārīkh*, more or less, summarizes the past two accounts. Al-Ṭabarī said: Ibn Ḥumayd informed us, he said: Jarīr informed us, on the authority of Mughīra, from Ziyād b. Kulayb that he said:

> ʿUmar b. al-Khaṭṭāb approached ʿAlī's house when Ṭalḥa, al-Zubayr and men from the *Muhājirīn* were there. He said, "By Allah, I shall burn the house upon you if you do not come out to pledge allegiance!"
>
> Al-Zubayr hence went out to him with his sword drawn, and he tripped, to which his sword fell out of his hand. They rushed to him and acquired the sword.

---

1 Aḥādīth Muntakhaba min Maghāzī Mūsā Ibn ʿUqba (p. 94-95). Al-Ḥākim described this tradition saying, "This ḥadīth is authentic according to the criteria of Bukhārī and Muslim, and they did not record it [in their Ṣaḥīḥs]." See al-Mustadrak ʿalā al-Ṣaḥīḥayn (3/70).

قال الطبري: حَدَّثَنَا ابْنُ حُمَيْدٍ، قَالَ: حَدَّثَنَا جَرِيرٌ، عَنْ مُغِيرَةَ، عَنْ زِيَادِ بْنِ كُلَيْبٍ، قَالَ: أَتَى عُمَرُ بْنُ الْخَطَّابِ مَنْزِلَ عَلِيٍّ وَفِيهِ طَلْحَةُ وَالزُّبَيْرُ وَرِجَالٌ مِنَ الْمُهَاجِرِينَ، فَقَالَ: وَاللَّهِ لأَحْرِقَنَّ عَلَيْكُمْ أَوْ لَتخْرُجُنَّ إِلَى الْبَيْعَةِ فَخَرَجَ عَلَيْهِ الزُّبَيْرُ مصلتا بالسيف، فَعَثَرَ فَسَقَطَ السَّيْفُ مِنْ يَدِهِ، فَوَثَبُوا عَلَيْهِ فاخذوه.

This tradition is weak, for Ibn Ḥumayd (d. 248) used to forge isnāds, and the isnād is disconnected after Ziyād b. Kulayb (d. 119).[1] Nevertheless, this tradition's weakness is inconsequential, as its general contents were relayed in other more reliable traditions.

In later accounts, one begins to observe gradual developments in the descriptions of these events. Abū Bakr al-Jawharī said: Abū Zayd ʿUmar b. Shabba informed me, he said: Ibrāhīm b. al-Mundhir informed me, he said: Ibn Wahb informed us, on the authority of Ibn Lahīʿah, from Abū al-Aswad that he said:

> Men from the Muhājirīn were angered at Abū Bakr's pledge of allegiance without council. ʿAlī and al-Zubayr were angered, and they entered Fāṭima's house armed. ʿUmar thus came with a band that included Usayd b. Ḥuḍayr and Salama b. Salāma, who were from the clan of Banī ʿAbdilʾAshhal. They both stormed into the house, and Fāṭima screamed and asked them by Allah. They took both ʿAlī and al-Zubayr's swords and struck the stone with them until the swords were broken. ʿUmar then took them outside and drove them until they pledged allegiance.
>
> Abū Bakr then got up and gave a sermon before the people. He said, "My pledge of allegiance was an undeliberate affair (*falta*), and Allah protected from its evil. I feared *fitna*. By Allah, I never desired it in any day, nor did I ever ask Allah for it secretly or openly. I have been tasked with a grave matter for which I have no energy or power. I had wished that the there was someone more suitable for it in my place."[2]

قال أبو بكر الجوهري: حدثني أبو زيد عمر بن شبة، قال: حدثني ابراهيم بن المنذر قال: حدثنا ابن وهب، عن ابن لهيعة، عن أبي الأسود، قال: غضب رجال من المهاجرين في بيعة أبي بكر بغير مشورة، وغضب علي، والزبير، فدخلا بيت فاطمة، معهما السلاح، فجاء عمر في عصابة، فيهم اسيد بن حضير، وسلمة بن سلامة بن

1 See Ibn Ḥumayd's entry in Tahdhīb al-Kamāl (25/97-108).
2 Sharḥ Nahj al-Balāgha by Ibn Abī al-Ḥadīd (6/47)

قريش، وهما من بني عبد الأشهل، فاقتحما الدار، فاصحت فاطمة ونشادتهما الله، فأخذوا سيفيهما فضربوا بهما الحجر حتى كسروهما، فأخرجهما عمر يسوقهما حتى بايعا، ثم قام أبو بكر، فخطب الناس، فاعتذر إليهم وقال: أن بيعتي كانت فلتة، وقى الله شرها، وخشيت الفتنة، وأيم الله ما حرصت عليها يوما قط، ولا سألتها الله في سر ولا علانية قط، ولقد قلدت أمرا عظيما مالي به طاقة ولا يدان، ولقد وددت أن أقوى الناس عليه مكاني.

This tradition is weak, for Ibn Lahīʿa (d. 174) was a debased transmitter.[1] This rendition of the account hence cannot be dated before him. Asides from Ibn Lahīʿa's weakness, he was described by Ibn ʿAdī (d. 365) as someone who was excessive in his Shīʿism, which may further exacerbate his incompetence when transmitting traditions pertaining to such subjects.[2] Nonetheless, Ibn Lahīʿa's account embodies some accretions and developments, such as (1) the notion that ʿUmar and his band stormed the house, (2) the notion that both ʿAlī and al-Zubayr's swords were confiscated inside Fāṭima's house, (3) the notion that ʿUmar forcefully drove ʿAlī and al-Zubayr out of the house to pledge allegiance to Abū Bakr and (4) Fāṭima's screaming in response to these purported events. It should also be noted that Ibn Lahīʿa's alleged informant, Abū al-Aswad Muḥammad b. ʿAbdirraḥmān (d. 131), was a relatively later figure who did not directly transmit from the *ṣaḥāba*. Rather, his transmission mostly is from the *tābiʿīn*, so his transmission of this account is manifestly disconnected.

Around the time the past tradition developed, another account emerged which presents Abū Bakr regretting what he had purportedly done to Fāṭima's house, though it is vague and inexplicit. ʿUlwān d. Dāwūd (d. 180) narrated on the authority of Ṣāliḥ b. Kaysān, from ʿUmar b. ʿAbdirraḥmān b. ʿAwf, from his father that he said:

> I entered upon Abū Bakr when he was on his deathbed, [...] and he said, "I do not regret anything from the *Dunyā* except three things I did, which I wish I had never done. [...] I wish that I had not exposed Fāṭima's house for anything, even if they had locked it for war..."[3]

---

1 See his entry in Tahdhīb al-Kamāl (15/487-503)

2 Al-Kāmil fī Ḍuʿafāʾ al-Rijāl (3/289)

3 Al-Amwāl by Ibn Zanjawayh (1/301, 1/347), Tārīkh al-Rusul wa-l-Mulūk (3/429-431), al-Ḍuʿafāʾ al-Kabīr by al-ʿUqaylī (3/419-421), al-Muʿjam al-Kabīr by al-Ṭabarānī (1/62). Al-Ṭabarī, Ibn Zanjawayh and al-ʿUqaylī presented multiple isnāds that quote al-Layth b. Saʿd transmitting this tradition from ʿUlwān, an observation that will shortly prove to be relevant.

روى علوان بن داود عَنْ صَالِحِ بْنِ كَيْسَانَ، عَنْ عُمَرَ بْنِ عَبْدِ الرَّحْمَنِ بْنِ عَوْفٍ، عَنْ أَبِيهِ، أَنَّهُ دَخَلَ عَلَى أَبِي بَكْرٍ الصِّدِّيقِ رَضِيَ اللَّهُ تَعَالَى عَنْهُ فِي مَرَضِهِ [...] قال ابو بكر رضى الله عَنْهُ: أَجَلْ، إِنِّي لا آسَى عَلَى شَيْءٍ مِنَ الدُّنْيَا إِلا عَلَى ثَلاثٍ فَعَلْتُهُنَّ وَدِدْتُ أَنِّي تَرَكْتُهُنَّ، وَثَلاثٌ تَرَكْتُهُنَّ وَدِدْتُ أَنِّي فَعَلْتُهُنَّ، وَثَلاثٌ وَدِدْتُ أَنِّي سَأَلْتُ عَنْهُنَّ رَسُولَ اللَّهِ صَلَّى اللَّهُ عَلَيْهِ وَسَلَّمَ فَأَمَّا الثَّلاثُ اللاتِي وَدِدْتُ أَنِّي تَرَكْتُهُنَّ، فَوَدِدْتُ أَنِّي لَمْ أَكْشِفْ بَيْتَ فَاطِمَةَ عَنْ شَيْءٍ وَإِنْ كَانُوا قَدْ غَلَّقُوهُ عَلَى الْحَرْبِ.

This tradition seems to have been exclusively relayed by ʿUlwān b. Dāwūd, a disparaged transmitter who was deemed disapproved (*munkar*) in his transmission.[1] Some isnāds of this tradition present al-Layth b. Saʿd transmitting this tradition directly from Ṣāliḥ b. Kaysān with no mention of ʿUlwān b. Dāwūd, and these few reports merely omit al-Layth's original source in this tradition, ʿUlwān b. Dāwūd.[2] Barring the fact that al-Layth, on multiple occasions, explicitly mentioned that he had acquired the tradition from ʿUlwān b. Dāwūd, ʿUlwān later even acknowledged that he was al-Layth's source in this tradition. Yaḥyā b. ʿAbdillāh b. Bukayr, al-Layth's student, said:

> ʿUlwān then visited us after al-Layth's death, and I asked him about this ḥadīth. He relayed it to me as al-Layth had relayed to me letter-by-letter, and he informed me that he had informed al-Layth b. Saʿd of this ḥadīth.[3]

---

1 Al-ʿUqaylī said, "He is not corroborated in his ḥadīth, and he is only known by it." Al-Bukhārī said, "He is disapproved (*munkar*) in ḥadīth." Saʿīd b. Kathīr stated that he was a thief (of traditions?). See al-Ḍuʿafāʾ al-Kabīr of al-ʿUqaylī (3/419-421).

Ibn Rishdīn said, "I asked Aḥmed b. Ṣāliḥ about ʿUlwān b. Dāwūd's ḥadīth that our companions transmit. He said, 'This ḥadīth is a fabrication and lies. It should not be transcribed, written or transmitted,' and I felt that ʿUlwān b. Dāwūd was an abandoned (*matrūk*) transmitter according to him." See Tārīkh Asmāʾ al-Ḍuʿafāʾ wa-l-Kadhdhābīn of Ibn Shāhīn (p. 254). Abū Saʿīd b. Yūnus said, "He is disapproved (*munkar*) in ḥadīth." See al-Ḍuʿafāʾ wa-l-Matrūkūn of Ibn al-Jawzī (2/190).

2 See for example, Tārīkh Dimashq by Ibn ʿAsākir (30/419). Al-Dhahabī also noted that Ibn ʿĀʾidh relayed the tradition in this manner, though al-Dhahabī had mentioned beforehand that al-Layth had merely acquired this tradition from ʿUlwān b. Dāwūd. See Tārīkh al-Islām of al-Dhahabī (2/69-70). For further context, refer to footnote 1.

3 Tārīkh al-Rusul wa-l-Mulūk by al-Ṭabarī (3/431)

قال الطبري: قَالَ لِي يُونُسُ: قَالَ لَنَا يَحْيَى: ثُمَّ قَدِمَ عَلَيْنَا عُلْوَانُ بَعْدَ وَفَاةِ اللَّيْثِ، فَسَأَلْتُهُ عَنْ هَذَا الْحَدِيثِ، فَحَدَّثَنِي بِهِ كَمَا حَدَّثَنِي اللَّيْثُ بْنُ سَعْدٍ حَرْفًا حَرْفًا، وَأَخْبَرَنِي أَنَّهُ هُوَ حَدَّثَ بِهِ اللَّيْثَ بْنَ سَعْدٍ، وَسَأَلْتُهُ عَنِ اسْمِ أَبِيهِ، فَأَخْبَرَنِي أَنَّهُ عُلْوَانُ بْنُ دَاوُدَ.

Aḥmed b. Ḥanbal, on the other hand, blamed the forgery of this ḥadīth on other than ʿUlwān, revealing its true origins. Al-Khallāl said: Muhannā said:

> I asked Aḥmed about the ḥadīth of al-Layth b. Saʿd, from Ṣāliḥ b. Kaysān, from Ḥumayd b. ʿAbdirraḥmān, from his father that he entered upon Abū Bakr while he was on his deathbed and greeted him. Abū Bakr then said, 'I only regret three things I had done.'
>
> Aḥmed said, "It is not authentic." I asked, "How is it?" He said, "It was taken from the book of Ibn Dāb and then misattributed to al-Layth."

Al-Khallāl then said: Abū Bakr b. Ṣadaqa said:

> This ḥadīth is transmitted from ʿUlwān b. Dāwūd al-Bajalī, who was from the inhabitants of Qarqīsiā. He transmits these ḥadīths from Ibn Dāb, and I have found this ḥadīth among his transmission from Ibn Dāb. ʿUlwān, in and of himself, is not bad.[1]

قال الخلال: قَالَ مهنا: سألت أَحْمَدَ، عَنْ حَدِيثِ: اللَّيْثِ بْنِ سَعْدٍ، عَنْ صَالِحِ بْنِ كَيْسَانَ، عَنْ حُمَيْدِ بْنِ عَبْدِ الرَّحْمَنِ، عَنْ أَبِيهِ، أَنَّهُ دَخَلَ عَلَى أَبِي بَكْرٍ فِي مَرَضِهِ، فسلَّم عَلَيْهِ، فَقَالَ، "أَمَا إِنِي مَا آسَى إِلا عَلَى ثَلاثٍ فعلتُهنَّ" -الْحَدِيثَ؟.

فَقَالَ أَحْمَدُ: لَيْسَ صَحِيحًا. قَالَ: أُخذ مِنْ كِتَابِ ابْنِ دابٍ، فَوَضَعَهُ عَلَى اللَّيْثِ.

قَالَ الْخَلالُ: قَالَ أَبُو بَكْرِ بْنُ صَدَقَةَ رُوِيَ هَذَا الْحَدِيثُ، عَنْ عُلْوَانَ بْنِ دَاوُدَ الْبَجَلِيِّ، مِنْ أَهْلِ قرقيسيا، وَهُوَ يُحَدِّثُ بِهَذِهِ الأَحَادِيثِ، عَنِ ابْنِ دَابٍّ، ورأيتُ هذا الحديث من حديثه، عن [ابن] دابٍ، وَعُلْوَانُ فِي نَفْسِهِ لا بَأْسَ بِهِ.

Hence, it would be said that ʿUlwān b. Dāwūd in this tradition omitted his direct source, the suspect forger, ʿĪsā b. Yazīd b. Bakr b. Dāb, making the

1 Al-Muntakhab min ʿIlal al-Khallāl by Ibn Qudāma (p. 296-297)

isnād appear authentic.[1] Either way, ʿUlwān's tradition is an ahistorical account that is only relevant to the discussion at hand because it is regularly cited, despite its vagueness and unclarity, as some form of evidence to substantiate the narrative of *Kitāb Sulaym Ibn Qays.*

Al-Balādhurī relayed the previous account through a seemingly independent isnād that is, in reality, interdependent with those of ʿUlwān b. Dāwūd and Ibn Dāb. He relayed the tradition via Ḥafṣ b. ʿUmar al-ʿUmarī, fro, al-Haytham b. ʿAdī, from Yūnus b. Yazīd al-Aylī, from al-Zuhrī….[2]

قال البلاذري: حَدَّثَنِي حَفْصُ بْنُ عُمَرَ، ثنا الْهَيْثَمِ بْنِ عَدِيٍّ عَنْ يُونُسَ بْنِ يَزِيدَ الأَيْلِيِّ عَنِ الزُّهْرِيِّ أَنَّ عَبْدَ الرَّحْمَنِ بْنَ عَوْفٍ قَالَ: دَخَلْتُ عَلَى أَبِي بَكْرٍ فِي مَرَضِهِ .... الخبر.

I was unable to find any mention of Ḥafṣ b. ʿUmar al-ʿUmarī's status as a transmitter, and he appears to be obscure and unknown. Additionally, al-Haytham b. ʿAdī (d. 207) was a severely unreliable transmitter who was even declared a forger by several critics.[3] What is additionally noteworthy is how the unreliable al-Haytham b. ʿAdī was the exclusive source of this isnād that references al-Zuhrī, though al-Zuhrī was a man of many companions who regularly corroborated each other's transmission from him. In summary, this pseudo-corroboration evidently is unreliable, and it cannot be said to be independent of ʿUlwān b. Dāwūd's account.

Another slightly later tradition proceeds to add more details to the past accounts pertaining to this event. Abū Bakr al-Jawharī said: Abū Bakr al-Bāhilī informed me, on the authority of Ismāʿīl b. Mujālid, from al-Shaʿbī that he said:

> Abū Bakr said, "O ʿUmar, where is Khālid b. al-Walīd?" He said, "Here he is." Abū Bakr said, "Go to them both (ʿAlī and al-Zubayr) and bring them to me."
>
> They both set out, and ʿUmar entered the house while Khālid stood at the door outside. ʿUmar told al-Zubayr, "What is this sword?" He said, "I have prepared so that I can pledge my allegiance to ʿAlī," and there were many people at the house, among them was al-Miqdād b. al-Aswad and the majority of the Hashemites.

---

1 See Ibn Dāb's entry in Lisān al-Mīzān (6/287-290).
2 Jumalun min Ansāb al-Ashrāf by al-Balādhurī (10/346)
3 See his entry in Lisān al-Mīzān (8/361-363).

ʿUmar thus snatched the sword struck it on a stone inside the house. He then grabbed al-Zubayr's hand, lifted him and pushed him outside. ʿUmar then said, "O Khālid, take this man!" Khālid grabbed him, and there was a large band of people outside the house with Khālid sent by Abū Bakr to protect both men.

ʿUmar then entered the house and said to ʿAlī, "Get up and pledge your allegiance." ʿAlī slacked and stood behind, so ʿUmar grabbed his hand and said, "Get up!" He refused to get up, so ʿUmar lifted him and pushed him outside just as he did with al-Zubayr, and Khālid grabbed them both.

ʿUmar then violently drove both men, and the people congregated to witness what was taking place. The streets of Medīna were crowded, and Fāṭima witnessed what ʿUmar had done. She screamed and wailed, and many Hashemite and non-Hashemite women gathered around her. She went to her house's door and called out, "O Abū Bakr! How quickly have you raided the Prophet's ﷺ household?! By Allah, I shall never speak to ʿUmar till I meet Allah!"

When ʿAlī and al-Zubayr pledged their allegiance to Abū Bakr and Fāṭima calmed down from that outburst, Abū Bakr visited her, interceded on behalf of ʿUmar and requested that she be pleased with ʿUmar, so she was pleased with him.[1]

قال أبو بكر الجوهري: أخبرني أبو بكر الباهلي، عن اسماعيل بن مجالد، عن الشعبي، قال: قال أبو بكر: يا عمر، أين خالد بن الوليد، قال: هو هذا، فقال: انطلقا اليهما. يعني عليا والزبير. فأتياني بهما، فانطلقا فدخل عمر ووقف خالد على الباب من خارج، فقال عمر للزبير: ما هذا السيف؟ قال: اعددته لأبايع عليا، قال: وكان في البيت ناس كثير، منهم المقداد بن الاسود وجمهور الهاشميين، فاخترط عمر السيف فضرب به صخرة في البيت فكسره، ثم أخذ بيد الزبير فأقامه ثم دفعه فأخرجه، وقال: يا خالد، دونك هذا، فأمسكه خالد.

وكان خارج البيت مع خالد جمع كثير من الناس أرسلهم أبو بكر رداءا لهما، ثم دخل عمر فقال لعلي: قم فبايع فتلكأ واحتبس فأخذ بيده وقال: قم فأبى ان يقوم، فحمله ودفعه كما دفع الزبير ثم امسكهما خالد، وساقهما عمر ومن معه سوقا عنيفا، واجتمع الناس ينظرون، وامتلأت شوارع المدينة بالرجال، ورأت فاطمة ما صنع

1 Sharḥ Nahj al-Balāgha (6/48-49)

عمر. فصرخت وولولت، واجتمع معها نساء كثير من الهاشميات وغيرهن، فخرجت الى باب حجرتها، ونادت، يا أبا بكر، ما أسرع ما أغرتم على أهل بيت رسول الله، والله لا أكلم عمر حتى ألقى الله. قال: فلما بايع علي والزبير، وهدأت تلك الفورة، مشى إليها أبو بكر بعد ذلك فشفع لعمر، وطلب إليها فرضيت عنه.

This account clearly is a more dramatic presentation of the past accounts. Its dialogue is further developed into what resembles more of a script. More (erroneous) details are incorporated into the account, and, at this point, it becomes, more or less, a tragedy. It should hence not come as a surprise that Abū Bakr Aḥmed b. Muʿāwiya al-Bāhilī (d. mid-late third century) was severely disparaged by some.[1] Ismāʾīl b. Mujālid (d. 180-190) was also criticized as a truthful yet incompetent transmitter by various critics.[2] Though this tradition cannot be verifiably attributed to al-Shaʿbī, it should be noted that his transmission here is disconnected as well. This account developed after Ibn Lahīʿa's (d. 174) account, and its language seems more appropriately dated to Aḥmed b. Muʿāwiya's era in the third century.

Another contemporary account is that of Saʿīd b. Kathīr b. ʿUfayr (d. 226), which he relayed from anonymous sources. Abū Bakr al-Jawharī said: Aḥmed b. Isḥāq informed us, he said: Aḥmed b. Sayyār informed us, he said: Saʿīd b. Kathīr b. ʿUfayr al-Anṣārī said:

> [...] And ʿUmar went with a band of people to Fāṭima's house, and among the band was Usayd b. Ḥuḍayr and Salama b. Aslam. ʿUmar told those in the house, "Go and pledge your allegiance!" They refused to fulfill his orders.
>
> Al-Zubayr then went out to them with his sword drawn, and ʿUmar said, "Get the hound!" Salama b. Aslam thus leaped onto him, and he snatched his sword and struck it onto the wall. The band then drove al-Zubayr, ʿAlī and Banī Hāshim, and ʿAlī was saying, "I am the slave of Allah and the Messenger of Allah's ﷺ brother!" until they drove him to Abū Bakr.

1 Ibn ʿAdī described him saying, "He transmitted fabrications via reliable transmitters, and he used to steal ḥadīth." See al-Kāmil fī Ḍuʿafāʾ al-Rijāl (1/283-284). Al-Khaṭīb al-Baghdādī, however, did not seem to perceive him as a forger. He said, "There was nothing wrong in him." See Tārīkh Baghdād (6/380).

2 See his entry in Tahdhīb al-Kamāl (3/184-187).

It was then said to ʿAlī, "Pledge your allegiance," and he said, "I am more worthy of this matter than you! I shall not pledge my allegiance to you when you should pledge allegiance to me! You have taken this matter from the Anṣār, and you have cited your relationship to the Messenger of Allah ﷺ as evidence against them, so they granted you leadership. I cite against you the same argument you had made against the Anṣār, so be fair with us if you fear Allah from yourselves; and acknowledge our right in leadership just as the Anṣār had acknowledged yours. Otherwise, acknowledge your conscious oppression (*ẓulm*)."

ʿUmar then said, "You will not be left alone until you pledge your allegiance!" ʿAlī replied to him saying, "ʿUmar, milk a milking half of which will be given to you, and strengthen Abū Bakr's matter today so that he can compensate you in the future. By Allah, I will not accept your speech, and I will not pledge my allegiance to him."

Abū Bakr said to him, "If you do not pledge your allegiance to me, then I will not force you to do so."

ʿUbayda told ʿAlī, "O Abū Ḥasan, you are young, and these are the seniors of Quraysh, your tribe. You do not possess their experience and acquaintance in matters. I see Abū Bakr only more firm, enduring, and experienced in this matter than you, so concede the leadership to him and be content with it. If you are to live a long life, then you would be worthy and suitable for this matter due to your great status, relationship [to the Prophet], your precedent in Islam and your *jihad*."

ʿAlī thus said, "O Muhājirūn, I remind you of Allah, do not remove take away Muḥammad's authority outside his house to your houses. They have stripped his family from his status among the people and his right. By Allah, O Muhājirūn, we, *Ahlulbayt*, are more worthy of this matter than you. Was there not among us a reciter of Allah's book, a scholar in Allah's faith, a knowledgeable one in the *Sunna* and an acquainted one with the public's affairs? By Allah, he is within us, so do not follow your whims and hence become increasingly distanced from the Truth."

Bashīr b. Saʿd b. ʿUbāda said, "Had the Anṣār heard this speech from you, O ʿAlī, prior to their pledge of allegiance to Abū Bakr, then no two people would ever disagree in your regard. However, they have already pledged their allegiance."

ʿAlī went back to his house, and he did not pledge his allegiance. He was confined in his house until Fāṭima died, and he then pledged his allegiance [to Abū Bakr].[1]

قال أبو بكر الجوهري: أخبرني أحمد بن اسحاق قال: حدثنا أحمد بن سيار قال: حدثنا سعيد بن كثير ابن عفير الأنصاري، قال: [...] وذهب عمر ومعه عصابة الى بيت فاطمة، منهم اسيد بن حضير وسلمة بن أسلم، فقال لهم: انطلقوا فبايعوا، فأبوا عليه، وخرج إليهم الزبير بسيفه، فقال عمر: عليكم الكلب، فوثب عليه سلمة بن أسلم. فأخذ السيف من يده فضرب به الجدار، ثم انطلقوا به وبعلي ومعها بنو هاشم، وعلي يقول: انا عبد الله وأخو رسول الله صلى الله عليه وآله وسلم، حتى انتهوا به الى ابي بكر، فقيل له: بايع فقال: انا أحق بهذا الأمر منكم، لا أبايعكم وأنتم أولى بالبيعة لي، أخذتم هذا الأمر من الأنصار، واحتججتم عليهم بالقرابة من رسول الله، فأعطوكم المقادة، وسلموا اليكم الامارة، وانا احتج عليكم بمثل ما احتججتم به على الأنصار، فانصفونا ان كنتم تخافون الله من انفسكم، واعرفو لنا من الأمر مثل ما عرفت الأنصار لكم، وإلا فبؤوا بالظلم وأنتم تعلمون.

فقال عمر: انك لست متروكا حتى تبايع، فقال له علي: احلب يا عمر حلبا لك شطره، اشدد له اليوم أمره ليرد عليك غدا، الا والله لا اقبل قولك ولا ابايعه، فقال له أبو بكر: فإن لم تبايعني لم أكرهك، فقال له عبيدة: يا ابا الحسن، انك حديث السن، وهؤلاء مشيخة قريش قومك، ليس لك مثل تجربتهم ومعرفتهم بالأمور، ولا أرى أبا بكر الا أقوى على هذا الأمر منك، واشد احتمالا له، واضطلاعا به، فسلم له الأمر وارض به، فإنك ان تعش ويطل عمرك فأنت لهذا الأمر خليق وبه حقيق في فضلك وقرابتك وسابقتك وجهادك.

فقال علي: يا معشر المهاجرين، الله الله، لا تخرجوا سلطان محمد عن داره وبيته الى بيوتكم ودوركم، دفعوا أهله عن مقامه في الناس وحقه، فوالله يا معشر المهاجرين لنحن. أهل البيت. أحق بهذا الأمر منكم، أما كان منا القاريء لكتاب الله، الفقيه في دين الله، العالم بالسنة، المضطلع بأمر الرعية، والله انه لفينا، فلا تتبعوا الهوى، فتزدادوا من الحق بعدا.

---

1 Sharḥ Nahj al-Balāgha (6/11)

فقال بشير بن سعد: لو كان هذا الكلام سمعته منك الأنصار ياعلي قبل بيعتهم لأبي بكر، ما اختلف عليك اثنان، ولكنهم قد بايعوا. وانصرف علي الى منزله، ولم يبايع، ولزم بيته حتى ماتت فاطمة فبايع.

This tradition evidently is a more embellished weak account, for Saʿīd b. Kathīr b. ʿUfayr's (d. 226) sources in this tradition are anonymous. The report embodies certain additions and developments not outlined in the past traditions, and Fāṭima's role in the entire confrontation is significantly reduced when compared to some of the other accounts. This tradition forms the first portion of the account recorded in the anonymously authored book, *al-Imāma wa-l-Siyāsa* of pseudo-Ibn Qutayba.[1]

It appears to me that Saʿīd b. Kathīr's aforementioned tradition was an amalgamation of accounts he acquired from different sources. As an example, the Twelver scholar, al-Mufīd (d. 413), relayed a tradition via Saʿīd b. Kathīr that discloses one one of Saʿīd's sources in that tradition, and it shares obvious similarities and parallels with Saʿīd's aforementioned isnād-less account. Al-Mufīd said: Abū Bakr Muḥammad b. ʿUmar al-Jiʿābī informed me, he said: Abū al-Ḥusayn al-ʿAbbās b. al-Mughīra informed us, he said: Abū Bakr Aḥmed b. Manṣūr al-Ramādī informed us, he said: Saʿīd b. ʿUfayr informed us, he said: Ibn Lahīʿa informed me, on the authority of Khālid b. Yazīd, from Ibn Abī Hilāl, from Marwān b. ʿUthmān that he said:

> When the people pledged to Abū Bakr their allegiance, ʿAlī, al-Zubayr, and al-Miqdād entered Fāṭima's house, and they refused to come out. ʿUmar thus said, "Burn the house upon them!" Al-Zubayr then came out with his sword, to which Abū Bakr said, "Get the hound!"

---

1 Al-Imāma wa-l-Siyāsa by pseudo-Ibn Qutayba (p. 21-22). The anonymous authorship of this book is a topic which I do not wish to address in detail. Nonetheless, there are various internal and external indicators which indicate that this book actually was not authored by the Sunnī scholar, Ibn Qutayba al-Daynawarī (d. 276), as is asserted by some Shīʿite polemicists today. Either way, the report being cited in this text clearly is inauthentic.

It seems the anonymous author of *al-Imāma wa-l-Siyāsa* later incorporated into his narrative external details from Shīʿite and non-Shīʿite sources that effectively rendered his ahistorical account one of the more dramatic and emotive renditions of the historical events in question. It must be noted, however, that pseudo-Ibn Qutayba's account makes no mention of an attack on Fāṭima, which is quite noteworthy in this context.

> They then went towards him. His foot slipped, and he fell to the ground with the sword falling out of his hand. Abū Bakr thus said, "Strike the stone with it!" He then struck the rock with it until it broke.
>
> ʿAlī b. Abī Ṭālib departed to the ʿĀliya of Medīna, and Thābit b. Qays b. Shammās met him. He asked him, "What is your matter, O Abū al-Ḥasan?" ʿAlī replied, "They wanted to burn my house while Abū Bakr was on the pulpit, and he did not prevent it or criticizie it!" Thābit told him, "my hand shall not leave your hand until I am slain defending you!" They both departed until they eventually returned to Medīna, and Fāṭima was standing at her door. Her house did not have any of the people in it, and she was saying, "I am yet to witness a people worse in their gathering than you! You have left the Messenger of Allah as a funeral before us; and you have broken your matter among yourselves; and you did not consult us; and you did to us what you had done; and you did not see for us a right!"[1]

قال المفيد في أماليه: أخبرني أبو بكر محمد بن عمر الجعابي، قال: حدثنا أبو الحسين العباس بن المغيرة، قال: حدثنا أبو بكر أحمد بن منصور الرمادي، قال: حدثنا سعيد بن عفير، قال: حدثني ابن لهيعة، عن خالد بن يزيد، عن ابن أبي هلال، عن مروان بن عثمان، قال: لما بايع الناس أبا بكر دخل علي ع والزبير والمقداد بيت فاطمة ع وأبوا أن يخرجوا. فقال عمر بن الخطاب: أضرموا عليهم البيت نارا! فخرج الزبير ومعه سيفه، فقال أبو بكر: عليكم بالكلب! فقصدوا نحوه فزلت قدمه وسقط إلى الأرض، ووقع السيف من يده. فقال أبو بكر: اضربوا به الحجر! فضرب بسيفه الحجر حتى انكسر.

وخرج علي بن أبي طالب ع نحو العالية فلقيه ثابت بن قيس بن شماس، فقال: ما شأنك يا أبا الحسن؟ فقال: أرادوا أن يحرقوا علي بيتي وأبو بكر على المنبر يبايع له ولا يدفع عن ذلك ولا ينكره! فقال له ثابت: ولا تفارق كفي يدك حتى أقتل دونك. فانطلقا جميعا حتى عادا إلى المدينة، وإذا فاطمة ع واقفة على بابها وقد خلت دارها من أحد من القوم، وهي تقول: لا عهد لي بقوم أسوأ محضرا منكم! تركتم رسول الله ص جنازة بين أيدينا وقطعتم أمركم بينكم لم تستأمرونا وصنعتم بنا ما صنعتم ولم تروا لنا حقا!

This tradition is inauthentic: Ibn Lahīʿa (d. 176) is a debased transmitter, and Marwān b. ʿUthmān was criticized by some critics.[2] Furthermore,

---

1 Amālī al-Mufīd (p. 49-50)
2 Tahdhīb al-Kamāl fī Asmāʾ al-Rijāl (27/398)

Marwān's transmission of this account would be deemed disconnected, as he did not witness these events. What is noteworthy about this tradition of Saʿīd b. Kathīr is that it is relatively more concise than Saʿīd's past isnād-less account relayed by Abū Bakr al-Jawharī. This inauthentic tradition, which is to be dated to Ibn Lahīʿa's era, shares the general theme of several past traditions: (1) Abū Bakr is pledged allegienace, (2) ʿAlī and his associates withdraw to Fāṭima's house, (3) ʿUmar threatens to disband the congregation by force, (4) al-Zubayr comes out of the house with his sword drawn, (5) al-Zubayr is disarmed and the congregation is disbanded. This account, however, adds a few details, such as the notion that ʿAlī fled his house to al-ʿĀliya of Medīna, abandoning Fāṭima and leaving her behind. It also notably presents Thābit b. Qays b. Shammās as a loyalist of ʿAlī, though Thābit, according to some sources, was actually said to be part of the band that initially approached Fāṭima's house to dissolve the congregation therein.[1]

The account flirts with the notion of an attack taking place against ʿAlī's household, though it does explicitly state it nor does it seem to imply it. Rather, the grievances directed against Abū Bakr and ʿUmar primarily revolve around their intimidation of ʿAlī and Fāṭima and their supposed usurpation of power and disregard of the Hashemites, who were preoccupied with the Messenger of Allah's ﷺ funeral processions.

Around the time Saʿīd b. Kathīr relayed these accounts, a narrative began to develop in some Shīʿite circles that Fāṭima was physically assaulted during this controversy. One of the criticisms directed at the Shīʿite-leaning Muʿtazilite theologian, Ibrāhīm b. Sayyār al-Naẓẓām (d. 220+), was that he claimed ʿUmar had physically assaulted Fāṭima, resulting in the miscarriage of her fetus. Al-Shahrastānī (d. 548) criticized al-Naẓẓām saying:

> He added to the lie saying, "ʿUmar struck Fāṭima on the day of the pledge till she miscarried the fetus from her stomach, and he was yelling, 'Burn the house with those inside it!' and there was none in the house but ʿAlī, Fāṭima, al-Ḥasan and al-Ḥusayn."[2]

قال الشهرستاني: وزاد في الفرية فقال: إن عمر ضرب بطن فاطمة يوم البيعة حتى ألقت الجنين من بطنها، وكان يصيح: أحرقوا دارها بمن فيها، وما كان في الدار غير علي وفاطمة والحسن والحسين.

1 Refer to the tradition on pg. 222 of this book.
2 Al-Milal wa-l-Niḥal by al-Shahrastānī (1/57)

Abū al-Ḥusayn al-Malṭī (d. 377) similarly accused the Kūfan Rāfiḍite figure, Hishām b. al-Ḥakam (d. post-187), of claiming that Abū Bakr passed by Fāṭima and kicked her stomach, resulting in her miscarriage and eventual death.[1]

قال أبو الحسين الملطي: فَزعم هِشَام لَعنه الله أنّ [....]، وَأن أَبَا بكر مر بفاطمة عَلَيْهَا السَّلاَم فرفس فِي بَطنهَا فَأَسْقطت وَكَانَ سَبَب علتها وموتها.

The second century Muʿtazilite scholar, Ḍirār b. ʿAmr (d. pre-193) also referenced the claim that Abū Bakr and ʿUmar oppressed and beat Fāṭima till she miscarried her fetus as a belief that existed at the time among a sect or group of people. Ḍirār, however, proceeds to describe this belief and other referenced beliefs as "misguided, misguiding and fabricated ḥadīths."[2]

قال ضرار بن عمرو في «التحريش» واصفا مقالة بعضهم: وأن أبا بكر وعمر ظلما وضربا فاطمة بنت رسول الله حتى ألقت جنينا، وفي نحو هذا من الحديث الضال المضل المفتعل؛ فقبله قوم ودانوا إلى ما به...

This claim comes as a somewhat natural progression and development in the transmission of this narrative within some staunch second century Rāfiḍite circles in Kūfa that incessantly sought to exploit these controversies for their theological interests. Interestingly, this very notion was dismissed and challenged in certain Shīʿite circles at the time as well, and traditions that dismissed such notions were being ascribed to figures from *Ahlulbayt.*

In the Zaydī Shīʿite biographical work, *Tasmiyat Man Rawā ʿan al-Imām Zayd min al-Tābiʿīn*, Abū ʿAbdillāh Muḥammad b. ʿAlī b. al-Ḥasan al-ʿAlawī (d. 445) relayed a tradition via Yaḥyā b. Salama b. Kuhayl, from his father that he said:

> I told Zayd b. ʿAlī, "The people claim that Fāṭima was beaten." He replied, "O Abū Yaḥyā, she was more honorable to her family than for that to take place!"[3]

قال أبو عبد الله العلوي الزيدي في «تسمية من روى عن الإمام زيد من التابعين»: أخبرنا محمد بن علي بن الحكم الهمداني القارئ قراءة، قال: أخبرني محمد بن عمار العطار قراءة، قال: حدثنا أبو عمرو أحمد بن خازم

1 Al-Tanbīh wa-l-Rad ʿalā Ahl al-Ahwāʾ wa-l-Bidaʿ (p. 25-26)
2 Al-Taḥrīsh by Ḍirār b. ʿAmr al-Ghaṭafānī (p. 52)
3 Tasmiyat Man Rawā ʿan al-Imām Zayd min al-Tābiʿīn (p. 74)

[حازم]، عن علي، قال: حدثنا أبو غسان، قال حدثنا يحيى بن سلمة، قال: أخبرني أبي، عن أبي الحسن زيد بن علي، قال: قلت له: إن الناس يزعمون أن فاطمة لطمت. قال: كانت أكرم على أهلها من ذلك يا أبا يحيى!

It seems like there is a typographical error in the isnād, for Aḥmed b. Ḥāzim b. Abī Ghurza usually transmits directly from Abū Ghassān Mālik b. Ismāʿīl.[1] Hence, it seems that the unnamed ʿAlī mentioned in the isnād is not an actual transmitter in the chain, but a word that was misread as "ibn ʿAlī," presumably Aḥmed b. Ḥāzim's patronymic, "Ibn Abī Ghurza." If that is the case, then the isnād would be authentic to Yaḥyā b. Salama b. Kuhayl (d. 172), a weak Shīʿite transmitter.[2] Due to Yaḥyā's weakness, this tradition cannot be verifiably attributed to Zayd b. ʿAlī. Nevertheless, it can at least demonstrate that the Rāfiḍite narrative surrounding the attack on Fāṭima existed by the mid second century in certain Kūfan Shīʿite circles, and it was being rejected and contested within some contemporaneous Kūfan Shīʿite circles as well. Some contemporary Zaydī apologists cite this tradition to dismiss and undermine the Twelver Shīʿite narrative which claims that Fāṭima was physically assaulted by Abū Bakr and/or ʿUmar.

A late third and early fourth century Twelver traditionist, Muḥammad b. Jarīr b. Rustum al-Ṭabarī, relayed a tradition in his book, *al-Mustarshid*, regarding the attack at Fāṭima's house, and it similarly embodies accretions and developments to the narrative. Ibn Rustum al-Ṭabarī reported that Muḥammad b. Hārūn said: Mukhawwal b. Ibrāhīm al-Nahdī informed us, he said: Maṭar b. Arqam informed us, he said: Abū Ḥamza al-Thumālī informed us, on the authority of ʿAlī b. al-Ḥusayn that he said:

> When the Messenger of Allah ﷺ died and Abū Bakr was pledged as the leader, ʿAlī abstained [from paying his allegiance]. ʿUmar thus told Abū Bakr, "Shall you not send anyone to that man who has abstained from pledging so that he can come and pledge allegiance?"
>
> Abū Bakr thus said, "Qunfudh, go to ʿAlī and tell him, 'the Prophet's ﷺ successor commands you to come and pledge your allegiance'."
>
> Qunfudh went and knocked on the door, and ʿAlī said, "who is this?" He said, "I am Qunfudh." ʿAlī said, "What has brought you

1 Examples of Aḥmed b. Ḥāzim's direct transmission from Abū Ghassān can be observed in al-Mustadrak of al-Ḥākim (1/318, 1/754, 2/269, 3/132, 4/409, 4/632).

2 See his entry in Tahdhīb al-Kamāl (31/361-364)

here?" Qunfudh said, "The commander of the faithful commands you to come and pledge your allegiance." ʿAlī then raised his voice and said, "*subḥān Allāh!* How fast have you lied about the Messenger of Allah!"

Qunfudh went back and informed Abū Bakr of what had occurred. ʿUmar thus stood up and said, "Go to this man so that we can come to him!" A group of people went to ʿAlī, and they knocked on the door." When ʿAlī heard their voices, he did not speak. Instead, his wife spoke, and she said, "Who are they?" They replied, "Tell ʿAlī to come out and pledge his allegiance!" Fāṭima then raised her voice and said, "O Messenger of Allah, [how severe is] what have we faced from Abū Bakr and ʿUmar after you!"

When they heard her voice, many of those with ʿUmar cried and then left the scene, and ʿUmar stayed put with a group of people. They then brought ʿAlī out of his house and drove him to Abū Bakr until he was eventually seated before him. Abū Bakr said, "Pledge your allegiance," and ʿAlī replied, "What if I do not?" Abū Bakr said, "Then, by Allah there is no god but He, your neck shall be struck!" ʿAlī said, "I am the slave of Allah and the brother of His messenger!" Abū Bakr thus said, "Pledge your allegiance," and ʿAlī replied, "What if I do not?" Abū Bakr said, "Then, by Allah there is no god but He, your neck shall be struck!" ʿAlī then turned towards the Prophet's ﷺ grave and said, "O son of my mother! The people overpowered me and were about to kill me!" He then pledged his allegiance and left.[1]

قال ابن رستم الطبري في «المسترشد»: رواه محمد بن هارون [...] قال: وأخبرنا مخول بن إبراهيم النهدي، قال: حدثنا مطر بن أرقم قال: حدثنا أبو حمزة الثمالي: عن علي بن الحسين (عليهما لسلام)، قال: لما قبض النبي (صلى الله عليه وآله) و بويع أبو بكر، تخلف علي (عليه السلام) فقال عمر لابي بكر: الا ترسل إلى هذا الرجل المتخلف فيجيئ فيبايع ؟

قال [أبو بكر]: يا قنفذ اذهب إلى علي وقل له: يقول لك خليفة رسول الله (صلى الله عليه وآله وسلم) تعال بايع ! فذهب قنفذ، فضرب الباب، فقال علي عليه السلام: من هذا ؟ قال: أنا قنفذ، فقال: ما جاء بك ؟ قال: يقول لك أمير المؤمنين: تعالى فبايع ! فرفع علي (عليه السلام) صوته، وقال: سبحان الله ! لقد إدعى ما ليس

1 Al-Mustarshid fī Imāmat Amīr al-Muʾminīn (p. 376-378)

له، فجاء: فأخبره، فقام عمر: فقال: إنطلقوا إلى هذا الرجل حتى نجيئ إليه، فمضى إليه جماعة، فضربوا الباب، فلما سمع علي عليه السلام أصواتهم لم يتكلم، وتكلمت إمرأته، فقالت: من هؤلاء، فقالوا: قولي لعلي: يخرج ويبايع.

فرفعت فاطمة عليها السلام صوتها، فقالت: يارسول الله ما لقينا من ابي بكر وعمر بعدك ؟! فلما سمعوا صوتها، بكى كثير ممن كان معه، ثم أنصرفوا، وثبت عمر في ناس معه، فأخرجوه وانطلقوا به إلى أبي بكر حتى أجلسوه بين يديه !، فقال أبو بكر: بايع، قال: فإن لم أفعل ؟، قال: إذا والله الذي لا اله الا هو تضرب عنقك !، قال علي عليه السلام: فانا عبد الله وأخو رسوله قال (أبو بكر): بايع، قال: فإن لم أفعل، قال: إذا والله الذي لا اله الا هو، تضرب عنقك، فالتفت علي عليه السلام إلى القبر، وقال: يابن أم أن القوم استضعفوني وكادوا يقتلونني ثم بايع وقام.

As apparent, this tradition embodies several accretions not found in any of the past traditions. It presumably is the earliest source to introduce the obscure figure known as Qunfudh, who was not mentioned in any of the past accounts of this purported event. It also incorporates several details and developments to the text and dialogue, such as the claim that much of ʿUmar's band around the house dispersed in tears upon hearing Fāṭima's screams. All in all, it should not come as a surprise that this tradition's isnād is quite dubious: Maṭar b. Arqam is a transmitter who exclusively exists in Twelver Shīʿte sources, and he is an obscure transmitter whose reliability is unknown to Twelver scholarship.[1] Mukhawwal b. Ibrāhīm was a generally truthful Rāfiḍite transmitter, though his status is unknown in Twelver biographical sources.[2] Asides from that, the very author of *al-Mustarshid*, Muḥammad b. Jarīr b. Rustum al-Ṭabarī, was declared a forger by al-Sulaymānī (d. 404), though the later Twelver bibliographer, al-Najāshī (d. 450) claimed that he was a reliable transmitter.[3]

It also appears that this tradition constitutes the latter portion of pseudo-Ibn Qutayba's account in the anonymously authored *al-Imāma wa-l-Siyāsa*.[4] This observation should further attest to the unreliability of pseudo-Ibn Qutayba, the anonymous author of *al-Imāma wa-l-Siyāsa*, for he had merged

---

1 Al-Mufīd min Muʿjam Rijāl al-Ḥadīth by al-Jawāhirī (p. 607)
2 Lisān al-Mīzān (8/19), Mustadrakāt ʿIlm al-Rijāl (7/389-390)
3 Dhayl Mīzān al-Iʿtidāl by al-ʿIrāqī (p. 178-179), Lisān al-Mīzān (7/25, 7/29), Rijāl al-Najāshī (p. 360)
4 Al-Imāma wa-l-Siyāsa by pseudo-Ibn Qutayba (p. 22-23)

several accounts from different sources into a single tradition without properly partitioning and referencing them. This finding also illustrates that this purportedly Sunnī source was, on several occasions, non-transparently quoting Shīʿite sources. What is also noteworthy and potentially insightful is that some claims in *al-Imāma wa-l-Siyāsa* conflict with what Ibn Qutayba is recorded stating in his established works.[1]

The notion that ʿAlī faced the Prophet's ﷺ grave and excused himself after pledging allegiance to Abū Bakr is an interesting accretion that evolved differently in other Shīʿite accounts. In *Baṣā'ir al-Darajāt*, al-Ṣaffār (d. 290), for example, relayed a tradition from Aḥmed b. Muḥammad, on the authority of ʿAlī b. al-Ḥakam, from Rabīʿ b. Muḥammad al-Musallī, from ʿAbdullāh b. Sulaymān, from Jaʿfar al-Ṣādiq that he said:

> When ʿAlī was dragged out [of his house] and he stood at the Prophet's ﷺ grave, he said, "O son of my mother! The people overpowered me and were about to kill me!"
>
> A hand and voice then came out of the Messenger of Allah's ﷺ grave, which they recognized to be the Prophet's. It came towards Abū Bakr and said, "Have you disbelieved in the One who created you from dust, then from a small seed, then He made you a man?!"[2]

قال الصفار: حدثنا احمد بن محمد، عن على بن الحكم، عن ربيع بن محمد المسلى، عن عبدالله بن سليمان، عن ابى عبدالله عليه السلام قال: لما اخرج بعلى عليه السلام ملبيا وقف عند قبر النبى صلى الله عليه وآله قال: يابن ام ان القوم استضعفونى وكادوا يقتلونني. قال: فخرجت يد من قبر رسول الله صلى الله عليه وآله يعرفون انها يده وصوت يعرفون انها صوته نحو ابى بكر, "اكفرت بالذى خلقك من تراب ثم من نطفه ثم سواك رجلا."

This accreted detail about some hand and voice emerging from the Prophet's ﷺ grave is a further embellishment of this previously accreted element of the account, which states that ʿAlī faced the Prophet's ﷺ grave

1 For example, the author of *al-Imāma wa-l-Siyāsa* stated that Fāṭima only lived 75 days after her father's death. See al-Imāma wa-l-Siyāsa (p. 24). Ibn Qutayba, on the other hand, stated that Fāṭima died 100 days following her father's death. See al-Maʿārif of Ibn Qutayba (p. 142-143). This observation is supplementary to the aforementioned points about pseudo-Ibn Qutayba's account, for the dubiousness of the account in *al-Imāma wa-l-Siyāsa* would nonetheless be apparent.

2 Baṣā'ir al-Darajāt (p. 315)

and excused himself as an overpowered and subdued victim. Though inconsequential, it should be noted that the isnād of this tradition is unreliable according to Twelver standards: Rabīʿ b. Muḥammad and ʿAbdullāh b. Sulaymān are both unknown.[1]

The Twelver traditionist, al-Kulaynī (d.329), relayed an interesting tradition that introduces a new detail to these accounts. He relayed from al-Ḥusayn b. Muḥammad al-Ashʿarī, from Muʿallā b. Muḥammad, from al-Ḥasan b. ʿAlī al-Washshāʾ, from Abān b. ʿUthmān, from Abū Hāshim that he said:

> When ʿAlī was taken out of his house, Fāṭima came out with the Messenger of Allah's ﷺ shirt on her head, holding her two sons' hands. She said, "What have you and me, O Abū Bakr? Do you wish to orphan my two sons and widow me from my husband? By Allah, had it not been a sin, would have uncovered my hair and screamed to my Lord!"
>
> A man from the people then [told Abū Bakr], "What do you wish to achieve from this?" Fāṭima then took ʿAlī's hand and departed with him.

Al-Ḥasan b. ʿAlī al-Washshāʾ, from the past isnād, is then quoted relaying from Abān b. ʿUthmān, from ʿAlī b. ʿAbdulʿAzīz, from ʿAbdulḤamīd al-Ṭāʾī, from Abū Jaʿfar that he said, "By Allah, had she uncovered her hair, then they would have all instantly died."[2]

عن المعلى [بن محمد]، عن الحسن، عن أبان، عن أبي هاشم قال: لما أخرج بعلي (ع) خرجت فاطمة عليها السلام واضعة قميص رسول الله صلى الله عليه وآله على رأسها خذة بيدي ابنيها، فقالت: مالي ومالك يا أبا بكر! تريد أن تؤتم ابني وترملني من زوجي! والله لو لا أن تكون سيئة لنشرت شعري ولصرخت إلى ربي! فقال رجل من القوم: ما تريد إلى هذا، ثم أخذت بيده فانطلقت به.

أبان، عن علي بن عبدالعزيز، عن عبدالحميد الطائي، عن أبي جعفر (ع) قال: والله لونشرت شعرها ماتوا طرا.

This tradition constitutes a new prepostrous development in this narrative surrounding Fāṭima and her special powers and significance during this incident. The report clearly is inauthentic: Muʿallā b.

---

1 Rijāl al-Najāshī (p. 161, 216-217), Rijāl al-Ṭūsī (p. 101, 182, 244), Fihrist al-Ṭūsī (p. 120)

2 Al-Kāfī by al-Kulaynī (8/129)

Muḥammad, the source of both traditions, was an obscure Baṣran transmitter whose competence and meticulousness in transmission is criticized in Twelver biographical sources.[1] Other criticisms that transcend Twelver ḥadīth scholarship may be directed at this isnād, as the other transmitters in the isnād who were deemed reliable by Twelver scholarship were not necessarily reliable and trustworthy tradents. This emergent detail surrounding Fāṭima's threat was absorbed into other contemporaneous and later composite accounts that amassed various emergent accretions into a single tradition.

In the pseudepigraphical Twelver source, *al-Ikhtiṣās*, we find a later expanded account of the past tradition(s). The anonymous author of the book recorded an account relayed via Muḥammad b. ʿAlī b. al-Faḍl b. ʿĀmir, on the authority of al-Ḥusayn b. Muḥammad b. al-Farazdaq, from Muḥammad b. ʿAlī b. ʿAmrawayh al-Warrāq, from Abū Muḥammad al-Ḥasan b. Mūsā, from ʿAmr b. Abī al-Miqdām, from his father, from his grandfather that he said:

> No days were more severe upon ʿAlī than two specific days that came upon him. The first of them was the day in which the Messenger of Allah ﷺ died. As for the second day, by Allah I was sitting in the portico (*saqīfa*) of Banī Sāʿida on the right of Abū Bakr while the people were pledging allegiance to him.
>
> ʿUmar thus told him, "You have not accomplished anything if ʿAlī does not pledge his allegiance to you, so send for him so that he can come to you and pledge to you his allegiance."
>
> He then sent Qunfudh to him, and Qunfudh told ʿAlī, "Answer to the Prophet's ﷺ successor." ʿAlī replied, "How fast have you lied about the Messenger of Allah! The Messenger of Allah ﷺ left no one as a successor after him but me!"
>
> Qunfudh went back to Abū Bakr and informed him of what ʿAlī had said. Abū Bakr said, "Go to him and tell him, 'Abū Bakr summons

---

1 Ibn al-Najāshī described him as discrepant in his transmission and his *madhhab* (*muḍṭarib al-ḥadīth wa-l-madhhab*), and Ibn al-Ghaḍāʾirī mentioned that some of his transmission is verified while some of it is disapproved (*yuʿraf wa-yunkar ḥadīthuh*). He also noted that he transmits from weak transmitters, and he concluded that he may be cited as a corroborator but not individually relied upon. See Rijāl al-Najāshī (p. 400) and al-Rijāl of Ibn al-Ghaḍāʾirī (p. 96).

you,' and say, 'Come so that you may pledge your allegiance, for you are but a man among the Muslims'."

ʿAlī thus replied, "The Messenger of Allah ﷺ commanded me to not exit my house after his death until I compile the Book (the Quran), for it is dispersed in palm branches and the shoulder bones of camels."

Qunfudh returned to Abū Bakr and informed him of what ʿAlī had said. Thereupon, ʿUmar said, "Go to the man," and Abū Bakr, ʿUmar, ʿUthmān, Khālid b. al-Walīd, al-Mughīra b. Shuʿba, Abū ʿUbayda b. al-Jarrāḥ, Sālim the *mawlā* of Abū Ḥudhayfa, and I departed [to ʿAlī]. Fāṭima thought that none would be allowed into her house unless it were by her permission, and she hence closed the door and locked it. When they arrived at the door, ʿUmar struck the door with his foot and broke it, for it was made of fronds. They entered upon ʿAlī and took him out, dragging him.

Fāṭima came out and said, "O Abū Bakr and ʿUmar, do you wish to widow me from my husband? By Allah, if you do not leave him alone, I will uncover my hair, tear my clothes and go to my father's grave and scream to my Lord!" She went out holding al-Ḥasan and al-Ḥusayn's hand towards the grave, and ʿAlī thereupon told Salmān, "Catch up with Muḥammad's daughter, for I see both ends of Medīna flipping [upon the city]. By Allah, if she does [what she said] then Medīna and its inhabitants shall imminently be swallowed by the earth!"

Salmān caught up with her and said, "O daughter of Muḥammad, Allah sent your father as a mercy, so leave." She replied, "O Salmān, I have no patience, so let me go to my father's grave and scream to my lord." Salmān said, "ʿAlī has sent me to you, and he commands you to return." She said, "I listen to him and obey him," and she went back. They took ʿAlī out, dragging him.

Al-Zubayr approached with his sword drawn saying, "O people from Banī ʿAbdilMuṭṭalib, is this done to ʿAlī while you are alive?!" He then charged at ʿUmar to strike him with the sword. Khālid threw a stone that struck the back of his head, and the sword fell out of his hand. ʿUmar took the sword and struck it on a stone, breaking it.

ʿAlī then passed by the Prophet's ﷺ grave and said, "O son of my mother! The people overpowered me and were about to kill me!" ʿAlī was then brought to Abū Bakr's gathering in the portico, and ʿUmar told him, "Pledge your allegiance." ʿAlī said, "And what if I do not?" He said, "Then, by Allah, we shall strike your neck." ʿAlī replied, "Then, I shall be the slain slave of Allah and brother of the Messenger of Allah!" ʿUmar said, "As for the slain slave of Allah, then yes. As for the Messenger of Allah's ﷺ brother, then no," and he said it thrice.

Al-ʿAbbās then approached and said, "Be easy with my nephew, for I promise you that he will pledge his allegiance to you." Al-ʿAbbās then took ʿAlī's hand and rubbed it on Abū Bakr's hands. They then left ʿAlī angered, so he raised his head to the sky and said, "O Allah, you know that the Messenger of Allah ﷺ told me, 'if [your supporters] surmount to twenty, then resist them,' and it is your speech in your Book, 'if there are twenty patient ones of you, they shall overcome two hundred'. O Allah, they have not surmounted to that." He said that thrice and then left.[1]

قال المجلسي في «بحار الأنوار» ناقلا عن كتاب «الاختصاص»: أخبرني عبيد الله، عن أحمد بن علي بن الحسن بن شاذان عن محمد بن علي بن الفضل بن عامر، عن الحسين بن محمد بن الفرزدق، عن محمد بن علي بن عمرويه الوراق، عن أبي محمد الحسن بن موسى، عن عمرو بن أبي المقدام...

وفي المطبوع من كتاب «الاختصاص»: أبو محمد، عن عمرو بن أبي المقدام، عن أبيه، عن جده قال: ما أتاني على علي عليه السلام يوم قط أعظم من يومين أتياه، فأما أول يوم فاليوم الذي قبض فيه رسول الله صلى الله عليه وآله، وأما اليوم الثاني فوالله إني لجالس في سقيفة بني ساعدة عن يمين أبي بكر والناس يبايعونه إذ قال له عمر: يا هذا لم تصنع شيئا مالم يبايعك علي فابعث إليه حتى يأتيك فيبايعك.

قال: فبعث قنفذا، فقال له: أجب خليفة رسول الله صلى الله عليه وآله، قال علي عليه السلام: لأسرع ماكذبتم على رسول الله صلى الله عليه وآله ما خلف رسول الله صلى الله عليه وآله أحدا غيري، فرجع قنفذ وأخبر أبا بكر بمقالة علي عليه السلام فقال أبوبكر: انطلق إليه فقل له: يدعوك أبوبكر ويقول: تعال حتى تبايع فإنما أنت

1 Al-Ikhtiṣāṣ by pseudo-al-Mufīd (p. 184), Biḥār al-Anwār (28/229)

رجل من المسلمين، فقال علي عليه السلام: أمرني رسول الله صلى الله عليه وآله أن لا أخرج بعده من بيتي حتى اؤلف الكتاب فإنه في جرائد النخل وأكتاف الابل.

فأتاه قنفذ وأخبره بمقالة علي عليه السلام، فقال عمر: قم إلى الرجل، فقام أبوبكر وعمر وعثمان وخالد ابن الوليد والمغيرة بن شعبة وأبوعبيدة بن الجراح وسالم مولى أبي حذيفة وقمت معهم و ظنت فاطمة عليها السلام أنه لا تدخل بيتها إلا بإذنها، فأجافت الباب وأغلقته، فلما انتهوا إلى الباب ضرب عمر الباب برجله فكسره – وكان من سعف – فدخلوا على علي عليه السلام و أخرجوه ملببا. فخرجت فاطمة عليها السلام فقالت: يا أبا بكر وعمر تريدان أن ترملاني من زوجي؟ والله لئن لم تكفا عنه لانشرن شعري ولاشقن جيبي ولآتين قبر أبي ولاصيحن إلى ربي، فخرجت وأخذ بيد الحسن والحسين عليهما السلام متوجهة إلى القبر فقال علي عليه السلام لسلمان: يا سلمان أدرك ابنة محمد صلى الله عليه وآله فإني أرى جنبتي المدينة تكفئان، فوالله لئن فعلت لا يناظر بالمدينة أن يخسف بها وبمن فيها، قال: فلحقها سلمان فقال: يا بنت محمد صلى الله عليه وآله إن الله تبارك وتعالى إنما بعث أباك رحمة فانصرفي، فقالت: يا سلمان ما علي صبر فدعني حتى آتي قبر أبي، فأصيح إلى ربي، قال سلمان: فإن عليا بعثني إليك وأمرك بالرجوع فقالت: أسمع له وأطيع فرجعت.

وأخرجوا عليا ملببا قال: وأقبل الزبير مخترطا سيفه وهو يقول: يا معشر بني عبدالمطلب أيفعل هذا بعلي وأنتم أحياء وشد على عمر ليضربه بالسيف فرماه خالد بن الوليد بصخرة فأصابت قفاه وسقط السيف من يده فأخذه عمر وضربه على صخرة فانكسر ومر علي عليه السلام على قبر النبي صلى الله عليه وآله فقال, " يا ابن ام إن القوم استضعفوني وكادوا يقتلونني."

وأتي بعلي عليه السلام إلى السقيفة إلى مجلس أبي بكر، فقال له عمر: بايع، قال: فإن لم أفعل فمه؟ قال: إذا والله نضرب عنقك، قال علي عليه السلام: إذا والله أكون عبدالله وأخي رسول الله صلى الله عليه وآله المقتول، فقال عمر: أما عبدالله المقتول فنعم وأما أخا رسول الله صلى الله عليه وآله فلا – حتى قالها ثلاثا – وأقبل العباس فقال: يا أبا بكر ارفقوا بابن أخي، فلك علي أن يبايعك فأخذ العباس بيد علي عليه السلام فمسحها على يدي أبي بكر وخلوا عليا مغضبا فرفع رأسه إلى السماء، ثم قال: اللهم إنك تعلم أن النبي الامي – صلى الله عليه وآله – قال لي: إن تموا عشرين فجاهدهم، وهو قولك في كتابك, " فإن يكن منكم عشرون صابرون يغلبوا مائتين " اللهم إنهم لم يتموا – حتى قالها ثلاثا – ثم انصرف.

This account is a further embellishment of the narrative about the attack on Fāṭima's house: it embodies unprecedented accretions and developments in the dialogue and structure of the account. The isnād of this account is forged, and it is even inauthentic according to Twelver standards as well. First, the authorship of *al-Ikhtiṣās* is disputed. Though it is believed by some to be authored by the Twelver sholar, al-Mufīd (d. 413), several Twelver authorities have concluded that it cannot be verifiably ascribed to al-Mufīd.[1] Furthermore, Muḥammad b. ʿAlī b. al-Faḍl b. ʿĀmir and Muḥammad b. ʿAlī b. ʿAmrawayh are unknown to Sunnī and Shīʿite scholarship.[2] Additionally, ʿAmr b. Abī al-Miqdām (d. 172) is an unreliable transmitter.[3] More criticism may be directed at this isnād; nevertheless, the aforementioned points should suffice to briefly illustrate the report's dubious origins.

This account was referenced by the Twelver al-ʿAyyāshī (d. 320) in his *Tafsīr*, which would mean it was concocted sometime between the mid second century and early fourth century, presumably in the beginning or middle of the third century.[4] The final clause of the account represents a later Shiʿite polemic that attempts to explain away ʿAlī's noteworthy non-resistance to the purported assailants. All in all, the account of *al-Ikhtiṣās* clearly is the most developed and accumulated pre-*Kitāb Sulaym Ibn Qays* tradition that has absorbed material from a variety of past and contemporaneous sources.

Another noteworthy tradition that has been made relevant in the discussion surrounding Fāṭima's murder is a tradition found in the Twelver source, *Dalāʾil al-Imāma*. The anonymous fifth century author of the text relayed from Muḥammad b. Hārūn b. Mūsā, from his father, from Muḥammad b. Hammām b. Suhayl, from Aḥmed b. Muḥammad al-Barqī, from Aḥmed b. Muḥammad al-Ashʿarī, from ʿAbdurraḥmān b. Abī Najrān, from Ibn Sinān, from Ibn Muskān, from Abū Baṣīr, from Jaʿfar b. Muḥammad that he said:

> Fāṭima was born on the twentieth of *Jumādā al-Ākhira*, 45 years prior to the Prophet's ﷺ bith. She resided eight years in Mecca and ten years in Medīna, and [she lived] 75 days after her father's death. She died on Tuesday, the third of *Jumādā al-Ākhira* of 11 H. The

1 Mashraʾat Biḥār al-Anwār by Moḥsenī (1/443), Muʿjam Rijāl al-Ḥadīth by al-Khoei (8/130, 8/197, 8/307 etc.)

2 Mustadrakāt ʿIlm Rijāl al-Ḥadīth (7/239, 7/241)
Muḥammad b. ʿAlī b. ʿAmrawayh in this isnād is not to be confused with a later scholar from Naysābūr who shares the same name, Muḥammad b. ʿAlī b. ʿAmrawayh al-Wakīl.

3 Tahdhīb al-Kamāl (21/553-559)

4 Tafsīr al-ʿAyyāshī (2/204-206)

> reason behind her death was that Qunfudh, the *mawlā* of ʿUmar, struck her with the sword handle by ʿUmar's command. She hence miscarried Muḥassin and became severely ill because of that. She did not allow anyone who had harmed her visit her [before her death]."[1]

قال مصنف كتاب «دلائل الإمامة»: حدثني أبو الحسين محمد بن هارون بن موسى التلعكبري، قال: حدثني أبي، قال: حدثني أبو علي محمد بن همام بن سهيل رضي الله عنه، قال: روى أحمد ابن محمد بن البرقي، عن أحمد بن محمد الأشعري القمي، عن عبد الرحمن بن أبي نجران، عن عبد الله بن سنان، عن ابن مسكان، عن أبي بصير، عن أبي عبد الله جعفر بن محمد عليه السلام، قال: ولدت فاطمة عليها السلام في جمادى الآخرة، يوم العشرين منه، سنة خمس وأربعين من مولد النبي صلى الله عليه وآله. وأقامت بمكة ثمان سنين، وبالمدينة عشر سنين، وبعد وفاة أبيها خمسة وسبعين يوما. وقبضت في جمادي الآخرة يوم الثلاثاء لثلاث خلون منه، سنة إحدى عشرة من الهجرة. وكان سبب وفاتها أن قنفذا مولى عمر لكزها بنعل السيف بأمره، فأسقطت محسنا ومرضت من ذلك مرضا شديدا، ولم تدع أحدا ممن آذاها يدخل عليها.

This report is presented by some contemporary Twelver apologists as one of the few authentic texts regarding Fāṭima's murder according to Twelver ḥadīth standards. However, upon further inspection, its inauthenticity becomes quite apparent. Barring the anonymous authorship of *Dalāʾil al-Imāma*, the isnād cited therein is weak, in and of itself.[2] All-in-

---

1 Dalāʾil al-Imāma of pseudo-Ibn Rustum (p. 45-46), Biḥār al-Anwār (43/170)

2 The ahistoricity of this tradition transcends Twelver scholarship's debate on its isnād. Nevertheless, much of the discussion surrounding this tradition in Twelver circles revolves around the identity of one transmitter in the isnād: Ibn Sinān. Ibn Sinān may prove to be ʿAbdullāh b. Sinān, a reliable transmitter according to Twelver scholarship, or Muḥammad b. Sinān, a transmitter condemned by a plethora of Twelver critics.

My edition of *Dalāʾil al-Imāma* cites the reliable ʿAbdullāh b. Sinān, as the transmitter of this text; however, that probably is a typographical error. In other sources, such as *Tārīkh Mawālīd al-Aʾimma* of Ibn al-Khashshāb (d. 567), it becomes rather apparent that this tradition is but a fragment from a larger monograph transmitted via Ibn Muskān from the unreliable Muḥammad b. Sinān, which provides summarized biographical synopses for the Imāms of *Ahlulbayt.* See Biḥār al-Anwār of al-Majlisī (1/56-57, 47/5-6, 48/7, 49/8, 50/12). There are other reasons to assert that Ibn Sinān likely is Muḥammad b. Sinān, such as his position in the isnāds etc. All-in-all, the

all, this tradition is an inauthentic tradition that summarizes later claims and traditions that emerged surrounding Fāṭima's purported murder in Shīʿite literature.

It seems that the narrative surrounding Fāṭma's murder by Abū Bakr and ʿUmar became more popular and mainstream within the Twelver Shīʿite community and, perhaps, some other Shīʿte communities as well, by the fourth and fifth centuries.

In *Ithbāt al-Waṣiyya*, a polemical Shīʿite text ascribed to the Shīʿite historian, al-Masʿūdī (d. 346), it is said about ʿAlī the belligerents at the *Saqīfa*:

> They then set out towards his house, and they attacked it and burned its door; and they forcefully brought ʿAlī outside. They squeezed the Mistress of all women with the door until she miscarried Muḥassin...[1]

قال صاحب كتاب «إثبات الوصية»: فوجهوا إلى منزله فهجموا عليه وأحرقوا بابه واستخرجوا منه عليا كرها، وضغطوا سيدة النساء بالباب حتى أسقطت محسنا.

A recent study by the researcher, ʿAbdulHādī al-ʿAlawī, reasonably demonstrated that the present text known as *Ithbāt al-Waṣiyya*, which is ascribed to al-Masʿūdī (d. 346), is more appropriately attributed to the

---

tradition clearly is questionable, to say the least, according to Twelver standards, and it is inauthentic.

Additionally, one of the transmitters in the isnād, Muḥammad b. Hammām, transmitted this report saying, "Aḥmed b. Muḥammad al-Barqī relayed from Aḥmed b. Muḥammad b. ʿĪsā."

قال أبو علي محمد بن همام بن سهيل رضي الله عنه، قال: روى أحمد ابن محمد بن البرقي...

This statement of Muḥammad b. Hammām is vague, and it indicates that he may had not acquired this tradition directly from Aḥmed b. Muḥammad al-Barqī. The likelihood of a disconnection in this isnād between Muḥammad b. Hammām b. Suhayl and al-Barqī is confirmed when it is recognized that Muḥammad b. Hammām's transmission from al-Barqī elsewhere involves (at least) one intermediary between both men. See *Dalāʾil al-Imāma* (p. 142). This tradition's isnād is hence disconnected between Muḥammad b. Hammām and al-Barqī, further compounding its weakness.

Furthermore, I find it noteworthy, though perhaps inconsequential, that another variant of this tradition does not mention the clause about Fāṭima's death being the result of a blow by Qunfudh. See Dalāʾil al-Imāma (p. 13).

1 Ithbāt al-Waṣiyya by pseudo-al-Masʿūdī (p. 143)

nortorious Shīʿite figure, al-Shalmaghānī (d. 322).[1] This would entail that the aforementioned passage be dated to the early fourth century.

The seventh century historian, Ibn Shaddād (d. 684), quoted an earlier source, the *Tārīkh* of the Twelver Ibn Abī Ṭayy (d. ~ 630), describing an incident that involved the Ḥamdānid ruler of Aleppo in the year 351. Ibn Shaddād said: Ibn Abī Ṭayy said in his *Tārīkh*:

> In this year, referring to year 351, the shrine of al-Dikka appeared. The reason behind its emergence was that Sayf al-Dawla ʿAlī b. Ḥamdān, in one of his debates in his residence at the outskirt of the city, saw a light descending unto the site where the shrine is located several times. In the next morning, he rode to that site and dug it out. He found a stone therein upon which was written, "This is the grave of al-Muḥassin b. al-Ḥusayn b. ʿAlī b. Abī Ṭālib."
>
> Sayf al-Dawla hence summoned the Alids, and he asked them, "Did al-Ḥusayn have a son named al-Muḥassin?" Some of them replied, "That has not reached us. Rather, what has reached us is that Fāṭima was pregnant, and the Messenger of Allah told her, 'in your stomach is Muḥassin.' Then, on the day of the pledge, they assaulted her in her house to bring out ʿAlī to the pledge, so she miscarried."
>
> Some of them replied, "It is possible that the captives from al-Ḥusayn's wives, when they passed through this vicinity, laid this child, for we relay from out fathers that this vicinity was named Jawshan because Shimr b. Dhī al-Jawshan rested their with the captives and the severed heads; and it was a mine where gold was retrieved; and the people of the mine became happy regarding the captives, so Zanab bt. al-Ḥusayn made *duʿāʾ* against them; and the mine was spoiled because of that."
>
> Some of them replied "This writing on the rock is old, and the remnants of this place are old; and this miscarried child that they claimed has not spoiled; and its remnance till this day is evidence that he is al-Ḥusayn's son."

---

1 Al-ʿAlawī, ʿAbdulHādī, "Kitāb Ithbāt Al-Waṣiyya li-l-Masʿūdī am li-l-Shalmaghānī?" *Al-Khizāna*, no. 7 (2020): 67-171.

> News of this discussion spread among the people. They set out to this site, and they desired to construct it. Sayf al-Dawla hence said, "This is a site that Allah had given me permission to construct in the name of *Ahlulbayt.*"
>
> Ibn Abī Ṭayy then mentioned that the shrine was named after al-Muḥassin, the son of al-Ḥusayn.[1]

قال ابن شداد في «الأعلاق الخطيرة» ومنها مشهد الدكّة وهو في غربيّ حلب وسُمي بهذا الاسم لأنّ سيف الدولة كانت له دكّة على الجبل المطلّ على المشهد يجلس عليها للنظر إلى حلبة السبّاق فإنها كانت تجري بين يديه في ذلك الوطاء الّذي فيه المشهد.

قال يحيى بن أبي طيّ في تأريخه: وفي السنة – يعني سنة إحدى وخمسين وثلاثمائة – ظهر مشهد الدكة. وكان سبب ظهوره أن سيف الدولة عليّ ابن حمدان كان في أحد مناظره بداره الّتي ظاهر المدينة فرأى نوراً ينزل على المكان الّذي فيه المشهد عدّة مرّات. فلمّا أصبح ركب بنفسه إلى ذلك المكان وحفره فوجد حجراً عليه كتابة, " هذا " قبر " المحسن بن الحسين بن علي بن أبي طالب ". فجمع سيف الدولة العلويّين وسألهم هل كان للحسين ولد اسمه المحسّن. فقال بعضهم: ما بلغنا ذلك وإنما بلغنا أنّ فاطمة عم كانت حاملاً فقال لها النبيّ صلى الله عليه وسلم: في بطنك محسّن. فلمّا كان يوم البيعة هجموا عليها في بيتها لإخراج عليّ عم إلى البيعة فأخْدجت. وقال بعضهم: يُحتمل أنّ سبيّ نساء الحسين لمّا وردوا هذا المكان طرح بعض نسائه هذا الولد. فإنا نروي عن آبائنا أن هذا المكان سُمّي بجَوْشَن لأنّ شُمر ابن ذي الجَوْشَن نزل عليه بالسبي والرؤوس وأنّه معدناً يُعمَل فيه الصفر وأن أهل المعدن فرحوا بالسبي فدعت عليهم زينب بنت الحسين ففسد المعدن من يومئذ.

وقال بعضهم: إنّ هذه الكتابة ألّي على الحجر قديمة وأثر هذا المكان قديم وإن هذا الطِرْح الّذي زعموا لم يفسد وبقاؤه دليل على أنّه ابن الحسين. فشاع بين الناس هذه المفاوضة الّتي جرت وخرجوا إلى هذا المكان وأرادوا عمارته فقال سيف الدولة: هذا موضع قد أذن الله تع لي في عمارته على اسم أهل البيت.

قال يحيى بن أبي طيّء: ولحقتُ باب هذا المشهد وهو باب صغير من حجر أسود عليه قنطره مكتوبُ عليها بخطّ أهل الكوفة كتابة عريضة, " عمّر هذا المشهد المبارك ابتغاء وجه الله تع وقربةً إليه على اسم مولانا المحسّن ابن الحسين بن علي بن أبي طالب عم الأمير الأجل سيف الدولة أبو الحسن عليّ بن عبد الله بن حمدان ."

1 Al-Aʿlāq al-Khaṭīra fī Dhikr Umarāʾ al-Shām wa-l-Jazīra (1/147-150)

Al-Dhahābī (d. 748) quoted the Kūfān ḥadīthist, Muḥammad b. Aḥmed b. Ḥammād al-Ḥāfiẓ (d. 384), describing the Kūfan Rāfiḍite transmitter, Ibn Abī Dārim (d. 357), saying:

> He was upright for most of his life. Then, in his final days, most of what was read to him were the blunders [of the *ṣaḥāba*]. I sat with him while a man was reciting to him that ʿUmar kicked Fāṭima until she miscarried Muḥassin.[1]

قال الذهبي في «ميزان الاعتدال»: وقال محمد بن أحمد بن حماد الكوفي الحافظ – بعد أن أرخ موته: كان مستقيم الأمر عامة دهره، ثم في آخر أيامه كان أكثر ما يقرأ عليه المثالب، حضرته ورجل يقرأ عليه: إن عمر رفس فاطمة حتى أسقطت بمحسن.

The fifth century Twelver genealogist, ʿAlī b. Abī al-Ghanāʾim al-ʿUmarī al-ʿAlawī, when listing out ʿAlī b. Abī Ṭālib's children, said:

> They did not count Muḥassin, since he was born dead. The Shīʿa have relayed the story of al-Muḥassin and the kick. I found some book of geneology mentioning al-Muḥassin, but it did not mention the kick from a source that I rely upon.[2]

قال علي بن أبي الغنائم العلوي في «المجدي في أنساب الطالبيين»: ولم يحتسبوا بمحسن لأنه ولد ميتا، وقد روت الشيعة خبر المحسن والرفسة. ووجدت في بعض كتب أهل النسب يحتوي على ذكر المحسن، ولم يذكر الرفسة من جهة أعول عليها.

The anonymous fifth century Shīʿite author of *Dalāʾil al-Imāma* said regarding Fāṭima:

> She became pregnant with Muḥassin. When the Messenger of Allah died and what took place on the day the people entered upon her in her house; took her cousin, the Commander of the Faithful, outside; and what had been done to her by the man transpired, she miscarried him as a complete child. That was the cause of her illness and death.[3]

1 Mīzān al-Iʿtidāl by al-Dhahabī (p. 134)
2 Al-Majdī fī Ansāb al-Ṭālibiyyīn by al-ʿAlawī (p. 193)
3 Dalāʾil al-Imāma by pseudo-Ibn Rustum (p. 29)

قال مصنف كتاب «دلائل الإمامة»: وحملت بمحسن، فلما قبض رسول الله (صلى الله عليه وآله)، وجرى ما جرى في يوم دخول القوم عليها دارها، وإخراج ابن عمها أمير المؤمنين (عليه السلام)، وما لحقها من الرجل أسقطت به ولدا تماما، وكان ذلك أصل مرضها ووفاتها.

The fifth century Twelver scholar, al-Ṭūsī (d. 460), said:

> And among what he [Abū Bakr] was condemned for was their beating of Fāṭima. It has been reported that they struck her with whips. The famous position that is undisputed among the Shīʿa is that ʿUmar beat Fāṭima on her belly until she had a miscarriage, and the miscarried fetus was named Muḥassin. Transmission on that is well-known among them.
>
> And their desire to burn the house upon her when the people sought refuge in her and refused to pledge allegiance to Abū Bakr. No one can deny the transmission on this, for we had demonstrated its transmission through the *ʿĀmma* (non-Shīʿites), such as al-Balādhurī and others. The Shīʿa's transmission of this incident is overflowing: they do not disagree on it.[1]

قال الطوسي في «تلخيص الشافي»: ومما أنكر عليه ضربهم لفاطمة عليها السلام، وقد روي أنهم ضربوها بالسياط، والمشهور الذي لا خلاف فيه بين الشيعة أن عمر ضرب على بطنها حتى أسقطت فسمي السقط محسنا، والرواية بذلك مشهورة عندهم. وما أرادوا من إحراق البيت عليها حين التجأ إليها قوم وأمتنعوا من بيعته، وليس لأحد أن ينكر الرواية بذلك لأنّا قد بينا الرواية الواردة من جهة العامة من طريق البلاذري وغيره، ورواية الشيعة مستفيضة به لا يختلفون في ذلك.

This excerpt is worthy of several comments. It seems that al-Ṭūsī, when using the term "Shīʿa", was referring to the Twelver Shīʿite community, not all Shīʿite schools and sects spanned by the umbrella term. As an example, I referenced earlier a tradition relayed by the contemporaneous Zaydī Shīʿite scholar, Abū ʿAbdillāh al-ʿAlawī (d. 445), where Zayd b. ʿAlī b. al-Ḥusayn b. ʿAlī b. Abī Ṭālib was quoted denying that Fāṭima was physically beaten.[2] Furthermore, it is possible that al-Ṭūsī simply was exaggerating and inflating the degree of credibility this narrative maintained in Twelver sources.

1 Talkhīṣ al-Shāfī by al-Ṭūsī (3/156)
2 Tasmiyat Man Rawā ʿan al-Imām Zayd min al-Tābiʿīn (p. 74)

The Twelver scholar and teacher of al-Ṭūsī, al-Mufīd (d. 413), expressed uncertainty towards the existence and consequent miscarriage of al-Muḥassin. In *al-Irshād*, he said, "The children of the Commander of the Faithful are 27 in number, including males and females." After listing out their names, al-Mufīd said, "Among the Shīʿa are some who say that Fāṭima miscarried a boy after the Prophet's death who he had named al-Muḥassin as he was in the womb. According to the opinion of this group of the Shīʿa, the children of the Commander of the Faithful are 28 in number..."[1]

قال المفيد في «الإرشاد»: فأولاد أمير المؤمنين سبعة وعشرون ولدا ذكرا وأنثى. [...] وفي الشيعة من يذكر أن فاطمة (صلوات الله عليها) أسقطت بعد النبي ذكرا كان سماه رسول الله صلى الله عليه وسلم وهو محمل.

Al-Ṭūsī's claim that ʿUmar had physically beaten Fāṭima, resulting in her miscarriage, is a claim that predated his authorship of *Talkhīṣ al-Shāfī*, as demonstrated earlier. However, this is not the exact claim made in *Kitāb Sulaym Ibn Qays*, where it is stated that Fāṭima's miscarriage was caused by Qunfudh squeezing her body against the wall with a door.[2] The second portion of al-Ṭūsī's excerpt is referring to ʿUmar's preemptive threat to burn ʿAlī's house is a more general subject that can be found in various sources. Nonetheless, it is apparent that al-Ṭūsī unironically believed that ʿUmar had beaten Fāṭima and that he perceived this position to be undisputed within his sect.

The non-consensus of Zaydī Shīʿites on this event is observable elsewhere. Ibn Abī al-Ḥadīd (d. 656) quoted one of his Zaydī teachers, Abū Jaʿfar b. Abī Zayd al-ʿAlawī (d. 613), expressing some uncertainty towards the said event's historicity. Ibn Abī al-Ḥadīd said regarding a miscellaneous tradition:

> I read this report to the *naqīb* Abū Jaʿfar, may Allah bestow His mercy upon him. He thus said, "if the Messenger of Allah ﷺ made Habbār b. al-Aswad's blood permissible because he scared Zaynab, resulting her a miscarriage, then it becomes apparent that he would have done the same with whomever scared Fāṭima until she suffered a miscarriage."
>
> I hence said, "Shall I relay from you the claim made by some people that Fāṭima was scared such that she miscarried al-Muḥassin?" He

---

1 Al-Irshād by al-Mufīd (p. 233)
2 Kitāb Sulaym Ibn Qays (p. 153)

> replied, "No. Do not relay it from me, and do not relay that I deny it. I hold back on this matter due to the contradiction of its traditions in my opinion.[1]

قال ابن أبي الحديد: وهذا الخبر أيضا قرأته على النقيب أبي جعفر رحمه الله ، فقال إذا كان رسول الله صلى الله عليه وآله أباح دم هبار بن الأسود لأنه روع زينب فألقت ذا بطنها ، فظهر الحال إنه لو كان حيا لأباح دم من روع فاطمة حتى ألقت ذا بطنها.

فقلت: أروي عنك ما يقوله قوم إن فاطمة روعت فألقت المحسن؟ فقال: لا تروه عنى ولا ترو عني بطلانه ، فإني متوقف في هذا الموضع لتعارض الاخبار عندي فيه .

In this context, it should also be noted that Ibn Abī al-Ḥadīd quoted Ibn Abī Zayd al-ʿAlawī elsewhere praising Abū Bakr and ʿUmar and that he used to describe them saying, "They paved the path for the religion of Islam, and they laid down its foundations. It was in intense turmoil during the Messenger of Allah's ﷺ life, and they paved its way with what was available to the Arabs from the conquests and spoils during their reign."[2]

قال ابن أبي الحديد: وكان النقيب أبو جعفر رحمه الله ، غزير العلم ، صحيح العقل ، منصفا في الجدال ، غير متعصب للمذهب – وإن كان علويا – وكان يعترف بفضائل الصحابة ، ويثني على الشيخين . ويقول : إنهما مهدا دين الاسلام ، وأرسيا قواعده ، ولقد كان شديد الاضطراب في حياة رسول الله صلى الله عليه وآله ، وإنما مهداه بما تيسر للعرب من الفتوح والغنائم في دولتهما ...

The Zaydī Imām, al-Muʾayyad Billāh Yaḥyā b. Ḥamza (d. 749) said:

> [...] And what is relayed that he (ʿUmar) beat Fāṭima until she miscarried a fetus named al-Muḥassin, this is from the Imāmites' myths and forgeries.[3]

قال يحيى بن حمزة كما في مجموعه: وما يُروى أنه ضرب فاطمة حتى ألقت جنينا يُسمى المحسن، فهذا من خرافات الإمامية وتزويرهم.

---

1 Sharḥ Nahj al-Balāgha by Ibn Abī al-Ḥadīd (14/193)
2 Sharḥ Nahj al-Balāgha by Ibn Abī al-Ḥadīd (10/222)
3 Majmūʿ al-Imām al-Muʾayyad bi-Rabb al-ʿIzza Yaḥyā Ibn Ḥamza by Yaḥya Ibn Ḥamza (p. 201)

The eleventh century Yemenī scholar, Yaḥyā b. al-Ḥusayn b. al-Qāsim b. Muḥammad (d. 1100), quoted the Zaydī scholar, al-Najrī (d. 877), dismissing the emergent Shīʿite narrative surrounding Fāṭima. He said:

> What is relayed stating that ʿUmar burned ʿAlī b. Abī Ṭālib's house and that Fāṭima was beaten is from the lies of the Rāfiḍites. Al-Najrī, who was from the senior scholars of al-Hadawiyya,[1] mentioned in *Sharḥ al-Qalāʾid* that it is fabricated (*mawḍūʿ*).[2]

قال يحيى بن الحسين بن القاسم بن محمد في «الإيضاح لما خفا من الاتفاق على تعظيم صحابة المصطفى»: وما يُروى أن عمر أحرق بيت علي بن أبي طالب، وأن فاطمة لُطمت فهو من كذب الرافضة. ذكر النجري في «شرح القلائد» - وهو من كبار علماء الهدوية - وقال: موضوع...

Al-Najrī's book, *Sharḥ al-Qalāʾid*, has not been printed, and I hence painstakingly sifted through several manuscripts of the book until I was fortunately able to locate the aforementioned passage in a legible manuscript, as can be seen below.

1 Al-Hadawiyya or al-Hādawiyya is a reference to the Zaydī school named after the Zaydī Imām of Yemen, al-Hādī ilā al-Ḥaq Yaḥyā b. al-Ḥusayn al-Rassī (d. 298).

2 Al-Īḍāḥ li-mā Khafā min al-Ittifāq ʿalā Taʿẓīm Ṣaḥābat al-Muṣṭafā by Yaḥyā b al-Ḥusayn b. al-Qāsim b. Muḥammad (p. 241)

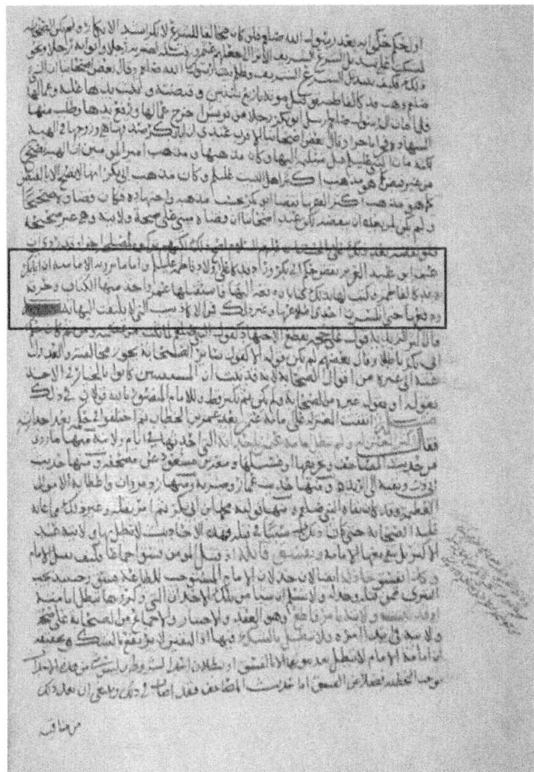

Figure 3.4 A leaf (pg. 226) from al-Najrī's *Sharḥ al-Qalāʾid wa-Taṣḥīḥ al-ʿAqāʾid* with the aforereferenced passage placed inside a black box. The manuscript at hand is labeled ZA: 095-05 at Maktabat Muʾassasat al-Imām Zayd al-Thaqāfiyya.

Al-Najrī's text reads:

> As for what the Imamites relay that Abū Bakr had returned Fadak to Fāṭima and that he had written to her a deed and handed it to her; and that ʿUmar then confronter her, snatched the book from her, and burnt it; and that he shoved her until one of her ribs broke; and other things; are among the inconsiderable lies.

قال النجري في «شرح القلايد»: وأما ما يرويه الإمامية أن أبا بكر رد فدكا لفاطمة وكتب لها بذلك كتابا ودفعه إليها، فاستقبلها عمر وأخذ منها الكتاب وحرقه، ودفعها حتى انكسرت إحدى أضلاعها، وغير ذلك، فمن الأكاذيب التي لا يُلتفت إليها.

Al-Najrī was referring to the tradition relayed in the pseudepigraphical Twelver source, *al-Ikhtiṣās,* via Abū Muḥammad (al-Ḥasan b. Mūsā al-Khashshāb), from ʿAbdullāh b. Sinān, from Jaʿfar al-Ṣādiq, that he said:

> [...] Abū Bakr then called for a deed, and he wrote it to her, returning Fadak to her. She then departed with the deed in her hand, and ʿUmar encountered her.
>
> He said, "O daughter of Muḥammad, what is this writing with you?" She said, "It is a deed written to me by Abū Bakr, returning Fadak to me." He thus said, "Hand it to me." She refused to do hand it to him, so he kicked her with his foot. She was pregnant with a son named al-Muḥassin, so she miscarried al-Muḥassin. He then struck her...[1]

قال مصنف كتاب «الاختصاص»: أبو محمد، عن عبدالله بن سنان، عن أبي عبدالله عليه السلام، قال: [...] فدعا بكتاب فكتبه لها برد فدك، فقال: فخرجت والكتاب معها، فلقيها عمر فقال: يا بنت محمد ما هذا الكتاب الذي معك، فقالت: كتاب كتب لي أبوبكر برد فدك، فقال: هلميه إلي، فأبت أن تدفعه إليه، فرفسها برجله وكانت حاملة بابن اسمه المحسن فأسقطت المحسن من بطنها ثم لطمها فكأني أنظر إلى قرط في اذنها حين نقفت.

This is a blunderous and worthless fabrication, as was rightfully stated by al-Najrī. There is a sizeable disconnection between the anonymous author of *al-Ikhtiṣāṣ* and Abū Muḥammad. Furthermore, it conflicts with the other Shīʿite accounts that place the attack and incursion inside Fāṭima's house as ʿAlī was being dragged out, where her miscarriage was hence caused by her being squeezed with the door. Certainly, the only historically accurate claim in this tradition is that Fāṭima approached Abū Bakr requesting that he grant her the land of Fadak as her inheritance from the Prophet ﷺ. Abū Bakr certainly did not hand her a deed and grant her the land after that. Rather, he informed her of a ḥadīth she did not know, which stated that the Prophets leave no material wealth behind as inheritance. Fāṭima was hence dismayed, and she then vowed to not speak with Abū Bakr until her death.[2]

---

1 Al-Ikhtiṣāṣ by pseudo-al-Mufīd (p. 181-183)

2 Ṣaḥīḥ al-Bukhārī (4/79), Ṣaḥīḥ Muslim (3/1380). This theme also exists in various non-Sunnī sources.

In this regard, it is interesting how some Zaydī accounts of the aforementioned event simply present Fāṭima casually handing ʿUmar the deeed upon his request. In this Zaydī account, ʿUmar then spat on the deed and ripped it apart, saddening Fāṭima. There is no mention of a physical assault, let alone a miscarriage, theirein.[1]

قال أبو العباس الحسني في «المصابيح»: أخبرنا عبد الله بن الحسن الإيوازي بإسناده عن زيد بن الحسن بن علي بن أبي طالب عليهم السلام، قال: جاءت فاطمة بنت رسول الله إلى أبي بكر فقالت: إن رسول الله أعطاني فدكاً في حياته. فقال أبو بكر ما يعلم بذلك. قالت: أم أيمن تعلم، وتشهد لي بذلك، وقد قال رسول الله: إنها من أهل الجنة. فجاءت أم أيمن فشهدت لها بذلك، فرد أبو بكر فدك عليها وكتب لها بذلك كتابا.

فخرجت فاطمة من عند أبي بكر والكتاب معها، فلقيها عمر بن الخطاب. فقال لها: من أين أقبلت يا بنت محمد؟ قالت: جئت من عند أبي بكر سألته أن يرد عليَّ فدكاً، وشهدت عنده أم أيمن أن رسول الله أعطانيها، فردها عليَّ أبو بكر وكتب لي بذلك كتاباً. فقال لها عمر: أريني الكتاب. فدفعته إليه فأخذه عمر، وتفل عليه ومحا ما فيه، وقال: إن رسول الله قال: إنا معاشر الأنبياء لا نورث ما تركنا فهو للمسلمين. فرجعت فاطمة باكيةً حزينة.

The presence of conflicting traditions and opinions within the Zaydī Shīʿite sect in this regard is observable, especially considering that Zaydism was not a monolith. The Zaydī *madhab* embodies a spectrum of schools and strands of varying staunchness in their Shīʿism, with some being more Rāfiḍite-leaning than others. As an example, the Zaydī Imām Yaḥyā b. al-Ḥusayn al-Rassī (d. 298), in a treatise titled, *Tathbīt al-Imāma*, is quoted affirming some of the Rāfiḍite narrative which states that Fāṭima was beaten, though he claimed that it was Khālid who had struck Fāṭima with a whip. He makes no mention of a miscarried fetus.[2]

قال يحيى بن الحسين الملقب بالهادي إلى الحق في كتاب «تثبيت الإمامة» المنسوب إليه: فحالت بينهم وبين البيت الذي فيه علي عليه السلام وهي ترى أنها أوجب عليهم حقا من علي عليه السلام لضعفها وقرابتها من رسول الله صلى الله عليه وآله، فوثب إليها خالد بن الوليد وضربها بالسوط على عضدها، حتى كان أثره في عضدها مثل الدملج، وصاحت عند ذلك.

1 See al-Maṣābīḥ fī al-Sīra by Abū al-ʿAbbās al-Ḥasanī (p. 263-266)
2 Tathbīt al-Imāma by Yaḥyā b. al-Ḥusayn al-Rassī (p. 17)

The claim in this text is not of much value, especially considering that Yaḥyā b. al-Ḥusayn (d. 298) cited no isnād to verify what he was claiming. Nonetheless, this example serves to demonstrate how Zaydī Shīʿite scholarship is not in agreement regarding the purported attack on Fāṭima, contrary to what is claimed by the Twelver scholar, al-Ṭūsī (d. 460), about the Shīʿa in general.

The Muʿtazilite scholar, al-Qāḍī ʿAbdulJabbār (d. 415), mentioned that the Imāmites of his time in Baghdād and al-Kūfa used to wail and mourn the murder of Fāṭima and al-Muḥassin at the hands of ʿUmar.[1]

قال القاضي عبد الجبار في «تثبيت دلائل النبوة»: وانه كان يقيم المناحات بالشعر على فاطمة وابنها الحسن [المحسن] الذي زعم الإمامية أن عمر قتله، كما يفعل الإمامية ذلك ببغداد والكوفة.

Al-Qāḍī ʿAbdulJabbār (d. 415) also listed a cohort of contemporaneous prominent Shīʿite figures in different regions of the world used to wail about Fāṭima and her son, al-Muḥassin, who they allege was murdered by ʿUmar.[2]

وقال القاضي عبد الحبار: وفي هذا الزمان منهم مثل أبي جبلة إبراهيم بن غسان، ومثل جابر المتوفي، وأبي الفوارس الحسن بن محمد الميمديّ، وأبي الحسين أحمد بن محمد بن الكميت، وأبي محمد الطبري، وأبي الحسن الحلبي، وأبي يتيم الرلباى، وأبي القاسم النجاري، وأبي الوفا الديلمي، وابن أبي الديس، وخزيمة، وأبي خزيمة، وأبي عبد الله محمد بن النعمان، فهؤلاء بمصر وبالرملة وبصور، وبعكا وبعسقلان وبدمشق وببغداد وبجبل البسماق. وكل هؤلاء بهذه النواحي يدّعون التشيع ومحبة رسول الله صلّى الله عليه وسلم وأهل بيته، فيبكون على فاطمة وعلى ابنها المحسن الذي زعموا أن عمر قتله، ويذكرون لهم تبديل القرآن والفرائض...

Al-Qāḍī ʿAbdulJabbār (d. 415) further addressed the Twelver Shīʿite claims regarding the beating of Fāṭima, saying:

> It would also be said to the Rāfiḍites, "if Abū Bakr had beaten Fāṭima and murdered al-Muḥassin, then knowledge of that incident must be among all those who had heard reports, and knowledge of that incident must be like the knowledge of Yazīd's murder of al-Ḥusayn, Muʿāwiya's murder of Ḥujr b. ʿAdī, and ʿUbaydullāh b. Ziyād's murder of Muslim b. ʿAqīl.

---

1 Tathbīt Dalāʾil al-Nubuwwa by al-Qāḍī ʿAbdulJabbār al-Hamadhānī (p. 276)
2 Tathbīt Dalāʾil al-Nubuwwa (p. 594-595)

Rather, knowledge of what you have claimed should be more manifest than the knowledge of the aforementioned slain individuals. That is because this incident that you have cited against Abū Bakr took place in Medīna, and it was witnessed by al-ʿAbbās and his children, ʿAlī b. Abī Ṭālib and his children, ʿAqīl and his children, all of Banī Hāshim and their clients and women, all of the Muhājirīn and the Anṣār, and their children and women.

When the Messenger of Allah ﷺ died, there were more than 100,000 people in Medīna. Knowledge of that incident hence would be greater than the knowledge of what took place at Karbalāʾ. However, the Rāfiḍites claims regarding the assault on Fāṭima and the murder of her fetus and Abū Bakr's order that Khālid kill ʿAlī b. Abī Ṭālib is akin to their claims regarding the Prophet's ﷺ designations [of their Imāms]. Anyone who observes their case is made aware of its invalidity, and it becomes as clear as the sun to him."[1]

وقال القاضي عبد الجبار: وقيل ايضا للرافضة: اذا كان أبو بكر قد ضرب فاطمة وقتل المحسن فقد كان ينبغي ان يحصل العلم بذلك عند كل من سمع الأخبار، وأن يكون العلم بذلك مثل العلم بقتل يزيد الحسين، ومثل قتل معاوية حجر بن عدي، وعبيد الله بن زياد مسلم بن عقيل. بل كان ينبغي ان يكون العلم بما ادعيتم اقوى من العلم بهؤلاء القتلى، لأن هذه الحادثة التي ادعيتموها على أبي بكر كانت بالمدينة، وقد شهدها العباس وولده، وعليّ بن أبي طالب وولده، وعقيل وولده، وجميع بن هاشم ومواليهم ونسائهم، وجميع المهاجرين والانصار وأولادهم ونسائهم؛ وقد كان بالمدينة حين توفي رسول الله صلّى الله عليه وسلم اكثر من مائة ألف إنسان، فكان يكون العلم بهذا أقوى مما كان بكربلاء، ولكن دعاوى الرافضة في ضرب فاطمة عليها السلام وقتل ولدها وأمر ابي بكر خالد بن الوليد بقتل عليّ بن ابي طالب، كدعواهم على رسول الله صلّى الله عليه وسلم النصوص التي يدّعونها، وكل من تأمل امرهم تبين له بطلان ذلك ووضح له وضوح الشمس.

The Muʿtazilite scholar, Ibn Abī al-Ḥadīd (d. 656), voiced similar objections to this Twelver Shīʿite narrative. He said:

As for the gruesome and reprehensible things that are claimed by the Shīʿa, such as the claim that Qunfudh was sent to Fāṭima's house and that he beat her with a whip until a bruise like a bracelet remained in her shoulder until her death; and that ʿUmar squeezed

1 Tathbīt Dalāʾil al-Nubuwwa (p. 240)

> her in between the door and the wall, to which she yelled, "O father! O Messenger of Allah!;" and that she miscarried her fetus; and that a rope was tied around ʿAlī's neck such that he was forcefully dragged while Fāṭima was screaming and wailing behind him, and his two sons, al-Ḥasan and al-Ḥusayn were crying with them; [...] all of this has no basis according to our companions, and none of them affirm it. The people of ḥadīth have not transmitted, and they do not know it. Rather, it is something exclusively relayed by the Shīʿa.[1]

قال ابن أبي الحديد: فأما الامور الشنيعة المستهجنة التي تذكرها الشيعة من إرسال قنفذ إلى بيت فاطمة ع ، وإنه ضربها بالسوط فصار في عضدها كالدملج وبقي أثره إلى أن ماتت ، وأن عمر أضغطها بين الباب والجدار ، فصاحت : يا أبتاه يا رسول الله ! وألقت جنينا ميتا ، وجعل في عنق علي ع حبل يقاد به وهو يعتل ، وفاطمة خلفه تصرخ ونادى بالويل والثبور ، وإبناه حسن وحسين معهما يبكيان . وأن عليا لما أحضر سلموه البيعة فامتنع ، فتهدد بالقتل ، فقال : إذن تقتلون عبد الله وأخا رسول الله ! فقالوا : أما عبد الله فنعم ! وأما أخو رسول الله فلا . وأنه طعن فيهم في أوجههم بالنفاق ، وسطر صحيفة الغدر التي إجتمعوا عليها ، وبأنهم أرادوا أن ينفروا ناقة رسول الله ص ليلة العقبة ، فكله لا أصل له عند أصحابنا ، ولا يثبته أحد منهم ، ولا رواه أهل الحديث ، ولا يعرفونه ، وإنما هو شئ تنفرد الشيعة بنقله .

Throughout my survey of the past accounts about the commotion at Fāṭima's house, my intention was not necessarily to grade the traditions' authenticity per se, though the analysis of their isnāds evidently is a crucial task of ample insight. Rather, my primary intention was to demonstrate the development and embellishment of these accounts with the progression of time, such that their final forms ended up embodying details, dialogues, characters, and events that are alien to the earlier accounts of this purported historical incident. The reader is hence able to observe how the downstreamness of weakness in an account's isnād generally tends to be directly correlated with the account's detail, embellishment, and development. To put it blatantly, the narrative surrounding Fatima's murder clearly was being developed and expanded with the progression of time, with increasing details and imagery being added to the story by later transmitters. Additionally, the reader can observe the subtle and blatant

1 Sharḥ Nahj al-Balāgha by Ibn Abī al-Ḥadīd (2/60)

contradictions between the varying weak accounts, which is yet another manifestation of these accounts' ahistorical nature.

In this regard, *Kitāb Sulaym Ibn Qays'* redaction of this historical event, disregarding its innumerable errors and discrepancies, evidently is the most developed and embellished of all accounts. I do not exaggerate when I say that it is exponentially more developed and embellished than any of the past Sunnī and Shīʿite accounts, and I shall quote the entire excerpt from *Kitāb Sulaym* here so that the reader is made aware of what I am exactly describing. In *Kitāb Sulaym,* Salmān al-Fārisī is quoted relaying the notorious account of the purported attack on Fāṭima and Abū Bakr's pledge. The account is quite extensive, and it commences on page 147 of *Kitāb Sulaym* and ends on page 159. Salmān is quoted saying:

> ʿUmar told Abū Bakr, "Send for ʿAlī so that he may pay allegiance, for we are upon nothing until he pays allegiance. If he pays allegiance, then we would be safe from him."
>
> Abū Bakr sent a messenger to ʿAlī saying, "Answer Messenger of Allah's ﷺ successor." ʿAlī replied, "*Subḥān Allāh*! How quickly have you lied about the Messenger of Allah! Abū Bakr and those around him know that Allah and His Messenger left none as a successor but me!"
>
> The messenger returned and informed Abū Bakr what ʿAlī had said. Abū Bakr asked the man to return and say, "Answer the Commander of the Faithful, Abū Bakr!" The man returned to ʿAlī and informed him of what Abū Bakr had told him. ʿAlī replied, "*Subḥān Allāh*! By Allah, it has not been long time such that he could have forgotten: by God, he knows that this title does not suit anyone but me! The Prophet ﷺ had commanded him as the seventh person in a group of seven people, and they saluted me as the commander of the faithful. Abū Bakr and his companion, ʿUmar, among the seven asked him, 'Is this an order from Allah and His Prophet?' The Prophet ﷺ told both of them, 'Yes, this truly is from Allah and His messenger. He is the commander of the faithful, master of the Muslims and the flag bearer of the brightly radiant ones [on the Day of Judgement from the traces of *wuḍūʾ*]. On the Day of Resurrection, Allah will position him on the *Ṣirāṭ*, and he will admit his loyalists into heaven and his enemies into hell'."

The messenger returned and informed Abū Bakr of what ʿAlī had told him, and they remained silent regarding ʿAlī on that day. At nighttime, ʿAlī placed Fāṭima on a donkey and held the hands of al-Ḥasan and al-Ḥusayn. He did not leave a single companion of the Messenger of Allah ﷺ except that he had visited him at his house. He asked them by Allah about his right and requested their support. None agreed to his pleas except us four, for we shaved our heads and offered our support. Al-Zubayr was the keenest in his support of ʿAlī.

When ʿAlī saw that people had let him down, abandoned his support and obeyed, revered and coalesced around Abū Bakr, he confined himself to his home.

ʿUmar then told Abū Bakr, "What prevents you from sending to ʿAlī so that he may pay his allegiance? There is not a single person that had not paid his allegiance except him and them four." Abū Bakr was the more soft-hearted, kinder, cleverer and more thoughtful of the two. The other one (ʿUmar) was the more short-tempered, hard-hearted and estranged of the two.

Abū Bakr asked, "Who shall we send to him?" ʿUmar said, "We shall send Qunfudh to him, for he is a rough, short-tempered and estranged man from the Ṭulaqāʾ from the clan of ʿAdī b. Kaʿb. Abū Bakr thus sent him to ʿAlī, and he sent aides alongside him.

Qunfudh departed and requested permission from ʿAlī to enter, and ʿAlī refused to grant them permission. Qunfudh's companions hence returned to Abū Bakr and ʿUmar, and both men were seated in the mosque surrounded by the people. They said, "We were not granted permission [to enter]." ʿUmar said, "Go! If he does not grant you permission to enter, then enter his house without permission!"

They departed and asked for permission to enter, to which Fāṭima said, "I bar you from entering my house without permission!" They returned, but Qunfudh, the damned, remained. They said, "Fāṭima said such and such, so we felt disconcerted from entering her house." ʿUmar became angered, and he said, "What have we with women?!"

ʿUmar commanded people around him to gather firewood, so they carried the firewood with ʿUmar and placed it around the house of

ʿAlī, Fāṭima and their two sons. ʿUmar then called out loud, such that ʿAlī and Fāṭima heard him, "By Allah, you will come outside and pay allegiance to the Prophet's ﷺ successor, O ʿAlī, or I shall otherwise set your house on fire!"

Fāṭima said, "O ʿUmar, what have we with you?!" He thus said, "Open the door, or we shall otherwise burn your house down upon you!" Fāṭima then said, "O ʿUmar, do you not fear Allah such that you would enter my house?!" He refused to leave.

ʿUmar asked for the fire to be brought, and he lit the door on fire. He then kicked it and entered the house. Fāṭima confronted him and yelled, "O father! O Messenger of Allah!" ʿUmar then raised the sword while it was sheathed, and he struck her side with it. She thus yelled, "O father!" He then raised the whip and struck her arm with it, to which she yelled, "O Messenger of Allah! Wretched is what Abū Bakr and ʿUmar have done after you!"

ʿAlī leaped and grabbed ʿUmar by his collar. He then shoved him, to which ʿUmar fell to the ground, and ʿAlī struck his ear and neck. ʿAlī intended to kill him, but he then remembered the Messenger of Allah's ﷺ speech and what he had advised him to do. ʿAlī thus said, "By the One Who had honored Muḥammad with prophethood, O son of Ṣuhāk, had it not been for a prior decree from Allah and an oath unto me by the Messenger of Allah, then you know you could not have entered my house!"

ʿUmar thus sent for assistance, and the people came and entered the house. ʿAlī leaped to his sword, and Qunfudh fled to Abū Bakr fearing that ʿAlī would confront him with his sword, since he was aware of ʿAlī's strength and severity.

Abū Bakr told Qunfudh, "Return to Ali's house. If he comes out then fine, otherwise enter his house. If he refrains, then set their house on fire!" Qunfudh the damned returned and impermissibly entered the house with his companions. ʿAlī leaped to his sword, but they beat him to it and outnumbered him. Some of them drew their swords, outnumbered ʿAlī and restrained him, and they tied a rope around his neck.

Fāṭima stood in between them and ʿAlī at the door, so the cursed Qunfudh struck her with a whip. When she died, a bruise from the strike, which resembled a shoulder bracelet, remained on her shoulder. May Allah curse him and the one who sent him.

He then set out with ʿAlī, violently dragging him until he reached Abū Bakr. ʿUmar was standing with the sword before him, and Khālid b. al-Walīd, Abū ʿUbayda b. al-Jarrāḥ, Sālim the *mawlā* of Abū Ḥudhayfa, Muʿādh b. Jabal, al-Mughīra b. Shuʿba, Usayd b. Ḥuḍayr, Bashīr b. Saʿīd and the remainder of the people were seated and armed around Abū Bakr.

[Sulaym said:] I asked Salmān, "Did they enter upon Fāṭima without permission?!" He said, "Yes, by Allah, and she was not covered. She thus yelled at her highest voice, 'O father! O Messenger of Allah! Wretched is what Abū Bakr and ʿUmar have done after you when your eyes are yet to close in your grave!' I saw Abū Bakr and all those around him cry and wail except ʿUmar, Khālid b. al-Walīd and al-Mughīra b. Shuʿba. ʿUmar was saying, "We have nothing to do with women and their opinions!"

They brought ʿAlī to Abū Bakr, and ʿAlī was saying, "By Allah, had my word been in my hand, then you know you would not have ever been able to get here! By Allah, I do not blame myself for resisting you, and had I had 40 men, then I would have disbanded your coalition! Alas, may Allah curse people who paid allegiance to me and then let me down!"

When Abū Bakr saw ʿAlī, he yelled, "Release him!" ʿAlī thus told him, "O Abū Bakr, how quickly have you rose against the Messenger of Allah! By what right and status have you called the people to your allegiance? Did you not pay allegiance to me in the past by Allah and the Messenger of Allah's ﷺ command?"

Qunfudh – may Allah curse him – had struck Fāṭima with a whip when she stood as a barrier between him and her husband. ʿUmar had written to him saying, "If Fāṭima stands as an obstacle between you and him, then hit her." Qunfudh had pushed her to seek refuge behind the door, and he squeezed her [with the door] and broke her rib, causing her to miscarry a fetus from her stomach. She remained bedridden until her death, may Allah bless her for the martyr she is.

When ʿAlī arrived to Abū Bakr, ʿUmar rebuked him and said, "Pay allegiance and leave these lies." ʿAlī replied, "If I do not, what will you do?" They said, "We would humiliatingly and disgracefully kill you!" ʿAlī said, "Then you would kill the slave of Allah and His Messenger's brother." Abū Bakr said, "As for the slave of Allah, then yes. As for the Messenger of Allah's ﷺ brother, then we do not concede that!" ʿAlī said, "Do you deny that the Messenger of Allah ﷺ took me as a brother?" He said, "Yes," and he repeated that three times to them.

ʿAlī then faced them and said, "O Muslims from the Muhājirīn and Anṣār, I ask you by Allah: did you hear the Messenger of Allah ﷺ say on the day of Ghadīr Khumm such and such and on the day of Tabūk such and such?" He did not leave out a single thing the Messenger of Allah ﷺ publicly said about him except that he reminded them of it. They replied, "By Allah, yes."

When Abū Bakr became fearful that the people may assist ʿAlī and thwart him [from fulfilling his plans], he quickly said, "What you have said is true, and we have heard it with our ears and understood it in our hearts. However, I have heard the Messenger of Allah ﷺ say after that, 'We are a household that Allah has chosen and honored. He chose for us the *Ākhira* over the *Dunyā*. Allah would not combine for us, *Ahlulbayt*, prophethood and the caliphate."

ʿAlī said, "Is there anyone from the Messenger of Allah's ﷺ companions who can attest to this with you?" ʿUmar said, "The Messenger of Allah's ﷺ successor has said the truth. I have heard it from him just has he had said." Abū ʿUbayda, Sālim the *mawlā* of Abū Ḥudhayfa and Muʿādh b. Jabal said, "He has said the truth. We have heard that from the Messenger of Allah."

ʿAlī thus said, "You have upheld the document which you have agreed upon at the Kaʿba, which stated that if Muḥammad were to die or be killed, you will prevent us *Ahlulbayt* from leadership." Abū Bakr said, "What do you know about that? We did not present it to you!" ʿAlī said, "Zubayr, Salmān, Abū Dharr and Miqdād, I ask you by Allah and Islam, did you not hear the Messenger of Allah ﷺ say that such-and-such person and such-and-such person – till he counted five people – have written among themselves a document. They have sworn oaths about what they would do if I were to die or be killed?" They said, "By Allah, yes. We have heard the Messenger of Allah ﷺ say that to you. We have heard the Messenger of Allah ﷺ say to you, 'They have sworn oaths regarding what they have done, and they have written among them a document saying that if I were to die or be killed, they would rise against you and prevent you from this O 'Alī'. You then told the Prophet, 'May my father and mother be ransom to you O Messenger of Allah, what do you command me to do if that happens?' He told you, 'If you find supporters against them, then resist them and fight them. If you do not find supporters, then pay allegiance and spare your life'."

'Alī said, "By God, had those forty men who paid allegiance to me been loyal to me then I would have resisted you for the sake of Allah. However, by Allah, none from your descendants until the Day of Resurrection will ever have it. What belies your ḥadīth from the Messenger of Allah ﷺ is Allah's saying, 'Or do they envy the people for Allah's bounties? Indeed, We have given the descendants of Abraham the Book and wisdom, along with great dominion.' The Book is prophethood; the wisdom is the Sunna; the dominion is the caliphate; and we are the descendants of Ibrāhīm."

Al-Miqdād then stood up and said, "O 'Alī, what do you command me to do? By Allah, if you were to command me, I would strike with my sword, and if you were to command me, I would halt." 'Alī told him, "Halt, O Miqdād, and remember the Messenger of Allah's ﷺ covenant and will to you."

Salmān then stood up and said, "By the One in whose hand is my soul, had I known that I would repel an evil and bring pride to Allah's religion, I would have placed my sword on my neck and struck with it by every step I take. Do you uprise against the Messenger of Allah's ﷺ brother, legatee and successor in his *Umma* and the father of his children?! Anticipate the tribulation and be despondent of any ease!"

Abū Dharr then stood up and said, "O Umma that is confused after its prophet and forsaken due to its disobedience, Allah says, 'Indeed, Allah chose Adam, Noah, the family of Ibrāhīm, and the family of 'Imrān above all people [of their time]. They are descendants of one another. And Allah is All-Hearing, All-Knowing.' The household of

Muḥammad are the successors from Nūḥ, the family of Ibrāhīm, the cream and progeny of Ismāʿīl, and the family of Muḥammad, the household of prophethood, the destination of the message (al-Risāla), and the visiting place of the angels. They are like the elevated sky, the fixed mountains, the enshrined Kaʿba, the pure spring, the guiding stars, the blessed tree: it brings light and its oil is blessed. Muḥammad is the seal of all prophets and the master of mankind, and ʿAlī is the legatee of all legatees, the Imām of the pious and the leader of the brightly radiant ones [on the Day of Judgement from the traces of wuḍūʾ]. He is the greater *ṣiddīq*, the great *fārūq*, the legatee (*waṣiī*) of Muḥammad, the inheritor of his knowledge, and most worthy of the believers than themselves, as Allah had said, 'Surely the Prophet ﷺ has a greater claim over the believers than they have over each other, and his wives are their mothers.' Hence, give precedence to whom Allah had given precedence, put back those who Allah had placed back, and place the *wilāya* among those whom Allah had placed it."

ʿUmar stood up and told Abū Bakr, as he was seated on the pulpit, "What makes you sit on the pulpit while this one is at war and does not get up to pay allegiance to you?! Shall you command that his neck be struck!" Al-Ḥasan and al-Ḥusayn were standing, and when they heard ʿUmar's words, they cried. ʿAlī then hugged them and said, "Do not cry, for, by Allah, they are unable to kill your father."

Umm Ayman, the woman who raised the Prophet, approached and she said, "O Abū Bakr, how quickly have you exposed your envy and hypocrisy!" ʿUmar then command that she be removed from the mosque, and he said, "What have we with women!"

Burayda al-Aslamī then stood up and said, "O ʿUmar, do you rise against the Messenger of Allah's ﷺ brother and the father of his children when you are identified within Quraysh for what you are known? Did the Messenger of Allah ﷺ not tell both of you, 'go to ʿAlī and salute him as the commander of the faithful.' So you both asked him, 'is this from Allah and His Messenger's command?' He said, 'yes.'"

Abū Bakr said, "That occurred, but the Messenger of Allah ﷺ said after that, 'The prophethood and caliphate shall not be combined for my household'." Burayda then said, "By Allah, the Messenger of

Allah ﷺ did not say that. By Allah, I shall never reside in a town where you are a leader!" ʿUmar then commanded that he be beaten, and he was beaten and thrown out.

He then said, "Get up O son of Abū Ṭālib and pay allegiance!" ʿAlī said, "And what if I do not?" He said, "Then, by Allah, we will strike your neck!" ʿAlī disputed with them for three times, and he then extended his hand without opening his palm. Abū Bakr then placed his hand on ʿAlī's hand, and he was content with that from him. Before paying allegiance and while the rope was tied around his neck, ʿAlī called out, "O son of my mother! The people overpowered me and were about to kill me!"

Al-Zubayr was then told to pledge allegiance, and he refused. ʿUmar, Khālid b. al-Walīd, al-Mughīra b. Shuʿba and others leaped onto him and snatched his sword from his hand. They then struck it on the ground, breaking it. They then restrained al-Zubayr, and while ʿUmar was atop his chest, al-Zubayr said, "O son of Ṣuhāk, by Allah, had my sword been in my hand, then you would not have gotten away from me!" He then paid allegiance.

[Salmān said:] They then took me, struck my neck such that it was like a tumor. They then took my hand and twisted it, and so I disapprovingly paid allegiance.

Abū Dharr and al-Miqdād then disapprovingly paid allegiance. None from the *Umma* disapprovingly paid allegiance to Abū Bakr besides ʿAlī and us four. None of us was more severe in his speech than al-Zubayr, for he, while paying allegiance, said, "O son of Ṣuhāk, by Allah, had it not been for these tyrants that have assisted you, then you would not have approached me while my sword was with me! I know of your cowardice and vileness, but you found tyrants with whom you have strength and power!"

ʿUmar then became angry and said, "Do you mention Ṣuhāk?!" Al-Zubayr replayed, "And who is Ṣuhāk, and what would prevent me from mentioning her?! Ṣuhāk was an adulteress. Do you deny that? Was she not an Abyssinian slave girl possessed by my grandfather, ʿAbdulMuṭṭalib, and your grandfather, Nufayl, committed *zinā* with her? She then gave birth to your father, al-Khaṭṭāb, so ʿAbdulMuṭṭalib granted her to your grandfather after he had committed adultery with her. She then gave birth to him, and he

> was a bastard slave of my grandfather?" Abū Bakr then reconciled between both of them and prevented each from attacking the other.

As evident in this excruciatingly lengthy excerpt from *Kitāb Sulaym*, this account bypasses all past authentic/inauthentic Sunnī and Shīʿite portrayals of the event in length, detail and polemicism. It is an exponentially more embellished and detailed conglomerate account that has absorbed many strands from the past accounts and traditions while also introducing new details to the narrative, hence fundamentally altering it in numerous ways. The dialogues in *Kitāb Sulaym's* account transcend those of most past accounts: they are expounded and anachronistic polemical appeals that have been embedded into the portrayedly historical text in an attempt to delegitimize and obliterate non-Rāfiḍite historiographies of these events.

When observing this account in light of the chronological development of the traditions surrounding the commotion at Fāṭima's house, one cannot help but notice how it is quite foreign in structure, lexicon, detail and nature to all first and second century accounts surrounding this event. Rather, it clearly is the latest of them all in authorship. Given my past observation when assessing passage 1 and related passages in this chapter, where it is demonstrated that portions of *Kitāb Sulaym* were authored after the third century, I find it likely that this account was concocted around (or after) that era and that it did not exist in the primitive recensions of the text. Such a dating not only takes into the account the tradition's extreme detail and verbosity, which is generally uncharacteristic of early traditions, but it also takes into consideration the tradition's standing with respect to other accounts of the same event(s).

Another possibility regarding this excerpt is that the kernel of *Kitāb Sulaym* contained a brief reference to the attack outside Fāṭima's house that was later expounded, developed and embellished after the third century. In this context, perhaps it should be noted that none of the references to *Kitāb Sulaym Ibn Qays* in third, fourth and fifth century Twelver sources mention the purported attack on Fāṭima. Rather, a survey of all references to Sulaym Ibn Qays in such sources will uncover a text that is different in nature to the extant recension of the book. Traditions of Sulaym b. Qays referenced in early Twelver sources, in reality, tend to revolve around two main subjects, (1) the special knowledge and hermeneutics of *Ahlulbayt* and (2) the religious and spiritual authority of *Ahlulbayt*. The only reference to Abū Bakr via Sulaym b. Qays in Twelver primary sources is a tradition in *al-Kāfī* where it is stated that the first to pledge allegiance to Abū Bakr at the *Saqīfa* was the devil, himself, and that ʿAlī, in fact, was delegated as the Prophet's ﷺ successor.[1]

Either way, most of *Kitāb Sulaym's* account of the assault on Fāṭima clearly was authored after the second and/or third centuries. The only difference between both propositions is that one asserts that the entire mention of Fāṭima's purported murder was later accreted into the book while the other proposition asserts that an initially brief reference to Fāṭima was exploded into the embellished tragedy we observe in the book today.

Passage 9

Passage 9 is a rather fascinating text that further provides us more insight on some of the original sources of *Kitāb Sulaym's* contents. Much of *Kitāb Sulaym*'s contents consist of traditions that Ḥammād b. ʿĪsā had disseminated elsewhere, occasionally through sources that seem independent of *Kitāb Sulaym.* As an example, in several Twelver ḥadīth collections, we find Ḥammād b. ʿĪsā relaying a tradition on the authority of Ibrāhīm b. ʿUmar al-Yamānī, from Abū al-Ṭufayl, from Abū Jaʿfar [al-Bāqir], as can be seen in figure 3.5 below.

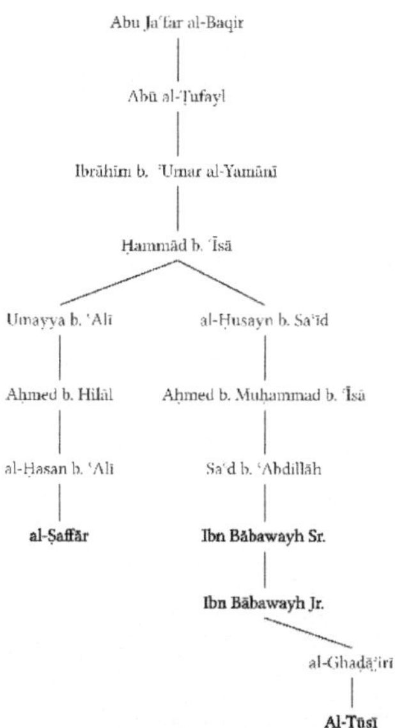

Figure 3.5 A diagram of the isnāds that cite Ḥammād relying this tradition via Abū al-Ṭufayl from al-Bāqir.

1 Al-Kāfī by al-Kulaynī (8/182-183)

In this tradition, Ḥammād b. ʿĪsā relayed that Abū Jaʿfar al-Bāqir said:

> The Messenger of Allah once told the Commander of the faithful, "Transcribe what I shall dictate to you." ʿAlī thus said, "O Prophet of Allah, do you fear that I may forget?"
>
> He said, "I do not fear any forgetfulness for you, as I had supplicated to Allah asking him to remember you and not forget you. Rather, write to your partners." ʿAlī said, "Who are my partnets, O Messenger of Allah?" He said, "The Imāms from your descendents. Through them my nation shall be given rain; and through them their suppplications shall be answered; and through them shall tribulations be repelled from them; and through them shall the mercy descend from the sky. This is the first of them," and he pointed at al-Ḥasan. He then pointed his hand at al-Ḥusayn and said, "The Imāms are from your descendents."[1]

عن حماد بن عيسى، عن ابراهيم بن عمر اليماني، عن أبي الطفيل، عن أبي جعفر عليه السلام، قال: قال رسول الله صلى الله عليه وآله لامير المؤمنين عليه السلام: اكتب ما أملي عليك. قال علي عليه السلام: يا نبي الله وتخاف النسيان؟ قال: لست أخاف عليك النسيان وقد دعوت الله لك ان يحفظك فلا ينساك، لكن اكتب لشركائك. قال: قلت: ومن شركائي يا نبي الله؟ قال: الائمة من ولدك، بهم يسقى [تسقى] أمتي الغيث وبهم يستجاب دعاؤهم وبهم يصرف البلاء عنهم ربهم [وبهم] تنزل الرحمة من السماء. هذا أولهم اوماء [وأومأ] بيده إلى الحسن ثم اوماء [أومأ] بيده إلى الحسين، ثم قال: الائمة من ولدك. اللفظ لفظ الصفار في «بصائر الدرجات» وألفاظهم متقاربة.

However, Ḥammād b. ʿĪsā, on other occasions, also claimed to relay this tradition from Ibrāhīm b. ʿUmar al-Yamānī, but via a different isnād unto the Prophet. In such instances, we observe Ḥammād relaying the tradition from Ibrāhīm b. ʿUmar ⟶ Abān b. Abī ʿAyyāsh ⟶ Sulaym b. Qays ⟶ ʿAlī b. Abī Ṭālib, as can be seen in figure 3.6 below.

1 Baṣāʾir al-Darajāt of al-Ṣaffār (p. 202-203), al-Imāma wa-l-Tabṣira min al-Ḥayra by Ibn Bābawayh Sr. (p. 54), Kamāl al-Dīn wa-Tamām al-Niʿma by Ibn Bābawayh Jr. (p. 198-199), al-Amālī of al-Ṭūsī (p. 655)

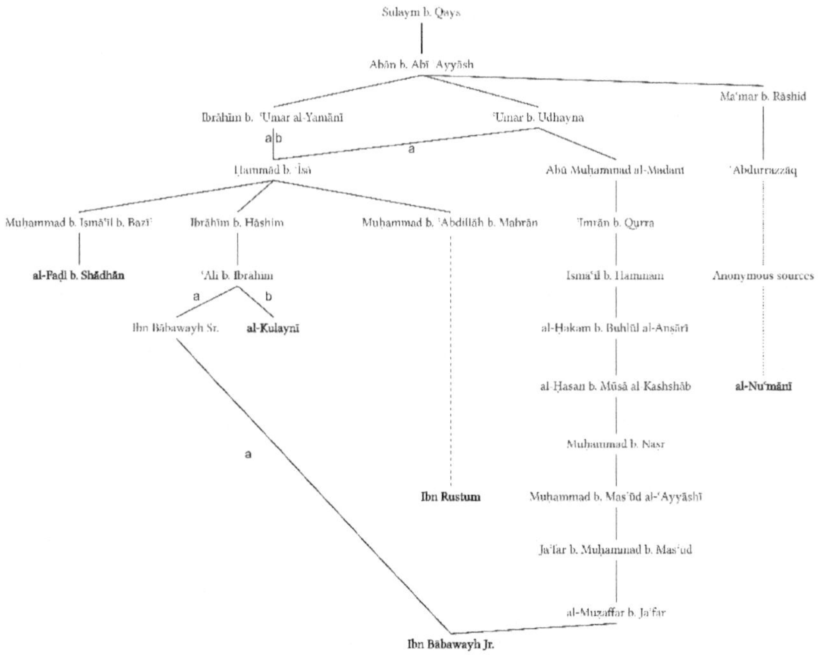

Figure 3.6 A diagram of the isnāds that cite Ḥammād relying this tradition via Sulaym b. Qays.

In this tradition, Ḥammād relayed that ʿAlī b. Abī Ṭālib said:

> [....] When the Messenger of Allah would inform me of all that, he would place his hand on my chest and supplicate to Allah that He fill my heart with knowledge, understanding, wisdom and light. He would say, "O Allah, give him knowledge and give him retention, and do not let him forget anything that I had informed and tought him."
>
> I thus said to him one day, "May my mother and father be your ransom, O Messenger of Allah, since you had supplicated to Allah for me with what you had supplicated, I have not forgetten a single thing. I have missed nothing from what you had tought me, and I have written down everything you have tought me. Do you fear that I may forget?"

He replied, "O brother, I do not fear for you of forgetfulness or ignorance, but I like to supplicate for you. Allah had informed me that he had made my succession in you and your partners, whose obedience Allah had paired with His obedience and mine. He said about them, 'O you who believe, obey Allah and obey the Messenger and those in authority among you.' [al-Nisāʾ: 59]."

I said, "Who are they, O Messenger of Allah?" He said, "They are the legatees (*awṣiyāʾ*) after me who shall not be bothered harmed by the betrayal of those who betray them. They are with the Quran, and the Quran is with them. They shall not separate from it, and it shall not separate from them until they arrive to me at the pond [of al-Kawthar]. Through them my nation shall be given victory; and through them they shall be given rain; and through them shall tribulation be repelled; and through them shall *duʿāʾ* be answered."

I thus said, "Name them to me, O Messenger of Allah." He said, "You, O ʿAlī, are the first of them. Then, this sone of mine," and he placed his hand on al-Ḥasan's head. [He said], "Then, this son of mine," and he placed his hand on al-Ḥusayn's head. [He said], "Then, his son who shares your name, Zayn al-ʿAbidīn. He will be born during your life, O brother, so convey my salutations to him. Then, his son, Muḥammad al-Bāqir, the Bāqir of my knowledge and storage of Allah's revelation. Then, his son, Jaʿfar al-Ṣādiq. Then, his son, Mūsā al-Kāẓim. Then, his son, ʿAlī al-Riḍā. Then, his son, Muḥammad al-Taqī. Then, his son, ʿAlī al-Naqī. Then, his son, al-Ḥasan al-Zakī. Then, his son, al-Ḥujja al-Qāʾim, the seal of my legatees and the one who avenges me from my enemies who shall fill the land with benevolence and justice as it had been filled with tyranny and oppresion."

The Commander of the Faithful then said, "By Allah, I know everyone who will pay their allegiance to him between the corner [of the Kaʿba] and the Maqām, and I know the names of his supporters and their tribes."

Muḥammad b. Ismāʿīl b. Bazīʿ said: Ḥammad b. ʿĪsā said:

I mentioned this ḥadīth to my master, Abū ʿAbdillāh (Jaʿfar al-Ṣādiq), to which he cried and said, "Sulaym has said the truth. My father had relayed this tradition to me, from his father ʿAlī b. al-Ḥusayn, from his father al-Ḥusayn b. ʿAlī, who said, 'I heard this ḥadīth from the Commander of the Faithful when Sulaym b. Qays asked him about it.'"[1]

قال حماد بن عيسى: حدثنا إبراهيم بن عمر اليماني، قال: حدثنا أبان بن أبي عياش، قال: حدثنا سليم بن قيس الهلالي، قال: قلت لامير المؤمنين عليه السلام: [....]. قال: فقال علي عليه السلام [...] وكان رسول الله صلى الله عليه وآله وسلم إذا أخبرني بذلك كله وضع يده على صدري ودعا الله لي أن يملأ قلبي علما وفهما وحكما ونورا، وكان يقول : اللهم علمه وحفظه ولا تنسه شيئا مما أخبرته وعلمته . فقلت له ذات يوم : بأبي أنت وأمي يا رسول الله إنك منذ دعوت لي الله بما دعوت لم أنس شيئا ولم يفتني شيء(مما علمتني، وكل ما علمتني كتبته، أتتخوف علي النسيان؟ فقال: يا أخي، لست أتخوف عليك النسيان ولا الجهل، وإني أحب أن أدعو لك، وقد أخبرني الله تعالى أنه قد أخلفني فيك وفي شركائك الذين قرن الله طاعتهم بطاعته وطاعتي وقال فيهم: (يا أيها الذين آمنوا أطيعوا الله وأطيعوا الرسول وأولي الامر منكم). قلت: من هم يا رسول الله؟ قال: الذين هم الاوصياء من بعدي، والذين لا يضرهم خذلان من خذلهم، وهم مع القرآن والقرآن معهم، لا يفارقونه ولا يفارقهم حتى يردوا علي الحوض، بهم تنصر أمتي، وبهم يمطرون، وبهم يدفع البلاء، وبهم يستجاب الدعاء. قلت : سمهم لي يا رسول الله؟ قال: أنت يا علي أولهم، ثم ابني هذا. ووضع يده على رأس الحسن. ثم ابني هذا .ووضع يده على رأس الحسين. ثم سميك علي ابنه زين العابدين، وسيولد في زمانك يا أخي فأقرئه مني السلام، ثم أبنه محمد الباقر، باقر علمي وخازن وحي الله تعالى، ثم ابنه جعفر الصادق، ثم ابنه موسى الكاظم، ثم ابنه علي الرضا، ثم ابنه محمد التقي، ثم ابنه علي النقي، ثم ابنه الحسن الزكي، ثم ابنه الحجة القائم، خاتم أوصيائي وخلفائي، والمنتقم من أعدائي، الذي يملا الارض قسطا وعدلا كما ملئت ظلما وجورا. ثم قال أمير المؤمنين عليه السلام: والله إني لا عرف جميع من يبايعه بين الركن والمقام، وأعرف أسماء أنصاره، وأعرف قبائلهم.

---

1 Mukhtaṣar Ithbāt al-Rajʿa of al-Faḍl b. Shādhān al-Naysābūrī (p. 45-50), Kitāb al-Ghayba of al-Nuʿmānī (p. 80-84), Kamāl al-Dīn wa-Tamām al-Niʿma by Ibn Bābawayh Jr. (p. 270-271). It is only al-Faḍl b. Shādhān's account that lists the names of each othe imams, and the other accounts merely mention that the Prophet listed the names of the imams to ʿAlī b. Abī Ṭālib.

Al-Kulaynī and Ibn Bābawayh Jr. also relayed this tradition via ʿAlī b. Ibrāhīm; however, they only cited the tradition until the point about forgetfulness. See al-Kāfī of al-Kulaynī (1/37-38) and al-Khiṣāl of Ibn Bābawayh Jr. (p. 255-257). Ibn Rustom al-Ṭabarī also cited another source relaying this tradition from Ḥammād, and he too only cited the tradition until the point about forgetfulness. See al-Mustarshid of Ibn Rustom al-Ṭabarī (p. 231-236).

قال محمد بن إسماعيل: ثم قال حماد بن عيسى: قد ذكرت هذا الحديث عند مولاي أبي عبد الله عليه السلام فبكى وقال: صدق سليم، فقد روى لي هذا الحديث أبي عن أبيه علي بن الحسين عن أبيه الحسين بن علي قال: سمعت هذا الحديث من أمير المؤمنين عليه السلام حين سأله سليم بن قيس.

هذا لفظ الحديث في كتاب «مختصر إثبات الرجعة» للفضل بن شاذان.

This tradition eventually made it way into *Kitāb Sulaym Ibn Qays*, and the account theirein has absorbed accretions from multiple reports and variants.[1] The Abū Muḥammad al-Madanī in one of Ibn Bābawayh's isnāds in figure 3.6 may prove to be Ḥammād b. ʿĪsā, as Ḥammād's *kunya* was Abū Muḥammad.[2]

Both reports outlined in figures 3.5 and 3.6 cite Ḥammad b. ʿĪsā relaying this tradition from Ibrāhīm b. ʿUmar al-Yamānī, yet they diverge in the isnād beyond Ibrāhīm and the level of detail in each account. In this regard, it is rather obvious that that the report which presents Ḥammād b. ʿĪsā relaying the tradition through Ibrāhīm b. ʿUmar, from Abū al-Ṭufayl, from Abū Jaʿfar per figure 3.5, is the earlier account and that report which cites Sulaym b. Qays per figure 3.6 is a later more embellished tradition.

In both cases, the corroborated transmission from Ḥammād b. ʿĪsā is indicative that he had played a role in not only disseminating the tradition, but also in spuriously ascribing it to Abān b. Abī ʿAyyāsh → Sulaym b. Qays. Ḥammād b. ʿĪsa's comment at the end of al-Faḍl b. Shādhān's report, where he is quoted relaying Jaʿfar al-Ṣādiq's approval of this tradition, may further demonstrate his involvement in the forgery of this tradition, especially considering that some early critics particularly condemned him for relaying fabricated traditions from Jaʿfar al-Ṣādiq. If one were to absolve Ḥammād b. ʿĪsā of the intentional forgery of this tradition, Ḥammād would still be the original source of the account, which was initially relayed via Abū al-Ṭufayl → Abū Jaʿfar.

Such examples should allows us to close in on Ḥammād b. ʿĪsā as one of the main redactors of *Kitāb Sulaym Ibn Qays*, and they should further allow us to understand the source material of the book and its consequent development with the progression of time. Al-Faḍl b. Shādhān's tradition, which names each of the twelve imams, clearly was developed after Ḥammād b. ʿĪsā's death as well, for Ḥammad b. ʿĪsā died during the life of

1 Kitāb Sulaym Ibn Qays (p. 183-184)
2 Rijāl al-Najāshī (p. 139)

the ninth imam of the Twelvers, Muḥammad al-Jawād. Hence, we observe that this tradition went through multiple developments, some of which occured prior to its admission into *Kitāb Sulaym*: (1) its original isnād was replaced with that of *Kitāb Sulaym*, (2) its contents were expanded and embellished, and (3) the names of the Twelve imams were incorporated into the text certainly after Ḥammād's death.

Dating Conclusion

After a careful study and examination of multiple passages from *Kitāb Sulaym Ibn Qays*, it becomes evident that the extant text today is but a later redaction of a text that had already been redacted and expanded several times before assuming its final form.

The book clearly has undergone multiple stages of development that are best culminated in my previous study of passage 5. At first, we have a text relayed via Sulaym b. Qays in a quite early source, namely the *Jāmiʿ* of Maʿmar b. Rāshid (d. 154). More than one century and a half after Maʿmar's death, we find this tradition in the Twelver collection, *al-Kāfī* of al-Kulaynī (d. 329), with serious changes in its context and structure. The passage is then found in *Kitāb Sulaym* with minor differences to al-Kulaynī's report. Passage 9 also is quite insightful in this regard: a relatively concise tradition initially relayed by Ḥammad b. ʿĪsā through other than Sulaym b. Qays is later presented as a tradition Ḥammad had relayed through Sulaym b. Qays with numerous developments and embellishments in its text.

The presence of multiple redactions of *Kitāb Sulaym* is further observed in my analysis of passages 2, 6 and 9, where a tradition relayed via Sulaym or others in early Twelver collections can be found redacted in *Kitāb Sulaym Ibn Qays* with various accretions, insertions and developments. This finding would indicate that the final redaction of *Kitāb Sulaym* was redacted after the third century, and it is aligned with another observation in my analysis of passage 1, where it is demonstrated that the final redactor of *Kitāb Sulaym* non-transparently utilized traditions relayed by ʿAbdullāh b. Aḥmed b. Ḥanbal (d. 290) and Abū Yaʿlā al-Mawṣilī (d. 307) (or a related source). This also may be the case in passage 7, albeit it may not be as clear of an example as the aforementioned passages.

Additionally, I believe my assessment of passage 3 is quite noteworthy: the presence of a voluminous tradition ascribed to Sulaym b. Qays in *al-Kāfī* of al-Kulaynī (d. 329) which cannot be found in the extant recension of *Kitāb Sulaym Ibn Qays* demonstrates that al-Kulaynī, when transmitting traditions via Sulaym b. Qays, was not necessarily referencing the extant document we possess today.

The extant recension of *Kitāb Sulaym Ibn Qays* is comprised of (at least) three layers. The first layer, which consists of a few oral traditions Abān relayed from Sulaym, is diluted, sparse and generally unidentifiable within the book today, and it has undergone serious corruption and distortion. It can be, nonetheless, dated to Abān b. Abī ʿAyyāsh (d. 138). An example of this layer would be Maʿmar b. Rāshid's (d. 154) report in his *Jāmiʿ*, which was analyzed in passage 5. In fact, there may even be an earlier layer that predates this layer, and it would consist of traditions relayed through various sources that would later be dubiously ascribed to Sulaym b. Qays, as was the case in passage 9. In that case, it would be said that *Kitāb Sulaym* consists of (at least) four layers.

The second layer of the book is a Shīʿite evolution of the first layer with significant additions and changes in the traditions and their contexts. This layer is readily observable in many third, fourth and fifth century Shīʿite ḥadīth collections that reference traditions from Sulaym b. Qays. The second layer, when incorporated into the extant redaction of *Kitāb Sulaym*, often was altered; however, it has mostly retained its general structure and outline within the book's final redaction. It is hence more recognizable than the first layer, which had been notably distorted and diluted within the second layer. The second layer can mostly be dated to the following isnād, Ḥammād b. ʿĪsā (d. 208) ⟶ Ibrāhīm b. ʿUmar ⟶ ʿUmar b. Udhayna ⟶ Abān b. Abī ʿAyyāsh ⟶ Sulaym b. Qays. One of the three transmitters, Ḥammād b. ʿĪsā, Ibrāhīm b. ʿUmar or ʿUmar b. Udhayna, is responsible for the development and distortion of this layer, and it is also possible that each of them partially contributed to its development and embellishment.

For several reasons, I am, however, inclined to conclude that Ḥammad b. ʿĪsā was a main forger and fabricator of this layer. First and foremost, Ḥammād is the first pivotal transmitter of the book and its traditions, and upon him revolve their isnāds. He was a known unreliable transmitter who was condemned for transmitting fabricated traditions from Jaʿfar al-Ṣādiq and others, and his corpus in non-Twelver and Twelver sources make it rather apparent that he was a flaming Shīʿite partisan. Secondly, Ḥammād effectively is the main and, arguably, only source of information on the obscure Ibrāhīm b. ʿUmar al-Yamānī, who purportedly was a transmitter of *Kitāb Sulaym*. Certain traditions found in *Kitāb Sulaym*, such as passage 9, can be said to have definitively originated from Ḥammād b. ʿĪsā. I believe that these observations, among other less notable ones, should point to

Ḥammād as a culprit who forged and disseminated this text, though it does not necessarily entail that he was the only forger involved in its development. All-in-all, layer two can be dated to the late second and early third century.

What is also noteworthy in this regard is that Ḥammād b. ʿĪsā was a propagator of the purported oppressorship of *Ahlulbayt*, the notion that *Ahlulbayt* lived in continuous fear, danger and persecution under their oppressors, which would perfectly fit with his dissemination of *Kitāb Sulaym Ibn* Qays.[1]

The third layer of the book is the extant recension of *Kitāb Sulaym*, and it was redacted by an unknown Twelver author/editor after 300 AH. It embodies notable accretions and embellishments to layer two alongside the introduction of new traditions and accounts to the book. In some instances, such as passage 6, the author of the third layer significantly diluted the second layer, which had been preserved in third and fourth century Twelver ḥadīth collections. Given the absence of any surviving manuscripts of *Kitāb Sulaym* from this era, it may be difficult to ascertain the identity of the book's final redactor. However, it is evident that this authors/editor/redactor was a deceitful forger who successfully led his Shīʿite readership into believing that his distortions and accretions originated from Sulaym b. Qays, himself.

The contemporary Twelver scholar and exegete, Abū al-Ḥasan b. Muḥammad al-Shaʿrānī (d. 1393/2015), concluded that the book was forged during the Umayyad era. He said:

> The reality of the matter is that *Kitāb Sulaym* was forged for a righteous cause in analogous manner to *Kitāb al-Ḥusayniyya*, the *Ṭarāʾif of Ibn* Dawud, *al-Riḥla al-Madrasiyya* of al-Balāghī and similar texts.
>
> Its forger compiled known and unknown details, and since he was fallible, he included incorrect things in it. It was apparently fabricated near the end of Umayyad rule...[2]

قال أبو الحسن الشعراني في هامش «شرح أصول الكافي» للمازندراني: وقد ذكرنا في غير موضع أن التكلم في سليم بن قيس وأبان بن أبي عياش ينبغي أن يخصص بهذا الكتاب الموجود بأيدينا المعروف بكتاب سليم.

1 Al-Ḍuʿafāʾ al-Kabīr by al-ʿUqaylī (4/177-178)
2 Sharḥ Uṣūl al-Kāfī by al-Māzandarānī (2/307)

والحق أن هذا كتاب موضوع لغرض صحيح نظير كتاب الحسنية وطرائف ابن طاووس والرحلة المدرسية للبلاغي وأمثاله وأن واضعه جمع امورا مشهورة وغير مشهورة ولما لم يكن معصوما أورد فيه أشياء غير صحيحة. والظاهر أنه وضع في أواخر دولة بني امية حين لم يجاوز عدد خلفاء الجور الاثني عشر إذ ورد فيه أن الغاصبين منهم اثنا عشر وبعدهم يرجع الحق إلى أهله مع أنهم زادوا ولم يرجع.

This generalization is somewhat inaccurate, as it does not account for the multi-layered nature of the book which is the byproduct of its continuous redaction at various points in history. Nonetheless, it seems to be the case that the first layer of the book, which was, compared to its later accretions, relatively insignificant, scarce and primitive, was composed during the late Umayyad epoch, only to be significantly distorted, developed, and embellished on multiple occasions after that.

Another contemporary Shīʿite scholar, Muḥammad Bāqir al-Behbūdī (d. 1393/2015), concluded that the book was a forgery. Though he held that Abān b. Abī ʿAyyāsh, the book's sole transmitter from Sulaym, was a weak transmitter, he concluded that it was, in fact, authored by a later forger who faslely attributed the text to Ibn Udhayna → Abān → Sulaym. He claimed that the book's forger, one of the *ghulāt*, chose to attribute the text to the absent Ibn Udhayna, who had fled his homeland in Baṣra to Yemen. This forger then disseminated the forged text among scribes and copyists who foolishly proceeded to spread the book without any verification.[1]

قال البهبودي في «معرفة الحديث»: ولكن الذي أعتقده بعد سبر الكتاب صدرا وذيلا ونقدها كلمة كلمة، أن الكتاب موضوع وضعه أحد الغلاة على لسان سليم بن قيس الهلالي ورواية ابن أذينة عن أبان بن أبي عياش. وإنما اختار عمرَ بن أذينة لأنه كان هاربا من موطنه – وهو البصرة – إلى مخاليف اليمن اتقاء شر المهدي العباسي في خلافته (158-168) ومات هناك. فدس الزنديق مصنف هذا الكتاب نسخته في الكوفة والبصرة واليمن بأيدي الوراقين المغفلين. وأخذه الأصحاب يروونها وجادة حسب الإجازات التي كانت لهم إلى روايات عمر بن أذينة من دون أن يتمكنوا من تحقيق النسخة وقراءتها على ابن أذينة، كل ذلك شوقا منهم في الكعن على أعداء أهل البيت وكسر شوكتهم.

Behbūdī's conclusion is more nuanced than contemporary appeals that pinpoint *Kitāb Sulaym's* forgery on Abān b. Abī ʿAyyāsh. He pinpoints its forgery on an anonymous contemporary of Ibn Udhayna who falsely

1 Maʿrifat al-Ḥadīth by al-Behbūdī (p. 363-364)

attributed the book to him, taking advantage of Ibn Udhayna's absence. Nevertheless, this conclusion is questionable in several regards: (1) it absolves Ibn Udhayna from any role in the authorship and forgery of the text, and (2) it disregards the book's multi-layered nature and development across several centuries. Hence, it would not necessarily be accurate to conclude that it was forged by a single perpetrator from the *ghulāt*. Rather, it would be more appropriate to conclude that it was composed by several *ghulāt* from various epochs who contributed to the text, including a final redactor who probably existed after 300 AH.

Contemporary scholar and academic, Hossein Modarresi, described the book saying, "the book is one written by commoners for commoners. It is a display of primitive, unsophisticated beliefs among the rank and file of the Shī'ites of Kufa during the late Umayyad period with clear residues of the usual Kaysani exaggerations on the virtues of the House of the Prophet." Modarresi additionally noted the texts development through later redactions. He said, "the original core of the work which is preserved to a great extent in the current version is definitely from the reign of Hishām b. ʿAbd al-Malik (r. 105–25), almost certainly from the final years of his reign when the long-established Umayyad hegemony was already under threat from troubles concerning his succession."[1] Modarresi then said:

> Owing to the fact that a number of insertions were made in the book, there are variations among its different manuscripts, as described by Āghā Buzurg 2: 152–9. Fortunately, later accretions seem always to have been in the form of insertions and additions rather than replacements and alterations. The old core is therefore preserved in most of the manuscripts, even at the cost of obvious contradictions. Some of these variations are noted in the editions of the book: a number of Najaf editions; Beirut, 1407; Qum, 1415 (the one used here is Najaf: Haydariyya, n.d., 236 pp.).[2]

This conclusion of Modarresi, by far, seems to be the most considerate of the book's nature and transmission. However, his claim that the accretions in the book always seemed to had been in the form of insertions/additions and not replacements/alterations seems to be the result of his limited assessment of the text's contents, which seemed generally

1 Tradition and Survival: A Bibliographical Survey of Early Shīʿite Literature (1/85, 1/83)

2 Tradition and Survival: A Bibliographical Survey of Early Shīʿite Literature (1/86)

confined to Shīʿite literature. A more comprehensive cross-examination of the text should demonstrate that some of its early contents had been seriously altered and distorted in later recensions, though it is difficult to estimate the prevalence of this phenomenon in the surviving recension of *Kitāb Sulaym*. This phenomenon can also be observed in some of Sulaym's traditions in Twelver ḥadīth collections, such as passage 6.

Patricia Crone, in her analysis of the 23rd report of *Kitāb Sulaym*, described the extreme (and often preposterous) Rāfiḍite polemic in that tradition saying:

> The letter is clearly fictitious. Muʿāwiya never wrote any such letter; nor is it obvious that the reader is being asked to believe that he did, though on this point opinions may defer. On the one hand, the sarcasm is so heavy that one would have thought that the other beyond attempts at verisimilitude: he works like a cartoonist by drawing an exaggerated and distorted picture of the practices he dislikes and then having Muʿāwiya recommend them with pride. But on the other hand, the naïve indignation expressed by some Shīʿite readers shows that the sarcasm was not always noticed, and the author may well have expected his audience to take his parody at face value. Either way, the letter is a clear piece of political satire.[1]

Amir-Moezzi, when referring to Crone's aforereferenced research, said, "the existence of portions added to an earlier text in accord with the needs of each epoch is stressed in equal measure by Patricia Crone in the study that she devoted to a fragment of *Kitāb Sulaym*, providing a letter supposedly from the Caliph Muʿāwiya to Ziyād b. Abīhi, his violently anti-Alid governor of Iraq."[2] Amir-Moezzi further stated that though accretions in *Kitāb Sulaym* were readily identifiable, reconstructing the primitive kernel of the text would prove to be difficult, if not impossible, due to its fragmentation and dilution within the book today.[3] This seems to be an accurate characterization of the book's early kernel. What is more accessible and reconstructible than the book's primitive kernel is a portion of the second layer of *Kitāb Sulaym*, which can be found in extant Twelver ḥadīth collections from the third, fourth and fifth centuries. This layer of the text occasionally made its way into the final redaction of *Kitāb Sulaym* without

---

1 From Arabian Tribes to Islamic Empire: Army State and Society in the Near East, *Mawālī* and the Prophet's ﷺ Family: An Early Shīʿite View (p. 167-168)

2 The Silent Qu'an and the Speaking Qur'an (p. 19)

3 The Silent Qu'an and the Speaking Qur'an (p. 19-20)

many serious and fundamental alterations, hence making it more recognizable and accessible in some instances.

In this regard, it is rather apparent (and ironic) that *Kitāb Sulaym's* account surrounding the attack on Fāṭima, which arguably is the main reason why the book has been granted much attention and relevance today, is the byproduct of a later redactor's creative imagination that was inserted into the book during the late third, fourth or fifth century. The entire account has no reference in Twelver primary sources via Sulaym Ibn Qays, though other (arguably) less significant portions of the book can be readily found in such sources attributed to Sulaym b. Qays. Furthermore, a careful analysis and cross-examination of the book's account on Fāṭima's murder with other related texts will demonstrate that *Kitāb Sulaym's* account is the most embellished, developed and lengthy account of them all: it is the latest conglomerate account that has absorbed and incorporated details from past and contemporaneous traditions while also introducing new details and plots to the greater narrative. This further lends credence to the notion that the account of Fāṭima's purported murder (or much of it) in *Kitāb Sulaym* merely is a later insertion and development.

When accounting for the aforementioned observations and conclusions, it would be unreasonable to reduce the discussion surrounding *Kitāb Sulaym Ibn Qays's* origins and authenticity to a mere debate surrounding the (un)reliability of Abān b. Abī ʿAyyāsh (d. 138), the purported sole transmitter of the book from Sulaym. Though Abān likely claimed to transmit a few relatively concise traditions from Sulaym b. Qays, as is observed in early Sunnī literature, the second and final redactions of *Kitāb Sulaym* only developed after his death. Hence, the emphasis on Abān b. Abī ʿAyyāsh's status by contemporary Shīʿite apologists and critics when discussing *Kitāb Sulaym Ibn Qays'* authenticity is, in reality, a red herring that distracts and detracts from the more serious issues that plague the text and its blunderous transmission. Nevertheless, Abān's unreliability, though effectively inconsequential, would be sufficient grounds to question and dismiss the text's authenticity.

ESSAY

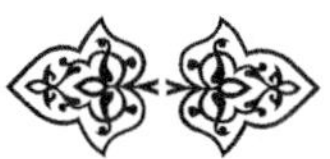

An Overview and Explanation of the *Saqīfa* Events and Their Aftermaths

Abū Bakr's inauguration at the *Saqīfa* of Banī Sāʿida is one of the perceivably more important and controversial events in early Islamic history. Its significance can be observed in the fact that divergent narratives about the event were eventually developed for various theological purposes: it clearly was a hotbed of forgery and fabrication within many partisan circles. I say this not to detract from our ability to ascertain the authentic historical narrative regarding Abū Bakr's rise as the Prophet's ﷺ successor, but rather to emphasize the need for a critical assessment of reports to piece together that narrative.

After carefully assessing the traditions surrounding Abū Bakr's inauguration and its aftermaths, I have come to the conclusion that outlining the authentic and more credible accounts of these events alongside their context tends to dispel the aura of controversy that has engulfed them as a result of their continuous polemicization. The problematization of these events today, which often occurs at the hands of Shīʿite polemicists attempting to justify Shīʿite dogma, tends to lead to the obfuscation of more genuine attempts to discern historical truths as the study of history is reduced to a sectarian conflict that is to be solely understood in light of a (false) Sunnī-Shīʿite dichotomy. Similarly, the naivety and unawareness exhibited by many Sunnī audiences towards these historical events often lead to the proliferation of romanticized, inaccurate narratives about the Prophet's ﷺ community within many Muslim circles. These two problematic approaches to history ironically are complementary to each other, effectively perpetuating the shallow debates that continue to take place about the *Saqīfa* till this day.

Unsurprisingly, understanding what took place at the *Saqīfa* of Banī Sāʿida requires understanding of the context behind these events. Though the entire *Sīra* of the Prophet ﷺ is inseparable from the aftermaths of his death, I will highlight a few select elements from the *Sīra* which I believe will allow the reader to put most things in place.

It is important for the reader to know that the communities that would later constitute the Muslim community of Prophet Muḥammad ﷺ were tribal in nature. Though the religion of Islam significantly weakened and undermined certain aspects of tribalism, tribal affiliation continued to function as the *modus operandus* for many different settings within the early Muslim community, as it continues to do in many Muslim societies today. Nonetheless, the tribalistic nature of the community at the time often allowed for its rapid polarization along tribal lines. This can be observed in numerous occasions within the *Sīra*. An example of this phenomenon can be seen in an event that occurred during the incident of *al-Ifk*, when the Prophet's ﷺ wife, ʿĀʾisha, was slanderously accused of adultery. Ibn Shihāb al-Zuhrī narrated an account from various sources on the authority of ʿĀʾisha that she said:

> [...] The Messenger of Allah ﷺ said while he was on the pulpit, "O Muslims, who shall suffice me from a man whose harm had reached my own household? By Allah, I have known nothing but good about my family (wife). They have also mentioned a man about whom I knew nothing but good, and he used to only enter upon my family along my side."
>
> Saʿd b. Muʿādh al-Anṣārī thus stood up and said, "O Messenger of Allah, I shall suffice you from him. If he is from the tribe of al-Aws, then I shall strike his neck. If he is from the tribe of al-Khazraj, then we shall do with him whatever you command us to do."
>
> Saʿd b. ʿUbāda, the chief of the Khazraj, then stood up. He was a pious man, but he had been overtaken by tribal zeal. He hence told Saʿd b. Muʿādh, "by Allah, you have lied! You would not kill him, nor would you be able to kill him!"
>
> Usayd b. Ḥuḍayr, Saʿd b. Muʿādh's cousin, stood up and told Saʿd b. ʿUbāda, "you have lied! By Allah, we shall kill him! You are but a hypocrite who defends hypocrites!"
>
> Both tribes of al-Aws and al-Khazraj then confronted each other until they were about to engage in combat while the Messenger of

> Allah ﷺ was on the pulpit. The Messenger of Allah ﷺ continued to assuage them until they became silent, and he was silent...[1]

عَنْ ابْنِ شِهَابٍ، قَالَ: أَخْبَرَنِي عُرْوَةُ بْنُ الزُّبَيْرِ، وَسَعِيدُ بْنُ الْمُسَيِّبِ، وَعَلْقَمَةُ بْنُ وَقَّاصٍ، وَعُبَيْدُ اللَّهِ بْنُ عَبْدِ اللَّهِ بْنِ عُتْبَةَ بْنِ مَسْعُودٍ، عَنْ حَدِيثِ عَائِشَةَ رَضِيَ اللَّهُ عَنْهَا زَوْجِ النَّبِيِّ حِينَ، قَالَ لَهَا، "أَهْلُ الإِفْكِ مَا قَالُوا فَبَرَّأَهَا اللَّهُ مِمَّا قَالُوا، وَكُلٌّ حَدَّثَنِي طَائِفَةً مِنَ الْحَدِيثِ وَبَعْضُ حَدِيثِهِمْ يُصَدِّقُ بَعْضًا، وَإِنْ كَانَ بَعْضُهُمْ أَوْعَى لَهُ مِنْ بَعْضٍ...

فَقَالَ رَسُولُ اللَّهِ وَهُوَ عَلَى الْمِنْبَرِ، "يَا مَعْشَرَ الْمُسْلِمِينَ، مَنْ يَعْذِرُنِي مِنْ رَجُلٍ قَدْ بَلَغَنِي أَذَاهُ فِي أَهْلِ بَيْتِي، فَوَاللَّهِ مَا عَلِمْتُ عَلَى أَهْلِي إِلَّا خَيْرًا وَلَقَدْ ذَكَرُوا رَجُلاً مَا عَلِمْتُ عَلَيْهِ إِلَّا خَيْرًا، وَمَا كَانَ يَدْخُلُ عَلَى أَهْلِي إِلَّا مَعِي "، فَقَامَ سَعْدُ بْنُ مُعَاذٍ الْأَنْصَارِيُّ، فَقَالَ: يَا رَسُولَ اللَّهِ، أَنَا أَعْذِرُكَ مِنْهُ إِنْ كَانَ مِنَ الْأَوْسِ ضَرَبْتُ عُنُقَهُ، وَإِنْ كَانَ مِنْ إِخْوَانِنَا مِنَ الْخَزْرَجِ أَمَرْتَنَا فَفَعَلْنَا أَمْرَكَ.

قَالَتْ: فَقَامَ سَعْدُ بْنُ عُبَادَةَ وَهُوَ سَيِّدُ الْخَزْرَجِ وَكَانَ قَبْلَ ذَلِكَ رَجُلاً صَالِحًا وَلَكِنْ احْتَمَلَتْهُ الْحَمِيَّةُ، فَقَالَ لِسَعْدٍ: كَذَبْتَ لَعَمْرُ اللَّهِ لَا تَقْتُلُهُ وَلَا تَقْدِرُ عَلَى قَتْلِهِ، فَقَامَ أُسَيْدُ بْنُ حُضَيْرٍ وَهُوَ ابْنُ عَمِّ سَعْدِ بْنِ مُعَاذٍ، فَقَالَ لِسَعْدِ بْنِ عُبَادَةَ: كَذَبْتَ لَعَمْرُ اللَّهِ لَنَقْتُلَنَّهُ، فَإِنَّكَ مُنَافِقٌ تُجَادِلُ عَنِ الْمُنَافِقِينَ، فَتَثَاوَرَ الْحَيَّانِ الْأَوْسُ وَالْخَزْرَجُ حَتَّى هَمُّوا أَنْ يَقْتَتِلُوا وَرَسُولُ اللَّهِ قَائِمٌ عَلَى الْمِنْبَرِ، فَلَمْ يَزَلْ رَسُولُ اللَّهِ يُخَفِّضُهُمْ حَتَّى سَكَتُوا وَسَكَتَ...

The Anṣār, which consisted of the tribes of al-Aws and al-Khazraj, were in a state of perpetual warfare and conflict among each other prior to the arrival of Islam to Medīna. Though both tribes eventually accepted Islam and consequently ceased their hostilities, there remained some underlying tensions between them. This report is but an example of these tensions between both tribes resurfacing in the presence of a catalyst: the chief of al-Aws casually offered to kill a man from al-Khazraj upon the Prophet's ﷺ command. After hearing that, the chief of al-Khazraj was enraged, and he interjected with the response mentioned in the report. Had the Prophet ﷺ not intervened and assuaged both parties, this standoff was bound to end with combat between both tribes.

There are other examples of this general phenomenon where we observe the community's susceptibility to polarizing tribalism in certain circumstances. Jābir b. ʿAbdillāh said:

---

1 Ṣāḥīḥ al-Bukhārī (6/101-105), Ṣaḥīḥ Muslim (4/2129-2136)

> We were once on an expedition, and a man from the Muhājirīn struck the buttocks of a man from the Anṣār. The Anṣārī man hence called out, "O Anṣār!" The Muhājirī man called out, "O Muhājirīn!"
>
> The Messenger of Allah ﷺ heard that, and he said, "What is the matter with the call of *Jāhiliyya*?" They said, "O Messenger of Allah, a man from the Muhājirīn struck the buttocks of a man from the Anṣār." Thereupon, the Prophet ﷺ said, "leave it, for it is putrid."
>
> ʿAbdullāh b. Ubayy heard of that, and he said, "So they have done it! By Allah, if we return to Medīna, the more honorable will expel the more humiliated!" News of what ʿAbdullāh b. Ubayy had said reached the Prophet, so ʿUmar stood up and said, "O Messenger of Allah, grant me permission to strike this hypocrite's neck!" The Prophet ﷺ replied, "Let him be, lest the people say that Muḥammad kills his companions."[1]

قَالَ عَمْرٌو: سَمِعْتُ جَابِرَ بْنَ عَبْدِ اللَّهِ رَضِيَ اللَّهُ عَنْهُمَا، قَالَ: كُنَّا فِي غَزَاةٍ، - قَالَ سُفْيَانُ مَرَّةً: فِي جَيْشٍ - فَكَسَعَ رَجُلٌ مِنَ الْمُهَاجِرِينَ رَجُلاً مِنَ الأَنْصَارِ، فَقَالَ الأَنْصَارِيُّ: يَا لَلأَنْصَارِ، وَقَالَ الْمُهَاجِرِيُّ: يَا لَلْمُهَاجِرِينَ، فَسَمِعَ ذَاكَ رَسُولُ اللَّهِ فَقَالَ، " مَا بَالُ دَعْوَى الْجَاهِلِيَّةِ "، قَالُوا: يَا رَسُولَ اللَّهِ، كَسَعَ رَجُلٌ مِنَ الْمُهَاجِرِينَ رَجُلاً مِنَ الأَنْصَارِ، فَقَالَ، " دَعُوهَا فَإِنَّهَا مُنْتِنَةٌ "، فَسَمِعَ بِذَلِكَ عَبْدُ اللَّهِ بْنُ أُبَيٍّ، فَقَالَ: فَعَلُوهَا أَمَا وَاللَّهِ لَئِنْ رَجَعْنَا إِلَى الْمَدِينَةِ لَيُخْرِجَنَّ الأَعَزُّ مِنْهَا الأَذَلَّ، فَبَلَغَ النَّبِيَّ فَقَامَ عُمَرُ، فَقَالَ: يَا رَسُولَ اللَّهِ، دَعْنِي أَضْرِبْ عُنُقَ هَذَا الْمُنَافِقِ، فَقَالَ النَّبِيُّ، " دَعْهُ لَا يَتَحَدَّثُ النَّاسُ أَنَّ مُحَمَّدًا يَقْتُلُ أَصْحَابَهُ."

This is an interesting tradition that sheds light on several issues, (1) an initially minute standoff between two men from different tribes in the right circumstances nearly resulted in a tribal conflict and (2) the hypocrites (*munāfiqūn*) attempted to capitalize on such standoffs within the Muslim community for their own interests. Near the end of the report, ʿUmar offers to kill the chief hypocrite, ʿAbdullāh b. Ubayy; however, the Prophet ﷺ prevents him from doing so due to the fact that such an action would lead to greater harm than the intended outcome: rumors would prevail among the ignorant that Muḥammad was a formidable leader who slayed his own companions.

1 Ṣāḥīḥ al-Bukhārī (6/154), Ṣaḥīḥ Muslim (4/1998-1999)

Other examples illustrate the role of tribal standing within the early Muslim community. Al-Aʿmash narrated on the authority of Saʿd b. ʿUbayda, from Abū ʿAbdirraḥmān al-Sulamī, from ʿAlī b. Abī Ṭālib that he said:

> I once said, "O Messenger of Allah, why is it that you marry from within Quraysh, yet you avoid us?" The Prophet ﷺ replied, "Do you have anything?" I said, "yes, Ḥamza's daughter." The Messenger of Allah ﷺ then said, "She is impermissible to me, as she is the daughter of my milk-brother."[1]

الْأَعْمَش، عَنْ سَعْدِ بْنِ عُبَيْدَةَ، عَنْ أَبِي عَبْدِ الرَّحْمَنِ، عَنْ عَلِيٍّ، قَالَ: قُلْتُ: يَا رَسُولَ اللَّهِ، مَا لَكَ تَنَوَّقُ فِي قُرَيْشٍ وَتَدعَنْا، فقَالَ, "وَعَنْدَكُمْ شَيْءٌ"، قُلْتُ: نَعَمْ، بِنْتُ حَمْزَةَ، فقَالَ رَسُولُ اللَّهِ, "إِنَّهَا لَا تَحِلُّ لِي، إِنَّهَا ابْنَةُ أَخِي مِنَ الرَّضَاعَةِ."

In this tradition, ʿAlī expressed his frustration at the fact that the Prophet, despite marrying multiple women from the tribe of Quraysh, never married a woman from the clan of Banī Hāshim. Such relationships clearly were perceived to have implications on tribal status and standing, even among different clans of the same tribe.

Other traditions highlight a sense of entitlement some Hashemites, such as al-ʿAbbās b. ʿAbdulMuṭṭalib and Rabīʿa b. al-Ḥārith b. ʿAbdilMuṭṭalib, espoused regarding the wealth that was managed by the Messenger of Allah due to their mere kinship with the Prophet ﷺ, and such sentiments evidently should not be discounted when attempting to understand the precursors to the post-Saqīfa events.[2]

It must also be noted that as the Prophet's ﷺ death became near, some individuals who felt entitled to the leadership of the community after him began to privately discuss his succession. Al-Zuhrī relayed from ʿAbdullāh b. Kaʿb b. Mālik, that ʿAbdullāh b. ʿAbbās informed him, he said:

> ʿAlī b. Abī Ṭālib once came outside after being with the Prophet ﷺ during his final illness, so the people said, "O Abū Ḥasan, how has the Messenger of Allah ﷺ awakened this day?"
>
> ʿAlī said, "He has, with thanks to Allah, awoken cured [from his illness.]" Al-ʿAbbās b. ʿAbdulMuṭṭalib then grabbed ʿAlī by his hand and said, "By Allah, after three days, you will become someone

1 Ṣaḥīḥ Muslim (2/1071)

2 Ṣaḥīḥ Muslim (2/752-753), Ṣaḥīḥ Ibn Ḥibbān (7/59)

> else's subject! By Allah, I see that the Messenger of Allah ﷺ will die from this illness of his, for I recognize the faces of ʿAbdulMuṭṭalib's descendants during death. Let us go to the Messenger of Allah ﷺ and ask him, 'with whom will this leadership be after him?' If it is within us, then we would become aware of that. If it is with other than us, then we would become aware of it, and he would advise [them] regarding us."
>
> ʿAlī thus said, "By Allah, if we are to ask the Messenger of Allah ﷺ for leadership, only for him to then deny us it, then the people will consequently never give it to us. By Allah, I will not ask the Messenger of Allah ﷺ for it."[1]

عَنْ الزُّهْرِيِّ، قَالَ: أَخْبَرَنِي عَبْدُ اللَّهِ بْنُ كَعْبِ بْنِ مَالِكٍ الْأَنْصَارِيُّ، وَكَانَ كَعْبُ بْنُ مَالِكٍ أَحَدَ الثَّلَاثَةِ الَّذِينَ تِيبَ عَلَيْهِمْ، أَنَّ عَبْدَ اللَّهِ بْنَ عَبَّاسٍ أَخْبَرَهُ: أَنَّ عَلِيَّ بْنَ أَبِي طَالِبٍ رَضِيَ اللَّهُ عَنْهُ، خَرَجَ مِنْ عِنْدِ رَسُولِ اللَّهِ فِي وَجَعِهِ الَّذِي تُوُفِّيَ فِيهِ، فَقَالَ النَّاسُ: يَا أَبَا حَسَنٍ، كَيْفَ أَصْبَحَ رَسُولُ اللَّهِ؟" فَقَالَ: أَصْبَحَ بِحَمْدِ اللَّهِ بَارِئًا، فَأَخَذَ بِيَدِهِ عَبَّاسُ بْنُ عَبْدِ الْمُطَّلِبِ، فَقَالَ لَهُ: أَنْتَ وَاللَّهِ بَعْدَ ثَلَاثٍ عَبْدُ الْعَصَا، وَإِنِّي وَاللَّهِ لَأَرَى رَسُولَ اللَّهِ سَوْفَ يُتَوَفَّى مِنْ وَجَعِهِ هَذَا، إِنِّي لَأَعْرِفُ وُجُوهَ بَنِي عَبْدِ الْمُطَّلِبِ عِنْدَ الْمَوْتِ، اذْهَبْ بِنَا إِلَى رَسُولِ اللَّهِ فَلْنَسْأَلْهُ فِيمَنْ هَذَا الْأَمْرُ؟ إِنْ كَانَ فِينَا عَلِمْنَا ذَلِكَ، وَإِنْ كَانَ فِي غَيْرِنَا عَلِمْنَاهُ، فَأَوْصَى بِنَا، فَقَالَ عَلِيٌّ، " إِنَّا وَاللَّهِ لَئِنْ سَأَلْنَاهَا رَسُولَ اللَّهِ فَمَنَعَنَاهَا لَا يُعْطِينَاهَا النَّاسُ بَعْدَهُ، وَإِنِّي وَاللَّهِ لَا أَسْأَلُهَا رَسُولَ اللَّهِ." هذا لفظ البخاري.

This tradition was also relayed by the Shīʿite-leaning traditionist, ʿAbdurrazzāq al-Ṣanʿānī (d. 211). At the end of the report, ʿAbdurrazzāq said:

> Maʿmar [d. 154] used to ask us, "Which of them is more correct in your opinion?" We would say, "al-ʿAbbās." Maʿmar then said, "Had ʿAlī asked him for it and then been granted it by the Prophet, then the people would have disbelieved if they denied him it."
>
> [ʿAbdurrazzāq said:] Ibn ʿUyayna informed me of the report, and he then said, "al-Shaʿbī said, 'ʿAlī asking him about it would have been better to him than his own wealth and progeny'."[2]

---

1 Ṣaḥīḥ al-Bukhārī (6/12, 8/59)

2 Al-Amālī fī Āthār al-Ṣaḥāba by ʿAbdurrazzāq al-Ṣanʿānī (p. 25-26). Maʿmar's statement regarding disbelief is in the context of the fact that there was a consensus among most of the Ṣaḥāba that Abū Bakr was more suitable for the role than ʿAlī.

قَالَ عَبْدُ الرَّزَّاقِ: فَكَانَ مَعْمَرٌ يَقُولُ لَنَا: أَيُّهُمَا كَانَ أَصْوَبَ عِنْدَكُمْ رَأْيًا؟ قَالَ: فَنَقُولُ: الْعَبَّاسُ، ثُمَّ قَالَ: لَوْ أَنَّ عَلِيًّا سَأَلَهُ عَنْهَا فَأَعْطَاهُ إِيَّاهَا فَمَنَعَهُ النَّاسُ كَانُوا قَدْ كَفَرُوا، قَالَ عَبْدُ الرَّزَّاقِ: فَحَدَّثَنِيهِ ابْنُ عُيَيْنَةَ، فَقَالَ: قَالَ الشَّعْبِيُّ: لَوْ أَنَّ عَلِيًّا سَأَلَهُ عَنْهَا كَانَ خَيْرًا لَهُ مِنْ مَالِهِ وَوَلَدِهِ.

Interestingly, the Muʿtazilite scholar, al-Qāḍī ʿAbdulJabbār (d. 415), cited this tradition as evidence that the Prophet ﷺ did not explicitly appoint ʿAlī as his successor at Ghadīr Khumm and elsewhere, as is believed and understood by the Shīʿa.[1]

قال القاضي عبد الجبار: فانظر كم في هذا من بيان على صحة ما قلنا؛ فهذا العباس، وهذا علي، وهؤلاء الصحابة، فلو كان النبي صلّى الله عليه وسلم قد نص لما جاز ان يذهب علمه عنهم، أو لو قال قولا يحتمل تأويله هذا المعنى لما ذهب عنهم، فإن البحث والنظر والخوض يخرج خفيات الأمور ويذكر بغوامضها وبما قد تقدم عهده وزمانه، فكيف بالشيء الواضح القريب العهد، ورسول الله صلّى الله عليه وسلم حي بينهم، فكيف لم يقل علي للعباس: يا عم، أما تعلم ان رسول الله صلّى الله عليه وسلم قد نص علي وجعلني حجة على العالم واستخلفني وولديّ على امته الى يوم القيامة، وكيف نسيت مع قرب العهد، أو ليس قد قال: من كنت مولاه فعليّ مولاه، وانت مني بمنزلة هرون من موسى ، وهذا نص واستخلاف. فإن كان امير المؤمنين علي رضي الله عنه نسي ان النبي صلّى الله عليه وسلم استخلفه كما نسي العباس فكيف لم يذكرهما الصحابة وهم يسمعون ما يجري، وهذا لا يخفى على متأمل، فقد وجدت رحمك الله عليا والعباس والصحابة قد اطبقوا على ان رسول الله صلّى الله عليه وسلم ما نص ولا استخلف رجلا بعينه، ولا قال قولا قصد به هذا المعنى. فان قيل: ومن سلم لكم ان هذا قد جرى بين علي والعباس رضي الله عنهما؟ قيل له: إن هذا كالذي جرى في السقيفة وفي الشورى، لا يرتاب بذلك اهل العلم، والعجب انكم تقولون أن النبي صلّى الله عليه وسلم قال: من كنت مولاه فعلي مولاه وتنكرون مثل هذا وهو أصح، والعلم به اقوى، وما زال ولد العباس وولد علي من قديم الدهر يتذاكرون هذا الذي جرى من آبائهما في أنهما أصوب رأيا، ويخوض اهل العلم في ذلك، كالشعبيّ وعبد الرزاق، وإنما يذهب مثل هذا على معاند أو من لا نصيب له في العلم.

ʿAbdurrazzāq said: Ibn ʿUyayna informed us, on the authority of ʿAmr [b. Dīnār], from Abū Jaʿfar that he said:

> When the Prophet ﷺ died, al-ʿAbbās went to ʿAlī and said, "Come so that I may pledge allegiance to you. If it is said, 'the Messenger

1 Tathbīt Dalāʾil al-Nubuwwa (1/255-257)

> of Allah's ﷺ uncle pledged allegiance to the Messenger of Allah's ﷺ cousin,' then no two people would ever disagree on you."
>
> ʿAlī told him, "I would never force a matter upon the people. If they desire me, then they know where I am."[1]

قال عبد الرزاق: أنا ابْنُ عُيَيْنَةَ، عَنْ عَمْرٍو، عَنْ أَبِي جَعْفَرٍ، قَالَ: لَمَّا مَاتَ النَّبِيُّ جَاءَ الْعَبَّاسُ إِلَى عَلِيٍّ فَقَالَ: تَعَالَ أُبَايِعْكَ فَإِذَا قِيلَ عَمُّ رَسُولِ اللَّهِ صَلَّى اللَّهُ عَلَيْهِ بَايَعَ ابْنَ عَمِّ رَسُولِ اللَّهِ لَمْ يَخْتَلِفْ عَلَيْكَ اثْنَانِ، قَالَ: فَقَالَ لَهُ عَلِيٌّ: مَا كُنْتُ لأَفْتَئِتَ عَلَى النَّاسِ بِأَمْرٍ إِنْ أَرَادُونِي فَقَدْ عَرَفُوا مَكَانِي.

This tradition can be authentically traced back to Abū Jaʿfar al-Bāqir, who is Muḥammad b. ʿAlī b. al-Ḥusayn b. ʿAlī b. Abī Ṭālib and the fifth Imām according to Twelver and Ismāʿīlī Shīʿites. Though it is a valuable report, its isnād is disconnected, for there is at least one omitted intermediary between Abū Jaʿfar and ʿAlī b. Abī Ṭālib. This report shares a general theme with the past account of al-ʿAbbās and ʿAlī's exchange prior to the Messenger of Allah's ﷺ death, and it can also substantiate al-Qāḍī ʿAbdulJabbār's assessment of the authentically recorded exchange between both men. However, it should be noted that the particular dialogue in Abū Jaʿfar's report should be cited with discretion due to its inauthenticity. The past two traditions highlight an early Hashemite desire for rulership near the end of the Prophet's life ﷺ.

Nonetheless, the past reports and notes shed light on some of the context surrounding the Prophet's ﷺ death. It should hence not come as a surprise to the reader that the Muslim community of Medīna, barring some exceptions, was initially polarized along tribal lines after the Prophet's ﷺ death in the absence of an explicitly designated successor. Ibn Isḥāq (d. 151) said:

> When the Messenger of Allah ﷺ died, this tribe of the Anṣār aligned with Saʿd b. ʿUbāda at the portico (*saqīfa*) of Banī Sāʿida. ʿAlī b. Abī Ṭālib, al-Zubayr b. al-ʿAwwām and Ṭalḥa b. ʿUbaydillāh withdrew to Fāṭima's house. The remainder of the Muhājirīn aligned with Abū Bakr, and with them was Usayd b. Ḥuḍayr with the clan of Banī ʿAbdilʾAshhal [from the Anṣār].[2]

---

1 Al-Amālī fī Āthār al-Ṣaḥāba by ʿAbdurrazzāq al-Ṣanʿānī (p. 26-27)
2 Al-Sīra al-Nabawiyya by Ibn Hishām (2/656)

قَالَ ابْنُ إِسْحَاقَ: وَلَمَّا قُبِضَ رَسُولُ اللهِ صَلَّى اللهُ عَلَيْهِ وَسَلَّمَ انْحَازَ هَذَا الْحَيُّ مِنْ الْأَنْصَارِ إِلَى سَعْدِ بْنِ عُبَادَةَ فِي سَقِيفَةِ بَنِي سَاعِدَةَ، وَاعْتَزَلَ عَلِيُّ بْنُ أَبِي طَالِبٍ وَالزُّبَيْرُ ابْنِ الْعَوَّامِ وَطَلْحَةُ بْنُ عُبَيْدِ اللهِ فِي بَيْتِ فَاطِمَةَ، وَانْحَازَ بَقِيَّةُ الْمُهَاجِرِينَ إِلَى أَبِي بَكْرٍ، وَانْحَازَ مَعَهُمْ أُسَيْدُ بْنُ حُضَيْرٍ فِي بَنِي عَبْدِ الْأَشْهَلِ.

This is an accurate characterization of the situation at the time. Shortly after the Prophet's ﷺ death, Medīna was polarized into three main factions. The Anṣār generally coalesced around their chief, Saʿd b. ʿUbāda. The Muhājirūn coalesced around the most senior of them in rank, Abū Bakr. Interestingly, we find that the clan of Banī ʿAbdilʾAshhal from the Anṣār are said to have joined Abū Bakr, not Saʿd b. ʿUbāda. Perhaps that decision was influenced by the fact that Saʿd b. ʿUbāda was the chief of al-Khazraj, while Banī ʿAbdilʾAshhal were from al-Aws, al-Khazraj's pre-Islamic rival tribe. It is also noteworthy that ʿAbdilʾAshhal was the clan of Saʿd b. Muʿādh, the aforementioned chief of al-Aws and rival of Saʿd b. ʿUbāda. The third faction consisted of ʿAlī b. Abī Ṭālib, Ṭalḥa, al-Zubayr, and (possibly) other Hashemite figures and associates.

The initial events in this narrative are briefly described in an authentic tradition of ʿĀʾisha. Al-Bukhārī, in his *Ṣaḥīḥ*, said: Yaḥyā b. Bukayr informed us, he said: al-Layth informed us, on the authority of ʿUqayl, from Ibn Shihāb, he said: Abū Salama informed me that ʿĀʾisha informed him, she said:

> Abū Bakr came riding on his horse from al-Sunḥ until he arrived. He entered the mosque and did not speak to the people until he entered upon ʿĀʾisha. He approached the Messenger of Allah, whose body was covered in a *ḥibara* cloth. He uncovered his face and then fell onto it, kissed it and cried. He then said, "My father and mother are ransom to you. By Allah, Allah shall not give you two deaths. As for the death that was written upon you, you have [now] fulfilled it."

Al-Zuhrī then said: Abū Salama informed me on the authority of Ibn ʿAbbās that he said:

> Abū Bakr went out while ʿUmar was addressing the people, so Abū Bakr said, "Sit down, ʿUmar," and ʿUmar refused to sit down. The people hence approached Abū Bakr and abandoned ʿUmar. Abū Bakr then said, "Whoever among you worships Muḥammad, then Muḥammad has died. Whoever among you worships Allah, then Allah is alive, and He does not die. Allah had said, 'Muḥammad is

> but a messenger who was preceded by other messengers before him' [until he reached] 'the thankful. [Quran 3:144]'
>
> It was as though the people were unaware that Allah had revealed this verse until Abū Bakr recited it, and they all then acquired it from him. I would not hear a person except that he was reciting it.

Al-Zuhrī then said: Saʿīd b. al-Musayyab said: ʿUmar said:

> By Allah, as soon as I heard Abū Bakr reciting it, I was in awe such that my feet could not carry me, and I collapsed to the ground. When I heard him reciting it, I realized that the Prophet ﷺ had died."[1]

قال البخاري في صحيحه: حَدَّثَنَا يَحْيَى بْن بُكَيْرٍ، حَدَّثَنَا اللَّيْثُ، عَنْ عُقَيْلٍ، عَنْ ابْنِ شِهَابٍ، قَالَ: أَخْبَرَنِي أَبُو سَلَمَةَ، أَنَّ عَائِشَةَ أَخْبَرَتْهُ: أَنَّ أَبَا بَكْرٍ رَضِيَ اللَّهُ عَنْهُ أَقْبَلَ عَلَى فَرَسٍ مِنْ مَسْكَنِهِ بِالسُّنْحِ حَتَّى نَزَلَ، فَدَخَلَ الْمَسْجِدَ فَلَمْ يُكَلِّمْ النَّاسَ حَتَّى دَخَلَ عَلَى عَائِشَةَ، فَتَيَمَّمَ رَسُولَ اللهِ وَهُوَ مُغَشًّى بِثَوْبِ حِبَرَةٍ، فَكَشَفَ عَنْ وَجْهِهِ، ثُمَّ أَكَبَّ عَلَيْهِ فَقَبَّلَهُ وَبَكَى، ثُمَّ قَالَ: بِأَبِي أَنْتَ وَأُمِّي، وَاللَّهِ لَا يَجْمَعُ اللَّهُ عَلَيْكَ مَوْتَتَيْنِ، أَمَّا الْمَوْتَةُ الَّتِي كُتِبَتْ عَلَيْكَ فَقَدْ مُتَّهَا.

قَالَ الزُّهْرِيُّ: وَحَدَّثَنِي أَبُو سَلَمَةَ، عَنْ عَبْدِ اللَّهِ بْنِ عَبَّاسٍ، أَنَّ أَبَا بَكْرٍ خَرَجَ وَعُمَرُ بْنُ الْخَطَّابِ يُكَلِّمُ النَّاسَ، فَقَالَ: اجْلِسْ يَا عُمَرُ، فَأَبَى عُمَرُ أَنْ يَجْلِسَ، فَأَقْبَلَ النَّاسُ إِلَيْهِ وَتَرَكُوا عُمَرَ، فَقَالَ أَبُو بَكْرٍ، "أَمَّا بَعْدُ، فَمَنْ كَانَ مِنْكُمْ يَعْبُدُ مُحَمَّدًا فَإِنَّ مُحَمَّدًا قَدْ مَاتَ، وَمَنْ كَانَ مِنْكُمْ يَعْبُدُ اللَّهَ، فَإِنَّ اللَّهَ حَيٌّ لَا يَمُوتُ، قَالَ اللَّهُ: (وَمَا مُحَمَّدٌ إِلا رَسُولٌ قَدْ خَلَتْ مِنْ قَبْلِهِ الرُّسُلُ إِلَى قَوْلِهِ: الشَّاكِرِينَ)، وَقَالَ: وَاللَّهِ لَكَأَنَّ النَّاسَ لَمْ يَعْلَمُوا أَنَّ اللَّهَ أَنْزَلَ هَذِهِ الْآيَةَ حَتَّى تَلَاهَا أَبُو بَكْرٍ فَتَلَقَّاهَا مِنْهُ النَّاسُ كُلُّهُمْ، فَمَا أَسْمَعُ بَشَرًا مِنَ النَّاسِ إِلَّا يَتْلُوهَا.

فَأَخْبَرَنِي سَعِيدُ بْنُ الْمُسَيَّبِ أَنَّ عُمَرَ، قَالَ: وَاللَّهِ مَا هُوَ إِلَّا أَنْ سَمِعْتُ أَبَا بَكْرٍ تَلَاهَا فَعَقِرْتُ حَتَّى مَا تُقِلُّنِي رِجْلَايَ وَحَتَّى أَهْوَيْتُ إِلَى الْأَرْضِ حِينَ سَمِعْتُهُ تَلَاهَا، عَلِمْتُ أَنَّ النَّبِيَّ قَدْ مَاتَ."

A similar account was relayed via Sulaymān b. Bilāl, from Hishām b. ʿUrwa, from his father, from ʿĀʾisha. In the report, it is clarified that ʿUmar initially was in denial that the Prophet ﷺ had died, and he claimed that the Prophet ﷺ would return and fulfill justice from certain individuals before leaving this world.[2]

---

1 Ṣaḥīḥ al-Bukhārī (6/13-14)

2 Al-Ṭabaqāt al-Kabīr by Ibn Saʿd (2/235), Ṣaḥīḥ al-Bukhārī (5/6-7)

An extensive account of the ensuing events was authentically recorded from Ibn ʿAbbās in various early sources. In it, Ibn ʿAbbās relayed the account of Abū Bakr's inauguration as he had heard it in a sermon of ʿUmar b. al-Khaṭṭāb. Al-Zuhrī narrated on the authority of ʿUbaydillāh b. ʿAbdillāh b. ʿUtba, from Ibn ʿAbbās that he said:

> [...] When ʿUmar ascended the pulpit, the *muʿadhdhin* commenced the call to prayer (*adhān*). When he finished the call to prayer, ʿUmar stood up, and he praised Allah with suitable praise and said, "[...] So no one should be deceived by one who says, 'Abū Bakr's inauguration was a hasty, sudden matter (*falta*).' Indeed, it was so, but Allah had dispelled its evil. There is none among you who is as outstanding as is Abū Bakr. He was from the best among us when the Messenger of Allah ﷺ died. ʿAlī, al-Zubayr and whoever was with them withdrew to Fāṭima's house. The entirety of the Anṣār evaded our congregation [and were present] at the portico of Banī Sāʿida. The Muḥājirūn gathered with Abū Bakr.
>
> I said, "O Abū Bakr, set us out to our brothers from the Anṣār," so we set out to lead them. We met two righteous men from the Anṣār who had witnessed Badr, and they both said, "where are you going, O assembly of the Muhājirūn?" We said, "We are going to our brethren from the Anṣār." They both then said, "Return and settle on who will lead you among yourselves." I then said, "Make way, for we will go to them."
>
> We then came to them, only to find them congregated at the portico of Banī Sāʿida, and among them was a man who was wrapped [in cloth]. I asked, "Who is this man?" They said, "He is Saʿd b. ʿUbāda." I then asked, "What is his matter?" They replied, "He is in pain."
>
> The speaker of the Anṣār then stood up, and he praised Allah and extolled him with worthy praise. He said, "We are the Anṣār (supporters) and the battalion of Islam, and you, O company of Quraysh, are but a troop in our ranks, a small band that had migrated to us."
>
> It then turned out that they sought to rip us out by the roots and seize power from us. I had contemplated [what to say], and I wished to say it afront Abū Bakr so that he might soften its harshness, for he was more tranquil and dignified than me. When I wished to speak, he told me, "rest easy," so I did not want to disobey him.

Abū Bakr then praised Allah and extolled him with suitable praise. By Allah, he did not leave out a single word I had contemplated saying except that he had intuitively expressed it or said something even better. He then said, "the eminence you had mentioned about yourselves, O Anṣār, you are worthy of it. The Arabs will never recognize leadership among anyone except this tribe of Quraysh, for it is the greatest of Arabs in abode and in lineage. I am pleased with either of these two men for you, so pay allegiance to whomever you want from them." He then took my hand and Abū ʿUbayda b. al-Jarrāḥ's hand. By Allah, I disliked nothing from his speech except this sentence, for I would rather be brought forth and be beheaded than be appointed as a leader over a people in whose midst is Abū Bakr.

When Abū Bakr concluded his statement, a man from the Anṣār stood up and cried, "I am the stout rubbing post and the short palm heavily laden with fruit! There shall be leader from us and a leader from you, O company of Quraysh; lest a war break out from our dispute and ensnare us once again!"

Maʿmar said: Qatāda said:

ʿUmar b. al-Khaṭṭāb hence replied, "Two swords cannot fit into a single scabard. Rather, the leaders are from our ranks, and the aides are from yours."

Maʿmar said: al-Zuhrī then said in his report with the [earlier] isnād:

[ʿUmar said:] Voices were then raised from both directions, and clamor heightened such that I feared mischief. I thus said, "O Abū Bakr, stretch out your hand so that I may pledge my allegiance to you!"

He stretched out his hand, and I pledged my allegiance to him. Then the Muhājirūn pledged their allegiance to him, and then the Anṣār pledged their allegiance to him. We pounced on Saʿd until someone cried out, "You have killed Saʿd!" I replied, "May Allah kill Saʿd!"

By Allah, we did not see anything that had transpired during these events graver than Abū Bakr's pledge of allegiance. We feared that the people (the Anṣār), had we left them to their own devices, would commence another pledge of allegiance immediately after our departure. Thus, we would either end up pledging allegiance to someone of whom we did not approve or we would oppose them, resulting in chaos. So no one should be deceived into saying, "Abū Bakr's pledge of allegiance was a hasty, sudden matter." Though it indeed was so, Allah dispelled its evil, and there is none among you who is as outstanding as is Abū Bakr...[1]

عَنْ مَعْمَرٍ، عَنِ الزُّهْرِيِّ، عَنْ عُبَيْدِ اللَّهِ بْنِ عَبْدِ اللَّهِ بْنِ عُتْبَةَ، عَنِ ابْنِ عَبَّاسٍ، قَالَ: [...]

فَلَمَّا ارْتَقَى عُمَرُ الْمِنْبَرَ أَخَذَ الْمُؤَذِّنُ فِي أَذَانِهِ، فَلَمَّا فَرَغَ مِنْ أَذَانِهِ قَامَ عُمَرُ، فَحَمِدَ اللَّهَ وَأَثْنَى عَلَيْهِ بِمَا هُوَ أَهْلُهُ، ثُمَّ قَالَ: [...] فَلا يَغُرَّنَّ امْرأً، أَنْ يَقُولَ: إِنَّ بَيْعَةَ أَبِي بَكْرٍ كَانَتْ فَلْتَةً وَقَدْ كَانَتْ كَذَلِكَ إِلا أَنَّ اللَّهَ وَقَى شَرَّهَا، وَلَيْسَ فِيكُمْ مَنْ يُقْطَعُ إِلَيْهِ الأَعْنَاقُ مِثْلُ أَبِي بَكْرٍ، إِنَّهُ كَانَ مِنْ خَيْرِنَا حِينَ تُوُفِّيَ رَسُولُ اللَّهِ وَإِنَّ عَلِيًّا وَالزُّبَيْرَ وَمَنْ مَعَهُ تَخَلَّفُوا عَنْهُ فِي بَيْتِ فَاطِمَةَ، وَتَخَلَّفَتْ عَنَّا الأَنْصَارُ بِأَسْرِهَا فِي سَقِيفَةِ بَنِي سَاعِدَةَ، وَاجْتَمَعَ الْمُهَاجِرُونَ إِلَى أَبِي بَكْرٍ رَحِمَهُ اللَّهُ، فَقُلْتُ: يَا أَبَا بَكْرٍ، انْطَلَقْ بِنَا إِلَى إِخْوَانِنَا مِنَ الأَنْصَارِ، فَانْطَلَقْنَا نَؤُمُّهُمْ، فَلَقِينَا رَجُلَيْنِ صَالِحَيْنِ مِنَ الأَنْصَارِ قَدْ شَهِدَا بَدْرًا، فَقَالا: أَيْنَ تُرِيدُونَ يَا مَعْشَرَ الْمُهَاجِرِينَ؟ قُلْنَا: نُرِيدُ إِخْوَانَنَا هَؤُلاءِ الأَنْصَارَ، قَالا: فَارْجِعُوا فَاقْضُوا أَمْرَكُمْ بَيْنَكُمْ، قَالَ: قُلْتُ: فَاقْضُوا وَلَنَأْتِيَنَّهُمْ، فَأَتَيْنَاهُمْ فَإِذَا هُمْ مُجْتَمِعُونَ فِي سَقِيفَةِ بَنِي سَاعِدَةَ بَيْنَ أَظْهُرِهِمْ رَجُلٌ مُزَمَّلٌ، قُلْتُ: مَنْ هَذَا؟ فَقَالُوا: هَذَا سَعْدُ بْنُ عُبَادَةَ، قُلْتُ: وَمَا شَأْنُهُ؟ قَالُوا: هُوَ وَجِعٌ، قَالَ: فَقَامَ خَطِيبُ الأَنْصَارِ، فَحَمِدَ اللَّهَ وَأَثْنَى عَلَيْهِ بِمَا هُوَ أَهْلُهُ، ثُمَّ قَالَ: أَمَّا بَعْدُ، فَنَحْنُ الأَنْصَارُ، وَكَتِيبَةُ الإِسْلامِ، وَأَنْتُمْ يَا مَعْشَرَ قُرَيْشٍ رَهْطٌ مِنَّا، وَقَدْ دَفَّتْ إِلَيْنَا دَافَّةٌ مِنْكُمْ، فَإِذَا هُمْ يُرِيدُونَ أَنْ يَخْتَزِلُونَا مِنْ أَصْلِنَا وَيَحْضُونَا مِنَ الأَمْرِ، وَكُنْتُ قَدْ رَوَّيْتُ فِي نَفْسِي، وَكُنْتُ أُرِيدُ أَنْ أَقُومَ بِهِ بَيْنَ يَدَيْ أَبِي بَكْرٍ، وَكُنْتُ أُدَارِئُ مِنْ أَبِي بَكْرٍ بَعْضَ الْحَدِّ وَكَانَ هُوَ أَوْقَرَ مِنِّي وَأَجَلَّ، فَلَمَّا أَرَدْتُ الْكَلامَ، قَالَ: عَلَى رِسْلِكَ، فَكَرِهْتُ أَنْ أَعْصِيَهُ.

فَحَمِدَ اللَّهَ أَبُو بَكْرٍ رَضِيَ اللَّهُ عَنْهُ، وَأَثْنَى عَلَيْهِ بِمَا هُوَ أَهْلُهُ، ثُمَّ قَالَ: وَاللَّهِ مَا تَرَكَ كَلِمَةً كُنْتُ رَوَّيْتُهَا فِي نَفْسِي إِلا جَاءَ بِهَا أَوْ بِأَحْسَنَ مِنْهَا فِي بَدِيهَتِهِ، ثُمَّ قَالَ: أَمَّا بَعْدُ، فَمَا ذَكَرْتُمْ فِيكُمْ مِنْ خَيْرٍ يَا مَعْشَرَ الأَنْصَارِ، فَأَنْتُمْ لَهُ أَهْلٌ وَلَنْ تَعْرِفَ الْعَرَبُ هَذَا الأَمْرَ إِلا لِهَذَا الْحَيِّ مِنْ قُرَيْشٍ فَهُوَ أَوْسَطُ الْعَرَبِ دَارًا وَنَسَبًا، وَإِنِّي قَدْ رَضِيتُ لَكُمْ هَذَيْنِ الرَّجُلَيْنِ، فَبَايِعُوا أَيَّهُمَا شِئْتُمْ، قَالَ: فَأَخَذَ بِيَدِي وَبِيَدِ أَبِي عُبَيْدَةَ بْنِ الْجَرَّاحِ، قَالَ: فَوَاللَّهِ مَا كَرِهْتُ مِمَّا قَالَ شَيْئًا إِلا هَذِهِ الْكَلِمَةَ، كُنْتُ لأَنْ أُقَدَّمَ فَيُضْرَبَ عُنُقِي لا يُقَرِّبُنِي ذَلِكَ إِلَى إِثْمٍ أَحَبُّ إِلَيَّ مِنْ أَنْ أُؤَمَّرَ عَلَى قَوْمٍ فِيهِمْ أَبُو بَكْرٍ، فَلَمَّا قَضَى أَبُو بَكْرٍ مَقَالَتَهُ قَامَ رَجُلٌ مِنَ الأَنْصَارِ، فَقَالَ: أَنَا جُذَيْلُهَا الْمُحَكَّكُ وَعُذَيْقُهَا الْمُرَجَّبُ، مِنَّا أَمِيرٌ وَمِنْكُمْ

1 Muṣannaf ʿAbdirrazzāq al-Ṣanʿānī (5/439-445), Ṣaḥīḥ al-Bukhārī (8/168-170). In several instances throughout this report, I benefited from Sean Anthony's translation of this passage in *The Expeditions: An Early Biography of Muḥammad* (p. 193-199).

أَمِيرٌ يَا مَعْشَرَ قُرَيْشٍ، وَإِلا أَجْلَبْنَا الْحَرْبَ فِيمَا بَيْنَنَا وَبَيْنَكُمْ جَذَعًا، قَالَ مَعْمَرٌ، قَالَ قَتَادَةُ، فَقَالَ عُمَرُ بْنُ الْخَطَّابِ: لا يَصْلُحُ سَيْفَانِ فِي غِمْدٍ وَاحِدٍ، وَلَكِنْ مِنَّا الأُمَرَاءُ وَمِنْكُمُ الْوُزَرَاءُ، قَالَ مَعْمَرٌ: قَالَ الزُّهْرِيُّ فِي حَدِيثِهِ بِالإِسْنَادِ: فَارْتَفَعَتِ الأَصْوَاتُ بَيْنَنَا، وَكَثُرَ اللَّغَطُ حَتَّى أَشْفَقْتُ الاخْتِلافَ، فَقُلْتُ: يَا أَبَا بَكْرٍ، ابْسُطْ يَدَكَ أُبَايِعْكَ، قَالَ: فَبَسَطَ يَدَهُ فَبَايَعْتُهُ، فَبَايَعَهُ الْمُهَاجِرُونَ وَبَايَعَهُ الأَنْصَارُ، قَالَ: وَنَزَوْنَا عَلَى سَعْدٍ حِينَ قَالَ قَائِلٌ: قَتَلْتُمْ سَعْدًا، قَالَ: قُلْتُ: قَتَلَ اللَّهُ سَعْدًا وَإِنَّا وَاللَّهِ مَا رَأَيْنَا فِيمَا حَضَرْنَا مِنْ أَمْرِنَا أَمْرًا كَانَ أَقْوَى مِنْ مُبَايَعَةِ أَبِي بَكْرٍ، خَشِينَا إِنْ فَارَقْنَا الْقَوْمَ أَنْ يُحْدِثُوا بَيْعَةً بَعْدَنَا، فَإِمَّا أَنْ نُبَايِعَهُمْ عَلَى مَا لا نَرْضَى، وَإِمَّا أَنْ نُخَالِفَهُمْ فَيَكُونَ فَسَادًا، فَلا يَغُرَّنَّ امْرَأً أَنْ يَقُولَ إِنَّ بَيْعَةَ أَبِي بَكْرٍ كَانَتْ فَلْتَةً، فَقَدْ كَانَتْ كَذَلِكَ غَيْرَ أَنَّ اللَّهَ وَقَى شَرَّهَا، وَلَيْسَ فِيكُمْ مَنْ يُقْطَعُ إِلَيْهِ الأَعْنَاقُ مِثْلُ أَبِي بَكْرٍ، فَمَنْ بَايَعَ رَجُلا عَنْ غَيْرِ مَشُورَةٍ مِنَ الْمُسْلِمِينَ فَإِنَّهُ لا يُتَابَعُ هُوَ وَلا الَّذِي بَايَعَهُ تَغِرَّةَ أَنْ يُقْتَلا. "

In this tradition, we observe the polarization that ensued following the Prophet's ﷺ death. Upon learning that the Anṣār had congregated to elect the next leader among themselves, ʿUmar directed Abū Bakr to disband this emergent political entity, for he recognized the stark risks associated with the simultaneous rise of multiple leaders within Medīna. Furthermore, as stated in the tradition, the Anṣār would not be granted the political recognition that Quraysh would be granted, so an Anṣārī leader would not be suitable for such a role. The Muhājirūn's concern with the Anṣār political incompetence was confirmed when the Anṣār proposed that there be two rulers from the Muslim community from both tribes, a disastrous administrative proposition that precisely was the precursor to al-Anṣār's pre-Islamic internal strife, and the proposition was justifiably shot down by the Muhājirūn. I suppose what further warranted Abū Bakr and ʿUmar's concern in this regard is the fact that the Anṣār were to choose, Saʿd b. ʿUbāda, a tribal leader whose tribalistic impulses often affected his judgement (as can be seen in the Propehtic tradition at the beginning of this essay). Other reports multifactedly hint at Saʿd's unsuitableness to be the leader of the greater Muslim community as well, though I do not wish to expound them all here.

Nevertheless, while both parties were engaged in dialogue, tensions began to rise, and combat seemed imminent. Recognizing that a swift move was needed, ʿUmar cleverly pledged his allegiance to Abū Bakr on the spot, and the Muhājirūn and Anṣār thus followed his track. Saʿd b. ʿUbāda was disgruntled with the outcome, and it appears he caused some commotion after Abū Bakr's inauguration. He was hence beaten and silenced by the congregants. Following this event, the ill Saʿd b. ʿUbāda was beaten, and his politicial career effectively came to an end. Saʿd proceeded to live a life of relative irrelevance after this event, and he died away from Medīna in al-Shām around three to five years after this event.

Following the Muhājirīn and the Anṣār's coalition around Abū Bakr, there remained an issue: the Hāshemites avoided this congregation and gathered at Fāṭima's house where they were armed. Muḥammad b. ʿAmr b. ʿAlqama (d. 145) narrated on the authority of Abū Salama b. ʿAbdirraḥmān b. ʿAwf (d. 94) that he said:

> [...] ʿAlī and al-Zubayr entered the house of Fāṭima, the Prophet's ﷺ daughter. ʿUmar thus came, and he said, "Come out for the pledge of allegiance! By Allah, you will come out or I will otherwise burn the house down upon you!"
>
> Al-Zubayr thus came out with his sword drawn, and a man from the Anṣār and Ziyād b. Labīd al-Anṣārī, who was from the clan of Bayāḍa, embraced him, struck him, and the sword fell out of his hand.
>
> Ziyād thus took the sword, and [Abū Bakr] said, "No! Strike the stone with it!"

This report's transmitter, Muḥammad b. ʿAmr, then said:

> Abū ʿAmr b. Ḥimās, who was from the Laythī clan, informed me, he said, "I witnessed that rock that was struck by the sword."
>
> Abū Bakr then said, "Let them be, for Allah will eventually bring them." They then went out after that and pledged allegiance to Abū Bakr. They said, "There was no one more worthy of the position than you, but we felt that ʿUmar was extorting our matter from us." The people hence pledged allegiance to him on Monday [...].[1]

مُحَمَّدُ بْنُ عَمْرٍو، عَنْ أَبِي سَلَمَةَ قَالَ: [....] وَدَخَلَ عَلِيٌّ وَالزُّبَيْرُ بَيْتَ فَاطِمَةَ بِنْتِ رَسُولِ اللَّهِ صَلَّى اللهُ عَلَيْهِ وَسَلَّمَ، فَجَاءَ عُمَرُ فَقَالَ: اخْرُجُوا لِلْبَيْعَةِ، وَاللَّهِ لَتَخْرُجُنَّ، أَوْ لَأُحَرِّقَنَّهُ عَلَيْكُمْ، فَخَرَجَ الزُّبَيْرُ صَلْتًا بِالسَّيْفِ، فَاعْتَنَقَهُ زِيَادُ بْنُ لَبِيدٍ الْأَنْصَارِيُّ مِنْ بَيَاضَةَ فَدَقَّ بِهِ، وَبَدَرَ السَّيْفُ مِنْ يَدِهِ مِنْهُ، فَأَخَذَهُ زِيَادٌ قَالَ: لَا، وَلَكِنِ اضْرِبْ بِهِ الْحَجَرَ، قَالَ مُحَمَّدُ بْنُ عَمْرٍو: فَحَدَّثَنِي أَبُو عَمْرِو بْنُ حِمَاسٍ مِنَ اللَّيْثِيِّينَ قَالَ: أَدْرَكْتُ ذَلِكَ الْحَجَرَ الَّذِي فِيهِ

1 Ḥadīth Hishām Ibn ʿAmmār (p. 122-125), Sharḥ Nahj al-Balāgha by Ibn Abī al-Ḥadīd (2/56)

ضُرِبَ السَّيْفُ، فَقَالَ أَبُو بَكْرٍ رَضِيَ اللَّهُ عَنْهُ: دَعُوهُمْ فَسَيَأْتِي اللَّهُ بِهِمْ، فَخَرَجُوا بَعْدَ ذَلِكَ فَبَايَعُوهُ، قَالُوا: مَا كَانَ أَحَدٌ أَحَقَّ بِهَا، وَلَا أَوْلَى بِهَا مِنْكَ، وَلَكِنَّا قَدْ عَهِدْنَا مِنْ عُمَرَ يَبْتَزُّنَا أَمْرَنَا، فَبَايَعَهُ النَّاسُ يَوْمَ الِاثْنَيْنِ [...].

قلت: وروى نحو هذا الخبر أبو بكر الجوهري في «كتاب السقيفة» بإسناده إلى محمد بن عمرو بن علقمة، وقد أورد ذلك ابن أبي الحديد في شرحه لنهج البلاغة.

Similar claims can be found in another report. ʿAbdullāh b. Aḥmed b. Ḥanbal said: Muḥammad b. Isḥāq b. Muḥammad al-Makhzūmī al-Musayyabī informed us, he said: Muḥammad b. Fulayḥ b. Sulaymān informed us, on the authority of Mūsā b. ʿUqba, from Ibn Shihāb that he said:

> And some men from the Muhājirīn were angered by Abū Bakr's inauguration, among them was ʿAlī b. Abī Ṭālib and al-Zubayr b. al-ʿAwwām. They both entered the house of Fāṭima, the Messenger of Allah's ﷺ daughter, bearing arms. ʿUmar hence came to them with a band of Muslims that included Usayd and Salama b. Salāma b. Waqsh, who were both from Banī ʿAbdilʾAshhal. It is said that Thābit b. Qays b. Shammās, who was from Banī al-Ḥārith b. al-Khazraj, was with them as well. One of them took al-Zubayr's sword and struck it onto a stone until the sword was broken.[1]

قال عبد الله في «كتاب السنة»: حَدَّثَنَا مُحَمَّدُ بْنُ إِسْحَاقَ بْنِ مُحَمَّدٍ الْمَخْزُومِيُّ الْمُسَيَّبِيُّ، نا مُحَمَّدُ بْنُ فُلَيْحِ بْنِ سُلَيْمَانَ، عَنْ مُوسَى بْنِ عُقْبَةَ، عَنِ ابْنِ شِهَابٍ، قَالَ، "وَغَضِبَ رِجَالٌ مِنَ الْمُهَاجِرِينَ فِي بَيْعَةِ أَبِي بَكْرٍ رَضِيَ اللَّهُ عَنْهُ، مِنْهُمْ عَلِيُّ بْنُ أَبِي طَالِبٍ، وَالزُّبَيْرُ بْنُ الْعَوَّامِ رَضِيَ اللَّهُ عَنْهُمَا، فَدَخَلَا بَيْتَ فَاطِمَةَ بِنْتِ رَسُولِ اللَّهِ وَمَعَهُمَا السِّلَاحُ فَجَاءَهُمَا عُمَرُ رَضِيَ اللَّهُ عَنْهُ فِي عِصَابَةٍ مِنَ الْمُسْلِمِينَ فِيهِمْ أُسَيْدُ وَسَلَمَةُ بْنُ سَلَامَةَ بْنِ وَقْشٍ وَهُمَا مِنْ بَنِي عَبْدِ الْأَشْهَلِ وَيُقَالُ فِيهِمْ ثَابِتُ بْنُ قَيْسِ بْنِ الشَّمَّاسِ أَخُو بَنِي الْحَارِثِ بْنِ الْخَزْرَجِ فَأَخَذَ أَحَدُهُمْ سَيْفَ الزُّبَيْرِ فَضَرَبَ بِهِ الْحَجَرَ حَتَّى كَسَرَهُ."

This report's contents can be found in other stronger reports, and its authenticity is hence mostly inconsequential. Nevertheless, its isnād embodies weakness: (1) Muḥammad b. Fulayḥ b. Sulaymān was not the most reliable in transmission and (2) Ibn Shihāb's transmission of this account is disconnected.

When ʿUmar commanded that the congregants inside the house disperse, al-Zubayr rushed out of the house with his sword drawn, effectively

1 Kitāb al-Sunna by ʿAbdullāh b. Aḥmed b. Ḥanbal al-Shaybānī (2/553)

validating ʿUmar's preemptive concerns with this gathering: bloodshed and strife were imminent if these competing factions were left to grow and fester within Medīna. Al-Zubayr was quickly disarmed and the congregation was disbanded.

Mūsā b. ʿUqba (d. 141) said: Saʿd b. Ibrāhīm informed me, he said: Ibrāhīm b. ʿAbdirraḥmān b. ʿAwf informed me, he said:

> ʿAbdurraḥmān b. ʿAwf was with ʿUmar b. al-Khaṭṭāb on that day, and he was the one who broke al-Zubayr's sword. (God knows best as to who actually broke it.)
>
> Abū Bakr then got up, gave a sermon before the people, and he apologized to them. He said, "By Allah, I was never eager for leadership in any day or night, nor was I ever interested in it, nor did I ever ask Allah for it in secret or in open. Rather, I was wary of the *fitna*, and I have no respite in leadership. I have been tasked with a grave matter that I cannot bare or withstand except through Allah's assistance. I had wished that the there was someone more suitable for it in my place."
>
> The Muhājirūn thus accepted what he said and what he mentioned as an excuse, and ʿAlī b. Abī Ṭālib and al-Zubayr said, "We were only angered because we were excluded from the council. We see Abū Bakr as the worthiest of it after the Messenger of Allah. He is the companion of the cave where he was the second of two. We know his honor and seniority, and the Messenger of Allah ﷺ had commanded him to lead the people in prayer while he was alive."[1]

قال موسى بن عقبة: قَالَ سَعْدُ بْنُ إِبْرَاهِيمَ: حَدَّثَنِي إِبْرَاهِيمُ بْنُ عَبْدِ الرَّحْمَنِ بْنِ عَوْفٍ أَنَّ عَبْدَ الرَّحْمَنِ بْنَ عَوْفٍ رَضِيَ اللَّهُ عَنْهُ كَانَ مَعَ عُمَرَ بْنِ الخطاب رضي الله عنه يومئذ، وَأَنَّهُ هُوَ كَسَرَ سَيْفَ الزُّبَيْرِ، وَاللَّهُ أَعْلَمُ من كَسْرِهِ ,ثُمَّ قَامَ أَبُو بَكْرٍ فَخَطَبَ النَّاسَ وَاعْتَذَرَ إِلَيْهِمْ، فَقَالَ: وَاللَّهِ مَا كُنْتُ حَرِيصًا عَلَى الإِمَارَةِ يَوْمًا قَطُّ وَلا لَيْلَةً، وَلا كُنْتُ فِيهَا رَاغِبًا، وَلا سَأَلْتُهَا اللَّهَ قَطُّ فِي سِرٍّ وَلا عَلانِيَةٍ، وَلَكِنِّي أَشْفَقْتُ مِنَ الْفِتْنَةِ، وَمَا لِي فِي الإِمَارَةِ مِنْ رَاحَةٍ، ولكن قلدت أمرا عظيما ما لي به طاقة ولا يدان إلا بِتَقْوِيَةِ اللَّهِ عَزَّ وَجَلَّ، وَلَوَدِدْتُ أَنَّ أَقْوَى النَّاسِ عَلَيْهَا مَكَانِي، فَقَبِلَ الْمُهَاجِرُونَ - مِنْهُ مَا قَالَ وَمَا اعْتَذَرَ بِهِ، وَقَالَ عَلِيُّ بْنُ أَبِي طَالِبٍ وَالزُّبَيْرُ بْنُ الْعَوَّامِ: مَا غضبنا إلا أنا أخرنا

1 Aḥādīth Muntakhaba Min Maghāzī Mūsā Ibn ʿUqba (p. 94-95), al-Mustadrak ʿalā al-Ṣaḥīḥayn by al-Ḥākim al-Naysābūrī (3/70). Al-Ḥākim described this tradition saying, "This ḥadīth is authentic according to the criteria of Bukhārī and Muslim, and they did not record it [in their Ṣaḥīḥs]."

عن المشاورة، وَإِنَّا لَنَرَى أَبَا بَكْرٍ أَحَقَّ النَّاسِ بِهَا بَعْدَ رَسُولِ اللَّهِ صَلَّى اللَّهُ عَلَيْهِ وَسَلَّمَ، إنه لصاحب الغار، ثاني اثنين، وإنا لنعرف لَهُ شَرَفَهُ وَكِبَرَهُ، وَلَقَدْ أَمَرَهُ رَسُولُ اللَّهِ صَلَّى اللَّهُ عَلَيْهِ وَسَلَّمَ بِالصَّلَاةِ لِلنَّاسِ وَهُوَ حي.

قال الحاكم في «المستدرك»: صَحِيحٌ عَلَى شَرْطِ الشَّيْخَيْنِ، وَلَمْ يُخَرِّجَاهُ.

It is in this context that Abū Bakr's inauguration was described as a hasty and sudden matter (*falta*), for it barely saved the Medinite community from plunging into the strife and turmoil of a civil war following the Prophet's ﷺ death. Nonetheless, such reports, which are occasionally cited by Shīʿite polemicists to vilify ʿUmar, should rather be illustrative of his foresightedness and political adeptness.

ʿAbdulʾAʿlā b. ʿAbdilʾAʿlā said: Dāwūd b. Abī Hind informed us, on the authority of Abū Naḍra (d. 108) that he said:

> When the people congregated around Abū Bakr, he said, "Why do I not see ʿAlī?" Men from the Anṣār then went and brought ʿAlī. Abū Bakr then told him, "O ʿAlī, you said, '[I am] the son of the Messenger of Allah's ﷺ uncle, and [I am] his brother-in-law'?" ʿAlī said, "There is no reproach O successor of the Prophet. Stretch out your hand so that I may pay allegiance to you." Abū Bakr then put forth his hand, and ʿAlī pledged his allegiance to him.
>
> Abū Bakr then said, "Why do I not see al-Zubayr?" Men from the Anṣār then went and brought him. Abū Bakr then told him, "O Zubayr, you said, '[I am] the son of the Messenger of Allah's ﷺ aunt, and [I am] his apostle [*ḥawārī*]'?" Al-Zubayr then said, "There is no reproach, O successor of the Messenger of Allah. Stretch out your hand so that I may pay allegiance to you." Abū Bakr then put forth his hand, and al-Zubayr paid allegiance to him.[1]

قال عبد الله بن أحمد في «كتاب السنة»: حَدَّثَنِي عُبَيْدُ اللَّهِ بْنُ عُمَرَ الْقَوَارِيرِيُّ، نا عَبْدُ الأَعْلَى بْنُ عَبْدِ الأَعْلَى، نا دَاوُدُ بْنُ أَبِي هِنْدٍ، عَنْ أَبِي نَضْرَةَ، قَالَ، " لَمَّا اجْتَمَعَ النَّاسُ عَلَى أَبِي بَكْرٍ رَضِيَ اللَّهُ عَنْهُ فَقَالَ مَا لِي لا أَرَى عَلِيًّا، قَالَ: فَذَهَبَ رِجَالٌ مِنَ الأَنْصَارِ فَجَاءُوا بِهِ، فَقَالَ لَهُ: يَا عَلِيُّ قُلْتَ ابْنُ عَمِّ رَسُولِ اللَّهِ وَخَتَنُ رَسُولِ اللَّهِ؟ فَقَالَ عَلِيٌّ رَضِيَ اللَّهُ عَنْهُ: لا تَثْرِيبَ يَا خَلِيفَةَ رَسُولِ اللَّهِ ابْسُطْ يَدَكَ فَبَسَطَ يَدَهُ فَبَايَعَهُ، ثُمَّ قَالَ أَبُو بَكْرٍ: مَا لِي لا أَرَى

1 Al-Sunna by ʿAbdullāh b. Aḥmed b. Ḥanbal (2/554)

الزُّبَيْرَ؟ قَالَ: فَذَهَبَ رِجَالٌ مِنَ الأَنْصَارِ فَجَاءُوا بِهِ، فَقَالَ: يَا زُبَيْرُ قُلْتَ ابْنُ عَمَّةِ رَسُولِ اللَّهِ وَحَوَارِيُّ رَسُولِ اللَّهِ؟ قَالَ الزُّبَيْرُ: لا تَثْرِيبَ يَا خَلِيفَةَ رَسُولِ اللَّهِ ابْسُطْ يَدَكَ فَبَسَطَ يَدَهُ فَبَايَعَهُ."

قلت: وروى نحوه حماد بن سلمة، عن الجريري، عن أبي نضرة. ورواه باختصار ابن علية عن الجريري عن أبي نضرة. وروى ذا الخبر وهيب بن خالد، عن داود بن أبي هند، عن أبي نضرة فأسنده من حديث أبي سعيد الخدري، والظاهر أنه قد وهم في هذا الأثر وسلك الجادة المعهودة في حديث أبي نضرة، والله أعلم.

This tradition was also relayed via (1) Ḥammād b. Salama ⟶ al-Jurayrī ⟶ Abū Naḍra and (2) Ibn ʿUlayya ⟶ al-Jurayrī ⟶ Abū Naḍra.[1] Abū Naḍra was a *tạbiʿī* who met several companions of the Prophet. Though this report is a relatively early account, its isnād is disconnected, for Abū Naḍra was not an eyewitness to these events. One later transmitter added Abū Saʿīd al-Khudrī as Abū Naḍra's source for this report, hence rendering its isnād authentic; however, there are reasons to believe that this was a slight error on that transmitter's part.[2]

Other unrelated reports similarly highlight the direness of the situation at hand following the Prophet's ﷺ death. Mālik b. Mighwal (d. 159) narrated on the authority of Ibn Abjar that he said:

> When Abū Bakr was pledged allegiance, Abū Sufyān went to ʿAlī and said, "The most inferior of households within Quraysh has beat you to this matter. By Allah, I will fill it (Medīna) with cavalry and men!"
>
> ʿAlī said, "O Abū Sufyān, you have always shown animosity to Islam and its people, and that has never harmed Islam nor its people. We have deemed Abū Bakr worthy of it."[3]

مَالِك بْن مِغْوَلٍ، عَنِ ابْنِ أَبْجَرَ، قَالَ، " لَمَّا بُويِعَ لأَبِي بَكْرٍ رَضِيَ اللَّهُ عَنْهُ جَاءَ أَبُو سُفْيَانَ إِلَى عَلِيٍّ، فَقَالَ: غَلَبَكُمْ عَلَى هَذَا الأَمْرِ أَذَلُّ أَهْلِ بَيْتٍ فِي قُرَيْشٍ، أَمَا وَاللَّهِ لأَمْلأَنَّهَا خَيْلا وَرِجَالا، قَالَ: فَقُلْتُ: مَا زِلْتَ عَدُوًّا لِلإِسْلامِ وَأَهْلِهِ فَمَا ضَرَّ ذَلِكَ الإِسْلامَ وَأَهْلَهُ شَيْئًا، إِنَّا رَأَيْنَا أَبَا بَكْرٍ لَهَا أَهْلا."

This report is weak: Ibn Abjar's transmission is disconnected, and he is a relatively later figure. A stronger report that reiterates Abū Sufyān's past

1 Al-Sunna by ʿAbdullāh b. Aḥmed b. Ḥanbal (2/554), Jumalun min Ansāb al-Ashrāf by al-Balādhurī (1/585)
2 Al-Mustadrak ʿalā al-Ṣaḥīḥayn by al-Ḥākim (3/80)
3 Muṣannaf ʿAbdirrazzāq (5/450), Tārīkh al-Rusul wa-l-Mulūk (3/209)

sentiment can be found relayed by al-Ṭabarī. He said: Muḥammad b. ʿUthmān al-Thaqafī informed me, he said: Umayya b. Khālid informed us, he said: Ḥammād b. Salama informed us, on the authority of Thābit (d. 127) that he said:

> When Abū Bakr was inaugurated, Abū Sufyān said, "What have we with the father of the calf (Abū Bakr)? Rather, it is Banū ʿAbdManāf [who are worthy of leadership]!"
>
> It was then said to Abū Sufyān, "Abū Bakr has appointed your son [to an official post]." Abū Sufyān hence said, "the kinship has reached him."[1]

قال الطبري: حدثني محمد بْن عثمان الثقفي، قَالَ: حَدَّثَنَا أمية بْن خالد، قَالَ: حَدَّثَنَا حماد بْن سلمة، عن ثابت، قَالَ: لما استخلف أبو بكر، قَالَ أبو سفيان: مالنا ولأبي فصيل، إنما هي بنو عبد مناف. قَالَ: فقيل لَهُ: إنه قد ولى ابنك. قَالَ: وصلته رحم.

This report is weak: Thābit b. Aslam al-Bunānī (d. 127) was a reliable *tābiʿī* who also occasionally transmitted from some *tābiʿīn*, and his transmission here is disconnected. Nonetheless, this report is a relatively early and relevant *mursal* tradition. It is not farfetched that Abū Sufyān, a man renowned for his sense of pride, would feel frustrated that a man from a weaker and less relevant clan of Quraysh, Banū Taym, would surpass the more noble clans of Quraysh in the leadership of the Arabs and the greater Muslim community.

One day after the events at the Saqīfa, Abū Bakr's public pledge of allegiance took place in the Prophet's ﷺ mosque. Maʿmar narrated on the authority of al-Zuhrī, he said:

> Anas b. Mālik informed me that he heard ʿUmar's later sermon when he sat on the Prophet's ﷺ pulpit. That was in the day after the day when the Prophet ﷺ died.
>
> ʿUmar uttered the *shahada* while Abū Bakr was silent. ʿUmar then said, "I have claimed something, and the matter turned out to be not as I had claimed. By Allah, I did not find the claim I had made within Allah's book nor within a promise made to me by the Messenger of Allah. Rather, I hoped that the Messenger of Allah ﷺ would live such that he would direct us (meaning that he would be the last of

---

1 Tārīkh al-Rusul wa-l-Mulūk of al-Ṭabarī (3/209)

> the Muslims). If Muḥammad had died, then Allah had kept among you a light through which you shall be guided. Here is the book of Allah, so hold onto it, and you shall be guided to what Allah had guided Muḥammad ﷺ. Furthermore, Abū Bakr is the Messenger of Allah's ﷺ companion and the second of two [in the cave], and he is most worthy of your affairs; so get up and pay allegiance to him."
>
> A group of the people had pledged allegiance to him prior to that at the portico of Banī Sāʿida, and the public pledge of allegiance was on the Prophet's ﷺ pulpit."
>
> Al-Zuhrī said: and Anas informed me, he said, "I saw ʿUmar push Abū Bakr up to the pulpit."[1]

مَعْمَرٌ، عَنِ الزُّهْرِيِّ، قَالَ: أَخْبَرَنِي أَنَسُ بْنُ مَالِكٍ، أَنَّهُ سَمِعَ خُطْبَةَ عُمَرَ رَحِمَهُ اللَّهُ الآخِرَةَ حِينَ جَلَسَ عَلَى مِنبَرِ النَّبِيِّ وَذَلِكَ الْغَدَ مِنْ يَوْمِ تُوُفِّيَ رَسُولُ اللَّهِ قَالَ: فَتَشَهَّدَ عُمَرُ، وَأَبُو بَكْرٍ صَامِتٌ لا يَتَكَلَّمُ، ثُمَّ قَالَ عُمَرُ: أَمَا بَعْدُ، فَإِنِّي قُلْتُ مَقَالَةً، وَإِنَّهَا لَمْ تَكُنْ كَمَا قُلْتُ، وَإِنِّي وَاللَّهِ مَا وَجَدْتُ الْمَقَالَةَ الَّتِي قُلْتُ فِي كِتَابِ اللَّهِ تَعَالَى وَلا فِي عَهْدٍ عَهِدَهُ إِلَيَّ رَسُولُ اللَّهِ وَلَكِنِّي كُنْتُ أَرْجُو أَنْ يَعِيشَ رَسُولُ اللَّهِ حَتَّى يَدْبُرَنَا يُرِيدُ بِذَلِكَ حَتَّى يَكُونَ آخِرَهُمْ، فَإِنْ يَكُ مُحَمَّدٌ قَدْ مَاتَ، فَإِنَّ اللَّهَ قَدْ جَعَلَ بَيْنَ أَظْهُرِكُمْ نُورًا تَهْتَدُونَ بِهِ: هَذَا كِتَابُ اللَّهِ فَاعْتَصِمُوا بِهِ تَهْتَدُونَ لِمَا هَدَى اللَّهُ بِهِ مُحَمَّدًا ثُمَّ إِنَّ أَبَا بَكْرٍ رَحِمَهُ اللَّهُ صَاحِبُ رَسُولِ اللَّهِ وَثَانِي اثْنَيْنِ، وَإِنَّهُ أَوْلَى النَّاسِ بِأُمُورِكُمْ، فَقُومُوا فَبَايِعُوهُ وَكَانَتْ طَائِفَةٌ مِنْهُمْ قَدْ بَايَعُوهُ قَبْلَ ذَلِكَ فِي سَقِيفَةِ بَنِي سَاعِدَةَ، وَكَانَتْ بَيْعَةُ الْعَامَّةِ عَلَى الْمِنْبَرِ.

قَالَ الزُّهْرِيُّ: وَأَخْبَرَنِي أَنَسٌ، قَالَ: لَقَدْ رَأَيْتُ عُمَرَ يُزْعِجُ أَبَا بَكْرٍ إِلَى الْمِنْبَرِ إِزْعَاجًا. اللفظ لفظ عبد الرزاق في مصنفه.

ʿUmar's claim that is referenced at the beginning of this tradition is referring to the claim he made on the first day the Prophet ﷺ died, where he initially denied the Prophet's ﷺ death.

ʿAlī b. Hāshim b. al-Barīd narrated on the authority of his father, from Abū al-Jaḥḥāf that he said:

> When allegiance was paid to Abū Bakr and ʿAlī and his companions had pledged their allegiance to him, Abū Bakr stood thrice facing the people. He would say, "O people, I have absolved you of your

1 Muṣannaf ʿAbdirrazzāq (5/437), Ṣaḥīḥ al-Bukhārī (9/81)

pledges, so is there anyone who is displeased [with his pledge to me]?"

ʿAlī would then stand up at the forefront of the people and say, "No, by Allah, we shall not relinquish you nor ever ask you to relinquish [your duty]. The Messenger of Allah ﷺ put you forth to lead the people, so who shall dare put you back?"[1]

قال عبد الله بن أحمد: حَدَّثَنِي عَبْدُ اللَّهِ بْنُ عُمَرَ أَبُو عَبْدِ الرَّحْمَنِ الْقُرَشِيُّ، قثنا عَلِيُّ بْنُ هَاشِمِ بْنِ الْبَرِيدِ، عَنْ أَبِيهِ، عَنْ أَبِي الْجَحَّافِ، قَالَ: لَمَّا بُويِعَ أَبُو بَكْرٍ، فَبَايَعَهُ عَلِيٌّ وَأَصْحَابُهُ، قَامَ ثَلاثًا يَسْتَقْبِلُ النَّاسَ، يَقُولُ، " أَيُّهَا النَّاسُ، قَدْ أَقَلْتُكُمْ بَيْعَتَكُمْ، هَلْ مِنْ كَارِهٍ؟ " قَالَ: فَيَقُومُ عَلِيٌّ فِي أَوَائِلِ النَّاسِ، فَيَقُولُ: وَاللَّهِ لا نُقِيلُكَ، وَلا نَسْتَقِيلُكَ أَبَدًا، قَدَّمَكَ رَسُولُ اللَّهِ تُصَلِّي بِالنَّاسِ، فَمَنْ ذَا يُؤَخِّرُكَ؟

قلت: هذا إسناد مرسل، وجُلّ رواته – ما عدا عبد الله بن أحمد – من شيعة أهل الكوفة. وقد روى ذا الخبر عن علي بن هاشم جماعة، ورواه كذلك تليد بن سليمان عن أبي الجحاف.

This account can be authentically traced back to Abū al-Jaḥḥāf. Its isnād, however, is disconnected, for Abū al-Jaḥḥāf was a Kūfan Shīʿite figure who died in the early second century. What is noteworthy about this report, however, is that its isnād consists of Kūfan Shīʾites, (1) ʿAlī b. Hāshim b. al-Barīd, (2) his father and (3) Abū al-Jaḥḥāf. Another extreme Kūfan Shīʿite, Talīd b. Sulaymān (d. 191), also relayed this tradition from Abū al-Jaḥḥāf.[2] Such traditions should, if anything, indicate that the early Shīʿite community of Kūfa was not a monolith with regards to Abū Bakr's inauguration, and some staunch Shīʿites had a favorable perception of Abū Bakr's caliphate. Nonetheless, I must not that none of the reports that present ʿAlī pledging allegiance to Abū Bakr immediately after his inauguration are authentic. Rather, stronger evidence, which shall shortly be presented, states that ʿAlī withheld paying allegiance to Abū Bakr until Fāṭima's death several months after his inauguration.

Shortly after Abū Bakr's inauguration and its aftermaths, Fāṭima requested from Abū Bakr to hand her what she perceived to be her rightful inheritance from her father, the Messenger of Allah ﷺ. The details of this

---

1 Faḍāʾil al-Ṣaḥāba by Aḥmed b. Ḥanbal (1/131), al-Sharīʿa by al-Ājurrī (4/1719, 5/2332), Talkhīṣ al-Mutashābih fī al-Rasm by al-Khaṭīb al-Baghdādī (2/608)

2 Faḍāʾil al-Ṣaḥāba by Aḥmed b. Ḥanbal (1/132, 1/151), al-Sharīʿa by al-Ājurrī (4/1720, 4/1840)

event and its aftermaths are authentically recorded via Ibn Shihāb, on the authority of ʿUrwa b. al-Zubayr, from ʿĀʾisha that she informed him:

> Fāṭima, the Messenger of Allah's ﷺ daughter, sent to Abū Bakr requesting from him her inheritance from the Messenger of Allah, which Allah had granted to His Messenger in Medīna, Fadak and what remained from the *khums* of Khaybar.
>
> Abū Bakr hence said, "The Messenger of Allah ﷺ said, 'we are not inherited. Whatever we leave behind is *ṣadaqa*.' Muḥammad's household (wives) shall eat from this wealth. By Allah, I shall not alter anything from the Messenger of Allah's charities beyond their status during his reign, and I shall do with them as did the Messenger of Allah ﷺ. Abū Bakr hence refused to give Fāṭima anything, and Fāṭima was dismayed with Abū Bakr for that. She estranged Abū Bakr, so she did not speak with him until her death.
>
> She lived after the Messenger of Allah ﷺ for six months. When she died, her husband, ʿAlī b. Abī Ṭālib, buried her at night. ʿAlī did not inform Abū Bakr about her, and he prayed her funeral prayer.
>
> ʿAlī was of status among the people during Fāṭima's life. When she died, ʿAlī felt a change in the people's faces. He hence desired to reconcile with Abū Bakr and pay allegiance to him, as he had not paid allegiance to him throughout those months. ʿAlī sent to Abū saying, "come to us, and let no one come with you," not wanting ʿUmar to come with him.
>
> ʿUmar thus told Abū Bakr, "By Allah, you shall not enter upon them alone." Abū Bakr said, "And what could they do to me? By Allah, I will go to them." Abū Bakr then entered upon them, so ʿAlī uttered the *shahāda* and said, "O Abū Bakr, we have known your merit and what Allah had granted you. We are not envious of you for a good Allah had granted you, but you have excluded us in the matter. We used to see that we had a right in it due to our relationship to the Messenger of Allah ﷺ."
>
> ʿAlī continued to speak with Abū Bakr until Abū Bakr's eyes began to tear. When Abū Bakr spoke, he said, "By the One in Whose Hand is my soul, maintaining ties with the Messenger of Allah's kin is more beloved to me than maintaining ties with my own kin. As for the dispute between me and you about this wealth, I did not sway

away from the Truth in it, and I did not leave a single thing I saw the Messenger of Allah ﷺ do except that I upheld it."

ʿAlī thus told Abū Bakr, "Your appointment is this afternoon for the pledge of allegiance." After praying *Dhuhr*, Abū Bakr ascended the pulpit. He uttered the *shahāda*, and he mentioned ʿAlī's matter, his withdrawal from the pledge of allegiance and his excuse that he had cited. ʿAlī then prayed for forgiveness and uttered the *shahāda*. He extolled Abū Bakr's status and mentioned that his past actions were not done out of envy to Abū Bakr nor out of denial to what Allah had granted him. Rather it was because he believed he had a share in the matter, but Abū Bakr excluded him from it, to which he was disgruntled.

The Muslims were elated by that, and they said, "You have done what is correct." The Muslims were close to ʿAlī once he returned to the enjoinment of good.[1]

عَنْ ابْنِ شِهَابٍ، عَنْ عُرْوَةَ بْنِ الزُّبَيْرِ، عَنْ عَائِشَةَ، أَنَّهَا أَخْبَرَتْهُ أَنَّ فَاطِمَةَ بِنْتَ رَسُولِ اللَّهِ أَرْسَلَتْ إِلَى أَبِي بَكْرٍ الصِّدِّيقِ تَسْأَلُهُ مِيرَاثَهَا مِنْ رَسُولِ اللَّهِ مِمَّا أَفَاءَ اللَّهُ عَلَيْهِ بِالْمَدِينَةِ، وَفَدَكٍ وَمَا بَقِيَ مِنْ خُمْسِ خَيْبَرَ، فَقَالَ أَبُو بَكْرٍ: إِنَّ رَسُولَ اللَّهِ قَالَ: لَا نُورَثُ مَا تَرَكْنَا صَدَقَةٌ "، إِنَّمَا يَأْكُلُ آلُ مُحَمَّدٍ فِي هَذَا الْمَالِ، وَإِنِّي وَاللَّهِ لَا أُغَيِّرُ شَيْئًا مِنْ صَدَقَةِ رَسُولِ اللَّهِ عَنْ حَالِهَا، الَّتِي كَانَتْ عَلَيْهَا فِي عَهْدِ رَسُولِ اللَّهِ وَلَأَعْمَلَنَّ فِيهَا بِمَا عَمِلَ بِهِ رَسُولُ اللَّهِ فَأَبَى أَبُو بَكْرٍ أَنْ يَدْفَعَ إِلَى فَاطِمَةَ شَيْئًا، فَوَجَدَتْ فَاطِمَةُ عَلَى أَبِي بَكْرٍ فِي ذَلِكَ.

قَالَ: فَهَجَرَتْهُ فَلَمْ تُكَلِّمْهُ حَتَّى تُوُفِّيَتْ وَعَاشَتْ بَعْدَ رَسُولِ اللَّهِ سِتَّةَ أَشْهُرٍ، فَلَمَّا تُوُفِّيَتْ دَفَنَهَا زَوْجُهَا عَلِيُّ بْنُ أَبِي طَالِبٍ لَيْلاً، وَلَمْ يُؤْذِنْ بِهَا أَبَا بَكْرٍ، وَصَلَّى عَلَيْهَا عَلِيٌّ وَكَانَ لِعَلِيٍّ مِنَ النَّاسِ وِجْهَةٌ حَيَاةَ فَاطِمَةَ، فَلَمَّا تُوُفِّيَتِ اسْتَنْكَرَ عَلِيٌّ وُجُوهَ النَّاسِ، فَالْتَمَسَ مُصَالَحَةَ أَبِي بَكْرٍ وَمُبَايَعَتَهُ وَلَمْ يَكُنْ بَايَعَ تِلْكَ الْأَشْهُرَ، فَأَرْسَلَ إِلَى أَبِي بَكْرٍ أَنِ ائْتِنَا وَلَا يَأْتِنَا مَعَكَ أَحَدٌ كَرَاهِيَةَ مَحْضَرِ عُمَرَ بْنِ الْخَطَّابِ، فَقَالَ عُمَرُ، لِأَبِي بَكْرٍ: وَاللَّهِ لَا تَدْخُلْ عَلَيْهِمْ وَحْدَكَ، فَقَالَ أَبُو بَكْرٍ: وَمَا عَسَاهُمْ أَنْ يَفْعَلُوا بِي إِنِّي وَاللَّهِ لَآتِيَنَّهُمْ.

فَدَخَلَ عَلَيْهِمْ أَبُو بَكْرٍ، فَتَشَهَّدَ عَلِيُّ بْنُ أَبِي طَالِبٍ، ثُمَّ قَالَ: إِنَّا قَدْ عَرَفْنَا يَا أَبَا بَكْرٍ فَضِيلَتَكَ وَمَا أَعْطَاكَ اللَّهُ، وَلَمْ نَنْفَسْ عَلَيْكَ خَيْرًا سَاقَهُ اللَّهُ إِلَيْكَ وَلَكِنَّكَ اسْتَبْدَدْتَ عَلَيْنَا بِالْأَمْرِ، وَكُنَّا نَحْنُ نَرَى لَنَا حَقًّا لِقَرَابَتِنَا مِنْ رَسُولِ اللَّهِ فَلَمْ يَزَلْ يُكَلِّمُ أَبَا بَكْرٍ، حَتَّى فَاضَتْ عَيْنَا أَبِي بَكْرٍ، فَلَمَّا تَكَلَّمَ أَبُو بَكْرٍ، قَالَ: وَالَّذِي نَفْسِي بِيَدِهِ لَقَرَابَةُ رَسُولِ

1 Ṣaḥīḥ al-Bukhārī (5/139-140), Ṣaḥīḥ Muslim (3/1380)

اللَّهِ أَحَبُّ إِلَيَّ أَنْ أَصِلَ مِنْ قَرَابَتِي، وَأَمَّا الَّذِي شَجَرَ بَيْنِي وَبَيْنَكُمْ مِنْ هَذِهِ الْأَمْوَالِ، فَإِنِّي لَمْ آلُ فِيهَ عَنِ الْحَقِّ وَلَمْ أَتْرُكْ أَمْرًا رَأَيْتُ رَسُولَ اللَّهِ يَصْنَعُهُ فِيهَا إِلَّا صَنَعْتُهُ، فَقَالَ عَلِيٌّ، لِأَبِي بَكْرٍ: مَوْعِدُكَ الْعَشِيَّةُ لِلْبَيْعَةِ، فَلَمَّا صَلَّى أَبُو بَكْرٍ صَلاَةَ الظُّهْرِ رَقِيَ عَلَى الْمِنْبَرِ، فَتَشَهَّدَ وَذَكَرَ شَأْنَ عَلِيٍّ وَتَخَلُّفَهُ عَنِ الْبَيْعَةِ وَعُذْرَهُ بِالَّذِي اعْتَذَرَ إِلَيْهِ، ثُمَّ اسْتَغْفَرَ وَتَشَهَّدَ عَلِيُّ بْنُ أَبِي طَالِبٍ، فَعَظَّمَ حَقَّ أَبِي بَكْرٍ وَأَنَّهُ لَمْ يَحْمِلْهُ عَلَى الَّذِي صَنَعَ نَفَاسَةً عَلَى أَبِي بَكْرٍ، وَلَا إِنْكَارًا لِلَّذِي فَضَّلَهُ اللَّهُ بِهِ وَلَكِنَّا كُنَّا نَرَى لَنَا فِي الْأَمْرِ نَصِيبًا، فَاسْتُبِدَّ عَلَيْنَا بِهِ فَوَجَدْنَا فِي أَنْفُسِنَا فَسُرَّ بِذَلِكَ الْمُسْلِمُونَ، وَقَالُوا: أَصَبْتَ فَكَانَ الْمُسْلِمُونَ إِلَى عَلِيٍّ قَرِيبًا حِينَ رَاجَعَ الْأَمْرَ الْمَعْرُوفَ.

In a variant of the tradition, Maʿmar b. Rāshid (d. 154) noted that a man asked Ibn Shihāb amidst the report, "So ʿAlī did not pledge his allegiance to him for six months?" Ibn Shihāb replied, "No, nor did anyone from Banī Hāshim pledge his allegiance to him until ʿAlī pledged his allegiance to him."[1] Maʿmar's tradition also mentioned that al-ʿAbbās and Fāṭima were both requesting the inheritance of the land of Fadak from Abū Bakr.[2]

عَنْ مَعْمَرٍ، عَنِ الزُّهْرِيِّ، عَنْ عُرْوَةَ، عَنْ عَائِشَةَ، أَنَّ فَاطِمَةَ، وَالْعَبَّاسَ، أَتَيَا أَبَا بَكْرٍ يَلْتَمِسَانِ مِيرَاثَهُمَا مِنْ رَسُولِ اللَّهِ صَلَّى اللهُ عَلَيْهِ وَسَلَّمَ - وَهُمَا حِينَئِذٍ يَطْلُبَانِ أَرْضَهُ مِنْ فَدَكَ، وَسَهْمَهُ مِنْ خَيْبَرٍ. [....] قَالَ مَعْمَرٌ: فَقَالَ رَجُلٌ لِلزُّهْرِيِّ: فَلَمْ يُبَايِعْهُ عَلِيٌّ سِتَّةَ أَشْهُرٍ؟ قَالَ: لَا، وَلَا أَحَدٌ مِنْ بَنِي هَاشِمٍ حَتَّى بَايَعَهُ عَلِيٌّ....

Such traditions only serve to highlight the nature of the dispute that ensued following the Prophet's death, especially its tribalistic and materialistic underpinnings. It appears that ʿAlī b. Abī Ṭālib and his uncle, al-ʿAbbās, perpetuated their dispute over over the Prophet's inheritance well into ʿUmar's reign after Abū Bakr's death.

Al-Bukhārī said in his *Ṣaḥīḥ*: Abū al-Yamān informed us, he said: Shuʿayb informed us, on the authority of al-Zuhrī that he said: Mālik b. Aws b. al-Ḥadathān al-Naṣrī informed me:

> That ʿUmar b. al-Khaṭṭāb once summoned him. His doorkeeper, Yarfā, then approached and said, "Would you let in ʿUthmān, ʿAbdurraḥmān, al-Zubayr and Saʿd, as they are asking for permission [to enter]?" ʿUmar said, "Yes," so he let them in.

---

1 Muṣannaf ʿAbdirrazzāq (5/472)
2 Muṣannaf ʿAbdirrazzāq (5/471)

The doorkeeper remained put for a bit, and he then came and said, "Would you let in ʿAlī and al-ʿAbbās, as they are asking for permission [to enter]?" ʿUmar said, "Yes," so they both came in.

Al-ʿAbbās thus said, "O Commander of the Faithful, judge between me and this man," as they were disputing one another over the spoils that Allah had granted His Messenger from Banī al-Naḍīr. ʿAlī and al-ʿAbbās then began to curse at each other, and so the assembly said, "O Commander of the Faithful, judge between them and relieve each of them from the other."

ʿUmar hence said, "I ask you by Allah, the One by Whose permission the sky and land become upright, do you know that the Messenger of Allah said, 'we are not inherited. Whatever we leave behind is *ṣadaqa*,' referring to himself?" They replied, "He had said that."

ʿUmar thus approached al-ʿAbbās and ʿAlī, and he said, "I ask you both by Allah, do you two know that the Messenger of Allah said that?" They replied, "Yes." Umar said, "Then, I shall tell you about this matter. Allah *subḥānah* had uniquely given to His messenger something from the spoils that He had not given to anyone else. He, glorified be His mention, hence said [in the Quran], 'As for the gains Allah has turned over to His Messenger from them—you did not [even] spur on any horse or camel for such gains. But Allah gives authority to His messengers over whoever He wills. For Allah is Most Capable of everything. [Quran 59:6]' This share was hence solely for the Messenger of Allah. By Allah, he did not possess it in exclusion to you. He had given you it and split it among you until this portion of the wealth had remained. The Messenger of Allah hence used to utilize this wealth for the annual provisions of his household, and he would take whatever remained from it and treat it as the wealth belonging to Allah.

The Messenger of Allah did so throughout his life, and he then died. Abū Bakr then said, 'I am the *walī* of Allah's Messenger,' so he possessed the wealth and dealt with it as the Messenger of Allah did, and you were there."

ʿUmar then approached ʿAlī and al-ʿAbbās, and he said, "You mentioned that Abū Bakr is as you had said, but Allah knows that he is truthful, dutiful, guided and pursuant of the Truth. Then, Abū

> Bakr died, so I said, 'I am the *walī* of the Messenger of Allah and Abū Bakr.' I hence possessed the wealth for two years of my reign dealing with it as the Messenger of Allah and Abū Bakr had dealt with it [during their lives], and Allah knows that I am truthful, dutiful, guided and pursuant of the Truth in that. Both of you then approached me in agreement, so you approached me, O ʿAbbās. I then had told both of you that the Messenger of Allah said, 'We are not inherited. Whatever we leave behind is charity.'
>
> When I decided to hand it over to you two, I said, 'if you wish, I shall hand it to both of you, but you must give me God's oath and covenant that you shall run it as the Messenger of Allah, Abū Bakr and I ran it during my reign. Otherwise, do not speak to me.' You both then said, 'hand it over to us in accordance to that,' so I handed it over to you. Do you expect from me a verdict other than that? By Allah, the One by Whose permission the sky and land become upright, I will not issue a verdict other than that in this regard until the Hour commences. If you are unable to run it, then hand it over to me, and I shall suffice you."

Ibn Shihāb then said, I informed ʿUrwa b. al-Zubayr of this ḥadīth, so he said, "Mālik b. Aws has said the truth." Ibn Shihāb's tradition from ʿUrwa concludes saying:

> This *ṣadaqa* eventually was in ʿAlī's hands. ʿAlī had prevented al-ʿAbbās from it, so he beat him to it. It then was in the hands of al-Ḥasan b. ʿAlī. Then, it was in the hands of ʿAlī b. Ḥusayn and al-Ḥasan b. al-Ḥasan, both of them used to run it. Then, it was in the hands of Zayd b. al-Ḥasan, and it truly is the Messenger of Allah's *ṣadaqa*.[1]

قال البخاري في صحيحه: حَدَّثَنَا أَبُو اليَمَانِ، أَخْبَرَنَا شُعَيْبٌ، عَنِ الزُّهْرِيِّ، قَالَ: أَخْبَرَنِي مَالِكُ بْنُ أَوْسِ بْنِ الحَدَثَانِ النَّصْرِيُّ، أَنَّ عُمَرَ بْنَ الخَطَّابِ رَضِيَ اللَّهُ عَنْهُ دَعَاهُ، إِذْ جَاءَهُ حَاجِبُهُ يَرْفَا، فَقَالَ: هَلْ لَكَ فِي عُثْمَانَ، وَعَبْدِ

1 Ṣaḥīḥ al-Bukhārī (5/89-90), Ṣaḥīḥ Muslim (3/1377-1378).
Several transmitters relayed this tradition from Ibn Shihāb, and Ibn Shihāb was also corroboted in his transmission of this report from Mālik b. Aws. ʿIkrima b. Khālid relayed it from Mālik. See Al-Sunan al-Kubrā by al-Nasāʾī (4/333). Muḥamamd b. ʿAmr b. ʿAṭā also relayed a related, abridged tradition in this regard from Mālik. See the Musnad of Aḥmed (1/389).

الرَّحْمنِ، وَالزُّبَيْرِ، وَسَعْدٍ يَسْتَأْذِنُونَ؟ فَقَالَ: نَعَمْ فَأَدْخِلْهُمْ، فَلَبِثَ قَلِيلاً ثُمَّ جَاءَ فَقَالَ: هَلْ لَكَ فِي عَبَّاسٍ، وَعَلِيٍّ يَسْتَأْذِنَانِ؟ قَالَ: نَعَمْ، فَلَمَّا دَخَلاَ قَالَ عَبَّاسٌ: يَا أَمِيرَ الْمُؤْمِنِينَ اقْضِ بَيْنِي وَبَيْنَ هَذَا، وَهُمَا يَخْتَصِمَانِ فِي الَّذِي أَفَاءَ اللَّهُ عَلَى رَسُولِهِ صَلَّى اللهُ عَلَيْهِ وَسَلَّمَ مِنْ بَنِي النَّضِيرِ، فَاسْتَبَّ عَلِيٌّ، وَعَبَّاسٌ، فَقَالَ الرَّهْطُ: يَا أَمِيرَ الْمُؤْمِنِينَ اقْضِ بَيْنَهُمَا، وَأَرِحْ أَحَدَهُمَا مِنَ الآخَرِ.

فَقَالَ عُمَرُ: اتَّئِدُوا أَنْشُدُكُمْ بِاللَّهِ الَّذِي بِإِذْنِهِ تَقُومُ السَّمَاءُ وَالأَرْضُ، هَلْ تَعْلَمُونَ أَنَّ رَسُولَ اللَّهِ صَلَّى اللهُ عَلَيْهِ وَسَلَّمَ، قَالَ، "لاَ نُورَثُ مَا تَرَكْنَا صَدَقَةٌ" يُرِيدُ بِذَلِكَ نَفْسَهُ؟ قَالُوا: قَدْ قَالَ ذَلِكَ، فَأَقْبَلَ عُمَرُ عَلَى عَبَّاسٍ، وَعَلِيٍّ فَقَالَ: أَنْشُدُكُمَا بِاللَّهِ، هَلْ تَعْلَمَانِ أَنَّ رَسُولَ اللَّهِ صَلَّى اللهُ عَلَيْهِ وَسَلَّمَ قَدْ قَالَ ذَلِكَ؟ قَالاَ: نَعَمْ.

قَالَ: فَإِنِّي أُحَدِّثُكُمْ عَنْ هَذَا الأَمْرِ، إِنَّ اللَّهَ سُبْحَانَهُ كَانَ خَصَّ رَسُولَهُ صَلَّى اللهُ عَلَيْهِ وَسَلَّمَ فِي هَذَا الفَيْءِ بِشَيْءٍ لَمْ يُعْطِهِ أَحَدًا غَيْرَهُ، فَقَالَ جَلَّ ذِكْرُهُ: {وَمَا أَفَاءَ اللَّهُ عَلَى رَسُولِهِ مِنْهُمْ فَمَا أَوْجَفْتُمْ عَلَيْهِ مِنْ خَيْلٍ وَلاَ رِكَابٍ} إِلَى قَوْلِهِ – {قَدِيرٌ}، فَكَانَتْ هَذِهِ خَالِصَةً لِرَسُولِ اللَّهِ صَلَّى اللهُ عَلَيْهِ وَسَلَّمَ، ثُمَّ وَاللَّهِ مَا احْتَازَهَا دُونَكُمْ، وَلاَ اسْتَأْثَرَهَا عَلَيْكُمْ، لَقَدْ أَعْطَاكُمُوهَا وَقَسَمَهَا فِيكُمْ حَتَّى بَقِيَ هَذَا المَالُ مِنْهَا، فَكَانَ رَسُولُ اللَّهِ صَلَّى اللهُ عَلَيْهِ وَسَلَّمَ يُنْفِقُ عَلَى أَهْلِهِ نَفَقَةَ سَنَتِهِمْ مِنْ هَذَا المَالِ، ثُمَّ يَأْخُذُ مَا بَقِيَ فَيَجْعَلُهُ مَجْعَلَ مَالِ اللَّهِ، فَعَمِلَ ذَلِكَ رَسُولُ اللَّهِ صَلَّى اللهُ عَلَيْهِ وَسَلَّمَ حَيَاتَهُ، ثُمَّ تُوُفِّيَ النَّبِيُّ صَلَّى اللهُ عَلَيْهِ وَسَلَّمَ، فَقَالَ أَبُو بَكْرٍ: فَأَنَا وَلِيُّ رَسُولِ اللَّهِ صَلَّى اللهُ عَلَيْهِ وَسَلَّمَ، فَقَبَضَهُ أَبُو بَكْرٍ فَعَمِلَ فِيهِ بِمَا عَمِلَ بِهِ رَسُولُ اللَّهِ صَلَّى اللهُ عَلَيْهِ وَسَلَّمَ، وَأَنْتُمْ حِينَئِذٍ، فَأَقْبَلَ عَلَى عَلِيٍّ، وَعَبَّاسٍ وَقَالَ: تَذْكُرَانِ أَنَّ أَبَا بَكْرٍ فِيهِ كَمَا تَقُولاَنِ، وَاللَّهُ يَعْلَمُ: إِنَّهُ فِيهِ لَصَادِقٌ بَارٌّ رَاشِدٌ تَابِعٌ لِلْحَقِّ؟ ثُمَّ تَوَفَّى اللَّهُ أَبَا بَكْرٍ، فَقُلْتُ: أَنَا وَلِيُّ رَسُولِ اللَّهِ صَلَّى اللهُ عَلَيْهِ وَسَلَّمَ، وَأَبِي بَكْرٍ، فَقَبَضْتُهُ سَنَتَيْنِ مِنْ إِمَارَتِي أَعْمَلُ فِيهِ بِمَا عَمِلَ فِيهِ رَسُولُ اللَّهِ صَلَّى اللهُ عَلَيْهِ وَسَلَّمَ، وَأَبُو بَكْرٍ، وَاللَّهُ يَعْلَمُ: أَنِّي فِيهِ صَادِقٌ بَارٌّ رَاشِدٌ تَابِعٌ لِلْحَقِّ؟ ثُمَّ جِئْتُمَانِي كِلاَكُمَا، وَكَلِمَتُكُمَا وَاحِدَةٌ وَأَمْرُكُمَا جَمِيعٌ، فَجِئْتَنِي – يَعْنِي عَبَّاسًا – فَقُلْتُ لَكُمَا: إِنَّ رَسُولَ اللَّهِ صَلَّى اللهُ عَلَيْهِ وَسَلَّمَ، قَالَ، "لاَ نُورَثُ مَا تَرَكْنَا صَدَقَةٌ" فَلَمَّا بَدَا لِي أَنْ أَدْفَعَهُ إِلَيْكُمَا قُلْتُ: إِنْ شِئْتُمَا دَفَعْتُهُ إِلَيْكُمَا، عَلَى أَنَّ عَلَيْكُمَا عَهْدَ اللَّهِ وَمِيثَاقَهُ: لَتَعْمَلاَنِ فِيهِ بِمَا عَمِلَ فِيهِ رَسُولُ اللَّهِ صَلَّى اللهُ عَلَيْهِ وَسَلَّمَ وَأَبُو بَكْرٍ وَمَا عَمِلْتُ فِيهِ مُنْذُ وَلِيتُ، وَإِلَّا فَلاَ تُكَلِّمَانِي، فَقُلْتُمَا ادْفَعْهُ إِلَيْنَا بِذَلِكَ، فَدَفَعْتُهُ إِلَيْكُمَا، أَفَتَلْتَمِسَانِ مِنِّي قَضَاءً غَيْرَ ذَلِكَ، فَوَاللَّهِ الَّذِي بِإِذْنِهِ تَقُومُ السَّمَاءُ وَالأَرْضُ، لاَ أَقْضِي فِيهِ بِقَضَاءٍ غَيْرِ ذَلِكَ حَتَّى تَقُومَ السَّاعَةُ، فَإِنْ عَجَزْتُمَا عَنْهُ فَادْفَعَا إِلَيَّ فَأَنَا أَكْفِيكُمَاهُ.

قَالَ: فَحَدَّثْتُ هَذَا الحَدِيثَ عُرْوَةَ بْنَ الزُّبَيْرِ، فَقَالَ: صَدَقَ مَالِكُ بْنُ أَوْسٍ: أَنَا سَمِعْتُ عَائِشَةَ رَضِيَ اللَّهُ عَنْهَا، زَوْجَ النَّبِيِّ صَلَّى اللهُ عَلَيْهِ وَسَلَّمَ، تَقُولُ، " أَرْسَلَ أَزْوَاجُ النَّبِيِّ صَلَّى اللهُ عَلَيْهِ وَسَلَّمَ عُثْمَانَ إِلَى أَبِي بَكْرٍ، يَسْأَلْنَهُ

ثُمُنَهُنَّ مِمَّا أَفَاءَ اللَّهُ عَلَى رَسُولِهِ صَلَّى اللهُ عَلَيْهِ وَسَلَّمَ فَكُنْتُ أَنَا أَرُدُّهُنَّ، فَقُلْتُ لَهُنَّ: أَلاَ تَتَّقِينَ اللَّهَ، أَلَمْ تَعْلَمْنَ أَنَّ النَّبِيَّ صَلَّى اللهُ عَلَيْهِ وَسَلَّمَ كَانَ يَقُولُ, "لاَ نُورَثُ، مَا تَرَكْنَا صَدَقَةٌ - يُرِيدُ بِذَلِكَ نَفْسَهُ - إِنَّمَا يَأْكُلُ آلُ مُحَمَّدٍ صَلَّى اللهُ عَلَيْهِ وَسَلَّمَ فِي هَذَا المَالِ،" فَانْتَهَى أَزْوَاجُ النَّبِيِّ صَلَّى اللهُ عَلَيْهِ وَسَلَّمَ إِلَى مَا أَخْبَرَتْهُنَّ، قَالَ: فَكَانَتْ هَذِهِ الصَّدَقَةُ بِيَدِ عَلِيٍّ، مَنَعَهَا عَلِيٌّ عَبَّاسًا فَغَلَبَهُ عَلَيْهَا، ثُمَّ كَانَ بِيَدِ حَسَنِ بْنِ عَلِيٍّ، ثُمَّ بِيَدِ حُسَيْنِ بْنِ عَلِيٍّ، ثُمَّ بِيَدِ عَلِيِّ بْنِ حُسَيْنٍ، وَحَسَنِ بْنِ حَسَنٍ، كِلاَهُمَا كَانَا يَتَدَاوَلاَنِهَا، ثُمَّ بِيَدِ زَيْدِ بْنِ حَسَنٍ، وَهِيَ صَدَقَةُ رَسُولِ اللَّهِ صَلَّى اللهُ عَلَيْهِ وَسَلَّمَ حَقًّا.

This tradition highlights the nature of Fāṭima and ʿAlī's dispute with Abū Bakr on inheritance, and it is not farfetched to argue that ʿAlī's initial uneasiness with Abū Bakr's inauguration was of similar nature and underpinnings. Furthermore, when ʿAlī and al-ʿAbbās were eventually granted the authority to run and maintain the Prophet's charities, they disputed the wealth among themselves, eventually resorting to ʿUmar b. al-Khaṭṭāb as a judge between them. Later in history, ʿAlī fully usurped the admisntration of the charities from his uncle, al-ʿAbbās, and its maintenance was then passed along among some of his descendents.[1]

All in all, the past traditions shed light on the aftermaths of the Prophet's death in the city of Medīna. The only historical aspects from the Shīʿite narrative surrounding the commotion at Fāṭima's house are as follow, (1) ʿUmar approached the house and threatened to burn it if the congregation within is not dispersed, (2) al-Zubayr then came out of the house with his sword drawn, (3) al-Zubayr was subdued and the congregation was dispersed. All other claims that cite Fāṭima being beaten, let alone miscarrying a fetus after a beating, are fabrications and byproducts of extreme Rāfiḍite myths and fantasies.

In this regard, I am aware that some readers may express concern or confusion towards ʿUmar's threat at the congregation within Fāṭima's house, though I do not believe any of it should actually be a cause of concern. Rather, I would invite the reader to consider this event from ʿUmar's perspective, which I will shortly illustrate.

---

1 In this regard, I find it noteworthy to mention that several historical sources have claimed that Zayd b. ʿAlī b. al-Ḥusayn b. ʿAlī b. Abī Ṭālib's revolt against Umayyad authorities in 122 was initially sparked by a dispute over these charities between al-Ḥasan and al-Ḥusayn's descendents. I have dissected this narrative alongside many others in my upcoming biography of Zayd b. ʿAlī, may Allah hasten its completion.

The threat to burn down the house in which ʿAlī and his associates congregated should be assessed in its greater context: did ʿUmar actually intend to murder ʿAlī, Fāṭima, and al-Zubayr as he approached the house? I do not believe that to be the case. Rather, there are a few instances where this threat was made by ʿUmar in a non-violent and non-murderous context. Take for example this authentic tradition relayed by Ibn Abī Shayba, from Yaʿlā b. ʿUbayd, from Fuḍayl b. Ghazwān, from Nāfiʿ, from Ibn ʿUmar that he said:

> News once reached ʿUmar that a son of his draped his walls in fabric. ʿUmar thus said, "By Allah, if it is true, then I shall burn down his house!"[1]

قال ابن أبي شيبة: حَدَّثَنَا يَعْلَى بْنُ عُبَيْدٍ ، عَنْ فُضَيْلِ بْنِ غَزْوَانَ ، عَنْ نَافِعٍ ، عَنِ ابْنِ عُمَرَ ، قَالَ : بَلَغَ عُمَرَ أَنَّ ابْنًا لَهُ سَتَرَ حِيطَانَهُ ، فَقَالَ : وَاللَّهِ لَئِنْ كَانَ كَذَلِكَ لأَحْرِقَنَّ بَيْتَهُ!

The practice of draping one's walls with fabric was a luxury at the time, and ʿUmar was furious that a son of his would engage in such a wasteful and unnecessary luxury, especially when many subjects of his were destitute and in need. This theme is readily observable in ʿUmar's relationship with his children throughout his reign.

The threat to burn down one's house in the face of a *fitna* has precedent in the Prophet's *sīra*. Abū Hurayra reported that the Messenger of Allah ﷺ said:

> By the One in Whose Hand is my soul, I have wanted to command that firewood be gathered. I would then command that the prayer start, to which *adhān* is hence called. I would then command a man to lead the people in prayer. Then, I would depart to the households of men and burn their houses upon them. By the One in Whose hand is my soul, if one of them were to expect a fatty piece of meat or two nice pieces of meat, he would have attended ʿIshāʾ prayer![2]

عَنْ أَبِي هُرَيْرَةَ، أَنَّ رَسُولَ اللَّهِ قَالَ، " وَالَّذِي نَفْسِي بِيَدِهِ لَقَدْ هَمَمْتُ أَنْ آمُرَ بِحَطَبٍ فَيُحْطَبَ، ثُمَّ آمُرَ بِالصَّلاَةِ فَيُؤَذَّنَ لَهَا، ثُمَّ آمُرَ رَجُلاً فَيَؤُمَّ النَّاسَ، ثُمَّ أُخَالِفَ إِلَى رِجَالٍ فَأُحَرِّقَ عَلَيْهِمْ بُيُوتَهُمْ، وَالَّذِي نَفْسِي بِيَدِهِ لَوْ يَعْلَمُ أَحَدُهُمْ أَنَّهُ يَجِدُ عَرْقًا سَمِينًا أَوْ مِرْمَاتَيْنِ حَسَنَتَيْنِ لَشَهِدَ الْعِشَاءَ."

1 Muṣannaf Ibn Abī Shayba (12/622)
2 Ṣaḥīḥ al-Bukhārī (1/131), Ṣaḥīḥ Muslim (1/451)

Furthermore, there are a variety of obvious and implicit reasons to conclude that ʿUmar did not intend to murder the congregants at Fāṭima's house. Take for example the tradition relayed via al-Zuhrī, from ʿUbaydillāh b. ʿAbdillāh b. ʿUtba, from Abū Hurayra that he said:

> When the Messenger of Allah died and Abū Bakr became his successor and those who had apostatized from the Arabs had apostatized, ʿUmar told Abū Bakr, "how do you fight the people when the Messenger of Allah had said, 'I was commanded to fight the people until they say, there is no God but Allah. Whosoever says that, then he has secured his wealth and life from me, except when warranted by law, and his judgement is upon Allah?!"
>
> Thereupon, Abū Bakr retorted, "by Allah, I will fight whoever differentiates between prayer and *zakat*, for *zakat* is the obligation upon the wealth. By Allah, if they were to prevent me from a camel's rope that they used to pay the Messenger of Allah, I would fight them for preventing it!"
>
> ʿUmar said, "By Allah, I then recognized that Allah had eased Abū Bakr's chest [to combat the deniers of *zakat*], so I recognized that it is the Truth."[1]

قال الزهري: حدَّثَنَا عُبَيْدُ اللَّهِ بْنُ عَبْدِ اللَّهِ بْنِ عُتْبَةَ بْنِ مَسْعُودٍ، أَنَّ أَبَا هُرَيْرَةَ رَضِيَ اللَّهُ عَنْهُ، قَالَ, " لَمَّا تُوُفِّيَ رَسُولُ اللَّهِ وَكَانَ أَبُو بَكْرٍ رَضِيَ اللَّهُ عَنْهُ وَكَفَرَ مَنْ كَفَرَ مِنْ الْعَرَبِ، فَقَالَ عُمَرُ رَضِيَ اللَّهُ عَنْهُ: كَيْفَ تُقَاتِلُ النَّاسَ؟ وَقَدْ قَالَ رَسُولُ اللَّهِ: أُمِرْتُ أَنْ أُقَاتِلَ النَّاسَ حَتَّى يَقُولُوا لَا إِلَهَ إِلَّا اللَّهُ، فَمَنْ قَالَهَا فَقَدْ عَصَمَ مِنِّي مَالَهُ، وَنَفْسَهُ إِلَّا بِحَقِّهِ، وَحِسَابُهُ عَلَى اللَّهِ، فَقَالَ: وَاللَّهِ لَأُقَاتِلَنَّ مَنْ فَرَّقَ بَيْنَ الصَّلَاةِ، وَالزَّكَاةِ، فَإِنَّ الزَّكَاةَ حَقُّ الْمَالِ، وَاللَّهِ لَوْ مَنَعُونِي عَنَاقًا كَانُوا يُؤَدُّونَهَا إِلَى رَسُولِ اللَّهِ لَقَاتَلْتُهُمْ عَلَى مَنْعِهَا، قَالَ عُمَرُ رَضِيَ اللَّهُ عَنْهُ: فَوَاللَّهِ مَا هُوَ إِلَّا أَنْ قَدْ شَرَحَ اللَّهُ صَدْرَ أَبِي بَكْرٍ رَضِيَ اللَّهُ عَنْهُ، فَعَرَفْتُ، أَنَّهُ الْحَقُّ."

The events described in this tradition occurred several days after Abū Bakr's inauguration and the events of the Saqīfa and their immediate aftermaths. What is noteworthy about this tradition is that it illustrates ʿUmar's initial caution and reservation against combatting individuals who believed in the *shahada* yet refused to pay *zakat*. ʿUmar, at the time, did not believe it was permissible to fight the emergent "Muslim" entities that refused to pay *zakāt* following the Prophet's death. Hence, it should be

1 Ṣaḥīḥ al-Bukhārī (2/105), Ṣaḥīḥ Muslim (1/51)

apparent that ʿUmar was not planning to murder the handful of individuals who merely avoided Abū Bakr's inauguration and reserved themselves to Fāṭima's house. Rather, his primary motive was to disband this congregation which would inevitably give rise to strife and polarization within Medīna, especially after the Muhājirūn and the Anṣār had coalesced around Abū Bakr.

In fact, a Muslim leader around whom the Muslims had coalesced possesses the authority to disband and combat a minority of dissidents who declare war upon him, cause *fitna* and/or refuse to submit to his authority. In this regard, ʿUmar's concerns were rather founded, for as soon as he had approached Fāṭima's house, al-Zubayr leapt out of the house with his sword drawn. Had this congregation been left to fester within Medīna, then it evidently could have given rise to an emergent political faction within the city that would further divide the already distraught and unstable Muslim community. The Prophet's companion, ʿArfaja, is authentically quoted saying: I heard the Messenger of Allah ﷺ say:

> There shall be trials and tribulations. Whosoever desires to divide the matter of this *Umma* when it is united, then strike him with the sword, whosoever he may be.[1]

قَالَ عرفجة: سَمِعْتُ رَسُولَ اللَّهِ يَقُولُ, " إِنَّهُ سَتَكُونُ هَنَاتٌ وَهَنَاتٌ، فَمَنْ أَرَادَ أَنْ يُفَرِّقَ أَمْرَ هَذِهِ الْأُمَّةِ وَهِيَ جَمِيعٌ، فَاضْرِبُوهُ بِالسَّيْفِ كَائِنًا مَنْ كَانَ.

Luckily, ʿUmar was able to nip any potential for strife within the city of Medīna in the bud before any turmoil and bloodshed could become manifest. However, it is clear that the circumstances were dire at the time. Furthermore, ʿUmar's threat directed at the congregants within Fāṭima's house is akin to what the Messenger of Allah ﷺ is quoted saying elsewhere. Ibn Shihāb narrated on the authority of ʿUrwa b. al-Zubayr that he said:

> A woman once committed theft during the Messenger of Allah's life during the conquest of Mecca. Her clan hence rushed to Usāma b. Zayd asking him to intercede. When Usāma then spoke to the Messenger of Allah, the Messenger of Allah's face became colored [in anger]. He said, "Do you intercede with me with regards to one of Allah's boundaries!"

---

1 Ṣaḥīḥ Muslim (3/1479)

Usāma said, "Pray for my forgiveness, O Messenger of Allah." In the evening, the Messenger of Allah got up and gave a sermon. He praised Allah with due praise and then said, "The people before you were merely perished because they would exonerate the honorable one among them when he would commit theft. However, if the weak among them were to commit theft, they would implement the prescribed punishment (*ḥadd*) upon him. By the One in Whose hand is my soul, if Fāṭima the daughter of Muḥammad were to commit theft, I would sever her hand!"

The Messenger of Allah then gave a command with regards to that woman, and her hand was cut off. She then repented a candid repentance, and she became married. ʿĀʾisha said, "She would visit [us] after that, and I would raise her request(s) to the Messenger of Allah."[1]

يُونُسُ، عَنْ الزُّهْرِيِّ، قَالَ: أَخْبَرَنِي عُرْوَةُ بْنُ الزُّبَيْرِ: أَنَّ امْرَأَةً سَرَقَتْ فِي عَهْدِ رَسُولِ اللَّهِ فِي غَزْوَةِ الْفَتْحِ، فَفَزِعَ قَوْمُهَا إِلَى أُسَامَةَ بْنِ زَيْدٍ يَسْتَشْفِعُونَهُ، قَالَ عُرْوَةُ: فَلَمَّا كَلَّمَهُ أُسَامَةُ فِيهَا تَلَوَّنَ وَجْهُ رَسُولِ اللَّهِ فَقَالَ, " أَتُكَلِّمُنِي فِي حَدٍّ مِنْ حُدُودِ اللَّهِ "، قَالَ أُسَامَةُ: اسْتَغْفِرْ لِي يَا رَسُولَ اللَّهِ، فَلَمَّا كَانَ الْعَشِيُّ قَامَ رَسُولُ اللَّهِ خَطِيبًا فَأَثْنَى عَلَى اللَّهِ بِمَا هُوَ أَهْلُهُ، ثُمَّ قَالَ, " أَمَّا بَعْدُ، فَإِنَّمَا أَهْلَكَ النَّاسَ قَبْلَكُمْ أَنَّهُمْ كَانُوا إِذَا سَرَقَ فِيهِمُ الشَّرِيفُ تَرَكُوهُ، وَإِذَا سَرَقَ فِيهِمُ الضَّعِيفُ أَقَامُوا عَلَيْهِ الْحَدَّ، وَالَّذِي نَفْسُ مُحَمَّدٍ بِيَدِهِ لَوْ أَنَّ فَاطِمَةَ بِنْتَ مُحَمَّدٍ سَرَقَتْ لَقَطَعْتُ يَدَهَا "، ثُمَّ أَمَرَ رَسُولُ اللَّهِ بِتِلْكَ الْمَرْأَةِ، فَقُطِعَتْ يَدُهَا، فَحَسُنَتْ تَوْبَتُهَا بَعْدَ ذَلِكَ وَتَزَوَّجَتْ، قَالَتْ عَائِشَةُ: فَكَانَتْ تَأْتِي بَعْدَ ذَلِكَ، فَأَرْفَعُ حَاجَتَهَا إِلَى رَسُولِ اللَّهِ. "

In this tradition, one is able to observe the Messenger of Allah's ﷺ multifaceted sense of justice. His statement regarding his daughter, Fāṭima, is especially insightful in this regard. Indeed, it is quite profound how the Messenger of Allah ﷺ, the supreme leader within his community, would candidly say, "even if Fāṭima, my daughter, were to commit theft, I would sever her hand." Such a statement evidently is not intended to detract from Fāṭima's status. Rather, it emphasizes her close connection to the Messenger of Allah while further illustrating that the Prophet ﷺ would not be deterred

1 Ṣaḥīḥ al-Bukhārī (5/151), Ṣaḥīḥ Muslim (3/1315). This tradition was also relayed via Abū al-Zubayr from Jābir b. ʿAbdillāh. See the Ṣaḥīḥ of Muslim (3/1316). ʿAmr b. Dīnār also relayed a similar tradition from al-Ḥasan b. Muḥammad b. ʿAlī b. Abī Ṭālib. See the Muṣannaf of ʿAbdurrazzāq (10/202).

from implementing justice on his own loved ones. I believe this point is not to be overlooked when considering ʿUmar's statement, especially considering that some reports in this context highlighted this theme.

Ibn Abī Shayba (d. 235) said: Muḥammad b. Bishr informed us, he said: ʿUbaydullāh b. ʿUmar informed us, he said: Zayd b. Aslam informed us, on the authority of his father that he said:

> When Abū Bakr was pledged allegiance after the Messenger of Allah, ʿAlī and al-Zubayr used to enter upon Fāṭima and consult her and discuss their affairs. When news of that reached ʿUmar b. al-Khaṭṭāb, he set out and entered upon Fāṭima. He said, "O daughter of the Messenger of Allah, none is more beloved to me than your father, and none after him is more beloved to me than you. By Allah, that would not prevent me from commanding that the house is burnt upon them if they congregate with you."
>
> When ʿUmar left, they came to her, and she said, "You are aware that ʿUmar has approached me and swore that he would burn the house upon you! By Allah, he will fulfill what he had sworn to do, so depart in peace! See what you shall do, and do not come back to me!" They thus left her, and they only came back after pledging allegiance to Abū Bakr.[1]

قال ابن أبي شيبة: حَدَّثَنَا مُحَمَّدُ بْنُ بِشْرٍ، حدثنا عُبَيْدُ اللَّهِ بْنُ عُمَرَ، حَدَّثَنَا زَيْدُ بْنُ أَسْلَمَ، عَنْ أَبِيهِ أَسْلَمَ: أَنَّهُ حِينَ بُويِعَ لِأَبِي بَكْرٍ بَعْدَ رَسُولِ اللَّهِ كَانَ عَلِيٌّ وَالزُّبَيْرُ يَدْخُلَانِ عَلَى فَاطِمَةَ بِنْتِ رَسُولِ اللَّهِ فَيُشَاوِرُونَهَا، وَيَرْتَجِعُونَ فِي أَمْرِهِمْ. فَلَمَّا بَلَغَ ذَلِكَ عُمَرَ بْنَ الْخَطَّابِ خَرَجَ حَتَّى دَخَلَ عَلَى فَاطِمَةَ، فَقَالَ، "يَا بِنْتَ رَسُولِ اللَّهِ وَاللَّهِ مَا مِنْ أَحَدٍ أَحَبَّ إِلَيْنَا مِنْ أَبِيكَ، وَمَا مِنْ أَحَدٍ أَحَبَّ إِلَيْنَا بَعْدَ أَبِيكَ مِنْكَ، وَايْمُ اللَّهِ مَا ذَاكَ بِمَانِعِي إِنِ اجْتَمَعَ هَؤُلَاءِ النَّفَرُ عِنْدَكِ، أَنْ آمُرَ بِهِمْ أَنْ يُحَرَّقَ عَلَيْهِمُ الْبَيْتُ." قَالَ: فَلَمَّا خَرَجَ عُمَرُ، جَاءُوهَا فَقَالَتْ: تَعْلَمُونَ أَنَّ عُمَرَ قَدْ جَاءَنِي، وَقَدْ حَلَفَ بِاللَّهِ لَئِنْ عُدْتُمْ لَيُحَرِّقَنَّ عَلَيْكُمُ الْبَيْتَ، وَايْمُ اللَّهِ لَيَمْضِيَنَّ لِمَا حَلَفَ عَلَيْهِ، فَانْصَرِفُوا رَاشِدِينَ، فَرَوْا رَأْيَكُمْ وَلَا تَرْجِعُوا إِلَيَّ. فَانْصَرَفُوا عَنْهَا فَلَمْ يَرْجِعُوا إِلَيْهَا حَتَّى بَايَعُوا لِأَبِي بَكْرٍ."

Earlier in this book, I criticized some aspects of this tradition, as I do not believe its ending provides an accurate summary of what historically took place following ʿUmar's threat. Nonetheless, this tradition, which is regularly cited by Twelver polemicists attempting to substantiate the narrative within *Kitāb Sulaym*, reiterates the theme found in the past

---

1 Muṣannaf Ibn Abī Shayba (20/579)

Prophetic tradition. ʿUmar's rationale stems from his concern that this congregation would result in downstream strife, bloodshed and disunity within the Muslim nation. His love of Fāṭima hence would not deter him from taking the necessary measures to disband this potentially inciteful congregation at her house. Luckily, however, the confusion was quickly contained and put to ease before any of ʿUmar's concerns could become manifest. I believe ʿUmar's threat towards the congregation must be understood and perceived in light of these observations and conclusions, which should assuage any misunderstanding or concern brought forth by misinformed and/or dishonest polemicists.

I would further add: much of the self-righteous outrage that Twelver Shīʿite polemicists attempt to invoke with regards to the verified historical post-*saqīfa* events stems from a dogmatic Twelver reading of history. Take for example a rather neutral scenario where an unspecified Muslim community hypothetically coalesces around a leader who they deem fit for the management of their administrative affairs during a time of turmoil and confusion. The majority from within the community, including the knowledgeable among them, agree upon this man, recognizing that he possessed the qualifications and skills needed to lead them and manage their affairs/interests during such times. Following the general consensus of that community on the suitability of that leader, a fractional and negligible minority within that community withdraws from the greater body and refuses to acknowledge that leader's legitimacy, potentially causing a rift and polarization within the previously unified community. Shortly after that, the leader is informed that this reserved minority is, as a matter of fact, armed and congregated within a specific vicinity in his jurisdiction. I believe most reasonable individuals would agree that the usage of force to disband this potentially tumultuous congregation is justified and (arguably) warranted.

Though this essentially is a summary and characterization of the events that took place between Abū Bakr, ʿUmar and the congregants at Fāṭima's house, the Twelver Shiʿite interlocutor is unable to concede this reality for two main reasons: (1) he/she believes that ʿAlī and Fāṭima are infallible, supreme and divinely inspired humans and (2) he/she believes that Abū Bakr and ʿUmar were mere hypocrites during the Prophet's life and deplorable individuals who certainly were not rightful rulers of the Muslim community. These presumptions, however, merely are byproducts of Twelver Shīʿite dogma, and they evidently influence the manner in which the Shīʿite reader approaches and interprets these numerous historical events. The Twelver Shīʿite reader cannot fathom a world where ʿAlī could have committed an error, let alone a world where both Abū Bakr and ʿUmar could have possessed valid grievances against ʿAlī b. Abī Ṭālib. In this regard, the downfall of the Twelver Shīʿite narrative about Fāṭima's purported murder is most apparent: a flimsy and dubious story that is based on a cluster of unreliable sources and accounts which are weaved together and then circularly interpreted in light of Twelver dogma... What a convenient and self-serving approach to history! Furthermore, when the reader becomes aware of the fact that this Twelver Shīʿite narrative is only viable via a selective reading of historical sources where anything that portrays Abū Bakr and ʿUmar in a positive light is discarded and dismissed, he/she will further recognize the spurious nature of most Twelver polemics regarding the purported attack on Fāṭima.

In summary, this chapter contains the most reliable texts that outline the aftermaths of the Prophet's ﷺ death, namely the pledge at the Saqīfa and the commotion outside Fāṭima's house. It also includes some inauthentic texts which I thought were relevant and/or valuable to the discussion at hand. Though some polemicists attempt to self-righteously problematize some of these reports' contents, I believe, as stated in this chapter, that there should be nothing shocking or problematic in ʿUmar and Abū Bakr's handling of the events that ensued after the Prophet's ﷺ death. Such reports and accounts provide the historical and more plausible narrative surrounding Abū Bakr's inauguration, which was later bastardized and polemicized within extreme Shīʿite circles, finally giving rise to the notorious and mythical narrative of *Kitāb Sulaym Ibn Qays.*

Addendum

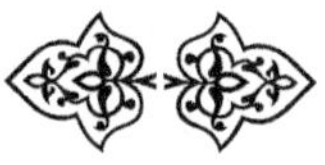

Other Shīʿite Traditions – Can the Multiplicity of Twelver Reports Entail the *Tawātur* of the Assault on Fāṭima?

Asides from the cluster of inauthentic Twelver traditions that I had referenced throughout my assessment of passage 8 in chapter 3, which claim that a physical assault against Fāṭima took place, there are a few other Twelver traditions that I had not referenced for the sake of brevity. Nonetheless, I will entertain a pivotal question regarding those Shīʿite reports: can the multiplicity of Twelver Shīʿite isnāds behind the claim that Fāṭima was murdered be cited as evidence of this event's *tawātur* or authenticity?

Barring the fact that much of the Twelver literature in this regard is demonstrably inauthentic according to Twelver standards, let alone non-Twelver ones, I will assess an unrelated Prophetic tradition recorded in some sources to provide the reader with a live example that should contextualize the theoretical element of this discussion. The report at hand is a bizarre prophetic tradition relayed in several Sunnī and Zaydī sources where the Prophet is essentially quoted stating that there shall be a misguided group of people after him known as the *Rāfiḍa* and that they must be combatted since they shared the same status as polytheists (*mushrikūn*) etc.

Here is an example of one of this tradition's variants. Abū Yaʿlā al-Mawṣilī (d. 307) relayed via Abū al-Jaḥḥāf Dāwūd b. Abī ʿAwf, on the authority of Muḥamad b. ʿAmr al-Hāshimī, from Zaynab bt. ʿAlī, from Fāṭima bt. Muḥammad that she said:

> The Prophet ﷺ once looked at ʿAlī and said, "This one shall be in heaven. Among his Shīʿa are a group of people who know Islam and then reject it. They have a nickname, and they are called the *Rāfiḍa.*

> Whosoever encounters them must slay them, for they are polytheists (*mushrikūn*)."[1]

عَنْ أَبِي الْجَحَّافِ دَاوُدَ بْنِ أَبِي عَوْفٍ، عَنْ مُحَمَّدِ بْنِ عَمْرٍو الْهَاشِمِيِّ، عَنْ زَيْنَبَ بِنْتِ عَلِيٍّ، عَنْ فَاطِمَةَ بِنْتِ مُحَمَّدٍ، قَالَتْ: نَظَرَ النَّبِيُّ إِلَى عَلِيٍّ، فَقَالَ, "هَذَا فِي الْجَنَّةِ، وَإِنَّ مِنْ شِيعَتِهِ قَوْمًا يَعْلَمُونَ الإِسْلامَ، ثُمَّ يَرْفُضُونَهُ، لَهُمْ نَبَزٌ يُسَمَّوْنَ الرَّافِضَةَ، مَنْ لَقِيَهُمْ فَلْيَقْتُلْهُمْ فَإِنَّهُمْ مُشْرِكُونَ."

The Sunnī and Shīʿite reader alike may be surprised to learn that this tradition was recorded through many isnāds in various sources. What is further noteworthy about this tradition is that it was mostly relayed through Shīʿite transmitters, and it was recorded in several Zaydī sources as well![2] For context, I have constructed a series of schematics that outline some of this tradition's routes of transmission through ʿAlī b. Abī Ṭālib, Ibn ʿAbbās, Fāṭima, Umm Salama and Ibn ʿUmar.

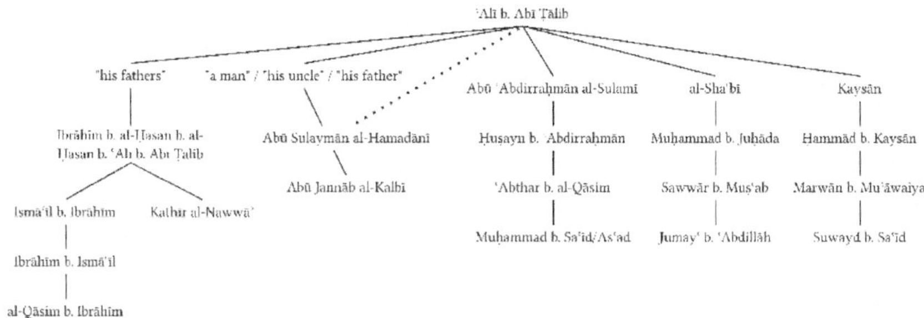

Figure 4.1 A schematic outlining some routes of transmission for the aforementioned ḥadīth via ʿAlī b. Abī Ṭālib

1 Musnad Abī Yaʿlā al-Mawṣilī (12/116)
2 Kitāb al-ʿUlūm by al-Murādī (2/305), al-Aḥkām by Yaḥyā b. al-Ḥusayn al-Rassī (1/401)

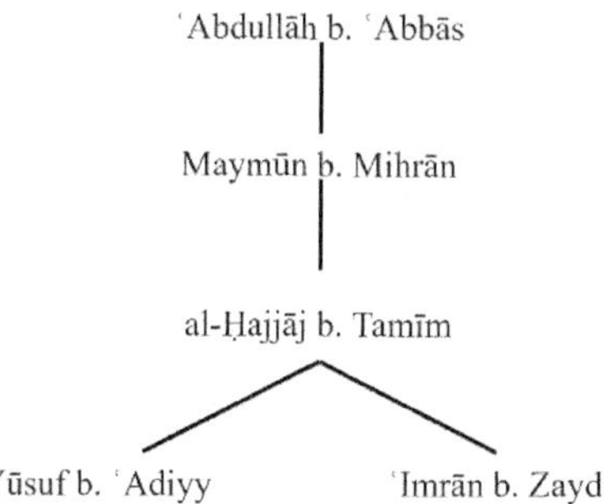

Figure 4.2 A schematic outlining some routes of transmission for the aforementioned ḥadīth via Ibn ʿAbbās

Asides from the past sources, the tradition is also relayed from Fāṭima,[1] Umm Salama,[2] and ʿAbdullāh b. ʿUmar b. al-Khaṭṭāb through other isnāds.[3]

Despite what appears to be a multitude of independent isnāds for this alleged prophetic tradition, several scholars, such as Ibn Taymiyya (d. 728) and Sheikh Nāṣiruddīn al-Albānī (d. 1420), rightfully declared this tradition to be a fabrication.[4] Why is that the case? Do these numerous isnāds not corroborate each other such that the report can be elevated to the rank of *ḥasan*, *ṣaḥīḥ* or even *mutawātir*?

The answer to that question lies in the fact that the numerous isnāds cited for this tradition, which appear to be independent of each other, actually are quite interdependent. The isnāds that cite seemingly different sources relaying this ḥadīth all the way back to the Prophet ﷺ merely are pseudo-corroborations that falsely provide the illusion of independence: they actually originate from a shared source. A careful assessment of this tradition's isnāds will demonstrate that it was exclusively relayed by a slew of forgers and unreliable transmitters. Forgers often stole traditions from other sources and then invented their own isnāds for those traditions, and severely incompetent and unreliable transmitters often attributed traditions to incorrect isnāds isnāds and delusionally claimed to relay them through those imaginary routes. Hence, a tradition that is relayed through a bundle

1 Al-ʿIlal al-Wārida fī al-Aḥādīth al-Nabawiyya by al-Dāraquṭnī (15/180)
2 Al-Muʿjam al-Awsaṭ by al-Ṭabarānī (6/354), al-Sharīʿa by al-Ājurrī (5/2514), al-Sunna by Ibī ʿĀṣim (2/475)
3 Al-Sharīʿa by al-Ājurrī (5/2513), Tārīkh Dimashq by Ibn ʿAsākir (42/335)
4 Minhāj al-Sunna al-Nabawiyya by Ibn Taymiyya (1/36), Silsilat al-Aḥādīth al-Ḍaʿīfa wa-l-Mawḍūʿa by al-Albānī (12/186)

of apparently independent isnāds may, in fact, prove to originate from a single unreliable source. The number of isnāds for that dubious tradition would then only proliferate with the progression of time, giving rise to what appears to be a mass-transmitted ḥadīth from ʿAlī b. Abī Ṭālib and others, as can be observed with this tradition.

In this context, I am certain that Twelver Shīʿite readers of this tradition would not be flattered by its contents, let alone convinced in its authenticity, despite its seemingly prolific transmission in early Zaydī and Kūfan Shīʿite circles. I believe Sunnī and Twelver Shīʿite scholarship should generally be in agreement, albeit for different reasons, that a mere abundance of flimsy and questionable isnāds attached to this tradition does not necessarily lend it credibility and authority. It is in this context where one would hope for consistency and fairness from all participants in such historical discussions.

The belief that Fāṭima was physically assaulted by ʿUmar and his aides is, in multiple regards, an analogous scenario to the past prophetic tradition, if not an even more evidently dubious claim. A cluster of late second, third and fourth century Rāfiḍite transmitters (mainly from the city of Kūfa) ascribed traditions to figures from *Ahlulbayt* stating that Fāṭima was physically assaulted by the Prophet's companions following his death. Though these traditions may appear to be mass-transmitted in Twelver Shīʿite sources today, they are far from that. Rather, these claims and traditions are not independent of each other: they originate from a quite narrow geographic range within a very particular Shīʿite subcommunity that was, more or less, a minority among the Shīʿa at one point in history, let alone the greater Muslim body. Furthermore, the staunchly Rāfiḍite individuals who relayed these traditions had a vested interest in proliferating traditions that vilified Abū Bakr and ʿUmar, for they were in desperate search of any material to nullify both men's legitimacy and authority. When that is taken into account, alongside the fact that numerous internal and external contradictions and discrepancies plague this Rāfiḍite narrative, one becomes even more assured in these claims' dubious origins.

What should further highlight the unreliability and ahistoricity of this narrative is the fact that many of the traditions cited in Twelver sources about this purported historical event actually are unreliable and inauthentic according to Twelver ḥadīth standards, let alone Sunnī and other non-Twelver ones! Hence, the handful of traditions found in Twelver sources that reiterate some of the claims found in *Kitāb Sulaym* merely are the byproduct of direct and indirect collusion between their transmitters, and they cannot be deemed independent, organic accounts.

The narrative found in *Kitāb Sulaym* merely is a polemical Rāfiḍite attempt to exploit the otherwise benign historical event where ʿUmar is said to have directed a threat at the congregants in Fāṭima's house to disband their gathering. Some Rāfiḍite transmitters found an opportunity in this historical event to vilify Abū Bakr and ʿUmar and undermine their legitimacy, hence developing and embellishing accounts about this incident that were increasingly more vilifying and damning with the progression of time. What initially commenced as a mere threat directed at ʿAlī and his associates followed by a brief brawl outside Fāṭima's house eventually was exploded into a dramatic tragedy where the purportedly pregnant Fāṭima was violently struck with a whip, squeezed with a door and made to miscarry her fetus as the alleged assailants dramatically stormed her house, among a host of other dramatic theatrical accretions.

I shall finally conclude this book with a statement by Ibn Taymiyya (d. 728) in his *magnum opus* refutation against Twelver theology, *Minhāj al-Sunna al-Nabawiyya fī Naqḍ Kalām al-Shīʿa wa-l-Qadariyya*, regarding the alleged assault on Fāṭima. Though his statement(s) are quite harsh in their wording, my intention merely is to convey his perspective, which should be representative of the majority of Muslim scholarship in this context. Ibn Taymiyya said:

> Some of them claim that they beat Fāṭima's stomach until she suffered a miscarriage; that they demolished her house's roof upon whomever was inside it; and similar lies that anyone with minimal knowledge would recognize as lies. They always approach known and mass-transmitted matters, and they proceed to deny them; and [they then approach] nonexistent things that have no reality to them, and they proceed to affirm them. They have the greatest share in Allah's statement, "Who could be more wicked than the person who invents lies about God or denies the truth? [Quran: 29:68]." They invent lies and bely the Truth...[1]

قال أبو العباس بن تيمية في «منهاج السنة»: وَمِنْهُم مَنْ يَقُولُ: إِنَّهُمْ بَعَجُوا بَطْنَ فَاطِمَةَ حَتَّى أُسْقِطَتْ، وَهَدَمُوا سَقْفَ بَيْتِهَا عَلَى مَنْ فِيهِ، وَأَمْثَالُ هَذِهِ الْأَكَاذِيبِ الَّتِي يَعْلَمُ مَنْ لَهُ أَدْنَى عِلْمٍ وَمَعْرِفَةٍ أَنَّهَا كَذِبٌ، فَهُمْ دَائِمًا يَعْمِدُونَ إِلَى الْأُمُورِ الْمَعْلُومَةِ الْمُتَوَاتِرَةِ يُنْكِرُونَهَا، وَإِلَى الْأُمُورِ الْمَعْدُومَةِ الَّتِي لَا حَقِيقَةَ لَهَا يُثْبِتُونَهَا. فَلَهُمْ أَوْفَرُ نَصِيبٍ مِنْ قَوْلِهِ تَعَالَى: (وَمَنْ أَظْلَمُ مِمَّنِ افْتَرَى عَلَى اللَّهِ كَذِبًا أَوْ كَذَّبَ بِالْحَقِّ) فَهُمْ يَفْتَرُونَ الْكَذِبَ وَيُكَذِّبُونَ بِالْحَقِّ...

1 Minhāj al-Sunna al-Nabawiyya (4/493)

Elsewhere, Ibn Taymiyya also said:

> No one transmits things like this except the ignorant of the liars, and it is believed by the fools of people who claim that the *ṣaḥāba* demolished Fāṭima's house and beat her stomach until she suffered a miscarriage. All of these are made-up lies and claims, per agreement of the people of Islam. It is only believed by whomever is from the category of animals.[1]

وقال أيضا: وَإِنَّمَا يَنْقُلُ مِثْلَ هَذَا جُهَّالُ الْكَذَّابِينَ، وَيُصَدِّقُهُ حَمْقَى الْعَالَمِينَ، الَّذِينَ يَقُولُونَ: إِنَّ الصَّحَابَةَ هَدَمُوا بَيْتَ فَاطِمَةَ، وَضَرَبُوا بَطْنَهَا حَتَّى أَسْقَطَتْ. وَهَذَا كُلُّهُ دَعْوَى مُخْتَلِقٍ، وَإِفْكٌ مُفْتَرًى، بِاتِّفَاقِ أَهْلِ الْإِسْلَامِ، وَلَا يَرُوجُ إِلَّا عَلَى مَنْ هُوَ مِنْ جِنْسِ الْأَنْعَامِ.

All in all, I can finally say that the ending of this book marks the end to this chapter of my life which has spanned more than two years of research as I assessed and evaluated this Twelver Shīʿite narrative pertaining to Fāṭima's demise. Hopefully, it should not only educate the reader about the particular subject of this book, but it should also help him/her understand and contextualize many of the important questions, quandaries and problems that arise throughout discussions on history, especially the rise, proliferation and downfall of ahistorical polemical narratives in later subcommunities within the Muslim world.

1 Minhāj al-Sunna al-Nabawiyya (8/291). I particularly conclude with Ibn Taymiyya's comments because some Shīʿite polemicists today dishonestly claim that Ibn Taymiyya affirmed that an assault on Fāṭima's residence took place, blatantly misrepresenting some comment of his elsewhere.

هذا تمام الكتاب بفضل الله ورحمته، فيه نقض «كتاب سليم بن قيس» الذي هو واد من أودية الكذب التي لم يفتأ الجهلة من الرعاع وأضرابهم يثبتونه مقلّدين في ذلك من قد لبّس عليهم أمرهم من بعض مشيخة الإمامية.

ثم إنك – أيها القارئ – إذا استمعت إلى مزاعم القوم في إطراء هذا الكتاب وتثبيت حجيته والثناء على رواته حسبته في أول الأمر جبلاً صعبَ المرتقى لا سبيل إلى نقضه؛ حتى إذا ما أمعنت النظر في هذا الكتاب وأسانيده المزعومة ومتونه الركيكة المنظومة بان لك وهنُ تلك الدعاوي الخاوية، فكان لسان حال القوم قول القائل «تمخّض الجبل فولد فأرا»، وقول القائل «سمعنا جعجعة ولم نر طحينا»، وقول الشاعر:

مِمّا يُزهّدني في أرْضِ أنْدَلُسٍ ... أَسماءُ مُقْتَدِرٍ فيْها ومُعْتَضِدِ

أَلْقابُ مَمْلَكَةٍ في غَيْرَ مَوْضِعِهَا ... كالهِرِّ يَحْكِي انتِفاخًا صَولَةَ الأَسَدِ

فالحمد لله دائما وأبدا، والحمد لله أولا وآخرا، والحمد لله ظاهرا وباطنا، وصلى الله على المصطفى وعلى آله وأصحابه وأزواجه وذريته وأمته وإخوانه من الأنبياء إلى يوم الدين، آمين يا رب العالمين.

وكتب عبد الله بن محمد الرباط حامدًا مصلّيًا مسلّما.

BIBLIOGRAPHY

Al-Ābī, Manṣūr b. al-Ḥusayn, *Nathr al-Dur fī al-Muḥāḍarāt*, Khālid ʿAbdulGhanī Maḥfūẓ, ed., 1st ed., (Beirut, 1424/2004).

Al-Ājurrī, Abū ʿUbayd, *Su'ālāt Abī ʿUbayd al-Ājurrī li-Abī Dāwūd al-Sijistānī fī al-Jarḥ wa-l-Taʿdīl*, Muḥammad ʿAlī Al-ʿUmarī, ed., 1st ed., (Medina, 1403/1983).

Al-Ājurrī, Muḥammad b. al-Ḥusayn, *al-Sharīʿa*, ʿAbdullāh bin ʿUmar Al-Damījī, ed., 2nd ed., (Riyadh, 1420/1999).

Al-ʿAlawī, ʿAbdulHādī, "Kitāb Ithbāt Al-Waṣiyya li-l-Masʿūdī am li-l-Shalmaghānī?" *Al-Khizāna*, no. 7 (2020): 67-171.

Al-ʿAlawī, Abū ʿAbdillāh Muḥammad b. ʿAlī b. al-Ḥusayn, *Tasmiyat man Rawā ʿan al-Imām Zayd min al-Tābiʿīn*, Ṣāliḥ ʿAbdullāh Qarbān, ed., 1st ed., (Sanaa, 1423/2003).

Al-ʿAlawī, ʿAlī b. Muḥammad Abī al-Ghanā'im, *al-Majdī fī Ansāb al-Ṭālibiyyīn*, Aḥmed Al-Dāmghānī, ed., 2nd ed., (Qom, 1422).

Al-Albānī, Nāṣiruddīn Muḥammad, *Silsilat al-Aḥādīth al-Ḍaʿīfa wa-l-Mawḍūʿa wa-Atharuhā al-Sayyi' fī al-Umma*, 1st ed., (Riyadh, 1412/1992).

Al-Amīn, Moḥsen, *Aʿyān al-Shīʿa*, Ḥasan Al-Amīn, ed., 5th ed., (Beirut, 1403/1983).

Amir-Moezzi, Mohammad Ali, *The Silent Qur'ān and the Speaking Qur'ān: Scriptural Sources of Islam Between History and Fervor*, New York, 2016.

Al-Asadī, al-Zubayr b. Bakkār, *al-Akhbār al-Muwaffaqiyyāt*, Sāmī Makkī Al-ʿĀnī, ed., Beirut, 1416/1996.

Al-Aṣbahānī, Abū Nuʿaym Aḥmed b. ʿAbdillāh, *al-Ḍuʿafā'*, Farūq Ḥamādah, ed., 1st ed., (Casablanca, 1405/1984).

——. *Maʿrifat al-Ṣaḥāba*, ʿĀdil bin Yūsuf Al-ʿAzzāzī, ed., 1st ed., (Riyadh, 1419/1998).

Al-ʿAyyāshī, Muḥammad b. Masʿūd, *al-Tafsīr*, 1st ed., (Qom, 1421).

Al-Azdī, Maʿmar b. Rāshid, *al-Jāmiʿ*, Ḥabīb Al-Raḥmān Al-Aẓmī, ed., 2nd ed., (s.l., 1390/1970).

——. *The Expeditions: An Early Biography of Muḥammad*, Translated by Sean Anthony, New York, 2014.

Al-Azdī, Muqātil b. Sulaymān, *Tafsīr Muqātil Ibn Sulaymān*, Aḥmed Farīd, ed., 2nd ed., (Beirut, 1441/2020).

Al-Baghdādī, al-Khaṭīb Aḥmed b. ʿAlī b. Thābit, *al-Asmāʾ al-Mubhama fī al-Anbāʾ al-Muḥkama*, ʿIzzaldine ʿAlī Al-Sayyed, ed., 3rd ed., (Cairo, 1417/1997).

——. *al-Jāmiʿ li-Akhlāq al-Rāwī wa-Ādāb al-Sāmiʿ*, Maḥmūd al-Ṭaḥḥān, ed., Riyadh, 1403/1983.

——. *al-Kifāya fī ʿIlm al-Riwāya*, Ibrāhīm Ḥamdī al-Madanī and Abū ʿAbdillāh al- Sūrqī, eds., Medīna, n.d.

——. *Muwaḍḍiḥ Awhām al-Jamʿ wa-l-Tafrīq Bayn al-Ruwāt*, ʿAbdulMuʿṭī Amīn Qalʿajī, ed., 1st ed., (Beirut, 1407).

——. *Talkhīṣ al-Mutashābih fī al-Rasm*, Sukayna Al-Shihābī, ed., 1st ed., (Damascus, 1985).

——. *Tārīkh Baghdād*, Bashar ʿAwwād Maʿrūf, ed., 1st ed., (Beirut, 1422/2002).

Al-Bakjarī, Mughulṭāy b. Qalīj, *Ikmāl Tahdhīb al-Kamāl fī Asmāʾ al-Rijāl*, ʿĀdil bin Muḥammad and Usāma bin Ibrāhīm, eds., 1st ed., (Cairo, 1422/2001).

Al-Balādhurī, Aḥmed b. Yaḥyā, *Jumalun min Ansāb al-Ashrāf*, Suhayl Zakkār, ed., 1st ed., (Beirut, 1417/1996).

Bāmakhrama, al-Ṭayyib b. ʿAbdillāh, *Qulādat al-Naḥr fī Wafayāt Aʿyān al-Dahr*, Būjumʿa Makrī and Khālid Zuwwārī, eds., 1st ed., (Jeddah, 1428/2008).

Al-Bardhaʿī, Saʿīd b. ʿAmr, *Suʾālāt al-Bardhaʿī li-Abī Zurʿa al-Rāzī*, Muḥammad bin ʿAlī Al-Azharī, ed., 1st ed., (Cairo, 2009).

Al-Barqī, Aḥmed b. ʿAbdillāh, *Rijāl al-Barqī*, Ḥaydar Al-Baghdādī, ed., 2nd ed., (Qom, 1433).

Al-Bayhaqī, Aḥmed b. al-Ḥusayn, *Dalāʾil al-Nubuwwa wa-Maʿrifat Aḥwāl Ṣāḥib al-Sharīʿa*, 1st ed., (Beirut, 1405).

——. *al-Sunan al-Kubrā*, Muḥammad ʿAbdulQādir ʿAṭā, ed., 3rd ed., (Beirut, 1424/2003).

Al-Bazzār, Aḥmed b. ʿAmr, *Musnad al-Bazzār*, Maḥfūẓ Al-Raḥmān Zaynallah et al., eds., 1st ed., (Medina, 1988-2009).

Al-Behbūdī, Muḥammad Bāqir, *Maʿrifat al-Ḥadīth*, 1st ed., (Beirut, 1427/2006).

Bentham, Jeremy, *A Treatise on Judicial Evidence*, London, 1825.

Al-Bukhārī, Muḥammad b. Ismāʿīl, *al-Adab al-Mufrad*, ʿAlī ʿAbdulBāsiṭ Mazīd and ʿAlī Riḍwān, eds., 1st ed., (Egypt, 1423/2003).

——. *Ṣāḥīḥ al-Bukhārī*, Muḥammad Zuhayr Al-Nāṣir, ed., 1st ed., (Beirut, 1422)

——. *al-Tārīkh al-Awsaṭ*, Maḥmūd Ibrāhīm Zāyid, ed., 1st ed., (Aleppo/Cairo, 1397/1997).

——. *al-Tārīkh al-Kabīr*, Muḥammad ʿAbdulMuʿīd Khān, ed., Hyderabad, n.d.

Crone, Patricia, *From Arabian Tribes to Islamic Empire: Army State and Society in the Near East*, (Ashgate, 2008).

Al-Dāraquṭnī, ʿAlī b. ʿUmar, *al-Ḍuʿafāʾ wa-l-Matrūkūn*, ʿAbdulRaḥīm Muḥammad Al-Qashqarī, ed., Medīna, 1403.

——. *al-ʿIlal al-Wārida fī al-Aḥādīth al-Nabawiyya*, Maḥfūẓ Al-Raḥmān Al-Salafī, ed., 1st ed., (Riyadh, 1405/1985).

——. *al-Muʾtalif wa-l-Mukhtalif*, Muwaffaq ʿAbdulQādir, ed., 1st ed., (Beirut, 1406/1986).

Al-Dhahabī, Muḥammad b. Aḥmed b. ʿUthmān, *Siyar Aʿlām al-Nubalāʾ*, Shuʿayb Al-Arnāʾūṭ et al., ed., 3rd ed., (Beirut, 1405/1985).

——. *Tārīkh al-Islām*, Bashār ʿAwwād Maʿrūf, ed., 1st ed., (Beirut, 2003).

Al-Dimashqī, Abū Zurʿa ʿAbdurraḥmān b. ʿAmr, *Tārīkh Abī Zurʿa al-Dimashqī*, Shukrullāh Al-Qūjānī, Damascus, n.d.

Al-Dūlābī, Muḥammad b. Aḥmed b. Ḥammād, *al-Dhurriyya al-Ṭāhira*, Saʿd Mubārak Al-Ḥasan, ed., 1st ed., (Kuwait, 1407).

——. *al-Kunā wa-l-Asmāʾ*, Naẓar Al-Fāryābī, ed., 1st ed., (Beirut, 1421/2000).

Al-Dūrī, ʿAbbās b. Muḥammad, *Tārīkh Ibn Maʿīn – Riwāyat al-Dūrī*, Aḥmed Muḥammad Nūr Sayf, ed., 1st ed., (Mecca, 1399/1979).

Ehrman, Bart, *Forged: Writing in the Name of God—Why the Bible's Authors Are Not Who We Think They Are*, New York, 2011.

Al-Fākihī, Abū Muḥammad ʿAbdullāh b. Muḥammad b. al-ʿAbbās, *Fawāʾid Abī Muḥammad al-Fākihī*, Muḥammad bin ʿAbdillāh b. ʿĀyiḍ Al-Ghibbānī, ed., 1st ed., (Riyadh, 1419/1998).

Al-Fallās, ʿAmr b. ʿAlī, *Kitāb al-Tārīkh*, Muḥammad Al-Ṭabarānī, ed., 2nd ed., (Riyadh, 1441/2020).

Al-Ghassānī, Muḥammad b. al-Fayḍ, *Akhbār wa-Ḥikāyāt*, Ibrāhīm Ṣāliḥ, ed., 1st ed., (Damascus, 1994).

Al-Ghaṭafānī, Ḍirār b. ʿAmr, *al-Tāḥrīsh*, Ḥusayn Khānṣo and Muḥammad Kasikīm eds., 1st ed., (Istanbul, 1435/2014)

Grafton, Anthony, *Forgers and Critics: Creativity and Duplicity in Western Scholarship*, London, 1990.

Al-Hamadhānī, al-Qāḍī ʿAbdulJabbār b. Aḥmed, *Tathbīt Dalāʾil al-Nubuwwa,* ʿAbdulKarīm ʿUthmān, ed., Beirut, 1966.

Al-Ḥamawī, Abū al-Fidāʾ Ismāʿīl b. ʿAlī, *al-Mukhtaṣar fī Akhbār al-Bashar*, 1st ed., (Cairo, 1907).

Al-Ḥarrānī, Abū ʿArūba al-Ḥusayn b. Muḥammad, *al-Muntaqā min Kitāb al-Ṭabaqāt li-Abī ʿArūba al-Ḥarrānī*, Ibrāhīm Ṣāliḥ, ed., 1st ed., (Damascus, 1994).

Al-Hārūnī, Abū Ṭālib Yaḥyā b. al-Ḥusayn, *al-Ifāda fī Tārīkh al-Aʾimma al-Sāda*, ed., 4th ed., (Ṣaʿda, 1435/2014).

——. *Taysīr al-Maṭālib fī Amālī Abī Ṭālib*, ʿAbdullāh Al-ʿAzzī, ed., 1st ed., (Sanaa, 1422/2002).

Al-Ḥasanī, Abū al-ʿAbbās Aḥmed b. Ibrāhīm, *al-Maṣābīḥ*, ʿAbdullāh bin ʿAbdullāh Al-Ḥūthī, ed., 2nd ed., (Sanaa, 1423/2002).

Al-Hilālī, Sulaym b. Qays, *Kitāb Sulaym Ibn Qays al-Hilālī*, Muḥammad Bāqir Al-Anṣārī Al-Zanjānī, ed., 1st ed., (Qom, 1420).

Al-Ḥillī, Ḥasan b. Sulaymān, *Mukhtaṣar Baṣāʾir al-Darājāt*, 1st ed., (Najaf, 1370/1950).

Al-Ḥillī, al-Ḥasan b. Yūsuf b. al-Muṭahhar, *Khulāsat al-Aqwāl fī Maʿrifat al-Rijāl*, Jawād Al-Qayyūmī, ed., 4th ed., (Qom, 1431).

Ibn ʿAbdilBarr, Yūsuf b. ʿAbdillāh, *al-Istīʿāb fī Maʿrifat al-Aṣḥāb*, ʿAlī Muḥammad Al-Bajjāwī, ed., 1st ed., (Beirut, 1412/1992).

Ibn Abī ʿĀṣim, Aḥmed b. ʿAmr b. al-Ḍaḥḥāk, *al-Āḥād wa-l-Mathānī*, Bāsim Al-Jawabrah, ed., 1st ed., (Riyadh, 1411/1991).

Ibn Abī al-Ḥadīd, ʿAbdulḤamīd b. Hibatullāh, *Sharḥ Nahj al-Balāgha*, Muḥammad Abū Al-Faḍl Ibrāhīm, ed., 1st ed., (s.l., 1378/1959)

Ibn Abī Ḥātim al-Rāzī, ʿAbdurraḥmān b. Muḥammad, *Bayān Khaṭaʾ al-Bukhārī fī Tarīkhih*, ʿAbdurraḥmān Al-Muʿallimī Al-Yamānī, ed., Hyderabad, n.d.

——. *al-Jarḥ wa-l-Taʿdīl*, ʿAbdurraḥmān Al-Muʿallimī Al-Yamānī, ed., 1st ed., (Beirut, 1371/1952).

——. *Tafsīr al-Qurʾān al-ʿAẓīm*, Asʿad Muḥammad Al-Ṭayyib, ed., 3rd ed., (KSA, 1419).

Ibn Abī Khaythama, Aḥmed, *al-Tārīkh al-Kabīr – al-Sifr al-Thālith*, Ṣalāḥ Fatḥī Hilāl, ed., 1st ed., (Cairo, 1427/2006).

Ibn Abī Shayba, Abū Bakr ʿAbdullāh, *al-Muṣannaf*, Muḥammad ʿAwwāma, ed., 1st ed., (Beirut, 1427/2006).

Ibn Abī Shayba, Muḥammad b. ʿUthmān, *Suʾālāt Muḥammad b. ʿUthmān b. Abī Shayba li-ʿAlī Ibn al-Madīnī*, Muḥammad bin ʿAlī Al-Azharī, ed., 1st ed., (Cairo, 2006).

Ibn ʿAdī, ʿAbdullah, *Al-Kāmil fī Ḍuʿafāʾ al-Rijāl*, ʿĀdil Aḥmed ʿAbdilMawjūd and ʿAlī Muḥammad Maʿwaḍ, eds., 1st ed., (Beirut, 1418/1997).

Ibn ʿAmmār, Hishām, *Ḥadīth Hishām Ibn ʿAmmār*, ʿAbdullāh bin Wakīl Al-Sheikh, ed., 1st ed., (KSA, 1419/1999).

Ibn ʿAsākir, ʿAlī b. al-Ḥasan, *Tārīkh Dimashq*, ʿAmr bin Gharāmah Al-ʿAmrawī, ed., 1st ed., (Beirut, 1415/1995).

Ibn al-Athīr, ʿAlī b. Muḥammad, al-Kāmil fī al-Tārīkh, ʿUmar Tadmurī, ed., 1st ed., (Beirut, 1417/1997).

——. *Usd al-Ghāba fī Maʿrifat al-Ṣaḥāba*, Beirut, 1409.

Ibn Bābawayh, ʿAlī b. al-Ḥusayn, *al-Imāma wa-l-Tabṣira min al-Ḥayra*, 1st ed., (Qom, 1404).

Ibn Bābawayh, al-Ṣadūq Muḥammad b. ʿAlī, *Kamāl al-Dīn wa-Tamām al-Niʿma*, Ḥusayn Al-Aʿlamī, ed., 1st ed., (Beirut, 1412/1991).

——. *al-Khiṣāl*, ʿAlī Akbar Ghaffārī, ed., (Qom, 1403).

——. *ʿUyūn Akhbār al-Riḍā*, 1st ed., (Qom, 1378 SH)

Ibn al-Ghaḍāʾirī, Aḥmed b. al-Ḥusayn, *al-Rijāl*, Muḥammad Reḍa Al-Ḥusaynī Al-Jalālī, ed., 1st ed., (Qom, 1422).

Ibn Ḥajar al-ʿAsqalānī, Aḥmed b. ʿAlī, *Fatḥ al-Bārī Sharḥ Ṣaḥīḥ al-Bukhārī*, Muḥib Al-Dīn Al-Khaṭīb, ed., Beirut, 1379.

——. *al-Iṣaba fī-Tamyīz al-Ṣaḥaba*, ʿĀdil Aḥmed ʿAbdulMawjūd and ʿAlī Muḥammad Miʿwaḍ, eds., 1st ed., (Beirut, 1415).

——. *Lisān al-Mīzān*, ʿAbdulFattāḥ Abū Ghudda, ed., 1st ed., (Beirut, 2002).

——. *Tahdhīb al-Tahdhīb*, Ibrāhīm Al-Zaybaq and ʿĀdil Murshid, eds., 1st ed., (Damascus, 1435/2014)

Ibn al-Ḥammāmī, ʿAlī b. Aḥmed b. ʿUmar, *Majmūʿ fīh Muṣannafāt Abī al-Ḥasan Ibn al-Ḥammāmī wa-Ajzāʾ Ḥadīthiyya Ukhrā*, Nabīl Jarrār, ed., 1st ed., (Riyadh, 1425/2004)

Ibn Ḥamza, Yaḥyā, *Majmūʿ al-Imām al-Muʾayyad bi-Rabb al-ʿIzza Yaḥyā Ibn Ḥamza*, Qāsim Ḥasan Al-Sirājī, ed., 1st ed., (Sanaa, 1431/2010).

Ibn Ḥanbal, Aḥmed b. Muḥammad, *Faḍāʾil al-Ṣaḥāba*, Waṣiyyullāh Muḥammad ʿAbbās, ed., 1st ed., (Beirut, 1403/1983).

——. *Musnad al-Imām Aḥmed Ibn Ḥanbal*, Shuʿayb Al-Arnāʾūṭ et al., eds., 1st ed., (Beirut, 1421/2001).

Ibn Ḥazm, ʿAlī b. Aḥmed, *Jamharat Ansāb al-ʿArab*, 1st ed., (Beirut, 1403/1983).

Ibn Ḥibbān, Muḥammad, *Kitāb al-Majrūḥīn min al-Muḥaddithīn wa-l-Ḍuʿafāʿ wa-l-Matrūkīn*, Maḥmūd Ibrāhīm Zāyed, ed., 1st ed., (Aleppo, 1396).

——. *Kitāb al-Thiqāt*, Muḥammad ʿAbdulMuʿīd Khān, ed., 1st ed., (Hyderabad, 1393/1973).

——. *Ṣaḥīḥ Ibn Ḥibbān*, Muḥammad ʿAlī Sonmez and Khāliṣ Aydemīr, eds., 1st ed., (Beirut , 1433).

Ibn Hishām, ʿAbdulMalik b. Hishām, *al-Sīra al-Nabawiyya*, Muṣṭafā Al-Saqqā et al., ed., 2nd ed., (Cairo, 1375/1955).

Ibn Isḥāq, Muḥammad, *al-Siyar wa-l-Maghāzī*, Suhayl Zakkār, ed., 1st ed., (Beirut, 1398/1978).

Ibn al-Jawzī, ʿAbdurraḥmān b. ʿAlī, *al-Ḍuʿafāʾ wa-l-Matrūkūn*, ʿAbdullāh Al-Qāḍī, ed., 1st ed., (Beirut, 1406).

——. *Talqīḥ Fuhūm Ahl al-Athar*, 1st ed., (Beirut, 1997).

Ibn Kathīr, Ismāʿīl b. ʿUmar, *al-Bidāya wa-l-Nihāya*, ʿAbdullāh bin ʿAbdilMuḥsen Al-Turkī, ed., 1st ed., (Giza, 1418/1998)

Ibn Khaldūn, ʿAbdurraḥmān b. Muḥammad, *Muqaddimat Ibn Khaldūn*, Darwīsh al-Jawīdī, ed., 2nd ed., (Sidon/Beirut, 1436/2015).

Ibn Manda, ʿAbdurraḥmān b. Muḥammad b. Isḥāq, *al-Mustakhraj min Kutub al-Nās li-l-Tadhkira wa-l-Mustaṭraf min Aḥwāl al-Rijāl li-l-Maʿrifa*, ʿĀmir Ḥasan Ṣabrī Al-Tamīmī, ed., Bahrain, n.d.

Ibn Miḥriz, Aḥmed b. Muḥammad, *Tārīkh Ibn Maʿīn – Riwāyat Ibn Miḥriz*, Muḥammad Kāmil Al-Qaṣṣār, ed., 1st ed., (Damascus, 1405/1985).

Ibn Muḥammad, Yaḥyā b al-Ḥusayn b. al-Qāsim, *al-Īḍāḥ li-mā Khafā min al-Ittifāq ʿalā Taʿẓīm Ṣaḥābat al-Muṣṭafā*, ʿAbdurraḥmān bin ʿAbdulQādir Al-Muʿallimī, ed., 1st ed., (Sharja/Cairo, 1426/2006).

Ibn al-Nadīm, Muḥammad b. Isḥāq, *al-Fihrist*, Ibrāhīm Ramaḍān, ed., 2nd ed., (Beirut, 1417/1997).

Ibn al-Qaysarānī, Muḥammad b. Ṭāhir, *Aṭrāf al-Gharāʾib wa-l-Afrād*, Jābir Al-Sarayyiʿ, ed., 1st ed., (Riyadh, 1428).

Ibn Qudāma, ʿAbdullāh b. Aḥmed, *al-Muntakhab min ʿIlal al-Khallāl*, Ṭāriq bin ʿAwaḍallāh, ed., 1st ed., (Riyadh, 1419/1998).

——. *al-Tabyīn fī Ansāb al-Qurashiyyīn*, Muḥammad Al-Dulaymī, ed., 1st ed., (Baghdād, 1982/1402).

Ibn Qutayba, ʿAbdullāh b. Muslim *Gharīb al-Ḥadīth*, ʿAbdullāh al-Jbūrī, ed., 1st ed., (Baghdād, 1397).

——. *al-Maʿārif*, Tharwat ʿUkāsha, ed., 2nd ed., (Cairo, 1982).

Ibn Rajab, ʿAbdurrāḥmān b. Aḥmed, *Sharḥ ʿIlal al-Tirmidhī*, Hammām ʿAbdurraḥīm Saʿīd, ed., 1st ed., (Zarqa, 1407/1987).

Ibn Saʿd, Muḥammad, *al-Ṭabaqāt al-Kabīr*, ʿAlī Muḥammad ʿUmar, ed., 1st ed., (Cairo, 1421/2001).

Ibn Shabba, ʿUmar, *Tārīkh al-Madīna*, Fahīm Muḥammad Shaltūt, ed., Jeddah, 1399.

Ibn Shaddād, Muḥammad b. ʿAlī, *al-Aʿlāq al-Khaṭīra fī Dhikr Umarāʾ al-Shām wa-l-Jazīra*, Yaḥyā ʿAbbāra, ed., 1st ed., (Damascus, 1991).

Ibn Shādhān al-Qummī, Muḥammad b. Aḥmed, *Miʾat Manqaba min Manāqib Amīr al-Muʾminīn wa-l-Aʾimma min Waladih min Ṭarīq al-ʿĀmma*, 2nd ed., (Qom, 1387 SH).

Ibn Shāhīn, ʿUmar b. Aḥmed, *Tārīkh Asmāʾ al-Ḍuʿafāʾ wa-l-Kadhdhābīn*, Muḥammad bin ʿAlī Al-Azharī, ed., 1st ed., (Cairo, 1430/2009).

Ibn Shahr Āshūb, Muḥammad b. ʿAlī, *Manāqib Āl Abī Ṭālib*, 2nd ed.m (Beirut, 1412/1991).

Ibn Taymiyya, Aḥmed b. ʿAbdilḤalīm, *Minhāj al-Sunna al-Nabawiyya fī Naqḍ Kalām al-Shīʿa al-Qadariyya*, Muḥammad Rashād Sālim, ed., 1st ed., (Riyadh, 1406/1986).

Ibn ʿUqba, Mūsā, *Aḥādīth Muntakhaba Min Maghāzī Mūsā Ibn ʿUqba*, selected by Yūsuf b. Muḥammad b. ʿUmar b. Qāḍī Shahba, Mashhūr bin Ḥasan Āl Salmān, ed., 1st ed., (Beirut, 1991).

Ibn Zabr al-Rabʿī, Muḥammad b. ʿAbdillāh, *Tārīkh Mawlid al-ʿUlamāʾ wa-Wafayātihim*, ʿAbdullāh Aḥmed Sulaymān Al-Ḥamad, ed., 1st ed., (Riyadh, 1410).

Ibn Zanjawayh, Ḥumayd b. Makhlad, *al-Amwāl*, Shākir Dhīb Fayyāḍ, ed., 1st ed., (Riyadh, 1406/1986).

Al-ʿIjlī, Aḥmed b. ʿAbdillāh b. Ṣāliḥ, *Tārīkh al-Thiqāt*, ʿAbdulMuʿṭī Qalʿajī, ed., 1st ed., (Beirut, 1405).

Al-ʿIrāqī, ʿAbdurrāḥīm, b. al-Ḥusayn, *Dhayl Mīzān al-Iʿtidāl*, ʿAlī Muḥammad Maʿwaḍ and ʿĀdil Aḥmed ʿAbdulMawjūd, eds., 1st ed., (Beirut, 1416/1995).

Al-Jawāhirī, Muḥammad, *al-Mufīd min Muʿjam Rijāl al-Ḥadīth*, 1st ed., (Beirut, 1430/2009).

Joe Nickell, *Detecting Forgery: Forensic Investigation of Documents*, Lexington, 2005.

Al-Karājikī, Muḥammad b. ʿAlī b. ʿUthmān, *al-Istinṣār fī al-Naṣṣ ʿalā al-Aʾimma al-Aṭhār*, Najaf, 1346.

Al-Kashshī, Muḥammad b. ʿUmar, *Rijāl al-Kashshī*, Aḥmed Al-Ḥusaynī, ed., 1st ed., (Beirut, 1430/2009).

Al-Khalīlī, Abū Yaʿlā al-Khalīl b. ʿAbdillāh, *al-Irshād fī Maʿrifat ʿUlamāʾ al-Ḥadīth*, Walīd Mitwallī Muḥammad, ed., 1st ed., (Cairo, 1431/2010).

Al-Khallāl, Abū Bakr Aḥmed b. Muḥammad, *al-Sunna,* ʿAṭiyyah Al-Zahrānī, ed., 1st ed., (Riyadh, 1410/1989).

Al-Kharsān, Muḥammad Mahdī, *al-Muḥassin al-Sibṭ Mawlud am Siqṭ,* 2nd ed., (Qom, 1430).

Al-Khoei, Abū al-Qāsim, *Muʿjam Rijāl al-Ḥadīth,* 5th ed., 1413/1992.

Al-Khuṣaybī, al-Ḥusayn b. Ḥamdān, *al-Hidāya al-Kubrā,* 4th ed., (Beirut, 1411/1991)

Al-Kūfī, Muḥammad b. Sulaymān, *Manāqib al-Imām Amīr al-Muʾminīn,* Muḥammad Bāqir al-Maḥmūdī, ed., 1st ed., (Qom, 1412). https://hz.turathalanbiaa.com/public/3453.pdf

Al-Kulaynī, Muḥammad b. Yaʿqūn, *al-Kāfī,* 1st ed., (Beirut, 1428/2007).

Al-Majlisī, Muḥammad Bāqir, *Biḥār al-Anwār al-Jāmiʿa li-Durar al-Aʾimma al-Akhyār,* 2nd ed., (Beirut, 1403/1983).

Al-Malṭī, Muḥammad b. Aḥmed, *al-Tanbīh wa-l-Radd ʿalā Ahl al-Ahwāʾ wa-l-Bidaʿ,* Muḥammad Zāhid Al-Kawtharī, ed., n.p., 1388/1968.

Al-Māmaqānī, ʿAbdullāh, *Tanqīḥ al-Maqāl fī ʿIlm al-Rijāl,* Muḥyīddīn Al-Māmaqānī ed., 1st ed., (Qom, 1430).

Al-Maqdisī, al-Muṭahhar b. Ṭāhir, *al-Badʾ wa-l-Tārīkh,* Port Said, n.d.

Al-Masʿūdī, ʿAlī b. al-Ḥusayn, *Murūj al-Dhahab wa-Maʿādin al-Jawhar,* Kamāl Ḥasan Mirʿī, ed., 1st ed., (Sidon/Beirut, 1425/2005).

——. *al-Tanbīh wa-l-Ishrāf,* ʿAbdullāh Al-Ṣāwī, ed., Baghdad, 1357/1938.

Al-Mawṣilī, Abū Yaʿlā Aḥmed b. ʿAlī, *Musnad Abī Yaʿlā,* Ḥusayn Salīm Asad, ed., 1st ed., (Damascus, 1404/1984).

Al-Māzandarānī, Muḥammad Ṣāliḥ, *Sharḥ Uṣūl al-Kāfī,* ʿAlī ʿĀshūr, ed., 2nd ed., (Beirut, 1429/2008).

Al-Mizzī, Abū al-Ḥajjāj Yūsuf, *Tahdhīb al-Kamāl fī Asmāʾ al-Rijāl,* Bashar ʿAwwād Maʿrūf, ed., 3rd ed., (Beirut, 1436/2015).

Modarresi, Hossein, *Tradition and Survival: A Bibliographical Survey of Early Shīʿite Literature,* Oxford, 2003.

Moḥṣenī, Āṣif, *Mashraʿat Biḥār al-Anwār,* 2nd ed., (Beirut, 1426/2005).

Al-Murādī, Muḥammad b. Manṣūr, *Kitāb al-ʿUlūm,* 1st ed., (n.p., 1401/1991)

Al-Najāshī, Aḥmed b. ʿAlī b. Aḥmed, *Rijāl al-Najāshī,* 1st ed., (Beirut, 1431/2010).

Al-Nasāʾī, Aḥmed b. Shuʿayb, *al-Mujtabā min al-Sunan,* ʿAbdulFattāḥ Abū Ghudda, 2nd ed., (Aleppo, 1406/1986).

Al-Naysābūrī, Abū Aḥmed al-Ḥākim Muḥammad b. Muḥammad, *al-Asāmī wa-l-Kunā,* Muḥammad bin ʿAlī Al-Azharī, ed., 1st ed., (Cairo, 1436/2015),

Al-Naysābūrī, al-Faḍl b. Shādhān, *Mukhtaṣar Ithbāt al-Rajʿa*, 1st ed., (Karbalāʾ, 1437/2016).

Al-Naysābūrī, al-Ḥākim Muḥammad b. ʿAbdillāh, *Faḍāʾil Fāṭima al-Zahrāʾ*, ʿAlī Riḍā bin ʿAbdillāh bin ʿAlī Riḍā, ed., 1st ed., (Cairo, 1429/2008).

——. *al-Madkhal ilā al-Ṣaḥīḥ*, Rabīʿ Al-Madkhalī, ed., 1st ed., (Beirut, 1404).

——. *al-Madkhal ilā Kitāb al-Iklīl*, Fuʾād ʿAbdulMunʿim Aḥmed, ed., Alexandria, n.d.

——. *al-Mustadrak ʿalā al-Ṣaḥīḥayn*, Muṣṭafā ʿAbdulqādir ʿAṭā, ed., 1st ed., (Beirut, 1411/1990).

Al-Naysābūrī, Muslim b. al-Ḥajjāj, *Ṣaḥīḥ Muslim*, Muḥammad Fuʾād ʿAbdilBāqī, ed., 1st ed., (Cairo, 1412/1991).

Al-Nuʿmānī, Muḥammad b. Ibrāhīm, *Kitāb al-Ghayba*, Fāris Ḥassūn Karīm, ed., 1st ed., (Beirut, 1432/2011).

Pseudo-Ibn Qutayba, ʿAbdullāh b. Muslim, *al-Imāma wa-l-Siyāsa,* Ibrāhīm Shams Al-Dīn, ed., 1st ed., (Beirut, 1427/2006).

Pseudo-Ibn Rustum al-Ṭabarī, Muḥammad b. Jarīr b. Rustum, *Dalāʾil al-Imāma*, 1st ed., (Beirut, 1439/2018).

Pseudo-al-Masʿūdī, ʿAlī b. al-Ḥusayn, *Ithbāt al-Waṣiyya li-l-Imām ʿAlī Ibn Abī Ṭālib*, 5th ed., (Qom, n.d.)

Pseudo-al-Mufīd, Muḥammad b. Muḥammad, *al-Ikhtiṣāṣ*, ʿAlī Akbar Ghaffārī, ed., 1st ed., (Beirut, 1430/2009).

Al-Qurṭubī, Aḥmed b. Muḥammad, *al-Taʿrīf bi-l-Ansāb wa-l-Tanwīh bi-Dhawī al-Aḥsāb*, Saʿd ʿAbdilMaqṣūd Ẓalām, ed., Cairo, 1990.

Al-Rassī, Yaḥyā b. al-Ḥusayn, *al-Aḥkām fī al-Ḥalāl wa-l-Ḥarām,* Al-Murtaḍā bin Zayd Al-Mahaṭwarī, ed., 1st ed., (Sanaa, 1434/2013).

——. *Tathbīt al-Imāma*, Muḥammad Reḍa Al-Jalālī, ed., 2nd ed., (Beirut, 1419).

Al-Rāzī, Aḥmed b. ʿAbdillāh, *Tārīkh Madīnat Ṣanʿāʾ*, Ḥusayn b. ʿAbdillāh al-ʿUmarī, ed., 3rd ed., (Damascus, 1409/1989).

Robert Gleave (2015). *Early Shiite hermeneutics and the dating of Kitāb Sulaym Ibn Qays*. Bulletin of the School of Oriental and African Studies, 78, pp 83-103
doi:10.1017/S0041977X15000038

Al-Ṣaffār, Muḥammad b. al-Ḥasan, *Baṣāʾir al-Darajāt*, 1st ed, (Beirut, 1431/2010).

Al-Sahmī, Ḥamza b. Yūsuf, *Tārīkh Jurjān*, Muḥammad ʿAbdulMuʿīd Khān, ed., 4th ed., (Beirut, 1407/1987).

Al-Ṣāliḥī, Muḥammad b. Yūsuf, ʿĀdil Aḥmed ʿAbdilMawjūd and ʿAlī Maʿwaḍ, eds., 1st ed., (Beirut, 1414/1993).

Al-Ṣanʿānī, ʿAbdurrazzāq b. Hammām, *al-Amālī fī Āthār al-Ṣaḥāba*, Majdī Al-Sayyid Ibrāhīm, ed., Cairo, n.d.

——. *al-Muṣannaf*, Ḥabīb Al-Raḥmān Al-ʿAẓmī, ed., 2nd ed., (Beirut, 1403).

Al-Saraqusṭī, Qāsim b. Thābit, *al-Dalāʾil fī Gharīb al-Ḥadīth*, Muḥammad b. ʿAbdillāh Al-Qannāṣ, ed., 1st ed., (Riyadh, 1422/2001).

Al-Shahrastānī, Muḥammad b. ʿAbdulKarīm, *al-Milal wa-l-Niḥal*, ʿAbdulʿAzīz Al-Wakīl, ed., Cairo, 1383/1968.

Al-Shāhrūdī, ʿAlī al-Namāzī, *Mustadrakāt ʿIlm Rijāl al-Ḥadīth*, 1st ed., (Qom, 1426).

Al-Shaybānī, ʿAbdullāh b. Aḥmed b. Ḥanbal, *al-ʿIlal wa-Maʿrifat al-Rijāl – Riwāyat ʿAbdillāh*, Waṣiyyullāh ʿAbbās, ed., 2nd ed., (Riyadh, 1422).

——. *Kitāb al-Sunna*, Muḥammad bin Saʿīd Al-Qaḥṭānī, ed., 1st ed., (Dammām, 1406/1986).

Al-Shihārī, Ibrāhīm b. al-Qāsim, *Ṭabaqāt al-Zaydiyya al-Kubrā*, ʿAbdulSalām bin ʿAbbās Al-Wajīh, ed., 1st ed., (Amman, 1421/2001).

Sibṭ Ibn al-Jawzī, Yūsuf b. Qizʾūghlī, *Mirʾāt al-Zamān fī Tawārīkh al-Aʿyān*, ʿAmmār Rayhāwī et al., eds., 1st ed., (Damascus, 1434/2013).

——. *Tadhkirat al-Khawāṣṣ*, Tehran, n.d.

Al-Suyūṭī, ʿAbdurraḥmān b. Abī Bakr, *al-Laʾāliʾ al-Maṣnūʿa fī al-Aḥādīth al-Mawḍūʿa*, Ṣalāḥ bin Muḥammad b. ʿAwīḍa, ed., 1st ed., (Beirut, 1417/1996).

Al-Ṭabarānī, Sulaymān b. Aḥmed, *al-Muʿjam al-Awsaṭ*, Ṭāriq bin ʿAwaḍallāh, ed., Cairo, 1416/1995.

——. *al-Muʿjam al-Kabīr*, Ḥamdī ʿAbdulMajīd Al-Salafī, ed., 2nd ed., (Cairo, 1404/1983).

——. *Musnad al-Shāmiyyīn*, Ḥamdī bin ʿAbdulMajīd Al-Salafī, ed., 1st ed., (Beirut, 1405/1984).

Al-Ṭabarī, Muḥammad b. Jarīr b. Rustom, *al-Mustarshid fī Imāmat Amīr al-Muʾminīn ʿAlī Ibn Abī Ṭālib*, Aḥmed Al-Maḥmūdī, ed., 1st ed., (Qom, n.d.).

Al-Ṭabarī, Muḥammad b. Jarīr b. Yazīd, *Tahdhīb al-Āthār*, Maḥmūd Muḥammad Shākir, ed., Cairo.

——. *Tārīkh al-Rusul wa-l-Mulūk*, 2nd ed., (Beirut, 1387).

Al-Ṭabarī, Muḥib al-Dīn Aḥmed b. ʿAbdillāh, *Dhakhāʾir al-ʿUqbā fī Manāqib Dhawī al-Qurbā*, Cairo, 1356,

Tamima Bayhom-Daou (2015). Kitāb Sulaym Ibn Qays revisited. Bulletin of the School of Oriental and African Studies, 78, pp 105-119 doi:10.1017/S0041977X14001062

Al-Ṭehrānī, Āghā Bozorg, *al-Dharīʿah ilā Taṣānīf al-Shīʿa*, 3rd ed., (Beirut, 1403/1983).

Al-Tirmidhī, Muḥammad b. ʿĪsā, *al-Jāmiʿ al-Kabīr*, Bashār ʿAwwād Maʿrūf, ed., Beirut, 1998.

Al-Ṭūsī, Muḥammad b. al-Ḥasan, *al-Amālī*, Bahrād Al-Jaʿfarī and ʿAlī Akbar Ghaffārī, eds., 1st ed., (Tehran, 1381 SH).

——. *al-Fihrist*, Muḥammad Ṣādiq Baḥr al-ʿUlūm, ed., 1st ed., (Beirut, 1436, 2015).

——. *Kitāb al-Ghayba*, ʿAlī Akbar Al-Ghaffārī, ed., 1st ed., (Beirut, n.d.)

——. *Rijāl al-Ṭūsī*, ʿAlāʾaldīn Al-Aʿlamī, ed., 1st ed., (Beirut, 1436/2015).

——. *Tahdhīb al-Aḥkām*, ʿAlī Akbar Al-Ghaffārī, ed., 1st ed., (Tehran, 1386 SH).

——. *Talkhīṣ al-Shāfī*, Ḥusayn Baḥr Al-ʿUlūm, ed., 1st ed., (Qom, 1382).

Al-Tustarī, Muḥammad Taqī, *al-Akhbār al-Dakhīla*, ʿAlī Akbār Ghaffārī, ed., 2nd ed., (Tehran, 1401).

Al-ʿUkbarī, Muḥammad b. Muḥammad b. al-Nuʿmān al-Mufīd, *Amālī al-Mufīd*, Ḥusayn Al-Istādūlī, ed., 1st ed., (Beirut, 1431/2010).

——. *al-Irshād*, 1st ed., (Beirut, 1429/2008).

——. *al-Jamal*, 1st ed., (Najaf, 1403/1983).

——. *Taṣḥīḥ Iʿtiqādāt al-Imāmiyya*, Ḥusayn Dargāhī, ed., 1st ed., (Qom, 1413).

Al-ʿUqaylī, Abū Jaʿfar Muḥammad b. ʿAmr, *al-Ḍuʿafāʾ al-Kabīr*, ʿAbdulMuʿṭī Amīn Qalʿajī, ed., 1st ed., (Beirut, 1404/1984).

Al-ʿUṣfurī, Khalīfa b. Khayyāṭ, *Ṭabaqāt Khalīfa b. Khayyāṭ*, Suhayl Zakkār, ed., Beirut, 1414/1993.

——. *Tārīkh Khalīfa Ibn Khayyāṭ*, Akram Ḍiyāʾ Al-ʿUmarī, ed., 2nd ed., (Damascus/Beirut, 1397).

Wheeler, G.J. "The Finding of Hidden Texts in Esoteric and Other Religious Traditions: Some Notes on 'Discovery Narratives.'" *Correspondences: Journal for the Study of Esotericism*, no. 2 (2019).

Al-Yaʿqūbī, Aḥmed b. Abī Yaʿqūb b. Jaʿfar, *Tārīkh al-Yaʿqūbī*, Najaf, 1384/1964.

Al-Zubayrī, Muṣʿab b. ʿAbdillāh, *Nasab Quraysh*, Évariste Lévi-Provençal, ed., 3rd ed., (Cairo, 1953).

Printed in Great Britain
by Amazon

72917807R10163